Jill & John.
Christmas
1976.

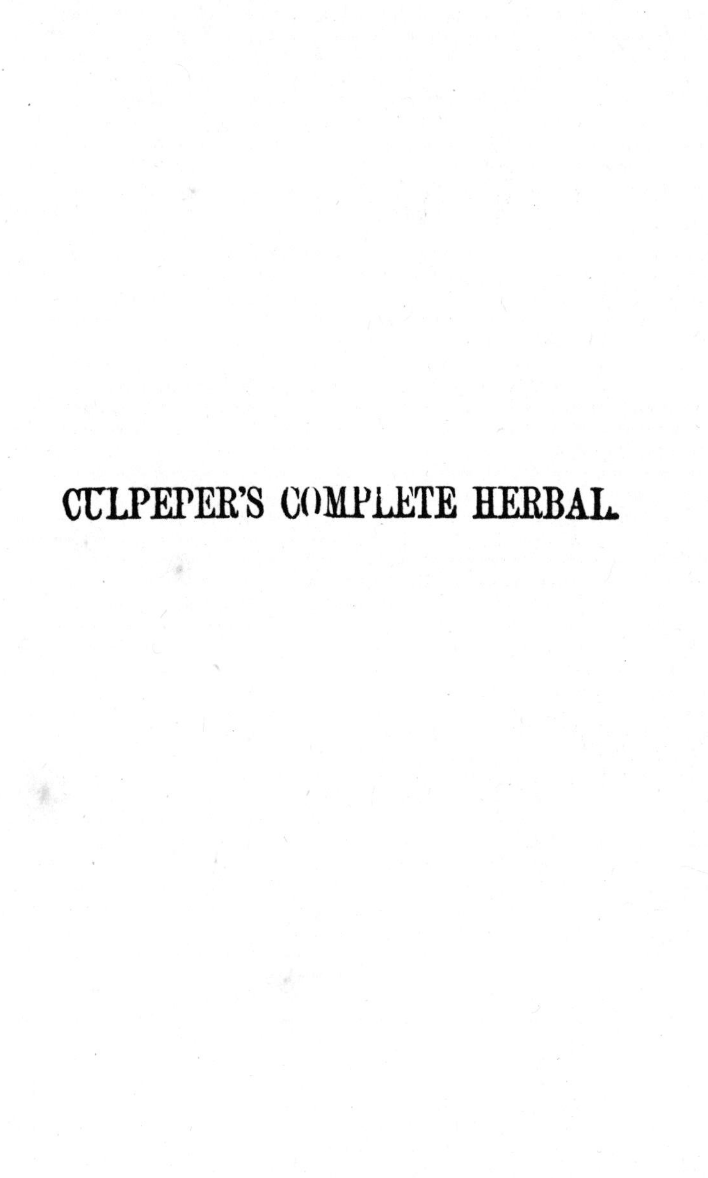

CULPEPER'S COMPLETE HERBAL

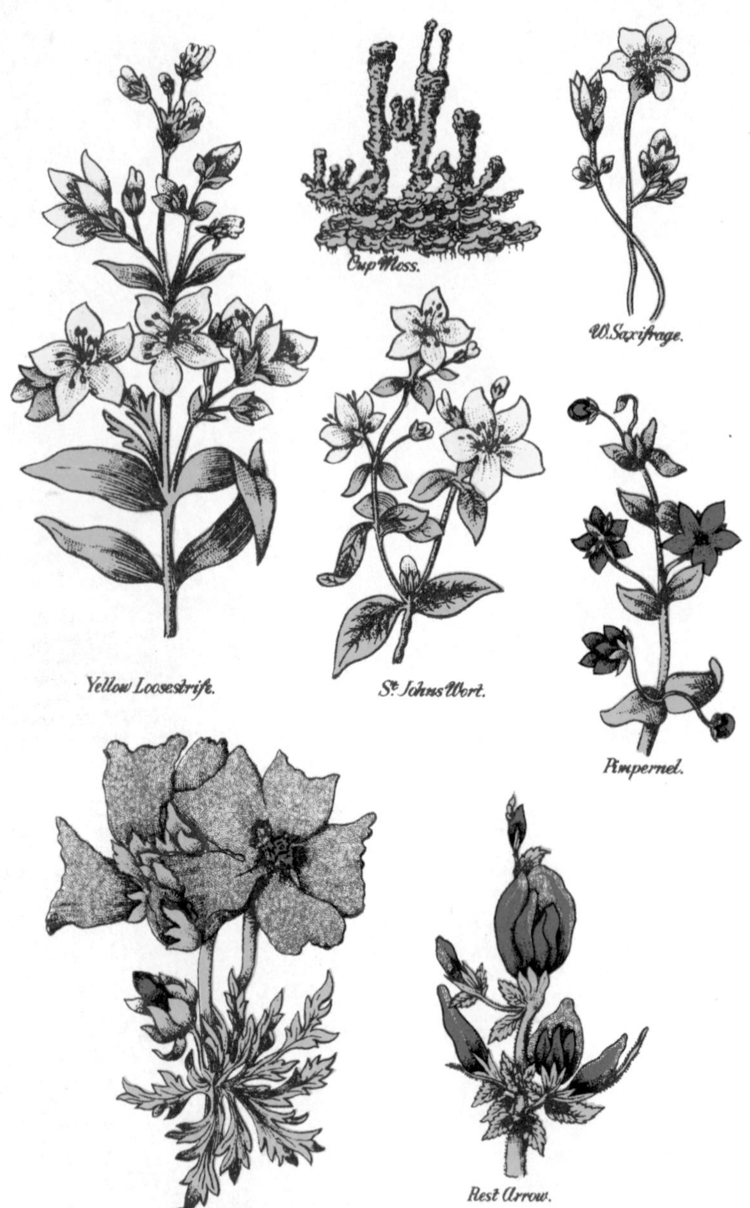
Cup Moss.
W. Saxifrage.
Yellow Loosestrife.
St. Johns Wort.
Pimpernel.
Rest Arrow.
Vervain Mallow.

CULPEPER'S
COMPLETE HERBAL:

CONSISTING OF

A COMPREHENSIVE DESCRIPTION
OF NEARLY ALL HERBS

WITH THEIR

MEDICINAL PROPERTIES

AND

DIRECTIONS FOR COMPOUNDING THE MEDICINES

EXTRACTED FROM THEM

LONDON
W. FOULSHAM & CO., LTD.
NEW YORK · TORONTO · CAPE TOWN · SYDNEY

W. FOULSHAM & CO. LTD.
Yeovil Road, Slough, Berks, England

ISBN 0-572 00203 3

MADE AND PRINTED IN GREAT BRITAIN
BY A. WHEATON & CO., EXETER.

CONTENTS.

CULPEPER'S COMPLETE HERBAL.

ACONITE.—(*Aconitum Anthora.*)

We have many poisonous Aconites growing in the fields, of which we ought to be cautious: but there is a medicinal one kept in the shop; this is called the Wholesome Aconite; *Anthora*, and Wholesome Wolf'sbane.

Descrip.—This a small plant, being a species of Wolf'sbane, or Monkshood, about a foot high, with pale divided green leaves, and yellow flowers. It grows erect, and the stalk is firm, angular, and hairy; the leaves do not stand in pairs; they are round almost, and cut into many divisions like those of Larkspur. The flowers are large and hooded, of a pleasant smell, and grow on the tops of the branches in spikes of a pale yellow colour, in shape like the flowers of Monkshood, but somewhat less, each succeeded by four or five horn-like pointed pods, containing black angular seeds. The root is tuberous, and sometimes consists of one lump or knob, sometimes of more.

Place.—This pant is a native of the Alps, but with us is planted in gardens.

Time.—It flowers in July, and the seeds are ripe at the latter end of August.

Government and Virtues.—This plant is under the government of Saturn. The shoot only is used, and that not often. However, it is said to be very serviceable against vegetable poisons. A decoction of the root is a good lotion to wash the parts bitten by venomous creatures but it is not much regarded at this time, and should be cautiously kept out of childrens' way, for there is a farina in the flower, which is very dangerous if blown in the eyes; the leaves also, if rubbed on the skin, will irritate and cause soreness.

AGARIC.—(*Agaricus.*)

Descrip.—This is a fungous substance, of a roundish, angular, unequal shape, from the size of a man's fist to his head, white as snow, and mealy when rubbed between the fingers; it has a few fibres, and a ash-coloured rind, the lower part being perforated, with small seeds in the holes. The taste is first sweetish, then bitter, acrid, and nauseous, with a slight astringency. There are a great variety of these excrescences; they differ both in virtue and the substances on which they grow. One kind grows at the foot of oak trees, which is pleasant to eat, weighing from an ounce to two pounds, of a fleshy juicy substance, without pores, dotted on the outside with red, tasting like the meat of a lobster's claw. It differs in colour, the upper surface is a brown red, the under approaches a buff colour, sometimes full of pores, the inner substance is fleshy and succulent, streaked with deeper and paler red. They are about a foot and a half round, apparently nothing but leaves encompassing each other ; these fungous leaves are halt an inch thick, all joining in one thick basis, by which it adheres to the stump of an oak tree. It consists of two sorts of fibres ; those which frame the outward surface are tough, and of a ligamentous firmness, placed horizontally; the others are soft and perpendicular to the first, forming the under surface, which is white and full of pores.

Touchwood, or Spunk, is made from another kind of fungus growing on willows, full of minuute pores, covered with a white substance on the under side when fresh. A third kind grows on the trunks of the larch trees.

Government and Virtues.—It is under the government of Mercury in the sign of Leo. The best is white, light, and brittle. It evacuates phlegm, and is given in defluxions and disorders of the breast, but that only to strong people. It is reckoned a useless medicine, or rather noxious, for it loads the stomach, distends the viscera, creates a nausea, and causes vomiting. Its powder has been prescribed from half a dram to two drams.

ALL-HEAL.—*(Prunella Vulgaris.)*

It is also called Hercules' All-heal, and Hercules' Wound-wort, because it is supposed that Hercules learned the herb and its virtues from Chiron, when he learned physic of him.

Descrip.—Its root is long, thick, and exceedingly full of juice, of a hot and biting taste : the leaves are great and large, and winged almost like Ash-tree leaves, but that they are something hairy, each leaf consisting of six pairs of such wings set one against the other upon foot-stalks, broad below, but narrow towards the end; one of the leaves is a little deeper at the bottom than the other, of a fair, yellowish, fresh green colour; they are of a bitterish taste being chewed in the mouth. From among these ariseth up a stalk, green in colour, round in form, great and strong in magnitude, five or six feet in altitude, with many joints and some leaves thereat: towards the top come forth umbles of small yellow flowers, after these are passed away, you may find whitish, yellow, short flat seeds, bitter also in taste.

Place.—Having given you the description of the herb from the bottom to the top, give me leave to tell you that there are other herbs called by this name; but because they are strangers in England, I give only the description of this, which is easily to be had in the gardens of divers places.

Time.—Although Gerard saith, That they flower from the beginning of May to the end of December, experience teacheth them that keep it in their gardens, that it flowers not till the latter end of the summer, and sheds its seed presently after.

Government and Virtues.—It is under the dominion of Mars, hot, biting, and choleric; and remedies what evils Mars afflicts the body of a man with, by sympathy, as vipers' flesh attracts poison, and the loadstone iron. It kills the worms, helps the gout, cramps, and convulsions; provokes urine, and helps all joint aches. It helps all cold griefs of the head, the vertigo, falling sickness, the lethargy, the wind colic, obstructions of the liver and spleen, stone in the kidneys and bladder. It provokes the terms, expels the dead birth: it is excellent for the griefs of the sinews, itch, stone, and tooth-ache, the bite of mad dogs and venomous beasts, and purgeth choler very gently.

ALKANET.—(*Anchusa Tinctoria.*)

Besides the common name, it is called orchanet, and Spanish bugloss, and by apothecaries, enchusa.

Descrip.—Of the many sorts of this herb, there is but one known to grow commonly in this nation; of which one takes this description:—It hath a great and thick root of a reddish colour; long, narrow, hairy leaves, green like the leaves of bugloss, which lie very thick upon the ground; the stalks rise up compassed round about, thick with leaves, which are lesser and narrower than the former; they are tender, and slender, the flowers are hollow, small, and of a reddish colour.

Place.—It grows in Kent, near Rochester, and in many places in the west country, both in Devonshire and Cornwall.

Time.—They flower in July and beginning of August, and the seed is ripe soon after, but the root is in its prime, as carrots and parsnips are, before the herb runs up to stalk.

Government and Virtues.—It is an herb under the dominion of Venus, and indeed one of her darlings, though somewhat hard to come by. It helps old ulcers, hot inflammations, burnings by common fire and St. Anthony's fire, by antipathy to Mars; for these uses your best way is to make it into an ointment; also if you make a vinegar of it, as you make vinegar of roses, it helps the morphy and leprosy; if you apply the herb to the privities, it draws forth the dead child. It helps the yellow jaundice, spleen, and gravel in the kidneys. Dioscorides saith, it helps such as are bitten by venomous beasts, whether it be taken inwardly or applied to the wound; nay, he saith further, if any that hath newly eaten it do but spit into the mouth of a serpent, the serpent instantly dies. It stays the flux of the belly, kills worms, helps the fits of the mother. Its decoction made in wine, and drank, strengthens the back, and easeth the pains thereof. It helps bruises and falls, and is as gallant a remedy to drive out the small pox and measles as any is: an ointment made of it is excellent for green wounds, pricks or thrusts,

ADDER'S TONGUE.—(*Ophioglossum Vulgatum.*)

Descrip.—This herb hath but one leaf, which grows with the stalk a finger's length above the ground, being flat and of a fresh green colour; broad like water plantain, but less, without any rib in it; from the bottom of which leaf on the inside riseth up, ordinarily, one, sometimes two or three slender stalks, the upper part whereof is somewhat bigger, and dented with small dents of a yellowish green colour, like the tongue of an adder serpent, (only this is as useful as they are formidable). The roots continue all the year.

Place.—It grows in moist meadows, and in such like places.

Time.—It is to be found in May or April, for it quickly perisheth with a little heat.

Government and Virtues.—It is an herb under the dominion of the Moon and Cancer, and therefore, if the weakness of the retentive faculty be caused by an evil influence in any part of the body governed by the moon, or under the dominion of Cancer, this herb cures it by sympathy. It cures these diseases after specified, in any part of the body under the influence of Saturn, by antipathy.

It is temperate in respect of heat, but dry in the second degree. The juice of the leaves drank with the distilled water of horse-tail, is a singular remedy of all manner of wounds in the breasts, bowels, or other parts of the body, and is given with good success unto those that are troubled with casting, vomiting, or bleeeding at the mouth and nose, or otherwards downwards. The said juice given in the distilled water of oaken buds, is very good for women who have their usual courses, or whites flowing down too abundantly. It helps sore eyes. Of the leaves infused or boiled in oil, omphacine, or unripe olives, set in the sun for certain days, or the green leaves sufficiently boiled in the said oil, is made an excellent green balsam, not only for green and fresh wounds, but also for old and inveterate ulcers, especially if a little fine clear turpentine be dissolved therein. It also stayeth and refresheth all inflammations that arise upon pains by hurts and wounds.

What parts of the body are under each planet and sign, and also what disease may be found in my astrological judgment of diseases; and for the internal work of nature in the body of man, as vital, animal, natural and procreative spirits of man; the apprehension, judgment, memory; the external senses, viz.—seeing, hearing, smelling, tasting, and feeling; the virtues attractive, retentive, digestive, expulsive, &c. under the dominion of what planets they are, may be fouud in my ephemeris for the year 1651: in both which you shall find the chaff of authors blown away by the fame of Dr. Reason, and nothing but rational truths left for the ingenious to feed upon.

AGRIMONY.—(*Agrimonia Eupatoria.*)

Descrip.—This hath divers long leaves, some greater, some smaller, set upon a stalk, all of them, dented about the edges, green above and greyish underneath, and a little hairy withal; among which ariseth up usually but one strong, round, hairy, brown stalk, two or three feet high, with smaller leaves set here and there upon it. At the top hereof grow many small yellow flowers, one above another, in long spikes, after which come round heads of seed, hanging downwards, which will cleave to and stick upon garments, or any thing that shall rub against them. The knot is black, long, and somewhat woody, abiding many years, and shooting afresh every spring; which root, though small, hath a reasonable scent.

Place.—It groweth upon banks, near the sides of hedges.

Time.—It flowereth in July and August, the seed being ripe shortly after.

Government and Virtues.—It is an herb under Jupiter and the sign Cancer; and strengthens those parts under the planet and sign, and removes diseases in them by sympathy; and those under Saturn, Mars, and Mercury, by antipathy, if they happen in any part of the body governed by Jupiter, or under the signs Cancer, Sagittary, or Pisces, and therefore must needs be good for the gout, either used outwardly in oil or ointment, or inwardly in an electuary, or syrup, or concerted juice; for which see the latter end of the work.

It is of a cleansing and cutting faculty, without any manifest heat, moderately drying and binding. It openeth and cleanseth the liver, helpeth the jaundice, and is very beneficial to the bowels, healing all inward wounds, bruises, hurts, and other distempers. The decoction of the herb made with wine, and drank, is good against the biting and stinging of serpents, and helps them that make foul, troubled or bloody water, and makes them part with clear urine speedily; it also helpeth the colic, cleanseth the breast, and rids away the cough. A draught of the decoction taken warm before the fit, first removes, and in time rids away the tertian or quartan agues. The leaves and seeds taken in wine stays the bloody flux; outwardly applied, being stamped with old swine's grease, it helpeth old sores, cancers, and inveterate ulcers, and draweth forth thorns and splinters of wood, nails, or any other such thing gotten into the flesh : it helpeth to strengthen the members that be out of joint ; and being bruised and applied, or the juice dropped in, it helpeth foul and imposthumed ears.

The distilled water of the herb is good to all the said purposes, either inward or outward, but a great deal weaker.

It is a most admirable remedy for such whose lives are annoyed either by heat or cold. The liver is the former of blood, and blood the nourisher of the body, and agrimony a strengthener of the liver.

I cannot stand to give you a reason in every herb why it cureth such diseases : but if you please to peruse my judgment in the herb wormwood, you shall find them there ; and it will be well worth your while to consider every herb—you shall find them true throughout the book.

AGRIMONY (WATER.)—(*Bidens Tripartita.*)

It is called in some countries Water Hemp, Bastard Hemp, and Bastard Agrimony ; Eupatorium and Hipatorium, because it strengthens the liver.

Descrip.—The root continues a long time, having many long slender strings : the stalk grows up about two feet high, sometimes higher ; they are of a dark purple colour : the branches are many, growing at distances the one from the other, the one from the one side of the stalk, the other from the opposite point : the leaves are winged, and much indented at the edges : the flowers grow at the top of the branches, of a brown yellow colour, spotted with black spots, having a substance within the midst of them like that of a daisy ; if you rub them between your fingers they smell like rosin or cedar when it is burnt : the seeds are long, and easily stick to any woollen thing they touch.

Place.—They delight not in heat, and therefore they are not so frequently found in the southern parts of England as in the northern, where they grow frequently. You may look for them in cold grounds by the sides of ponds and ditches, as also by running waters ; sometimes you shall find them grow in the midst of the waters.

Time.—They all flower in July or August, and the seed is ripe presently after.

Government and Virtues.—It is a plant of Jupiter, as well as the other agrimony, only this belongs to the celestial sign in Cancer. It healeth and drieth, cutteth and cleanseth thick and tough humours of the breast, and for this I hold it inferior to few herbs that grow; it helps the cachexia or evil disposition of the body, the dropsy, and yellow jaundice; it opens the obstructions of the liver, mollifies the hardness of the spleen, being applied outwardly: it breaks imposthumes, taken inwardly: it provokes urine and the terms: it kills worms, and cleanseth the body of sharp humours, which are the cause of itch and scabs; the herb being burnt, the smoke thereof drives away flies, wasps, &c.: It strengthens the lungs exceedingly. Country people give it to their cattle when they are troubled with the cough, or broken winded.

ALEHOOF, OR GROUND-IVY.—(*Glechoma Hederacea.*)

SEVERAL counties give it several names, so that there is scarce an herb growing of that bigness, that has got so many. It is called Cat's-Foot, Ground-ivy, Gill-go-by-ground, Gill-creep-by-ground, Turn-hoof, Hay-Maids, and Alehoof.

Descrip.—This well known herb lieth, spreadeth, and creepeth upon the ground, shooteth forth roots at the corners of tender jointed stalks, set with two round leaves at every joint, somewhat hairy, crumbled, and unevenly dented about the hedges with round dents; at the joints, likewise, with the leaves towards the end of the branches, come forth hollow long flowers, of a blueish purple colour, with small white spots upon the lips that hang down. The root is small, with strings.

Place.—It is commonly found under hedges and on the sides of ditches, under houses, or in shadowed lanes and other waste lands in almost every part of the land.

Time.—They flower somewhat early, and abide a great while; the leaves continue green until winter, and sometimes abide, except the winter be very sharp and cold.

Government and Virtues.—It is an herb of Venus, and therefore cures the diseases she causes by sympathy, and those of Mars by antipathy; you may easily find it all the year, except the year be extremely frosty; it is quick, sharp, and bitter in taste, and is thereby found to be hot and dry; a singular herb for all inward wounds, exulcerated lungs, or other parts, either by itself, or boiled with other the like herbs; and being drunk, in a short time it easeth all griping pains, windy and choleric humours in the stomach, spleen or belly; helps the yellow jaundice by opening the stoppings of the gall and liver, and melancholy, by opening the stoppings of the spleen; expelleth venom or poison, and also the plague: it provokes urine and women's courses. The decoction of it in wine drank for some time together, procureth ease unto them that are troubled with the sciatica, or hip gout; as also the gout in the hands, knees or feet; if you put to the decoction some honey and a little burnt alum, it is excellent good to gargle any sore mouth or throat, and to wash the sores and ulcers in the privy parts of man or woman; it speedily helpeth green wounds, being bruised and bound thereto. The juice of it boiled with a little honey and verdigris, doth wonderfully cleanse fistulas, ulcers, and stayeth the spreading or eating of cancers and ulcers; it helpeth the itch, scabs, weals, and other breakings out in any part of the body. The juice of celandine, field daises, and ground-ivy clarified and a little fine sugar dissolved therein, and dropped into the eyes, is a sovereign remedy for all pains, redness, and watering of them; as also for the pin and web, skins and films growing over the sight: it helpeth beasts as well as men. The juice dropped into the ear doth wonderfully help the noise and singing of them, and helpeth the hearing which is decayed. It is good to tun up with new drink, for it will clarify it in a night, that it will be the fitter to be drank the next morning; or if any drink be thick with removing or any other accident, it will do the like in a few hours.

ALEXANDER.—(*Smyrn ium Olusatrum.*)

It is also called Alisander, Horse Parsley, Wild Parsley, and the Black Pot-herb; the seed of it is that which is usually sold in apothecaries' shops for Macedonian parsley-seed.

Descrip.—It is usually sown in all the gardens in Europe, and so well known, that it needs no farther description.

Time.—It flowereth in June and July: the seed is ripe in August.

Government and Virtues.—It is an herb of Jupiter, and therefore friendly to nature, for it warmeth a cold stomach, and openeth a stoppage to the liver and spleen; it is good to move women's courses, to expel the after-birth, to break wind, to provoke urine, and helpeth the strangury; and these things the seeds will do likewise. If either of them be boiled in wine, or bruised and taken in wine, is alsc effectual in the biting of serpents. And you know what Alexander pottage is good for, that you may no longer eat it out of ignorance, but out of knowledge.

ALDER (BLACK.)—*(Alnus Nigra.)*

Descrip.—This tree seldom groweth to any great bigness, but for the most part abideth like a hedge-bush, or a tree spreading its branches, the woods of the body being white, and a dark red cole or heart ; the outward bark is of a blackish colour, with many whitish spots therein ; but the inner bark next the wood is yellow, which being chewed, will turn the spittle near into a saffron colour. The leaves are somewhat like those of an ordinary alder-tree, or the female cornet, or Dog-berry tree, called in Sussex dog-wood, but blacker, and not so long : the flowers are white, coming forth with the leaves at the joints, which turn into small round berries first green, afterwards red, but blackish when they are thoroughly ripe, divided as it were into two parts, wherein is contained two small round and flat seeds. The root runneth not deep into the ground, but spreads rather under the upper crust of the earth.

Place.—This tree or shrub may be found plentifully in St. John's wood by Hornsey, and the woods on Hampstead-heath ; as also in a wood called Old Park, in Barcomb, Essex, near the brook's side.

Time.—It flowereth in May, and the berries are ripe in September.

Government and Virtues.—It is a tree of Venus, and perhaps under the celestial sign Cancer. The inner yellow bark hereof purgeth downwards both choler and phlegm, and the watery humours of such as have the dropsy, and strengthens the inward parts again by binding. If the bark hereof be boiled with agrimony, wormwood, dodder, hops, and some fennel with smallage, endive, and succory roots, and a reasonable draught taken every morning for some time together, it is very effectual against the jaundice, dropsy, and the evil disposition of the body, especially if some suitable purging medicines have been taken before, to void the grosser excrements ; it purgeth and strengtheneth the liver and spleen, cleansing them from such evil humours and hardness as they are afflicted with. It is to be understood that these things are performed by the dry bark ; for the fresh green bark taken inwardly provokes strong vomitings, pains in the stomach, and gripings in the belly; yet if the decoction may stand and settle two or three days, until the yellow colour be changed black, it will not work so strongly as before, but will strengthen the stomach, and procure an appetite to meat. The outward bark contrariwise doth bind the body, and is helpful for all laxes and fluxes thereof, but this also must be dried first, whereby it will work the better. The inner bark thereof boiled in vinegar is an approved remedy to kill lice, to cure the itch, and take away scabs, by drying them up in a short time. It is singularly good to wash the teeth, and to take away the pains, to fasten those that are loose, to cleanse them, and keep them sound. The leaves are good fodder for kine, to make them give more milk.

In spring-time you use the herbs before-mentioned, and will take a handful of each of them, and to them add a handful of elder buds, and having bruised them all, boil them in a gallon of ordinary beer when it is new; and having boiled them half an hour, add to this three gallons more, and let them work together, and drink a draught of it every morning, half a pint, or thereabouts; it is an excellent purge for the spring to consume the phlegmatic quality the winter has left behind it, and withal to keep your body in health, and consume those evil humours which the heat of summer will readily stir up. Esteem it as a jewel.

ALDER (COMMON.)—*(Alnus Glutinosa.)*

Descrip.—Groweth to a reasonable height, and spreads much if it like the place. It is so generally well known unto country people, that I conceive it needless to tell that which is no news.

Place and Time.—It delighteth to grow in moist woods and watery places; flowereth in April and May, and yieldeth ripe seed in September.

Government and Use.—It is a tree under the dominion of Venus, and of some watery sign or other, I suppose Pisces, and therefore the decoction, or distilled water of the leaves, is excellent against burnings and inflammations, either with wounds or without, to bathe the place grieved with, and especially for that inflammation of the breast, which the vulgar call an ague.

If you cannot get the leaves, which in winter is impossible, make use of the bark in the same manner.

The leaves and bark of the alder tree are cooling, drying, and binding. The fresh leaves laid upon swellings dissolve them, and stay the inflammations. The leaves put under the bare feet galled with travelling, are a great refreshing to them. The said leaves gathered while the morning dew is on them, and brought into a chamber troubled with fleas, will gather them thereunto, which being suddenly cast out, will rid the chamber of these troublesome bed-fellows.

AMARANTHUS.—(*Amarantus Hypochondriacus.*)

Called also Flower-gentle, Flower-velure, Floramor, Velvet-flower, and Prince's Feather,

Descrip.—It being a garden flower, and well known to every one that keeps it, I might forbear the description; yet, notwithstanding, because some desire it, I shall give it. It runneth up with a stalk a cubit high, streaked, and somewhat reddish towards the root, but very smooth, divided towards the top with small branches, among which stand long broad leaves of a reddish green colour, slippery; the flowers are not properly flowers, but tufts, very beautiful to behold, but of no smell, of reddish colour; if you bruise them, they yield juice of the same colour; being gathered, they keep their beauty a long time: the seed is of a shining black colour.

Time.—They continue in flower from August till the time the frost nips them.

Government and Virtues.—It is under the dominion of Saturn, and is an excellent qualifier of the unruly actions and passions of Venus, though Mars should also join with her. The flowers dried and beaten into powder, stop the terms in women, and so do almost all other red things. And by the icon or image of every herb, the ancients at first found out their virtues. Modern writers laugh at them for it; but I wonder in my heart how the virtue of herbs came at first to be known, if not by their signatures; the moderns have them from the writings of the ancients; the ancients had no writings to have them from: but to proceed.—The flowers stop all fluxes of blood, whether in man or woman, bleeding either at the nose or wound. There is also a sort of amaranthus that bears a white flower, which stops the whites in women, and the running of the reins in men, and is a most gallant anti-venereal, and a singular remedy for the French pox.

ANGELICA.—(*Angelica Archangelica.*)

To write a description of that which is so well known to be growing almost in every garden, I suppose is altogether needless; yet for its virtues it is of admirable use.

In time of heathenism, when men had found out any excellent herb, they dedicated it to their god, as the bay-tree to Apollo, the oak to Jupiter, the vine to Bacchus, the poplar to Hercules. These the papists following as the patriarchs, they dedicated to their saints; as our lady's thistle to the Blessed Virgin, St. John's wort to St. John, and another wort to St. Peter, &c. Our physicians must imitate like apes, though they cannot come off half so cleverly, for they blasphemously call tansies, or heart's ease, *an herb for the Trinity*, because it is of three colours; and a certain ointment *an ointment of the Apostles*, because it consists of twelve ingredients. Alas! I am sorry for their folly, and grieved at their blasphemy. God send them wisdom the rest of their age, for they have their share of ignorance already. Oh! why must ours be blasphemous, because the heathens and papists were idolatrous? Certainly they have read so much in old rusty authors, that they have lost all their divinity, for unless it were amongst the ranters, I never read or heard of such blasphemy. The heathens and papists were bad, and ours worse; the papists giving names to herbs for their virtue's sake, not for their fair looks; and therefore some call this an herb of the Holy Ghost; others more moderate called it Angelica, because of its angelical virtues, and that name it retains still, and all nations follow it so near as their dialect will permit.

Government and Virtues.—It is an herb of the Sun in Leo; let it be gathered when he is there, the Moon applying to his good aspect; let it be gathered either in his hour, or in the hour of Jupiter: let Sol be angular: observe the like in gathering the herbs of other planets, and you may happen to do wonders. In all epidemical diseases caused by Saturn, that is as good a preservative as grows. It resists poison by defending and comforting the heart, blood, and spirits; it doth the like against the plague and all epidemical diseases, if the root be taken in powder to the weight of half a drachm at a time, with some good treacle in Carduus water, and the party thereupon laid to sweat in his bed; if treacle be not to be had, take it alone in Carduus water or Angelica water. The stalks or roots candied and eaten fasting, are good preservatives in time of infection ; and at other times to warm and comfort a cold stomach : the root also steeped in vinegar, and a little of that vinegar taken sometimes fasting, and the root smelled unto is good for the same purpose : a water distilled from the root simply, as steeped in wine and distilled in a glass, is much more effectual than the water of the leaves ; and this water drank two or three spoonfuls at a time, easeth all pains and torments coming of cold and wind, so that the body be not bound ; and taken with some of the root in powder at the beginning, helpeth the pleurisy, as also all other diseases of the lungs and breast, as coughs, phthisic, and shortness of breath ; and a syrup of the stalks doth the like. It helps pains of the cholic, the strangury and stoppage of the urine, procureth women's courses, and expelleth the after birth ; openeth the stoppage of the liver and spleen, and briefly easeth and discusseth all windiness and inward swellings. The decoction drank before the fit of an ague, that they may sweat, if possible, before the fit comes, will, in two or three times taking, rid it quite away ; it helps digestion, and is a remedy for a surfeit. The juice, or the water being dropped into the eyes or ears helps dimness of sight and deafness : the juice put into the hollow of the teeth easeth their pain. The root in powder, made up into plaister with a little pitch, and laid on the biting of mad dogs or any other venomous creature, doth wonderfully help. The juice or the water dropped, or tents wet therein, and put into filthy dead ulcers, or the powder of the root, in want of either, doth cleanse and cause them to heal quickly, by covering the naked bones with flesh : the distilled water applied to places pained with the gout, or sciatica, doth give a great deal of ease.

The Wild Angelica (*Angelica Sylvestris,*) may be safely used to all the purposes aforesaid.

ANEMONE.—(*Anemone Nemorosa.*)

Called also Wind-flower, because they say the flowers never open but when the wind bloweth. Pliny is my author ; if it be not so, blame him. The seed also, if it bears any at all, flies away with the wind.

Place and Time.—They are sown usually in the gardens of the curious, and flower in the spring-time. As for description, I shall pass it, being well known to all those that sow them.

Government and Virtues.—It is under the dominion of Mars, being supposed to be a kind of crow-foot. The leaves provoke the terms mightily, being boiled, and the decoction drank. The body being bathed with the decoction of them, cures the leprosy: the leaves being stamped, and the juice snuffed up the nose, purgeth the head mightily; so doth the root, being chewed in the mouth, for it procureth much spitting, and bringeth away many watery and phlegmatic humors, and is therefore excellent for the lethargy. And when all is done, let physicians prate what they please, all the pills in the dispensary purge not the head like to hot things held in the mouth. Being made into an ointment, and the eye-lids anointed with it, it helps inflammations of the eyes; whereby it is palpable, that every stronger draweth its weaker like. The same ointment is excellent good to cleanse malignant and corroding ulcers.

ARRACH (GARDEN.)—(*Atriplex Hortensis.*)

Called also Orach, and Arage.

Descrip.—It is so commonly known to every housewife, it were labour lost to describe it.

Time.—It flowereth and seedeth from June to the end of August.

Government and Virtues.—It is under the government of the Moon: in quality cold and moist like unto her. It softeneth and looseneth the body of man being eaten, and fortifieth the expulsive faculty in him. The herb, whether it be bruised and applied to the throat, or boiled, and in like manner applied, it matters not much, it is excellent good for swellings in the throat; the best way, I suppose, is to boil it, having drunk the decoction inwardly, and apply the herb outwardly. The decoction of it besides is an excellent remedy for the yellow jaundice.

ARRACH, WILD AND STINKING.—(*Atriplex Olida.*)

Called also Vulvaria, Dog's-arrach, Goat's-arrach, and Stinking Mother-wort.

Descrip.—This hath small and almost round leaves, yet a little pointed, and almost without dent or cut, of a dusky mealy colour, growing on the slender stalks and branches that spread on the ground, with small flowers in clusters set with the leaves, and small seeds succeeding like the rest, perishing yearly, and rising again with its own sowing. It smells like rotten fish, or something worse.

Place.—It grows usually upon dunghills.

Time.—They flower in June and July, and their seed is ripe quickly after.

Government and Virtues.—Stinking arrach is used as a remedy to help women pained, and almost strangled with the mother, by smelling to it; but inwardly taken there is no better remedy under the moon for that disease. I would be large in commendation of this herb, were I but eloquent. It is an herb under the dominion of Venus, and under the sign Scorpio; it is common almost upon every dunghill. The works of God are given freely to man, his medicines are common and cheap, and easy to be found. ('Tis the medicines of the College of Physicians that are so dear and scarce to find.) I commend it for a universal medicine of the womb, and such a medicine as will easily, safely, and speedily cure any diseases thereof, as fits of the mother, dislocation, or falling out thereof: it cools the womb being overheated. And let me tell you this, and I will tell you the truth—heat of the womb is one of the greatest causes of hard labour in child-birth. It makes barren women fruitful: it cleanseth the womb if it be foul, and strengthens it exceedingly: it provokes the terms if they be stopped, and stops them if they flow immoderately; you can desire no good to your womb but this herb will effect it; therefore if you love children, if you love health, if you love ease, keep a syrup always by you made of the juice of this herb, and sugar, or honey, if it be to cleanse the womb; and let such as be rich keep it for their poor neighbours, and bestow it as freely as I bestow my studies upon them, or else let them look to answer it another day, when the Lord shall come to make the inquisition of blood.

ARCHANGEL.—(*Lamium.*)

To put a gloss upon their practice, the physicians call an herb (which country people vulgarly know by the name of the dead nettle) archangel: whether they favour more of superstition or folly, I leave to the judicious reader. There is more curiosity than courtesy to my countrymen used by others in the explanation as well of the names, as description of this so well known herb; which, that I may not also be guilty of, take this short description, first of the red archangel.

Descrip.—This hath divers square stalks, somewhat hairy, at the joints whereof grow two sad green leaves dented about the edges, opposite to one another to the lowermost, upon long foot stalks, but without any toward the tops, which are somewhat round yet pointed, and a little crumpled and hairy; round about the upper joints, where the leaves grow thick, are sundry gaping flowers of a pale reddish colour; after which come the seed three or four in a husk: the root is smaller and thready, perishing every year; the whole plant hath a strong scent, but not stinking.

White archangel hath divers square stalks, none standing straight upward, but bending downward, wherein stand two leaves at a joint, larger and more pointed than the other, dented about the edges, and greener also, more like unto nettle leaves, but not stinking, yet hairy. At the joints with the leaves stand larger and more open gaping white flowers, husks round about the stalks, but not with such a bush of leaves as flowers set in the top, as is on the other, wherein stand small roundish black seed: the root is white, with many strings at it, not growing downward, but lying under the upper crust of the earth, and abideth many years increasing: this has not so strong a scent as the former.

Yellow archangel is like the white in the stalks and leaves; but that the stalks are more straight and upright, and the joints with leaves are farther asunder, having larger leaves than the former, and the flowers a little longer and more gaping, of a fair yellow colour in most, in some paler: the roots are like the white, only they creep not so much under the ground.

Place.—They grow almost every where, unless it be in the middle of the street; the yellow most usually in the wet grounds of woods, and sometimes in the drier, in divers counties of this nation.

Time.—They flower from the beginning of spring all the summer long.

Virtues and use.—The archangels are somewhat hot and drier than the stinging nettles, and used with better success for the stopping and hardness of the spleen, than by using the decoction of the herb in wine, and afterwards applying the herb hot into the region of the spleen as plaister, or the decoction with sponges. Flowers of the white archangel are preserved or conserved to be used to stay the whites, and the flowers of the red to stay the reds in women. It makes the heart merry, drives away melancholy, quickens the spirits, is good against the quartan agues, stauncheth bleeding at the mouth and nose if it be stamped and applied to the nape of the neck; the herb also bruised, and with some salt and vinegar and hog's-grease laid upon a hard tumour or swelling, or that vulgarly called the king's-evil, do help to dissolve or discuss them: and being in like manner applied, doth much allay the pains, and give ease to the gout, sciatica, and other pains of the joints and sinews. It is also very effectual to heal green wounds and old ulcers; also to stay their fretting, gnawing, and spreading: it draweth forth splinters, and such like things gotten into the flesh, and is very good against bruises and burnings. But the yellow archangel is most commended for old, filthy, corrupt sores and ulcers, yea, although they be hollow; and to dissolve tumours. The chief use of them is for women, it being an herb of Venus, and may be found in my Guide for women.

ARSSMART.—(*Polygonum.*)

THE hot Arssmart is called also Water-pepper, (*Polygonum Hydropiper.*) The mild Arssmart is called Dead Arssmart, (*Persicaria Maculata,*) or Peachwort, because the leaves are so like the leaves of a peach-tree: it also called Plumbago.

Descrip. of the Mild.—This hath broad leaves at the great red joints of the stalks, with semi-circular blackish marks on them usually either blueish or whitish, with such like seed following. The root is long with many strings thereat, perishing yearly; this hath no sharp taste (as another sort hath, which is quick and biting) but rather sour like sorrel, or else a little drying, or without taste.

Place.—It groweth in watery places, ditches, and the like, which for the most part are dry in summer.

Time.—It flowereth in June, and the seed is ripe in August.

Government and Virtues.—As the virtue of both these is various, so is also their government; for that which is hot and biting is under the dominion of Mars, but Saturn challengeth the other, as appears by that leaden coloured spot he hath placed upon the leaf.

It is of a cooling and drying quality, and very effectual for putrid ulcers in man or beast, to kill worms and cleanse putrefied places. The juice thereof dropped in, or otherwise applied, consumeth all cold swellings, and dissolveth the congealed blood of bruises by strokes, falls, &c. A piece of the root, or some of the seeds bruised and held to an aching tooth, taketh away the pain: the leaves bruised and laid to the joint that hath a felon thereon, taketh it away; the juice destroyeth worms in the ears, being dropped into them: if the hot arssmart be strewed in a chamber, it will soon kill all the fleas; and the herb or juice of the cold arssmart put to a horse or other cattle's sores, will drive away the fly in the hottest day of summer: a good handful of the hot bitter arssmart put under a horse's saddle, will make him travel the better, although he were half tired before. The mild arssmart is good against all imposthumes and inflammations at the beginning, and to heal all green wounds.

All authors chop the virtues of both sorts of arssmart together, as men chop herbs to the pot, when both of them are of clean contrary qualities. The hot arssmart groweth not so high or so tall as the mild doth, but hath many leaves of the colour of peach leaves, very seldom or never spotted; in other particulars it is like the former, but may easily be known from it if you will be pleased to break a leaf of it across your tongue; for the hot will make your tongue to smart, so will not the cold. If you see them together you may easily distinguish them, because the mild hath far broader leaves: and our College Physicians, out of their learned care of the public good, *anglicè*, their own gain, mistake the one for the other in their *New Master-piece*, whereby they discover,—1. Their ignorance; 2. Their carelessness; and he that hath but half an eye may see their pride without a pair of spectacles. I have done what I could to distinguish them in the virtues, and when you find not the contrary named, use the cold. The truth is, I have not yet spoken with Dr. Reason, nor his brother, Dr. Experience, concerning either of them.

ASARABACA.—(*Asarum Europæum.*)

Descrip.—Asarabaca hath many heads rising from the roots, from whence come many small leaves, every one upon his own foot stalks which are rounder and bigger than violet leaves, thicker also, and of a dark green shining colour on the upper side, and of a pale yellow green underneath, little or nothing dented about the edges, from among which rise small, round, hollow, brown green husks, upon short stalks, about an inch long, divided at the brims into five divisions, very like the cups or heads of the henbane seed, but that they are smaller ; and these be all the flowers it carrieth, which are somewhat sweet being smelled unto, and wherein, when they are ripe, are contained small corned rough seeds, very like the kernel or stones of grapes or raisins. The roots are small and whitish, spreading divers ways in the ground, increasing into divers heads : but not running or creeping under the ground as some other creeping herbs do. They are somewhat sweet in smell, resembling nardus, but more when they are dry than green ; and of a sharp but not unpleasant taste.

Place.—It groweth frequently in gardens.

Time.—They keep their leaves green all winter ; but shoot forth new in the spring, and with them come forth those heads or flowers which give ripe seed about Midsummer, or somewhat after.

Government and Virtues.—'Tis a plant under the dominion of Mars, and therefore inimical to nature. This herb being drunk, not only provoketh vomiting, but purgeth downward, and by urine also, purgeth both choler and phlegm. If you add to it some spikenard, with the whey of goat's milk, or honeyed water, it is made more strong ; but it purgeth phlegm more manifestly than choler, and therefore doth much help pains in the hips and other parts : being boiled in whey they wonderfully help the obstructions of the liver and spleen, and are therefore profitable for the dropsy and jaundice : being steeped in wine and drank, it helps those continual agues that come by the plenty of stubborn humours : an oil made thereof by setting in the sun, with some laudanum added to it, provoketh sweating, (the ridge of the back anointed therewith) and thereby driveth away the shaking fits of the ague. It will not abide any long boiling, for it loseth its chief strength thereby ; nor much beating, for the finer powder doth provoke vomits and urine, and the coarser purgeth downwards.

The common use hereof is to take the juice of five or seven leaves in a little drink to cause vomiting ; the roots have also the same virtue, though they do not operate so forcibly; they are very effectual against the biting of serpents, and therefore are put in as an ingredient both into Mithridate and Venice treacle. The leaves and root being boiled in lye, and the head often washed therewith while it is warm, comforteth the head and brain that is ill affected by taking cold, and helpeth the memory.

I shall desire ignorant people to forbear the use of the leaves: the roots purge more gently, and may prove beneficial to such as have cancers, or old putrefied ulcers, or fistulas upon their bodies, to take a dram of them in powder in a quarter of a pint of white wine in the morning. The truth is, I fancy purging and vomiting medicines as little as any man breathing doth, for they weaken nature, nor shall ever advise them to be used unless upon urgent necessity. If a physician be nature's servant, it is his duty to strengthen his mistress as much as he can, and weaken her as little as may be.

ASPARAGUS.—(*Asparagus Officinalis.*)

Descrip.—It riseth up at first with divers white and green scaly heads, very brittle or easy to break while they are young, which afterwards rise up in very long snd slender green stalks, of the bigness of an ordinary riding wand, at the bottom of most, or bigger or lesser, as the roots are of growth; on which are set divers branches of green leaves, shorter and smaller than fennel, to the top; at the joints whereof come forth small yellowish flowers, which run into round berries, green at first, and of an excellent red color when they are ripe, showing like bead or coral, wherein are contained exceeding hard black seeds: the roots are dispersed from a spongeous head into many long, thick, and round strings, wherein is sucked much nourishnent out of the ground, and increaseth plentifully thereby.

ASPARAGUS (PRICKLY.)—(*Asparagus Sativus.*)

Descrip.—It groweth usually in gardens, and some of it grows wild in Appleton meadows, in Gloucestershire, where the poor people do gather the buds of young shoots, and sell them cheaper than our garden asparagus is sold in London.

Time.—They do for the most part flower and bear their

berries late in the year, or not at all, although they are housed in winter.

Government and Virtues.—They are both under the dominion of Jupiter. The young buds or branches boiled in ordinary broth, make the belly soluble and open; and boiled in white wine, provoke urine being stopped, and is good against the strangury, or difficulty of making water; it expelleth the gravel and stone out of the kidnies, and helpeth pains in the reins: and boiled in white wine or vinegar, it is prevalent for them that have their arteries loosened, or are troubled with the hip-gout or sciatica. The decoction of the roots boiled in wine, and taken, is good to clear the sight, and being held in the mouth easeth the tooth-ache; and being taken fasting several mornings together, stirreth up bodily lust in man or woman, whatever some have written to the contrary. The garden asparagus nourisheth more than the wild, yet hath it the same effects in all the aforementioned diseases. The decoction of the roots in white wine, and the back and belly bathed therewith, or kneeling or lying down in the same, or sitting therein as a bath, hath been found effectual against pains of the reins and bladder, pains of the mother and colic, and generally against all pains that happen to the lower parts of the body, and no less effectual against stiff and benumbed sinews, or those that are shrunk by cramps and convulsions, and helpeth the sciatica.

ASH TREE.—*(Fraxinus Excelsior.)*

THIS is so well known, that time will be misspent in writing a description of it; and therefore I shall only insist upon the virtues of it.

Government and Virtues.—It is governed by the Sun and the young tender tops, with the leaves taken inwardly, and some of them outwardly applied, are singular good against the biting of an adder, viper, or any other venomous beast; and the water distilled therefrom being taken, a small quantity every morning fasting, is a singular medicine to those that are subject to the dropsy, or to abate the greatness of those that are too gross or fat. The decoction of the leaves in white wine helpeth to break the stone and expel it, and cure the jaundice. The ashes of the bark of the ash made into lye, and those heads bathed therewith which are leprous, scabby, or scald, they are thereby cured. The kernels within the husks, commonly called ashen key, prevail against stitches and pains in the side, proceeding of wind and voiding away the stone, by provoking urine.

I can justly except against none of this, save only the first, viz.—That ash-tree tops and leaves are good against the biting of serpents and vipers. I suppose this had its rise from Gerard or Pliny, both which hold, that there is such an antipathy between an adder and an ash-tree, that if an adder be encompassed around with ash-tree leaves, she would sooner run through fire than through the leaves; the contrary to which is the truth, as both my eyes are witness. The rest are virtues something likely, only if it be in winter when you cannot get the leaves, you may safely use the bark instead of them. The keys you may easily keep all the year, gathering them when they are ripe.

AVENS, CALLED ALSO COLEWORT, AND HERB BENNET.—(*Geum Herbanum.*)

Descrip.—The ordinary avens have many long, rough, dark green winged leaves rising from the root, every one made of many leaves set on each side of the middle rib, the largest three whereof grow at the end, and are snipped or dented round about the edges; the other being small pieces, sometimes two and sometimes more, standing on each side of the middle rib underneath them: among which do rise up divers rough or hairy stalks, about two feet high, branching forth with leaves at every joint, not so long as those below, but almost as much cut in on the edges, some into three, some into more. On the tops of the branches stand small, pale yellow flowers, consisting of five leaves, like the flowers of cinque-foil, but large, in the middle whereof standeth a small green herb, which when the flower is fallen, groweth to be sound, being made of many long purple seeds like grains, which will stick upon your clothes. The root consists of many brownish strings of fibres, smelling somewhat like unto cloves, especially those which grow in the higher, hotter, and drier grounds, and in free and clear air.

Place.—They grow wild in many places under hedges' sides, and by the path-way in fields; yet they rather delight to grow in shadowy than in sunny places.

Time.—They flower in May and June for the most part, and their seed is ripe in July at the farthest.

Government and Virtues.—It is governed by Jupiter, and that gives hope of a wholesome, healthful herb. It is good for the diseases of the chest or breast, for pains and stitches in the side, and to expel crude and raw humours from the belly and stomach, by the sweet savour and warming quality. It dissolves the inward congealed blood happening by falls or bruises, and the spitting of blood, if the roots, either green or dry, be boiled in wine and drunk: as also all manner of inward wounds or outward, if washed or bathed therewith. The decoction also being drunk, comforts the heart, and strengthens the stomach and a cold brain, and therefore is good in the springtime to open obstructions of the liver, and helpeth the wind colic: it also helps those that have fluxes, or are bursten, or have a rupture: it taketh away spots or marks in the face being washed therewith. The juice of the fresh root, or powder of the dried root, have the same effect as the decoction. The root in the spring-time, steeped in wine, doth give it a delicate flavor and taste, and being drunk fasting every morning, comforteth the heart, and is a good preservative against the plague or any other poison. It helpeth digestion, warmeth a cold stomach, and openeth obstructions of the liver and spleen.

It is very safe; you need have no dose prescribed; and is very fit to be kept in every body's house.

BALM.—(*Melissa Officinalis.*)

THIS herb is so well known to be an inhabitant almost in every garden, that I shall not need to give any description thereof, although the virtues thereof, which are many, should not be omitted.

Government and Virtues.—It is an herb of Jupiter, and under Cancer, and strengthens nature much in all its actions. Let a syrup made with the juice of it and sugar (as you shall be taught at the latter end of this book) be kept in every gentlewoman's house to relieve the weak stomachs and sick bodies of their poor and sickly neighbours; as also the herb kept dry in the house, that so with other convenient simples, you may make it into an electuary with honey, according as the disease is, you shall be taught at the latter end of my book. The Arabian physicians have extolled the virtues thereof to the skies; although the Greeks thought it not worth mentioning. Seraphio saith, it causeth the mind and heart to become merry, and reviveth the heart, faintings and swoonings, especially of such who are overtaken in sleep, and driveth away all troublesome cares and thoughts out of the mind, arising from melancholy and black choler: which Avicen also confirmeth. It is very good to help digestion, and open obstructions of the brain, and hath so much purging quality in it, (saith Avicen) as to expel those melancholy vapours from the spirits and blood which are in the heart and arteries, although it cannot do so in other parts of the body. Dioscorides saith, that the leaves steeped in wine, and the wine drank, and the leaves externally applied, is a remedy against the sting of a scorpion, and the biting of mad dogs; and commendeth the decoction for women to bathe or sit in to procure their courses; it is good to wash aching teeth therewith, and profitable for those that have the bloody-flux. The leaves also, with a little nitre taken in drink, are good against the surfeit of mushrooms, and help the griping pains of the belly; and being made into an electuary, it is good for them that cannot fetch their breath: used with salt, it takes away the wens, kernels, or hard swellings in the flesh or throat; it cleanseth foul sores, and easeth pains of the gout. It is good for the liver and spleen. A tansy or caudle made with eggs, and juice thereof, while it is young, putting to some sugar and rose-water, is good for a woman in child-bed, when the after birth is not thoroughly voided, and for their faintings upon or in their sore travail. The herb bruised and boiled in a little white wine and oil, and laid warm on a bile, will ripen and break it.

BARBERRY.—*(Berberis Vulgaris.)*

THE shrub is so well known by every boy and girl that has but attained to the age of seven years, that it needs no description.

Government and Virtues.—Mars owns the shrub, and presents it to the use of my countrymen to purge their bodies of choler. The inner rind of the barberry tree boiled in white wine, and a quarter of a pint drank every morning, is an excellent remedy to cleanse the body of choleric humours, and free it from such diseases as choler causeth, such as scabs, itch, tetters, ringworms, yellow jaundice, biles, &c. It is excellent for hot agues, burnings, scaldings, heat of the blood, heat of the liver, bloody flux, for the berries are as good as the bark, and more pleasing; they get a man a good stomach to his victuals, by strengthening the attractive faculty which is under Mars, as you may see more at large at the latter end of my Ephemeris. The hair washed with the lye made of ashes of the tree and water, will make it turn yellow, viz. of Mars own color. The fruit and rind of the shrub, the flowers of broom and heath, or furze, cleanse the body of choler by sympathy, as the flowers, leaves, and bark of the peach tree do by antipathy; because these are under Mars, that under Venus.

BARLEY.—(*Hordeum Vulgare.*)

THE continual usefulness hereof hath made all in general so acquainted herewith, that it is altogether needless to describe it, several kinds hereof plentifully growing, being yearly sown in this land. The virtues thereof take as followeth.

Government and Virtues.—It is a notable plant of Saturn; if you view diligently its effects by sympathy and antipathy, you may easily perceive a reason of them; as also why barley-bread is so unwholesome for melancholy people. Barley, in all the parts and composition thereof, except malt, is more cooling than wheat, and a little cleansing; and all the preparations thereof, as barley-water and other things made thereof, do give great nourishment to persons troubled with fevers, agues, and heats in the stomach. A poultice made of barley-meal or flour boiled in vinegar and honey, and a few dried figs put in them, dissolveth all hard imposthumes, and assuageth inflammations, being thereto applied: and being boiled with melilot and camomile flowers, and some linseed, fenugreek, and rue in powder, and applied warm, it easeth pains in the side and stomach, and windiness of the spleen. The meal of barley and flea-worts boiled in water and made a poultice with honey and oil of lilies, and applied warm, cureth swellings under the ears, throat, neck, and such like; and a plaister made thereof with tar, wax, and oil, helpeth the king's evil in the throat; boiled with sharp vinegar into a poultice, and laid on hot, helpeth the leprosy; being boiled in red wine with pomegranate rind, and myrtles, stayeth the lax or other flux of the belly; boiled with vinegar and quince, it easeth the pains of the gout: barley flour, white salt, honey, and vinegar mingled together taketh away the itch speedily and certainly. The water distilled from the green barley, in the end of May, is very good for those that have defluctions of humours fallen into their eyes, and easeth the pain being dropped into them; or white bread steeped therein, and bound on the eyes, doth the same.

BASIL (GARDEN OR SWEET.)—*(Ocymum Basilicum.)*

Descrip.—The greater or ordinary bazil riseth up usually with one upright stalk diversely branching forth on all sides, with two leaves at every joint, which are somewhat broad and round, yet pointed, of a pale green colour, but fresh; a little snipped about the edges, and of a strong healthy scent. The flowers are small and white, and standing at the tops of the branches, with two small leaves at the joints, in some places green, in others brown, after which come black seed. The root perisheth at the approach of winter, and therefore must be sown every year.

Place.—It groweth in gardens.

Time.—It must be sown late, and flowers in the heart of summer, it being a very tender plant.

Government and Virtues.—This is the herb which all authors are together by the ears about, and rail at one another, like lawyers. Galen and Dioscorides hold it not fitting to be taken inwardly, and Chrysippus rails at it with downright Billingsgate rhetoric: Pliny and the Arabian Physicians defend it.

For my own part, I presently found that speech true;

Non nostrum inter nos tantas componere lites.

And away to Dr. Reason went I, who told me it was an herb of Mars, and under the Scorpion, and therefore called basilicon, and it is no marvel if it carry a kind of virulent quality with it. Being applied to the place bitten by venemous beasts, or stung by a wasp or hornet, it speedily draws the poison to it.—*Every like draws its like.* Mizaldus affirms, that being laid to rot in horsedung, it will breed venomous beasts. Hilarius, a French physician, affirms upon his own knowledge, that an acquaintance of his, by common smelling to it, had a scorpion bred in his brain. Something is the matter; this herb and rue will never grow together, no, nor near one another; and we know rue is as great an enemy to poison as any that grows.

To conclude. It expelleth both birth and after-birth;

and as it helps the deficiency of Venus in one kind, so it spoils all her actions in another. I dare write no more of it.

BAY TREE.—(*Laurus Nobilis.*)

This is so well known, that it needs no description; I shall therefore only write the virtues thereof, which are many.

Government and Virtues.—I shall but only add a word or two to what my friend hath written. viz.—That it is a tree of the Sun, and under the celestial sign Leo, and resisteth witchcraft very potently, as also all the evils old Saturn can do the body of man, and they are not a few; for it is the speech of one, and I am mistaken if it were not Mizaldus, that neither witch nor devil, thunder nor lightning, will hurt a man where a bay tree is. Galen said, that the leaves or bark do dry and heal very much, and the berries more than the leaves; the bark of the root is less sharp and hot, but more bitter, and hath some astrictions withal, whereby it is effectual to break the stone, and good to open obstructions of the liver, spleen, and other inward parts which bring the jaundice, dropsy, &c. The berries are very effectual against all poisons of venomous creatures, and the sting of wasps and bees, as also against the pestilence, or other infectious diseases, and therefore put into sundry treacles for that purpose. They likewise procure women's courses; and seven of them given to a woman in sore travail of child-birth, do cause a speedy delivery, and expel the after birth, and therefore not to be taken by such as have not gone out of their time, lest they procure abortion, or cause labour too soon. They wonderfully help all cold and rheumatic distillations from the brain to the eyes, lungs, or other parts; and being made into an electuary with honey, do help the consumption, old coughs, shortness of breath, and thin rheums, as also the megrim. They mightily expel the wind, and provoke urine; help the mother, and kill the worms. The leaves also work the like effects. A bath of the decoction of the leaves and berries, is singular good for women to sit in that are troubled with the mother, or the diseases thereof, or the stoppings of their courses, or for the diseases of the bladder, pains in the bowels by wind and stopping of urine. A decoction likewise of equal parts of bay berries, cumin-seed, hyssop, origanum, and euphorbium, with some honey, and the head bathed therewith, doth wonderfully help distillations and rheums, and settleth the palate of the mouth into its place. The oil made of the berries is very comfortable in all cold griefs of the joints, nerves, arteries, stomach, belly, or womb; and helpeth palsies, convulsions, cramp, aches, trembling, and numbness in any part, weariness also, and pains that come by sore travailing. All griefs and pains proceeding from wind, either in the head, stomach, back, belly, or womb, by anointing the parts affected therewith; and pains of the ears are also cured by dropping in some of the oil, or by receiving into the ears the fume of the decoction of the berries through a funnel. The oil takes away the marks of the skin and flesh by bruises, falls, &c. and dissolveth the congealed blood in them. It helpeth also the itch, scabs, and weals in the skin.

BEANS.—(*Vicia Faba.*)

Both the garden and field beans are so well known, that it saveth me the labour of writing a description of them. Their virtues follow.

Government and Virtues.—They are plants of Venus, and the distilled water of the flower of garden beans is good to clean the face and skin from spots and wrinkles; and the meal or flower of them, or the small beans, doth the same. The water distilled from the green husks, is held to be very effectual against the stone, and to provoke urine. Bean flour is used in poultices to assuage inflammations rising upon wounds, and the swelling of women's breasts caused by curding of their milk, and represseth their milk. Flour of beans and fenugreek mixed with honey, and applied to felons, biles, bruises, or blue marks by blows, or the imposthumes in the kernels of the ears, helpeth them all, and with rose leaves, frankincense, and the white of an egg, being applied to the eyes, helpeth them that are swollen or do water, or have received any blows upon them, if used in wine. If a bean be parted in two, the skin being taken away, and laid on the place where the leech hath been set that bleedeth too much, it stayeth the bleeding. Bean flour boiled to a poultice with wine and vinegar, and some oil put thereto, easeth both pains and swelling of the testicles. The husks boiled in water to the consumption of a third part thereof, stayeth a lax, and the ashes of the husks, made up with hog's grease, helpeth the old pains, contusions, and wounds of the sinews, the sciatica and gout. The field beans have all the afore-mentioned virtues as the garden beans. Beans eaten are extremely windy meat ; but if after the Dutch fashion, when they are half boiled you husk them and then stew them, (I cannot tell you how, for I never was cook in all my life) they are wholesome food.

BEANS (FRENCH.)—(*Phaseolus Vulgaris.*)

Descrip.—This French or kidney bean ariseth at first but with one stalk, which afterwards divides itself into many arms or branches, but all so weak that if they be not sustained with sticks or poles, they will be fruitless upon the ground. At several places of these branches grow foot stalks, each with three broad, round and pointed green leaves at the end of them ; towards the top come forth divers flowers made like unto pea blossom, of the same colour for the most part that the fruit will be of—that is to say, white, yellow, red, blackish, or of a deep purple, but white is the most usual ; after which come long and slender flat pods, some crooked, some straight, with a string running down the back thereof, wherein is flattish round fruit made like a kidney : the root long, spreadeth with many strings annexed to it, and perisheth every year.

There is another sort of French beans commonly growing with us in this land, which is called the scarlet flowered bean.

This ariseth with sundry branches as the other, but runs higher to the length of hop poles, about which they grow twining, but turning contrary to the sun, having foot stalks with three leaves on each, as on the other ; the flowers also are like the other, and of a most orient scarlet colour. The beans are larger than the ordinary kind, of a dead purple colour, turning black when ripe and dry. The root perisheth in winter.

Government and Virtues.—These also belong to Dame Venus, and being dried and beat to powder, are as great strengtheners of the kidneys as any are ; neither is there a better remedy than it : a dram at a time taken in white wine, to prevent the stone, or to cleanse the kidneys of gravel or stoppage. The ordinary French beans are of an easy digestion ; they move the belly, provoke urine, enlarge the breast that is straitened with shortness of breath, engender sperm, and incite to venery. And the scarlet-coloured beans, in regard of the glorious beauty of their colour, being set near a quickset hedge, will bravely adorn the same by climbing up thereon, so that they may be discerned a great way, not without admiration of the beholders at a distance. But they will go near to kill the quicksets by clothing them in scarlet.

BED-STRAW (LADIES'.)—*(Galium Palustre.)*

Besides the common name above written, it is called Cheese-rennet, because it performs the same offices; as also Gallion, Pettimugget, and Maid-hair; and by some Wild Rosemary.

Descrip.—This riseth up with divers small, brown, and square upright stalks, a yard high or more; sometimes branches forth into divers parts full of joints, and with divers very fine small leaves at every one of them, little or nothing rough at all; at the tops of the branches grow many long tufts or branches of yellow flowers, very thick set together, from the several joints which consist of four leaves a piece, which smell somewhat strong, but not unpleasant. The seed is small and black like poppy seed, two for the most part joined together. The root is reddish, with many small threads fastened to it, which take strong hold of the ground, and creepeth a little; and the branches leaning a little down to the ground, take root at the joints thereof, whereby it is easily increased.

There is another sort of ladies' bed-straw growing frequently in England, which beareth white flowers, as the other doth yellow; but the branches of this are so weak, that unless it be sustained by the edges, or other things near which it groweth, it will lie down to the ground. The leaves a little bigger than the former, and the flowers not so plentiful as these, and the root hereof is also thready and abiding.

Place.—They grow in meadows and pastures, both wet and dry, and by the hedges.

Time.—They flower in May for the most part, and the seed is ripe in July and August.

Government and Virtues.—They are both herbs of Venus, and therefore strengthening the parts, both internal and external, which she rules. The decoction of the former of those being drank is good to fret and break the stone, provoke urine, stayeth inward bleeding, and healeth inward wounds: the herb or flower bruised and put into the nostrils, stayeth their bleeding likewise: the flowers and herb being made into an oil by being set in the sun, and changed after it hath stood ten or twelve days; or into an ointment, being boiled in axunga, or salad oil, with some wax melted therein after it is strained; either the oil made thereof, or the ointment, do help burnings with fire, or scaldings, with water. The same also, or the decoction of the herb and flower, is good to bathe the feet of travellers and lacqueys, whose long running causeth weariness and stiffness in their sinews and joints. If the decoction be used warm, and the joints afterwards anointed with ointment, it helpeth the dry scab and the itch in children; and the herb with the white flower is also very good for the sinews, arteries, and joints, to comfort and strengthen them after travel, cold, and pains.

BEETS.—(*Beta.*)

Of Beets there are two sorts which are best known generally, and whereof I shall principally treat at this time, viz. the White and Red Beets, and their virtues.

Descrip.—The common White Beet, (*Beta Vulgaris,*) hath many great leaves next the ground, somewhat large, and of a whitish green colour. The stalk is great, strong, and ribbed, bearing a great store of leaves upon it, almost to the very top of it: the flowers grow in very long tufts, small at the end, and turning down their heads, which are small, pale, greenish yellow buds, giving cornered prickly seeds. The root is great, long, and hard, and, when it hath given seed, it is of no use at all. The common Red Beet, (*Beta Hortensis,*) differeth not from the White, but only it is less, and the leaves and roots are somewhat red. The leaves are differently red, some only with red stalks or veins; some of a fresh red, and others of a dark red: the root thereof is red, spongy, and not used to be eaten.

Government and Virtues.—The government of these two sorts of beets are far different: the red beet being under Saturn, and the white under Jupiter: therefore take the virtues of them apart, each by itself. The white beet doth much loosen the belly, and is of a cleansing, digesting quality, and provoketh urine: the juice of it openeth obstructions both of the liver and spleen, and is good for the head-ache and swimming therein, and turnings of the brain: and is effectual also against all venomous creatures; and applied upon the temples stayeth inflammations in the eyes: it helpeth burnings being used without oil, and with a little alum put to it is good for St. Antony's fire. It is good for all weals, pustules, blisters, and blains in the skin: the herb boiled and laid upon chilblains or kibes, helpeth them: the decoction thereof in water and some vinegar, healeth the itch if bathed therewith, and cleanseth the head of dandruff, scurf, and dry scabs, and doth much good for fretting and running sores, ulcers, and cankers in the head, legs, or other parts, and is much commended against baldness and shedding the hair.

The red beet root is good to stay the bloody flux, women's courses, and the whites, and to help the yellow jaundice: the juice of the root put into the nostrils purgeth the head, helpeth the noise in the ears, and the tooth-ache: the juice snuffed up the nose helps a stinking breath, if the cause lies in the nose, as many times it doth, if any bruise had been there; as also want of smell coming that way.

BETONY (WATER.)—*(Betonica Aquatica.)*

Called also Brown-wort: and in Yorkshire, Bishop's-leaves.

Descrip.—First, of the water betony, which riseth up with square, hard, greenish stalks, sometimes brown, set with broad dark green leaves dented about the edges with notches, somewhat resembling the leaves of the wood betony, but much larger too, for the most part set at a joint. The flowers are many, set at the tops of the stalks and branches, being round bellied and opened at the brims, and divided into two parts the uppermost like a hood, and the lowermost like a hip hanging down, of a dark red colour, which passing, there comes in their places small round heads with small points at the ends, wherein lie small and brownish seeds. The root is a thick bush of strings and shreds growing from the head.

Place.—It groweth by the ditch side, brooks, and other water courses generally through this land, and is seldom found far from the water side.

Time.—It flowereth about July, and the seed is ripe in August.

Government and Virtues.—Water betony is an herb of Jupiter in Cancer, and is appropriated more to wounds and hurts in breasts than wood betony, which follows; it is an excellent remedy for sick hogs—it is of a cleansing quality. The leaves bruised and applied are effectual for old and filthy ulcers; and especially if the juice of the leaves be boiled with a little honey and dipped therein, and sores dressed therewith; as also for bruises or hurts, whether inward or outward. The distilled water of the leaves is used for the same purpose, as also to bathe the face and hands spotted or blemished, or discoloured by sun burning.

I confess I do not much fancy distilled waters, I mean such waters as are distilled cold; some virtues of the herb they may happily have, (it were a strange thing else) but this I am confident of, that being distilled in a pewter still, as the vulgar and apish fashion is, both chemical oil and salt is left behind, unless you burn them, and then all is spoiled, water and all, which was good for as little as can be by such a distillation in my translation of the London Dispensatory.

BETONY (WOOD.)—*(Betonica Officinalis.)*

Descrip.—Common, or wood betony, hath many leaves rising from the root, which are somewhat broad and round at the end, roundly dented about the edges, standing upon long foot stalks, from among which rise up small, square, slender, but upright hairy stalks, with some leaves thereon, to a piece at the joints, smaller than the lower, whereof are set several spiked heads of flowers like lavender, but thicker and shorter for the most part, and of a reddish or purple colour, spotted with white spots both in the upper and lower part, the seeds being contained in the husks that hold the flowers, are blackish, somewhat long and uneven. The roots are many white thready strings; the stalk perisheth, but the roots with some leaves thereon, abide all the winter. The whole plant is somewhat small.

Place.—It groweth frequently in woods and delighteth, in shady places.

Time.—It flowereth in July, after which the seed is quickly ripe, yet in its prime in May.

Government and Virtues.—The herb is appropriated to the planet Jupiter, and the sign Aries. Antonius Musa, physician to the Emperor Agustus Cæsar, wrote a peculiar book of the Virtues of this herb; and among other virtues saith of it, that it preserveth the liver and body of man from the danger of epidemical diseases, and from witchcraft also: it helpeth those that loathe or cannot digest their meat, those that have weak stomachs, or sour belchings, or continual rising in their stomach, using it familiarly either green or dry: either the herb or root, or the flowers in broth, drink, or meat, or made into conserve syrup, water, electuary, or powder, as every one may best frame themselves unto, or as the time or season requireth; taken any of the aforesaid ways, it helpeth the jaundice, falling sickness, the palsy, convulsions, shrinking of the sinews, the gout, and those that are inclined to dropsy, those that have continual pains in their heads, although it turn to frenzy. The powder mixed with pure honey is no less available for all sorts of coughs or colds, wheezing, or shortness of breath, distillations of thin rheums upon the lungs, which causeth consumptions. The decoction made with mead and a little pennyroyal, is good for those that are troubled with putrid agues, whether quotidian, tertian, or quartan, and to draw down and evacuate the blood and humours, that by falling into the eyes, do hinder the sight: the decoction thereof made in wine, and taken, killeth the worms in the belly, openeth obstructions both of the spleen and liver, cureth stitches and pains in the back or sides, the torments and griping pains of the bowels and the wind cholic: and mixed with honey purgeth the belly, helpeth to bring down women's courses, and is of special use for those that are troubled with the falling down of the mother, and pains thereof, and causeth an easy and speedy delivery of women in child-birth. It helpeth also to break and expel the stone, either in the bladder or kidneys: the decoction with wine gargled in the mouth easeth the tooth-ache. It is commended against the stinging or biting of venomous serpents, or mad dogs, being used inwardly and applied outwardly to the place. A dram of the powder of betony, taken with a little honey in some vinegar, doth wonderfully refresh those that are over wearied by travel. It stayeth bleeding at the mouth and nose, and helpeth those that evacuate blood, and those that are bursten or have a rupture, and is good for such as are bruised by any fall or otherwise. The green herb bruised, or the juice applied to any inward hurt, or outward green wound in the head or body, will quickly heal and close it up: as also any veins or sinews that are cut; and will draw forth a broken bone or splinter, thorn or other things got into the flesh. It is no less profitable for old and filthy ulcers; yea, though they be fistulous and hollow. But some do advise to put a little salt to this purpose, being applied with a little hog's lard, it helpeth a plague or sore and other biles and pushes. The fume of the decoction while it is warm received by a funnel into the ears, easeth the pains of them, destroys the worms, and cureth the running sores in them: the juice dropped into them doth the same. The root of betony is displeasing both to the taste and stomach, whereas the leaves and flowers, by their sweet and spicy taste, are comfortable both to meat and medicine.

These are some of the many virtues Antonius Musa, an expert physician, for it was not the practice of Octavius Cæsar to keep fools about him, appropriates to betony: it is a very precious herb, that is certain, and most fitting to be kept in a man's house, both in syrup, conserve, oil, ointment, and plaister. The flowers are usually conserved.

BEECH TREE.—(*Fagus Sylvatica.*)

In treating of this tree, you must understand that I mean the green Mast-beech, which is by way of distinction from that other small rough sort, called in Sussex the Smaller Beech, but in Essex, Hornbeam, (*Carpinus Betulus.*)

I suppose it is needless to describe it, being already too well known to my countrymen.

Place.—It groweth in woods among oaks and other trees, and in parks, forests, and chases to feed deer, and in other places to fatten swine.

Time.—It bloometh in the end of April or the beginning of May for the most part, and the fruit is ripe in September.

Government and Virtues.—It is a plant of Saturn, and therefore performs his qualities and proportion in these operations. The leaves of the beech tree are cooling and binding, and therefore good to be applied to hot swellings to discuss them: the nuts do much nourish such beasts as feed thereon. The water found in the hollow places of decaying beeches will cure both man and beast of any scurf, scab, or running tetters, if they be washed there-

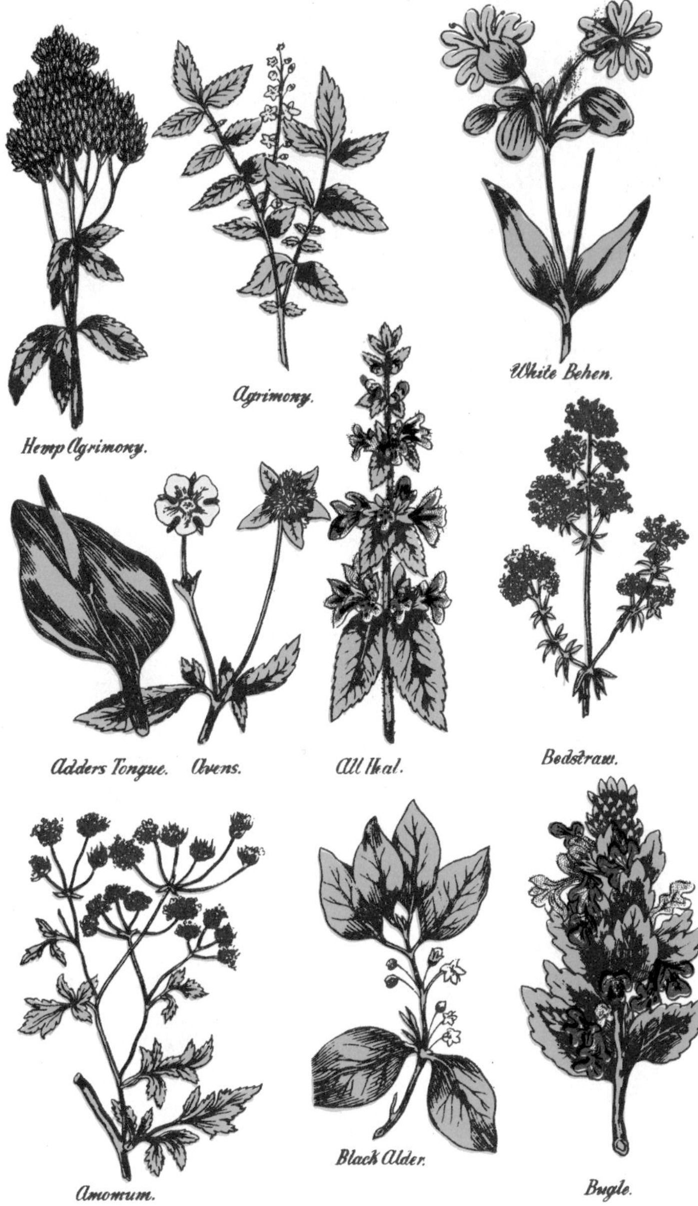

Hemp Agrimony.
Agrimony.
White Behen.
Adders Tongue.
Avens.
All Heal.
Bedstraw.
Amomum.
Black Alder.
Bugle.

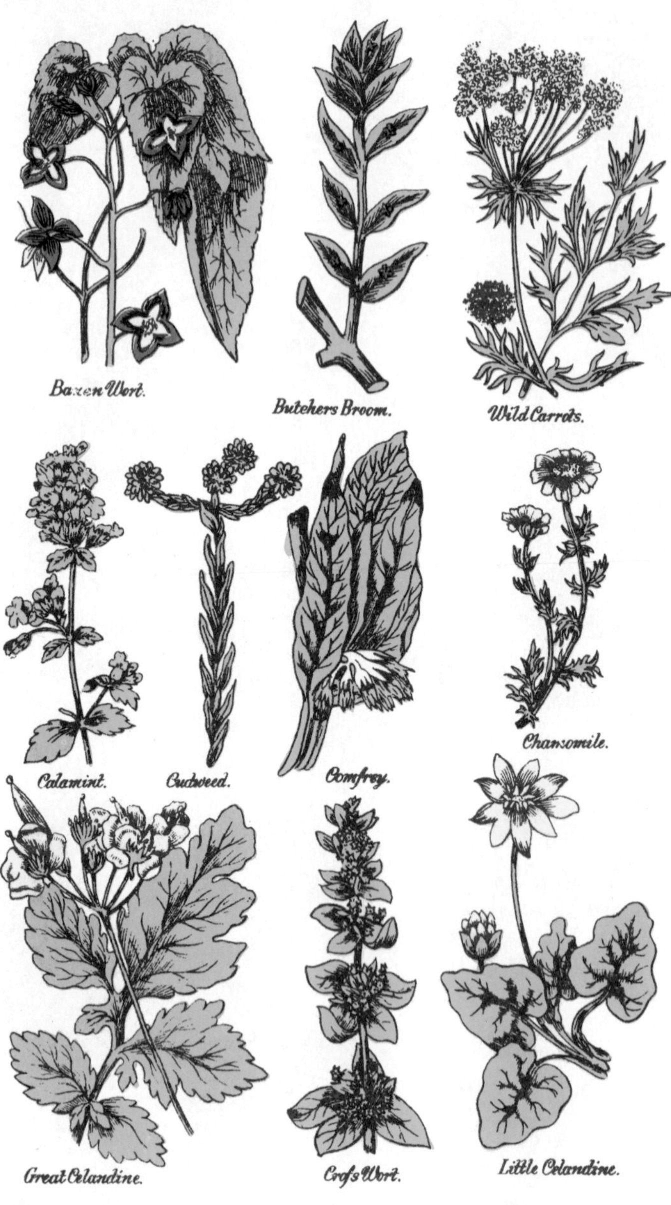
Baxen Wort.
Butchers Broom.
Wild Carrots.
Calamint.
Cudweed.
Comfrey.
Chamomile.
Great Celandine.
Croſs Wort.
Little Celandine.

with: you may boil the leaves into a poultice, or make an ointment of them when the time of year serves.

BILBERRIES, OR WHORTLEBERRIES.—(*Vaccinium Myrtillus.*)

Descrip.—Of these there are two sorts which are common in England, viz.—the black and red berries. And first of the black.

The small bush creepeth along upon the ground, scarce rising half a yard high, with divers small dark green leaves set in the green branches, not always one against the other, and a little dented about the edges; at the foot of the leaves come forth small, hollow, pale, blueish coloured flowers, the brims ending in five points, with a reddish thread in the middle, which pass into small round berries of the bigness and colour of the juniper berries, but of a purple, sweetish, sharp taste; the juice of them give a purplish colour to the hands and lips that eat and handle them, especially if they break them. The root groweth aslope under ground, shooting forth in sundry places as it creepeth. This loseth its leaves in winter.

The red bilberry, or whortle-bush, riseth up like the former, having sundry hard leaves, like the box-tree leaves, green and round pointed, standing on the several branches, at the top whereof only, and not from the sides as in the former, come forth divers round, reddish, sappy berries, of a sharp taste when they are ripe. The root runneth in the ground as in the former, but the leaves of this abide all the winter.

Place.—The first groweth in forests, on the heath, and such like barren places. The red grows in the north parts of this land, as Lancashire, Yorkshire, &c.

Time.—They flower in March and April, and the fruit of the black is ripe in July and August.

Government and Virtues.—They are under the dominion of Jupiter. It is a pity they are used no more in physic than they are. The black bilberries are good in hot agues, and to cool the heat of the liver and stomach: they do somewhat bind the belly, and stay the vomitings and loathings: the juice of the berries made into a syrup, or the pulp made into a conserve with sugar, is good for the purposes aforesaid, as also for an old cough, or an ulcer in the lungs, or other diseases therein. The red whorts are more binding, and stop women's courses, spitting of blood, or any other flux of blood or humours, being used as well outwardly as inwardly.

BIFOIL, OR TWABLADE.—(*Listera Ovata.*)

Descrip.—This small herb, from a root somewhat sweet, shooting downwards many long strings, riseth up a round green stalk, bare or naked next the ground for an inch, two or three to the middle thereof, as it is in age or growth : as also from the middle upward to the flowers, having only two broad plantain-like leaves, but whiter, set at the middle of the stalk, one against another, compasseth it round at the bottom of them.

Place.—It is an usual inhabitant in woods, copses, and in many other places in this land.

There is another sort groweth in wet grounds and marshes, which is somewhat different from the former. It is a smaller plant, and greener, having sometimes three leaves ; the spike of the flowers is less than the former, and the roots of this do run or creep in the ground.

They are much and often used by many to good purposes for wounds, both green and old, to consolidate or knit ruptures, as well it may, being a plant of Saturn.

BIRCH TREE.—(*Betula Alba.*)

Descrip.—This groweth a goodly tall straight tree, fraught with many boughs and slender branches bending downward ; the old being covered with a discoloured chopped bark, and the younger being browner by much. The leaves at the first breaking out are crumpled, and afterwards like beech leaves, but smaller and greener, and dented about the edges. It beareth small short catkins, somewhat like those of the hazel-nut tree, which abide on the branches a long time until growing ripe they fall upon the ground, and their seed with them.

Place.—It usually groweth in woods.

Government and Virtues.—It is a tree of Venus. The juice of the leaves, while they are young, or the distilled water of them, or the water that comes from the tree being bored with an auger, and distilled afterwards ; any of hese being drunk for some days together, is available to break the stone in the kidneys and bladder, and is good also to wash sore mouths.

BIRD'S FOOT.—(*Ornithopus Purpusillus.*)

THIS small herb groweth not above a span high, with many branches spread upon the ground, set with many wings of small leaves. The flowers grow upon the branches, many small ones of a pale yellow colour being set a head together, which afterwards turn into small jointed pods, well resembling the claws of small birds, whence it took its name.

There is another sort of bird's foot in all things like the former, but a little larger; the flowers of a pale whitish red colour, and the pods distinct by joints like the other, but a little more crooked, and the roots do carry many small white knots or kernels among the strings.

Place.—These grow on heaths, and many open untilled places of this land.

Time.—They flower and seed in the end of summer.

Government and Virtues.—They belong to Saturn, are of a drying, binding quality, and therefore very good to be used in wound drinks; as also to apply outwardly for the same purpose. But the latter bird's foot is found by experience to break the stone in the back or kidneys, and drives them forth, if the decoction thereof be taken; and it wonderfully helpeth the rupture, being taken inwardly, and outwardly applied to the place.

All salts have best operations upon the stone, as ointments and plasters have upon wounds; and therefore you may make a salt of this for the stone: the way how to do so may be found in my translation of the London Dispensatory; and it may be I may give you it again in plainer terms at the latter end of this book.

BISHOP'S WEED.—(*Ammi Majus.*)

BESIDES the common name, Bishop's Weed, it is usually known by the Greek name *Ammi* and *Ammios;* some call it Æthiopian Cumin-seed, and others Cumin-Royal, as also Herb-William, and Bull-Wort.

Descrip.—Common bishop's weed riseth up with a round straight stalk, sometimes as high as a man, but usually three or four feet high, beset with divers small, long, and somewhat broad leaves, cut in some places and dented about the edges, growing one against the other, of a dark green colour, having sundry branches on them, and at the top small umbels of white flowers which turn into small round seeds, little bigger than parsley-seeds, of a quick hot scent and taste ; the root is white and stringy, perishing yearly, and usually riseth again on its own sowing.

Place.—It groweth wild in many places in England and Wales, as between Greenhithe and Gravesend.

Government and Virtues.—It is hot and dry in the third degree, of a bitter taste, and somewhat sharp withal : it provokes lust to purpose ; I suppose Venus owns it. It digesteth humours, provoketh urine and women's courses, dissolveth wind, and being taken in wine it easeth pain and griping in the bowels, and is good against the biting of serpents : it is used to good effect in those medicines which are given to hinder the poisonous operation of cantharides upon the passage of the urine : being mixed with honey, and applied to black and blue marks coming of blows or bruises, it takes them away : and being drunk or outwardly applied, it abateth a high colour, and makes it pale ; and the fumes thereof taken with rosin or raisins, cleanseth the mother.

BISTORT, OR SNAKEWEED.—(*Polygonum Bistorta.*)

IT is called Snakeweed, English Serpentary, Dragon-wort, Osterick, and Passions.

Descrip.—This hath a thick short knobbed root, blackish without, and somewhat reddish within, a little crooked or turned together, of a hard astringent taste, with divers black threads hanging therefrom, whence spring up every year divers leaves standing upon long foot-stalks, being somewhat broad and long like a dock leaf, and a little pointed at the ends, but that it is of a blueish green colour on the upper side, and of an ash-colour grey and a little purplish underneath, with divers veins therein, from among which rise up divers small and slender stalks, two feet high, and almost naked and without leaves, or with a very few and narrow, bearing a spiky bush of pale-coloured flowers ; which being past, there abideth small seed, like unto sorrel seed, but greater.

There are other sorts of bistort growing in this land, but smaller, both in height, root, and stalks, and especially in the leaves. The root is blackish without, and somewhat whitish within ; of an austere binding taste, as the former.

Place.—They grow in shadowy moist woods and at the foot of hills, but are chiefly nourished up in gardens. The narrow leaved bistort groweth in the north, in Lancashire, Yorkshire, and Cumberland.

Time.—They flower about the end of May, and the seed is ripe about the beginning of July.

Government and Virtues.—It belongs to Saturn, and is in operation cold and dry: both the leaves and roots have a powerful faculty to resist all poison. The root in powder taken in drink expelleth the venom of the plague, the small-pox, measles, purples, or any other infectious disease, driving it out by sweating. The root in powder, the decoction thereof in wine being drunk, stayeth all manner of inward bleeding, or spitting of blood, and any fluxes in the body of either man or woman, or vomiting. It is also very available against ruptures, or burstings, or all bruises, or falls, dissolving the congealed blood, and easeth the pains that happen thereupon; it also helpeth the jaundice.

The water distilled from both leaves and roots, is a singular remedy to wash any place bitten or stung by any venomous creature; as also for any of the purposes before spoken of, and is very good to wash running sores or ulcers. The decoction of the root in wine being drunk, hindereth abortion or miscarriage in child-bearing. The leaves also kill the worms in children, and is a great help to them that cannot keep their water; if the juice of the plantain be added thereto, and outwardly applied, much helpeth the gonorrhœa, or running of the reins. A dram of the powder of the root taken in water thereof, wherein some red hot iron or steel hath been quenched, is also an admirable help thereto, so as the body be first prepared and purged from the offensive humours. The leaves, seed, or roots, are all very good in decoctions, drinks, or lotions, for inward or outward wounds or other sores; and the powder strewed upon any cut or wound in a vein, stayeth the immoderate bleeding thereof. The decoction of the root in water, whereunto some pomegranate peels and flowers are added, injected into the matrix, stayeth the immoderate flux of the courses. The root thereof with Pellitory of Spain and burnt alum, of each a little quantity, beaten small and made into paste with some honey, and a little piece thereof put into a hollow tooth, or held between the teeth if there be no hollowness in them, stayeth the defluxion of rheum upon them, which causeth pains, and helps to cleanse the head, and void much offensive water. The distilled water is very effectual to wash sores or cankers in the nose or any other part, if the powder of the root be applied thereunto afterwards. It is good also to fasten the gums, and to take away the heat and inflammations that happen in the jaws, almonds of the throat and mouth, if the decoction of the leaves, roots, or seeds be bruised, or the juice of them be applied; but the roots are most effectual to the purposes aforesaid.

BITTER SWEET.—(*Solanum Dulcamara.*)

CALLED also Mortal, Woody Nightshade, Felon-wort, and Amara Dulcis.

Descrip.—It grows up with wood stalks, even to a man's height, and sometimes higher. The leaves fall off at the approach of winter, and spring out of the same stalks at spring-time. The branch is compassed about with a whitish bark, and hath a pith in the middle of it; the main branch brancheth itself into many small ones with claspers, laying hold on what is next to them, as vines do. It bears many leaves; they grow in no order at all, or at least in no regular order. The leaves are longish, though somewhat broad, and pointed at the ends; many of them have two little leaves growing at the end of their footstalks; some have but one, and some none.

Place.—It grows commonly in moist and shady places.

Time.—The leaves shoot out in March; it flowereth in July, and the seeds are ripe soon after.

Government and Virtues.—It is under the planet Mercury. It is good to remove witchcraft both in men and beast, as all sudden diseases whatsoever. Being tied about the neck, it is a remedy for the vertigo or dizziness of the head; and that is the reason the Germans hang it about their cattle's necks, when they fear any such evil hath betided them: country people commonly used to take the berries of it, and having bruised them, they applied them to felons, and thereby soon rid their fingers of such troublesome guests.

BLACKBERRY BUSH (THE.)—(*Rubus Fruticosus.*)

IT is so well known that it needeth no description. The virtues thereof are as follows.

Government and Virtues.—It is a plant of Venus in Aries. You shall have some directions at the latter end of the book for the gathering of all herbs and plants, &c. If any ask the reason why Venus is so prickly? Tell them 'tis because she is in the house of Mars. The buds, leaves, and branches, while they are green, are of good use in the ulcers and putrid sores of the mouth and throat, and of the quinsey, and likewise to heal other fresh wounds and sores ; but the flowers and fruits unripe are very binding, and so profitable for the bloody flux, laxes, and are a fit remedy for spitting of blood. Either the decoction or powder of the root being taken is good to break or drive forth gravel and the stone in the reins and kidneys. The leaves and brambles, as well green as dry, are excellent good lotions for sores in the mouth or secret parts: the decoction of them and of the dried branches, do much bind the belly, and are good for too much flowing of women's courses : the berries of the flowers are a powerful remedy against the poison of the most venomous serpents : as well drank as outwardly applied, helpeth the sores of the fundament, and the piles : the juice of the berries mixed with the juice of mulberries do bind more effectually, and help all fretting and eating sores and ulcers whatsoever. The distilled water of the branches, leaves, and flowers, or of the fruit, is very pleasant in taste, and very effectual in fevers and hot distempers of the body, head, eyes, and other parts, and for the purposes aforesaid. The leaves boiled in lye, and the head washed therewith, healeth the itch and the running sores thereof, and maketh the hair black. The powder of the leaves strewed on cankers and running ulcers, wonderfully helps to heal them. Some used to condensate the juice of the leaves, and some the juice of the berries, to keep for their use all the year for the purposes aforesaid.

BLITES.—(*Amarantus Blitum.*)

Descrip.—Of these there are two sorts, white and red. The white hath leaves somewhat like unto beets, but smaller, rounder, and of a whitish green colour, every one standing upon a small long foot stalk ; the stalk rises up two or three feet high with such like leaves thereon ; the flowers grow at the top in long round tufts or clusters, wherein are contained small and round seeds : the root is very full of threads or strings.

The red blite is in all things like the white, but that its leaves and tufted heads are exceeding red at first, and after turn more purplish.

There are other kinds of blites whicn grow, differing from the two former sorts but little, but only the wild are smaller in every part.

Place.—They grow in gardens, and wild in many places in this land.

Time.—They seed in August and September.

Government and Virtues.—They are all of them cooling, drying, and binding, serving to restrain the fluxes of blood in either man or woman, especially the red; which also stayeth the overflowing of the women's reds, as the white blite stayeth the whites in women. It is an excellent secret; you cannot well fail in the use: they are all under the dominion of Venus.

There is another sort of wild blites like the other wild kinds, but have long and spiky heads of greenish seeds, seeming by the thick setting together to be all seed.

This sort fishes are delighted with, and it is a good and usual bait, for fishes will bite fast enough at them if you have but wit enough to catch them when they bite.

BORAGE.—(*Borago Officinalis.*) BUGLOSS.—(*Lycopsis Arvensis.*)

THESE are so well known to the inhabitants in every garden that I hold it needless to describe them.

To these I may add a third sort, which is not so common nor yet so well known, and therefore I shall give you its name and description.

It is called *langue de bœuf;* but why then should they call one herb by the name bugloss and another by the name *langue de bœuf?* It is some question to me, seeing one signifies ox-tongue in Greek, and the other signifies the same in French.

Descrip.—The leaves thereof are smaller than those of bugloss, but much rougher; the stalks arising up about a foot and a half high, and is most commonly of a red colour; the flowers stand in scaly rough heads, being composed of many small yellow flowers, not much unlike to those of dandelions, and the seed flieth away in down as that doth; you may easily know the flowers by their taste, for they are very bitter.

Place.—It groweth wild in many places of this land, and may be plentifully found near London, as between Rotherhithe and Deptford by the ditch side. Its virtues are held to be the same with borage and bugloss, only this is somewhat hotter.

Time.—They flower in June and July, and the seed is ripe shortly after.

Government and Virtues.—They are all three herbs of

Jupiter, and under Leo, all great cordials and great strengtheners of nature. The leaves and roots are to very good purpose used in putrid and pestilential fevers to defend the heart, and to resist and to expel the poison or venom of other creatures ; the seed is of the like effects ; and the seed and leaves are good to increase milk in women's breasts : the leaves, flowers, and seed, all or any of them, are good to expel pensiveness and melancholy : it helpeth to clarify the blood, and mitigate heat in fevers. The juice made into a syrup prevaileth much to all the purposes aforesaid, and is put with other cooling, opening, and cleansing herbs to open obstructions and help the yellow jaundice ; and mixed with fumitory, to cool, cleanse, and temper the blood thereby : it helpeth the itch, ringworms, and tetters, or other spreading scabs and sores. The flowers candied or made into a conserve, are helpful in the former cases, but are chiefly used as a cordial, and are good for those that are weak in long sickness, and to comfort the heart and spirits of those that are in a consumption, or troubled with often swoonings, or passions of the heart. The distilled water is no less effectual to all the purposes aforesaid, and helpeth the redness and inflammations of the eyes, being washed therewith : the dried herb is never used, but the green : yet the ashes thereof boiled in mead or honied water, is available against the inflammations and ulcers in the mouth or throat, to gargle it therewith : the roots of bugloss are effectual, being made into a licking electuary, for the cough, and to condensate phlegm, and the rheumatic distillations upon the lungs.

BLUE-BOTTLE.—*(Centaurea Cyanus.)*

It is called Cyanus, I suppose from the colour of it; Hurt-sickle, because it turns the edges of the sickles that reap the corn, Blue-blow, Corn-flower, and Blue-bottle.

Descrip.—I shall only describe that which is commonest, and in my opinion most useful : its leaves spread upon the ground, being of a whitish green colour, somewhat on the edges like those of corn scabious, amongst which ariseth up a stalk divided into divers branches beset with long leaves of a greenish colour, either but very little indented or not at all : the flowers are of a blue colour, from whence it took its name, consisting of an innumerable company of small flowers set in a scaly head, not much unlike those of knap-weed; the seed is smooth, bright, and shining, wrapped up in a woolly mantle; the root perisheth every year.

Place.—They grow in corn-fields, amongst all sorts of corn, peas, beans, and tares excepted. If you please to take them up from thence and transplant them in your garden, especially towards the full moon, they will grow more double than they are, and many times change colour.

Time.—They flower from the beginning of May to the end of harvest.

Government and Virtues.—As they are naturally cold, dry, and binding, so they are under the dominion of Saturn. The powder or dried leaves of the blue-bottle, or corn flower is given with good success to those that are bruised by a fall, or have broken a vein inwardly, and void much blood at the mouth: being taken in the water of plantain, horse-tail, or the greater comfrey, it is a remedy against the poison of the scorpion, and resisteth all venoms and poison. The seed or leaves taken in wine, is very good against the plague and all infectious diseases, and is very good in pestilential fevers: the juice put into fresh or green wounds doth quickly solder up the lips of them together, and is very effectual to heal all ulcers and sores in the mouth; the juice dropped into the eyes takes away the heat and inflammation of them: the distilled water of this herb hath the same properties, and may be used for the effects aforesaid.

BRANK URSINE.—(*Acanthus Spinosus.*)

Besides the common name Brank Ursine, it is also called Bear's Breech, and Acanthus, though I think our English names to be more proper; for the Greek word Acanthus signifies any thistle whatsoever.

Descrip.—This thistle shooteth forth very many large, thick, sad green smooth leaves upon the ground, with a very thick and juicy middle rib; the leaves are parted with sundry deep gashes on the edges; the leaves remain a long time before any stalk appears, afterwards riseth up a reasonable big stalk, three or four feet high, and bravely decked with flowers from the middle of the stalk upwards, for on the lower part of the stalk there is neither branches nor leaf: the flowers are hooded and gaping, being white in colour, and standing in brownish husks, with a long, small, undivided leaf under each leaf: they seldom seed in our country. Its roots are many, great, and thick, blackish without and whitish within, full of a clammy sap. A piece of them if you set it in the garden, and defend it from the first winter cold, will grow and flourish.

Place.—They are only nursed up in the gardens in England, where they will grow very well.

Time.—It flowereth in June and July.

Government and Virtues.—It is an excellent plant under the dominion of the moon. I could wish such as are studious would labour to keep it in their gardens: the leaves being boiled and used in clysters, are excellent good to mollify the belly, and make the passage slippery: the decoction drunk inwardly is excellent and good for the bloody flux: the leaves being bruised, or rather boiled, and applied like a poultice, are very good to unite broken bones, and strengthen joints that have been put out; the decoction of either leaves or roots being drunk, and the decoction of leaves applied to the place is excellent good for the king's evil that is broken and runneth: for by the influence of the moon it reviveth the ends of the veins which are relaxed; there is scarce a better remedy to be applied to such places as are burnt with fire than this is, for it fetches out the fire, and heals it without a scar: this is an excellent remedy for such as have ruptures, being either taken inwardly or applied to the place: in like manner used it helps the cramp and the gout: it is excellent good in hectic fevers, and restores radical moisture to such as are in consumptions.

BRIONY, OR WILD VINE.—*(Bryonia.)*

It is called Wild Vine, and Wood Vine, (*Bryonia Dioica.*) Tamus, or Ladies' Seal. The white is called White Vine, (*Bryonia Alba,*) and the black, Black Vine, (*Bryonia Nigra.*)

Descrip.—The common white briony groweth rampant upon the hedges, sending forth many long, rough, very tender branches at the beginning, with many rough and broad leaves thereon, cut (for the most part) into five partitions, in form like a vine leaf, but smaller, rough, and of a whitish hoary green color, spreading very far, and twining with its small claspers (that come forth at the joints with the leaves) very far on whatsoever standeth next to it. At the several joints also, especially towards the top of the branches, cometh forth a long stalk, bearing many white flowers together on a long tuft, consisting of five small leaves a-piece laid open like a star, after which come the berries separated one from another, more than a cluster of grapes, green at first and very red when they are thoroughly ripe, of no good scent, but of a very loathsome taste, provoking vomit. The root groweth to be exceeding great, with many long twines or branches going from it, of a pale whitish colour on the outside, and more white within, and of a sharp, bitter, loathsome taste.

Place.—It groweth on banks or under hedges, through this land : the roots lie very deep.

Time.—It flowereth in July and August, some earlier, and some later than the other.

Government and Virtues.—They are furious martial plants. The root of briony purges the belly with great violence, troubling the stomach and burning the liver, and therefore not rashly to be taken ; but being corrected, is very profitable for diseases of the head, as falling sickness, giddiness and swimmings, by drawing away much phlegm and rheumatic humours that oppress the head, as also the joints and sinews ; and is therefore good for palsies, convulsions, cramps, and stitches in the side, and the dropsy, and in provoking urine : it cleanses the reins and kidneys from gravel and stone, by opening the obstruction of the spleen, and consumeth the hardness and swelling thereof. The decoction of the root in wine drank once a week at going to bed, cleanseth the mother, and helpeth the rising thereof, and expelleth the dead child ; a drachm of the root in powder taken in white wine bringeth down the courses. An electuary made of the roots and honey doth mightily cleanse the chest of rotten phlegm, and wonderfully helps any old strong cough, to those that are troubled with shortness of breath, and is very good for them that are bruised inwardly, to help to expel the clotted or congealed blood. The leaves, fruit, and root do cleanse old and filthy sores, are good against all fretting and running cankers, gangrenes, and tetters, and therefore the berries are by some country-people called tetter berries. The root cleanseth the skin wonderfully from all black and blue spots, freckles, morphew, leprosy, foul scars, or other deformity whatsoever : also all running scabs and manginess are healed by the powder of the dried root or the juice thereof, but especially by the fine white hardened juice. The distilled water of the root worketh the same effects, but more weakly; the root bruised and applied of itself to any place where the bones are broken, helpeth to draw them forth, as also splinters and thorns in the flesh; and being applied with a little wine mixed therewith, it breaketh biles, and helpeth whitlows on the joints. For all these latter, beginning at sores, cankers, &c. apply it outwardly, and take my advice in my translation of the London Dispensatory, among the preparations at the latter end, where you have a medicine called *fæcula brionia*, which take and use, mixing it with a little hog's grease, or other convenient ointment.

As for the former diseases where it must be taken inwardly, it purgeth very violently, and needs an abler hand to correct it than most country people have; therefore it is a better way for them, in my opinion, to let the simple alone, and take the compound water of it

BROOK-LIME, OR WATER PIMPERNEL.—(*Veronica Becabung.*)

Descrip.—This sendeth forth from a creeping root that shooteth forth strings at every joint as it runneth, divers and sundry green stalks, round and sappy, with some branches on them, somewhat broad, round, deep green and thick leaves set by couples thereon; from the bottom whereof shoot forth long foot-stalks with sundry small blue flowers on them, that consist of five small round pointed leaves a-piece.

There is another sort nothing differing from the former but that it is greater, and the flowers are of a paler green colour.

Place.—They grow in small standing waters, and usually near water-cresses.

Time.—And flower in June and July, giving seed the next month after.

Government and Virtues.—It is a hot and biting martial plant. Brook-lime and water-cresses are generally used together in diet drink with other things serving to purge the blood and body from all ill humors that would destroy health, and are helpful to the scurvy. They do all provoke urine, and help to break the stone and pass it away; they procure women's courses, and expel the dead child. Being fried with butter and vinegar, and applied warm, it helpeth all manner of tumours swellings, and inflammations.

Such drinks ought to be made of sundry herbs according to the malady. I shall give a plain and easy rule at the latter end of this book.

BUTCHER'S BROOM.—(*Ruscus Aculeatus.*)

It is called Ruscus, and Bruscus, Kneeholm, Knee-Holy, Kneehulver, and Pettigree.

Descrip.—The first shoots that sprout from the roots of butcher's broom are thick, whitish, and short, somewhat like those of asparagus, but greater, they rising up to be a foot and a half high, are spread into divers branches, green, and somewhat cressed with the roundness, tough and flexible, whereon are set somewhat broad and almost round hard leaves, prickly, pointed at the end, and of a dark green colour; two for the most part set at a place very close and near together: about the middle of the leaf, on the back and lower side from the middle rib, breaketh forth a small whitish green flower, consisting of four small round pointed leaves standing upon little or no foot-stalk, and in the place whereof cometh a small round berry, green at the first and red when it is ripe, wherein are two or three white, hard round seeds contained. The root is thick, white, and great at the head, and from thence sendeth forth divers thick, white, long tough strings.

Place.—It groweth in copses, and upon heaths and waste grounds, and oftentimes under or near the holly bushes.

Time.—It shooteth forth its young buds in the spring, and the berries are ripe about September, the branches of leaves abiding green all the winter.

Government and Virtues.—It is a plant of Mars, being of a gallant cleansing and opening quality. The decoction of the root made with wine openeth obstructions, provoketh urine, helpeth to expel gravel and the stone, the strangury and women's courses, also the yellow jaundice and the head ache: and with some honey or sugar put thereunto, cleanseth the breast of phlegm, and the chest of such clammy humours gathered therein. The decoction of the root drank, and a poultice made of the berries and leaves being applied are effectual in knitting and consolidating broken bones or parts out of joint. The common way of using it is to boil the root, and parsley, fennel, and smallage in white wine, and drink the decoction, adding the like quantity of grass root to them: the more of the root you boil the stronger will the decoction be; it works no ill effects, yet I hope you have wit enough to give the strongest decoction to the strongest bodies.

BROOM, OR BROOM-RAPE.—(*Orobanche Major.*)

To spend time in writing a description hereof is altogether needless, it being so generally used by all the good housewives almost throughout this land to sweep their houses with, and therefore very well known to all sorts of people.

The broom-rape springeth up on many places from the roots of the broom, but more often in fields, as by hedge-sides and on heaths: the stalk whereof is of the bigness of a finger or thumb, above two feet high, having a show of leaves on them, and many flower at the tops of a reddish yellow colour, as also the stalks and leaves are.

Place.—They grow in many places of this land commonly, and as commonly spoil all the land they grow in.

Time.—They flower in the summer months, and give their seed before winter.

Government and Virtues.—The juice or decoction of the young branches, or seed, or the powder of the seed taken in drink purgeth downwards, and draweth phlegmatic and watery humours from the joints, whereby it helpeth the dropsy, gout, sciatica, and pains of the hips and joints; it also provoketh strong vomits, and helpeth the pains of the sides, and swelling of the spleen; cleanseth also the reins or kidneys, and bladder of the stone, provoketh urine abundantly, and hindereth the growing again of the stone in the body. The continual use of the powder of the leaves and seed doth cure the black jaundice: the distilled water of the flowers is profitable for all the same purposes: it also helpeth surfeits, and altereth the fit of agues, if three or four ounces thereof with as much of the water of the lesser centaury, and a little sugar put therein, be taken a little before the fit cometh, and the party be laid down in his bed: the oil or water that is drawn from the end of the green sticks heated in the fire, helpeth the tooth-ache: the juice of young branches made into an ointment of old hog's grease, and anointed, or the young branches bruised and heated in oil or hog's grease, and laid to the sides pained by wind, as in stitches or the spleen, easeth them in once or twice using it: the same boiled in oil is the safest and surest medicine to kill lice in the head or body, if any: and is an especial remedy for joint-aches and swollen knees, that come by the falling down of humours.

The broom-rape also is not without its virtues.

The decoction thereof in wine is thought to be as effectual to void the stone in the kidneys and bladder, and to provoke urine as the broom itself; the juice thereof is a singular good help to cure as well green wounds as old and filthy sores and malignant ulcers; the insolate oil, wherein there hath been three or four repetitions of infusions of the top stalks, with flowers strained and cleared, cleanseth the skin from all manner of spots, marks, and freckles that riseth either by the heat of the sun or the malignity of the humours. As for the broom and broom rape, Mars owns them: they are exceedingly prejudicial to the liver; I suppose by reason of the antipathy between Jupiter and Mars, therefore if the liver be disaffected, minister none of it.

BUCK'S-HORN PLANTAIN.—(*Plantago Coronopus.*)

Descrip.—This being sown of seed, riseth up at first with small, long, narrow, hairy, dark green leaves like grass, without any division or gash in them; but those that follow are gashed in on both sides, the leaves into three or four gashes, and pointed at the ends, resembling the knags of a buck's horn, (whereof it took its name) and being well ground round about the root upon the ground, in order one by another, thereby resembling the form of a star, from among which rise up divers hairy stalks about a hand's breadth high, bearing every one a long, small, spiky head, like those of the common plantain, having such like bloomings and seed after them. The root is single, long, and small, with divers strings at it.

Place.—They grow in sandy grounds as in Tothillfields, by Westminster, and divers other places of this land.

Time.—They flower and seed in May, June, and July, and their green leaves do in a manner abide fresh all the winter.

Government and Virtues.—It is under the dominion of Saturn, and is of gallant, drying, and binding quality. This boiled in wine, and drunk, and some of the leaves put to the hurt place, is an excellent remedy for the biting of the viper or adder, which I take to be one and the same. The same being also drunk, helpeth those that are troubled with the stone in the reins or kidneys, by cooling the heat of the parts afflicted, and strengthening them; also weak stomachs that cannot retain but cast up their meat. It stayeth all bleeding both at the mouth and nose, bloody urine, or the bloody flux, and stoppeth the lax of the belly and bowels. The leaves hereof bruised and laid to their sides that have an ague, suddenly easeth the fit; and the leaves and roots being beaten with some bay salt, and applied to the wrists, worketh the same effects. The herb boiled in ale or wine, and given for some mornings and evenings together, stayeth the distillation of hot and sharp rheums falling into the eyes from the head, and helpeth all sorts of sore eyes.

BUCKTHORN.—(*Rhamnus Catharticus.*)

It is called Harts'-horn, Herba-stellaria, Sanguinaria, Herb-eve, Herb-ivy. Wort-cresses, and Swine-cresses.

Descrip.—They have many small and weak straggling branches trailing here and there upon the ground; the leaves are many, small, and jagged, not much unlike to those of buck's horn plantain, but much smaller and not so hairy: the flowers grow among the leaves in small, rough, whitish clusters: the seeds are much smaller and brownish, of a bitter taste.

Place.—They grow in dry, barren sandy grounds.

Time.—They flower and seed when the rest of the plantains do.

Government and Virtues.—This is also under the dominion of Saturn; the virtues are held to be the same as buck's-horn plantain, and therefore by all authors it is joined with it: the leaves bruised and applied to the place, stop bleeding; the herb bruised and applied to warts, will make them consume and waste away in a short time.

BUGLE.—(*Ajuga Reptans.*)

Besides the name bugle, it is called middle confound and middle comfrey, brown bugle, and by some sickle-wort and herb-carpenter; though in Essex we call another herb by that name.

Descrip.—This hath larger leaves than those of the self-heal, but else of the same fashion, or rather longer, in some green on the upper side, and in others more brownish, dented about the edges, somewhat hairy, as the square stalk is also, which riseth up to be half a yard high sometimes, with the leaves set by couples from the middle almost, whereof upward stand the flowers, together with many smaller and browner leaves than the rest on the stalk below set at a distance, and the stalk bare betwixt hem ; among which flowers are also small ones of a blueish and sometimes of an ash colour, fashioned like the flowers of ground-ivy, after which come small, round, blackish seeds : the root is composed of many strings, and spreadeth upon the ground.

The white flowered bugle differeth not in form or greatness from the former, saving that the leaves and stalk are always green, and never brown like the other, and the flowers thereof are white.

Place.—They grow in woods, copses, and fields generally throughout England, but the white flowered bugle is not so plentiful as the former.

Time.—They flower from May until July, and in the meantime perfect their seed : the roots and leaves next thereunto upon the ground abiding all the winter.

Government and Virtues.—This herb belongeth to Dame Venus : if the virtues of it make you fall in love with it, (as they will if you be wise) keep a syrup of it to take inwardly, and an ointment and plaister of it to use outwardly, always by you.

The decoction of the leaves and flowers made in wine, and taken, dissolveth the congealed blood in those that are bruised inwardly by a fall or otherwise, and is very effectual for any inward wounds, thrusts, or stabs in the body or bowels ; and is an especial help in all wound-drinks, and for those that are liver-grown, as they call it. It is wonderful in curing all manner of ulcers and sores, whether new and fresh, or old and inveterate ; yea, gangrenes and fistulas also, if the leaves bruised and applied, or their juice be used to wash and bathe the place, and the same made into a lotion and some honey and alum, cureth all sores in the mouth and gums, be they ever so foul or of long continuance ; and worketh no less powerfully and effectually for such ulcers and sores as happen in the secret parts of men and women. Being also taken inwardly, or outwardly applied, it helpeth those that have broken any bone, or have any member out of joint. An ointment made with the leaves of bugle, scabious and sanicle bruised and boiled in hog's grease until the herbs be dry, and then strained into a pot for such occasions as shall require; it is so singular good for all sorts of hurts in the body, that none that know its usefulness will ever be without it.

The truth is, I have known this herb cure some diseases of Saturn, of which I thought good to quote one. Many times such as give themselves much to drinking are troubled with strange fancies, strange sights in the night time, and some with voices, as also with the disease ephialtes, or night-mare. I take the reason of this to be (according to Fernelius) a melancholy vapour made thin by excessive drinking strong liquor, and so flies up and disturbs the fancy, and breeds imaginations like itself, viz.—fearful and troublesome; these I have known cured by taking only two spoonfuls of the syrup of this herb after supper two hours, when you go to bed. But whether this does it by sympathy or antipathy is some doubt in astrology. I know there is a great antipathy between Saturn and Venus in matter of procreation; yea, such an one, that the barrenness of Saturn can be removed by none but Venus; nor the lust of Venus be repelled by none but Saturn, but I am not of opinion this is done this way, and my reason is, because these vapours, though in quality melancholy, yet by their flying upward seem to be somewhat aërial; therefore I rather think it is done by sympathy, Saturn being exalted in Libra in the house of Venus.

BURNET.—(*Pimpinella Saxifraga.*)

It is called Sanguisorbia, Meadow Pimpinel, Solbegrella, &c. The common garden burnet is so well known that it needeth no description.

Descrip.—The great wild burnet hath winged leaves rising from the root like the garden burnet, but not so many; yet each of these leaves are at the least twice as large as the other, and nicked in the same manner about the edges, of a greyish colour on the under side; the stalks are greater and rise higher, with many such like leaves thereon, and greater heads at the top of a brownish colour, and out of them come small dark purple flowers like the former, but great also. It hath almost neither scent nor taste therein, like the garden kind.

Place.—The first grows frequently in gardens. The wild kind groweth in divers counties of this island, especially in Huntingdon and Northamptonshire, in the meadows there; as also near London by Pancras church, and by a causeway-side in the middle of a field by Paddington.

Time.—They flower about the end of June and beginning of July, and their seed is ripe in August.

Government and Virtues.—This is an herb the Sun challengeth dominion over, and is a most precious herb, little inferior to betony: the continual use of it preserves the body in health and the spirit in vigour; for if the sun be the preserver of life under God, his herbs are the best in the world to do it. They are accounted to be both of one property, but the lesser is more effectual, because quicker and more aromatical. It is a friend to the heart, liver, and other principal parts of a man's body. Two or three of the stalks with leaves put into a cup of wine, especially claret, are known to quicken the spirits, refresh and clear the heart, and drive away melancholy. It is a special help to defend the heart from noisome vapours, and from infection of the pestilence, the juice thereof being taken in some drink, and the party laid to sweat thereupon. They have also a drying and an astringent quality, whereby they are available in all manner of fluxes of blood or humours, to staunch bleedings inward or outward, laxes, scourgings, the bloody-flux, women's too abundant flux of the courses, the whites, and the choleric belchings and castings of the stomach, and is a singular wound herb for all sorts of wounds both of the head and body, running cankers, and most sores, to be used either by the juice or decoction of the herb, or by the powder of the herb or root, or the water of the distilled herb or ointment by itself, or with other things to be kept; the seed is also no less effectual both to fluxes, and to dry up moist sores, being taken in powder inwardly in wine or steeled water, that is, wherein hot gads of steel have been quenched: or the powder, or the seed mixed with the ointment.

BUTTER-BUR.—(*Tussilago Hybrida.*)

Descrip.—This riseth up in February, with a thick stalk about a foot high, whereon are set a few small leaves, or rather pieces, and at the tops a long spike head; flowers of a blush or deep red colour, according to the soil where it groweth, and before the stalk with the flowers have abode a month above ground it will be withered and gone, and blown away with the wind, and the leaves will begin to spring, which being full grown are very large and broad, being somewhat thin and almost round, whose thick red foot stalks above a foot long, stand towards the middle of the leaves; the lower part being divided into two round parts close almost one to another, and are of a pale green colour, and hairy underneath: the root is long, and spreadeth under ground being in some places no bigger than one's finger, in others much bigger, blackish on the outside, and whitish within, of a bitter and unpleasant taste.

Place and Time.—They grow in low and wet grounds by rivers and water-sides; their flowers, as is said, rising and decaying in February and March before their leaves, which appear in April.

Government and Virtues.—It is under the dominion of the Sun, and therefore is a great strengthener of the heart and cheerer of the vital spirits: the roots thereof are by long experience found to be very available against the plague and pestilential fevers, by provoking sweat: if the powder thereof be taken in wine, it also resisteth the force of any other poison: the root hereof taken with zedoary and angelica, or without them, helps the rising of the mother: the decoction of the root, in wine, is singular good for those that wheeze much, or are short-winded. It provoketh urine also, and women's courses, and killeth the flat and broad worms in the belly. The powder of the root doth wonderfully help to dry up the moisture of the sores that are hard to be cured, and taketh away all spots and blemishes of the skin. It were well if gentlewomen would keep this root preserved to help their poor neighborus. *It is fit the rich should help the poor, for the poor cannot help themselves.*

BURDOCK.—(*Arctium Lappa.*)

It is also called Personata, and Happy-Major, Great Burdoak, and Clot-bur: it is so well known even by the little boys, who pull off the burs to throw at one another, that I shall spare to write any description of it.

Place.—They grow plentifully by ditches and water-sides, and by the high-ways almost every where through this land.

Government and Virtues.—Venus challengeth this herb

for her own: and by its leaf or seed you may draw the womb which way you please, either upward by applying it to the crown of the head in case it falls out; or downwards in fits of the mother, by applying it to the soles of the feet: or if you would stay it in its place, apply it to the navel, and that is one good way to stay the child in it. See more of it in my Guide for Women.

The Burdock leaves are cooling, moderately drying, and discussing withal, whereby it is good for old ulcers and sores. A dram of the roots taken with pine kernels, helpeth them that spit foul, mattery, and bloody phlegm. The leaves applied to the places troubled with the shrinking in of the sinews or arteries, give much ease: the juice of the leaves, or rather the roots themselves, given to drink with old wine, doth wonderfully help the biting of any serpents; the root beaten with a little salt, and laid on the place, suddenly easeth the pain thereof, and helpeth those that are bit by a mad dog: the juice of the leaves being drunk with honey, provoketh urine and remedieth the pain of the bladder: the seed being drunk in wine forty days together, doth wonderfully help the sciatica: the leaves bruised with the white of an egg and applied to any place burnt with fire, taketh out the fire, gives sudden ease, and heals it up afterwards; the decoction of them fomented on any fretting sore or canker, stayeth the corroding quality, which must be afterwards anointed with an ointment made of the same liquor, hog's grease, nitre, and vinegar boiled together. The root may be preserved with sugar, and taken fasting or at other times for the same purposes, and for consumptions, the stone, and the lax. The seed is much commended to break the stone, and cause it to be expelled by urine, and is often used with other seeds and things for that purpose.

CABBAGES.—(*Brassica Capitata.*) COLEWORTS.—(*Brassica Oleracea.*)

I SHALL spare labor in writing a description of these, since almost every one that can but write at all may describe them from his own knowledge, they being so well known that descriptions are altogether needless.

Place.—They are generally planted in gardens.

Time.—Their flower time is towards the middle or end of July, and the seed is ripe in August.

Government and Virtues.—The cabbages or coleworts boiled gently in broth, and eaten, do open the body, but the second decoction doth bind the body. The juice thereof drunk in wine helpeth those that are bitten by an adder, and the decoction of the flowers bringeth down women's courses ; being taken with honey it recovereth hoarseness or loss of the voice. The often eating of them well boiled helpeth those that are entering into a consumption. The pulp, or the middle ribs of coleworts boiled in almond milk, and made up into an electuary with honey, being taken often is very profitable for those that are puffy and short winded. Being boiled twice, and an old cock being boiled in the broth and drunk, it helpeth the pains, and the obstruction of the liver and spleen, and the stone in the kidneys. The juice boiled with honey, and dropped into the corners of the eyes, cleareth the sight by consuming any cloud or film beginning to dim it: it also consumeth the canker growing therein. They are much commended being eaten before meat to keep one from surfeiting, as also from being drunk with too much wine, or quickly makes a man sober that is drunk before ; for, as they say, there is such an antipathy or enmity between the vine and the coleworts, that one will die where the other groweth. The decoction of coleworts taketh away the pain and ache, and allayeth the swellings of sore and gouty legs and knees, wherein many gross and watery humours are fallen, the place being bathed therewith warm. It helpeth also old and filthy sores being bathed therewith, and healeth all small scabs, pushes, and wheals that break out in the skin : the ashes of colewort stalks mixed with old hog's grease, are very effectual to anoint the sides of those that have had long pains therein, or any other place pained with melancholy and windy humours. This was certainly Chrysippus's god, and therefore he wrote a whole volume about them and their virtues, and that none of the least neither, for he would be no small fool: he appropriates them to every part of the body, and to every disease in every part : and honest old Cato, they say, used no other physic. I know not what metal there bodies were made of ; this I am sure, cabbages are extremely windy whether you take them as meat or as medicine ; yea, as windy meat as can be eaten, unless you eat bag-pipes or bellows, and they are but seldom ate in our days ; and colewort flowers are something more tolerable, and the wholesomer food of the two : the moon challengeth the dominion of the herb.

COLEWORTS (THE SEA.)—(*Brassica Marina.*)

Descrip.—This hath divers somewhat long and broad, large, and thick wrinkled leaves somewhat crumpled about the edges, and growing each upon a foot-stalk, very brittle, of a greyish green colour, from among which riseth up a strong thick stalk two feet high and better, with some leaves thereon to the top, where it branches forth much ; on every branch standeth a large bush of pale whitish flowers, consisting of four leaves a-piece : the root is somewhat great, shooteth forth many branches under ground, keeping the leaves green all the winter.

Place.—They grow in many places upon the sea coasts, as well on the Kentish as Essex shores ; as at Lid, in Kent, Colchester, in Essex, and divers other places, and in other counties of this land.

Time.—They flower and seed about the time that other kinds do.

Government and Virtues.—The Moon claims the dominion of these also. The broth, or first decoction of the sea colewort doth by the sharp, nitrous, and bitter qualities therein, open the belly, and purge the body ; it cleanseth and digests more powerfully than the other kind : the seed hereof bruised and drunk, killeth worms ; the leaves or the juice of them applied to sores or ulcers cleanseth and healeth them, and dissolveth swellings, and taketh away inflammations.

CALAMINT.—(*Melissa Calaminta.*)

Descrip.—This is a small herb, seldom rising above a foot high, with square, hairy, and woody stalks, and two small hoary leaves set at a joint, about the bigness of marjorum, or not much bigger, a little dented about the edges, and of a very fierce or quick scent, as the whole herb is ; the flowers stand at several spaces of the stalks from the middle almost upwards, which are small and gaping like to those of mints, and of a pale blueish colour ; after which follow small, round, blackish seed : the root is small and woody, with divers small strings spreading within the ground, and dieth not, but abideth many years.

Place.—It groweth on heaths and uplands, and dry grounds in many places of this land.

Time.—They flower in July, and their seed is ripe quickly after.

Government and Virtues.—It is an herb of Mercury, and a strong one too, therefore excellent good in all afflictions of the brain; the decoction of the herb being drank bringeth down women's courses, and provoketh urine: it is profitable for those that have ruptures, or troubled with convulsions or cramps, with shortness of breath or choleric torments and pains in their bellies or stomach: it also helpeth the yellow jaundice, and stayeth vomiting being taken in wine: taken with salt and honey it killeth all manner of wounds in the body. It helpeth such as have the leprosy, either taken inwardly, drinking whey after it, or the green herb outwardly applied: it hindereth conception in women; but either burnt or strewed in a chamber it driveth away venomous serpents; it takes away black and blue marks in the face, and maketh black scars become well coloured, if the green herb (not the dry) be boiled in wine and laid to the place, or the place washed therewith. Being applied to the buckle-bone, by continuance of time it spends the humours which causeth the pain of the sciatica: the juice being dropped into the ears, killeth the worms in them; the leaves boiled in wine, and drank, provoke sweat, and open obstructions of the liver and spleen. It helpeth them that have a tertian ague (the body being first purged), by taking away the cold fits; the decoction hereof, with some sugar put thereto afterwards, is very profitable for those that are troubled with the overflowing of the gall, and that have an old cough, and that are scarce able to breathe by shortness of their wind, that have any cold distemper in their bowels, and are troubled with the hardness of the spleen, for all which purposes both the powder, called diacaluminthes, and compound syrup of calamint (which are to be had at the apothecaries) are the most effectual. Let not women be too busy with it, for it works very violently upon the feminine part.

CAMOMILE.—(*Anthemis Nobilis.*)

It is so well known every where, that it is but lost time and labour to describe it; the virtues thereof are as followeth.

A decoction made of camomile, taketh away all pains and stitches in the side: the flowers of camomile beaten and made up into balls with oil, drive away all sorts of agues, if the part grieved be anointed with that oil, taken from the flowers, from the crown of the head to the sole of the foot, and afterward laid to sweat in bed, and he sweats well ; this is Nechessor, an Egyptian's medicine. It is profitable for all sorts of agues that come either from phlegm, or melancholy, or from an inflammation of the bowels, being applied when the humours causing them shall be concocted : and there is nothing more profitable to the sides and region of the liver and spleen than it : the bathing with a decoction of camomile taketh away weariness, easeth pains to what parts soever they be applied. It comforteth the sinews that be over-strained, mollifieth all swellings : it moderately comforteth all parts that have need of warmth, digesteth and dissolveth whatsoever hath need thereof by a wonderful speedy property; it easeth all the pains of the colic and stone, and all pains and torments of the belly, and gently provoketh urine. The flowers boiled in posset-drink provoke sweat, and help to expel all colds, aches and pains whatsoever : is an excellent help to bring down women's courses. Syrup made of the juice of camomile, with the flowers in white wine, is a remedy against the jaundice and dropsy : the flowers boiled in lee, are good to wash the head and comfort both it and the brain : the oil made of the flowers of camomile is much used against all hard swellings, pains or aches, shrinking of the sinews, cramps or pains in the joints, or any other part of the body. Being used in clysters, it helps to dissolve the wind and pains in the belly ; anointed also, it helpeth pains and stitches in the sides.

Nechessor saith the Egyptians dedicated it to the Sun, because it cured agues, and they were like enough to do it, for they were the arrantest apes in their religion I ever read of. Bachinus, Bena, and Lobel commend the syrup made of the juice of it and sugar, taken inwardly, to be excellent for the spleen. Also this is certain, that it most wonderfully breaks the stone ; some take it in syrup or decoction, others inject the juice of it into the bladder with a syringe. My opinion is that the salt of it taken half a drachm in the morning, in a little white or rhenish wine, is better than either. That it is excellent for the stone appears in this which I have seen tried, viz.,—That a stone that hath been taken out of the body of a man, being wrapped in camomile, will in time dissolve, and in a little time too.

CALTROPS (WATER.)—(*Trapa Natans.*)

THEY are called also Tribulus Aquaticus, Tribulus Lacusoris, Tribulus Marinus, Caltrop, Saligos, Water Nuts and Water Chestnuts.

Descrip.—As for the greater sort of water caltrop, it is not found here, or very rarely: two other sorts there are, which I shall here describe. The first hath a long creeping and jointed root, sending forth tufts at each joint, from which joints arise long, flat, slender-knotted stalks, even to the top of the water, divided towards the top into many branches, each carrying two leaves on both sides, being about two inches long and half an inch broad, thin and almost transparent, they look as if they were torn; the flowers are long, thick, and whitish, set together almost like a bunch of grapes, which being gone, there succeeds for the most part sharp pointed grains altogether, containing a small white kernel in them.

The second differs not much from this, save that it delights in more clear water; its stalks are not flat, but round; its leaves are not so long, but more pointed. As for the place we need not determine, for their name showeth they grow in the water.

Government and Virtues.—They are under the dominion of the Moon, and being made into a poultice, are excellent good for hot inflammations, swellings, cankers, sore mouths and throats, being washed in the decoction. It cleanseth and strengtheneth the neck and throat, and helps those swellings which, when people have, they say the almonds of their ears are fallen down. It is excellent good for the rankness of the gums, a safe and present remedy for the king's evil. They are excellent good for the stone and gravel, especially the nuts being dried; they also resist poison and bitings of venomous beasts.

CAMPION (WILD.)—(*Cucubalus Behen.*)

Descrip.—The wild white campion hath many long and somewhat broad dark green leaves lying upon the ground, and divers ribs therein, somewhat like plantain, but somewhat hairy; broader and not so long; the hairy stalks rise up in the middle of them three or four feet high, and sometimes more, with divers great white joints at several places thereon, and two such like leaves thereat up to the top, sending forth branches at several joints also; all which bear on several footstalks white flowers at the tops of them, consisting of five broad-pointed leaves, every one cut in on the end unto the middle, making them seem to be two a-piece, smelling somewhat sweet, and each of them standing in a large green striped hairy husk, large and round below next to the stalk. The seed is small and greyish in the hard heads that come up afterwards: the root is white and long, spreading divers fangs in the ground.

The red wild campion groweth in the same manner as the white, but the leaves are not so plainly ribbed, somewhat shorter, rounder, and more woolly in handling. The flowers are of the same form and size, but in some of a pale, in others of a bright red colour, cut in at the ends more finely, which makes the leaves look more in number than the other. The seeds and the roots are alike, the roots of both sorts abiding many years.

There are forty-five kinds of campion more; those of them which are of a physical use having the like virtues with those above described, which I take to be the chiefest kinds.

Place.—They grow commonly through this land by fields and hedge sides and ditches.

Time.—They flower in summer, some earlier than others, and some abiding longer than others.

Government and Virtues.—They belong unto Saturn; and it is found by experience that the decoction of the herb, either in white or red wine, being drunk doth stay inward bleedings, and applied outwardly it doth the like; and being drunk helpeth to expel urine being stopped, and gravel or stone in the reins or kidneys. Two drams of the seed drunk in wine purgeth the body of choleric humours, and helpeth those that are stung by scorpions or other venomous beasts, and may be as effectual for the plague. It is of very great use in old sores, ulcers, cankers, fistulas, and the like, to cleanse and heal them by consuming the moist humours falling into them, and correcting the putrefaction of humours offending them.

CARDUUS BENEDICTUS.

IT is called Carduus Benedictus, or Blessed Thistle, or Holy Thistle. I suppose the name was put upon it by some that had little holiness in themselves.

I shall spare labour in writing a description of this, as

almost every one who can but write at all may describe them from his own knowledge.

Time.—They flower in August, and seed not long after.

Government and Virtues.—It is an herb of Mars, and under the sign of Aries. Now, in handling this herb, I shall give you a rational pattern of all the rest; and if you please to view them throughout the book, you shall to your content find it true. It helps giddiness and swimming of the head, or the disease called vertigo, because Aries is in the house of Mars. It is an excellent remedy against the yellow jaundice and other infirmities of the gall, because Mars governs choler. It strengthens the attractive faculty in man and clarifies the blood, because the one is ruled by Mars. The continually drinking the decoction of it helps red faces, tetters, and ringworms, because Mars causeth them. It helps the plague, sores, boils, and itch, the bitings of mad dogs and venomous beasts, all which infirmities are under Mars. Thus you see what it does by sympathy.

By antipathy to other planets it cureth the French pox. By antipathy to Venus, who governs it, it strengthens the memory, and cures deafness by antipathy to Saturn, who hath his fall in Aries, which rules the head. It cures quartan agues and other diseases of melancholy, and adjusts choler, by sympathy to Saturn, Mars being exalted in Capricorn. Also it provokes urine, the stopping of which is usually caused by Mars or the Moon.

CARROTS.—(*Daucus Carota.*)

GARDEN carrots are so well known that they need no description; but because they are of less physical use than the wild kind (as indeed almost in all herbs the wild are most effectual in physic, as being more powerful in operation than the garden kinds) I shall therefore briefly describe the wild carrot.

Descrip.—It groweth in a manner altogether like the tame, but that the leaves and stalks are somewhat whiter and rougher. The stalks bear large tufts of white flowers, with a deep purple spot in the middle, which are contracted together when the seed begins to ripen, that the middle part being hollow and low, and the outward stalk rising high, maketh the whole umbel look like a bird's nest; the root small, long, and hard, and unfit for meat, being somewhat sharp and strong.

Place.—The wild kind groweth in divers parts of this land, plentifully by the field sides and untilled places.

Time.—They flower and seed in the end of summer.

Government and Virtues.—Wild carrots belong to Mercury, and therefore break wind and remove stitches in the side, provoke urine and women's courses, and helpeth to break and expel the stone; the seed also of the same worketh the like effect, and is good for the dropsy, and those whose bellies are swollen with wind: helpeth the colic, the stone in the kidneys, and rising of the mother; being taken in wine, or boiled in wine and taken, it helpeth conception. The leaves being applied with honey to running sores or ulcers, do cleanse them.

I suppose the seeds of them perform this better than the roots: and though Galen commended garden carrots highly to break wind, yet experience teacheth they breed it first, and we may thank nature for expelling it, not they; the seeds of them expel wind indeed, and so mend what the root marreth.

CARAWAY.—(*Carum Carui.*)

Descrip.—It beareth divers stalks of fine cut leaves lying upon the ground, somewhat like the leaves of carrots, but not bushing so thick, of a little quick taste in them, from among which riseth up a square stalk, not so high as the carrot, at whose joint are set the like leaves, but smaller and flatter, and at the top small open tufts or umbels of white flowers, which turn into small blackish seed, smaller than the aniseed, and of a quicker and better taste. The root is whitish, small, and long, somewhat like unto parsnip, but with more wrinkled bark, and much less, of a little hot and quick taste, and stronger than the parsnip, and abideth after seed time.

Place.—It is usually sown with us in gardens.

Time.—They flower in June and July, and seed quickly after.

Government and Virtues.—This is also a Mercurial plant. Carraway seed hath a moderate sharp quality, whereby it breaketh wind and provoketh urine, which also the herb doth. The root is better food than the parsnips; it is pleasant and comfortable to the stomach, and helpeth digestion. The seed is conducing to all cold griefs of the head and stomach, bowels, or mother, as also the wind in them, and helpeth to sharpen the eye-sight.

The powder of the seed put into a poultice taketh away black and blue spots of blows and bruises. The herb itself, or with some of the seed bruised and fried. laid hot in a bag or double cloth to the lower parts of the belly, easeth the pains of the wind colic.

The roots of carraways eaten as men eat parsnips, strengthen the stomachs of old people exceedingly, and they need not to make a whole meal of them neither, and are fit to be planted in every garden.

Carraway confects, once only dipped in sugar, and a spoonful of them eaten in the morning fasting, and as many after each meal, is a most admirable remedy for those that are troubled with wind.

CELANDINE.—(*Chelidonium Majus.*)

Descrip.—This hath divers tender, round, whitish green stalks, with greater joints than ordinary in other herbs, as it were knees, very brittle and easy to break, from whence grow branches with large tender broad leaves divided into many parts, each of them cut in on the edges, set at the joint on both sides of the branches, of a dark blueish green colour on the upper side like columbines, and of a more pale blueish green underneath, full of yellow sap when any part is broken, of a bitter taste and strong scent. The root is somewhat great at the head, shooting forth divers long roots and small strings, reddish on the outside, and yellow within, full of yellow sap therein.

Place.—They grow in many places by old walls, hedges, and way-sides, in untilled places ; and being once planted in a garden, especially in some shady place, it will remain there.

Time.—They flower all the summer long, and the seed ripeneth in the mean time.

Government and Virtues.—This is an herb of the Sun, and under the celestial Lion, and is one of the best cures for the eyes, for all that know any thing in astrology know that the eyes are subject to the luminaries ; let it then be gathered when the Sun is in Leo, and the Moon in Aries, applying to this time ; let Leo arise, then may you make it into an oil or ointment, which you please, to anoint your sore eyes with : I can prove it both by my own experience and the experience of those to whom I have taught it, that most desperate sore eyes have been cured by this only medicine; and then I pray, is not this far better than endangering the eyes by the art of the needle? For if this doth not absolutely take away the film, it will so facilitate the work, that it may be done without danger: the herb or root boiled in white wine and drunk, a few aniseeds being boiled therewith, openeth obstructions of the liver and gall, helpeth the yellow jaundice; and often using it helps the dropsy and the itch, and those that have old sores in their legs or other parts of the body; the juice thereof taken fasting, is held to be of singular good use against the pestilence: the distilled water with a little sugar and a little good treacle mixed therewith (the party upon the taking being laid down to sweat a little) hath the same effect; the juice dropped into the eyes cleanseth them from films and cloudiness that darken the sight, but it is best to allay the sharpness of the juice with a little breast-milk. It is good in old filthy corroding creeping ulcers wheresoever, to stay their malignity of fretting and running, and to cause them to heal more speedily: the juice often applied to tetters, ring-worms, or other spreading cankers, will quickly heal them: and rubbed often upon warts will take them away: the herb with the root bruised and bathed with oil of camomile, and applied to the navel, taketh away the griping pains in the belly and bowels, and all the pains of the mother; and applied to women's breasts, stayeth the overmuch flowing of the courses: the juice or decoction of the herb gargled between the teeth that ache, easeth the pain, and the powder of the dried root laid upon any aching, hollow, or loose tooth, will cause it to fall out: the juice mixed with some powder of brimstone is not only good against the itch, but taketh away all discolourings of the skin whatsoever; and if it chance that in a tender body it causeth any itchings or inflammations, by bathing the place with a little vinegar it is helped.

Another ill-favoured trick have physicians got to use to the eye, and that is worse than the needle; which is to take away films by corroding or gnawing medicines; this I absolutely protest against.

1.—Because the tunicles of the eyes are very thin, and therefore soon eaten asunder.

2.—The callus or film that they would eat away is seldom of an equal thickness in every place, and then the tunicle may be eaten asunder in one place before the film

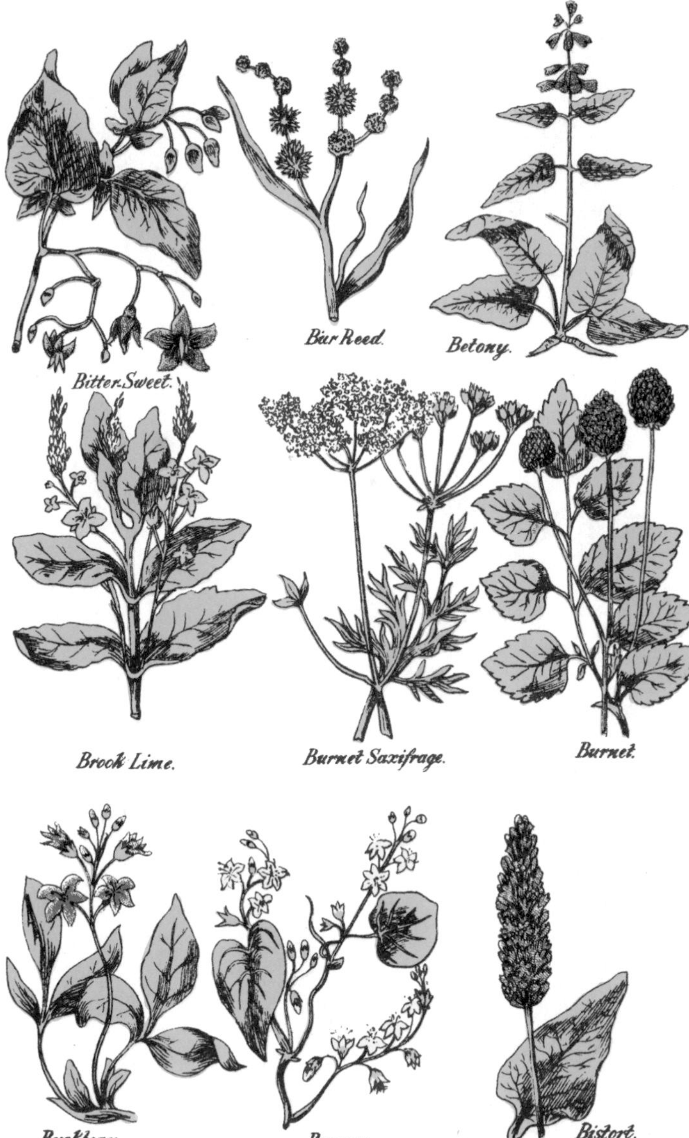

Bitter Sweet.
Bur Reed.
Betony.
Brook Lime.
Burnet Saxifrage.
Burnet.
Buckbean.
Bryony.
Bistort.

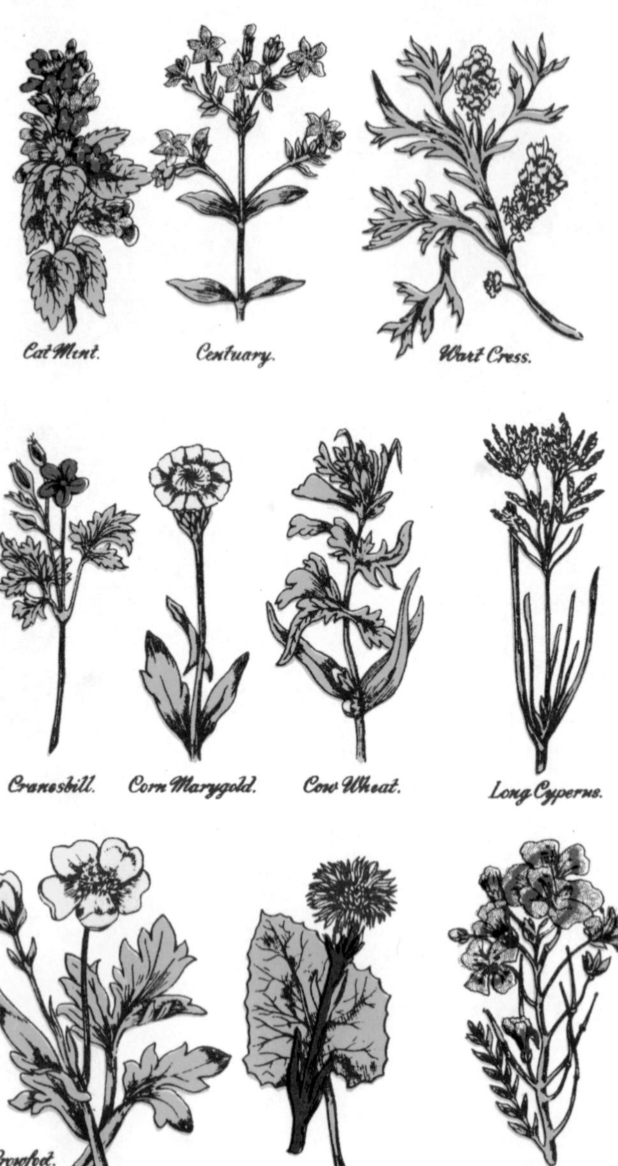
Cat Mint.
Centuary.
Wart Cress.
Cranesbill.
Corn Marygold.
Cow Wheat.
Long Cyperus.
Crowfoot.
Coltsfoot.
Cuckow Flower.

may be consumed in another, and so be a readier way to extinguish the sight than to restore it.

It is called chelidonium, from the Greek word *chelidon*, which signifies a swallow, because they say that if you put out the eyes of young swallows when they are in the nest, the old ones will recover them again with this herb: this I am confident, for I have tried it, that if we mar the very apple of their eyes with a needle she will recover them again; but whether with this herb or not I know not.

Also I have read, and it seems to be somewhat probable, that the herb, being gathered as I showed before, and the elements drawn apart from it by the art of the alchymist, and after they are drawn apart rectified, the earthly quality still in rectifying them added to the *terra damnata* (as alchymists call it,) or *terra sacratissima* (as some philosophers call it,) the elements so rectified are sufficient for the cure of all diseases, the humours offending being known, and the contrary elements given. It is an experiment worth the trying, and can do no harm.

CELANDINE (THE LESSER.) CALLED ALSO PILEWORT.—(*Ficaria Verna.*)

I WONDER what ailed the ancients to give this the name of celandine, which resembleth it neither in nature or form; it acquired the name of pilewort from its virtues, and it being no great matter where I set it down, so I set it down at all, I humoured Dr. Tradition so much as to set it down here.

Descrip.—This celandine or pilewort (which you please) doth spread many round pale green leaves, set on weak and trailing branches, which lie on the ground, and are flat, smooth, and somewhat shining, and in some places, though seldom, marked with black spots, each standing on a long foot-stalk, very like unto a crow's foot, whereunto the seed is not unlike, being many small kernels, like a grain of corn, sometimes twice as long as others, of a whitish colour, with some fibres at the end of them.

Place.—It groweth for the most part in moist corners of fields and places that are near water-sides, yet will abide in drier ground if it be but a little shady.

Time.—It flowereth about March or April, is quite gone by May, so it cannot be found till it springs again.

Government and Virtues.—It is under the dominion of

Mars, and behold here another verification of the learning of the ancients, viz. that the virtue of an herb may be known by its signature, as plainly appears in this: for if you dig up the root of it you shall perceive the perfect image of the disease which they commonly call the piles. It is certain by good experience that the decoction of the leaves and root doth wonderfully help piles and hæmorrhoides, also kernels by the ears and throat, called the king's evil, or any other hard wens or tumours.

Here is another secret for my countrymen and women, a couple of them together: pilewort made into an oil, ointment or plaster, readily cures both the piles, or hæmorrhoides, and the king's evil; the very herb borne about one's body next the skin helps in such diseases, though it never touches the place grieved; let poor people make much of it for those uses; with this I cured my own daughter of the king's evil, broke the sore, drew out a quarter of a pint of corruption, cured without any scar at all in one week's time.

CENTAURY (THE ORDINARY SMALL.)—(*Centaurea Cyanus.*)

Descrip.—This groweth up most usually but with one round and somewhat crusted stalk, about a foot high or better, branching forth at the top into many sprigs, and some also from the joints of the stalks below: the flowers thus stand at the tops as it were in one umbel or tuft, are of a pale red, tending to carnation colour, consisting of five, sometimes six small leaves very like those of St. John's wort, opening themselves in the day-time and closing at night, after which come seeds in little short husks, in form like unto wheat corn; the leaves are small and somewhat round: the root small and hard, perishing every year; the whole plant is of an exceeding bitter taste.

There is another sort in all things like the former, save only it beareth white flowers.

Place.—They grow ordinarily in fields, pastures, and woods, but that with the white flowers not so frequently as the other.

Time.—They flower in July or thereabouts, and seed within a month after.

Government and Virtues.—They are under the dominion of the Sun, as appears in that their flowers open and shut as the sun either sheweth or hideth his face: this herb boiled and drunk, purgeth choleric and gross humours, and helpeth the sciatica: it openeth obstructions of the liver, gall, and spleen, helpeth the jaundice, and easeth the pains in the sides, and hardness of the spleen, used outwardly, and is given with very good effect in agues. It helpeth those that have the dropsy, or the green sickness, being much used by the Italians in powder for that purpose: it killeth the worms in the belly, as is found by experience; the decoction thereof, viz. the tops of the stalks, with the leaves and flowers, is good against the colic, and to bring down women's courses, helpeth to void the dead birth, and easeth pains of the mother, and is very effectual in all old pains of the joints, as the gout, cramps, or convulsions. A dram of the powder thereof taken in wine, is a wonderful good help against the biting of an adder: the juice of the herb with a little honey put to it, is good to clear the eyes from dimness, mist, and clouds that offend or hinder the sight. It is singular good both for green and fresh wounds, as also for old ulcers and sores, to close up the one and cleanse the other, and perfectly to cure them both, although they are hollow or fistulous; the green herb especially being bruised and laid thereto: the decoction thereof dropped into the ears, cleanseth them from worms, cleanseth the foul ulcers and spreading scabs of the head, and taketh away all freckles, spots and marks in the skin, being washed with it; the herb is so safe you cannot fail in the using of it, only giving it inwardly for inward diseases: it is very wholesome, but not very toothsome.

There is, besides these, another small centaury, which beareth a yellow flower; in all other respects it is like the former, save that the leaves are bigger, and of a darker green, and the stalk passeth through the midst of them as it doth the herb thorowan. They are all of them, as I told you, under the government of the Sun; yet this if you observe it, you shall find an excellent truth: in diseases of the blood, use the red centaury; if of choler, use the yellow; but if phlegm or water, you will find the white best.

CHERRY-TREE (THE.)—(*Prunus Cerasus.*)

I SUPPOSE there are few but know this tree for its fruit's sake: and therefore I shall spare writing a description thereof.

Place.—For the place of its growth it is afforded room in every orchard.

Government and Virtues.—It is a tree of Venus. Cherries, as they are of different tastes, so they are of different qualities: the sweet pass through the stomach and the belly more speedily, but are of little nourishment: the tart or sour are more pleasing to a hot stomach, procure appetite to meat, and help to cut tough phlegm and gross humours: but when they are dried, they are more binding to the belly than when they are fresh, being cooling in hot diseases and welcome to the stomach, and provoke urine: the gum of the cherry-tree dissolved in wine, is good for a cold, cough, and hoarseness of the throat; mendeth the colour in the face, sharpeneth the eye-sight, provoketh appetite, and helpeth to break and expel the stone: the black cherries bruised with the stones and dissolved, the water thereof is much used to break the stone and to expel gravel and wind.

CHERRIES (WINTER.)—(*Physalis Alkekengi.*)

Descrip.—The winter cherry hath a running or creeping root in the ground, of the bigness many times of one's little finger, shooting forth at several joints in several places, whereby it quickly spreads over a great compass of ground; the stalk riseth not above a yard high, whereon are set many broad and long green leaves, somewhat like nightshade, but larger: at the joints whereof come forth whitish flowers made of five leaves a-piece, which afterwards turn into green berries inclosed with thin skins, which change to be reddish when they grow ripe, the berries likewise being reddish and as large as a cherry, wherein are contained many flat and yellowish seeds lying within the pulp, which being gathered and strung up, are kept all the year to be used upon occasion.

Place.—They grow not naturally in this land, but are cherished in gardens for their virtues.

Time.—They flower not until the middle or latter end of July; and the fruit is ripe in August or the beginning of September.

Government and Virtues.—This also is a plant of Venus. They are of great use in physic; the leaves being cooling, may be used in inflammations, but not opening as the berries and fruit are; which by drawing down the urine provoke it to be voided plentifully when it is stopped or grown hot, sharp, and painful in the passage; it is good to expel the stone and gravel out of the reins, kidneys, and bladder, helping to dissolve the stone, and voiding it by grit or gravel sent forth in the urine: it also helpeth much to cleanse inward imposthumes or ulcers in the reins or bladder, or those that void a bloody or foul urine, the distilled water of the fruit, or the leaves with them, or the berries green or dry, distilled with a little milk and drank morning and evening with a little sugar is effectual to all the purposes before specified, and especially against the heat and sharpness of the urinal. I shall mention one way amongst many others which might be used for ordering the berries, to be helpful for the urine and the stone, which is this:—take three or four good handfuls of the berries, either green, or fresh, or dried, and having bruised them, put them into so many gallons of beer or ale when it is new and tunned up: this drink taken daily hath been found to do much good to many, both to ease the pains and expel urine and the stone, and to cause the stone not to engender: the decoction of the berries in wine and water is the most usual way, but the powder of them taken in drink is more effectual.

CHERVIL.—(*Chærophyllum Sativum.*)

IT is called Cerefolium, Mirrhis, and Mirrha, Chervil, Sweet Chervil, and Sweet Cicely.

Descrip.—The garden chervil doth at first somewhat resemble parsley, but after it is better grown the leaves are more cut in and jagged, resembling hemlock, being a little hairy, and of a whitish green colour, sometimes turning reddish in the summer, with the stalks also; it riseth a little above half a foot high, bearing white flowers in spiked tufts, which turn into long and round seeds pointed at the ends, aud blackish when they are ripe; of a sweet taste but no smell, though the herb itself smelleth reasonably well: the root is small and long, and perisheth every year, and must be sown, in spring for seed, and after July for autumn salad.

The wild chervil groweth two or three feet high, with yellow stalks and joints, set with broader and more hairy leaves divided into sundry parts, nicked about the edges, and of a dark green colour, which likewise grow reddish with the stalks: at the tops whereof stand small white tufts of flowers, afterward smaller and longer seed: the root is white, hard, and endureth long. This hath little or no scent.

Place.—The first is sown in gardens for a salad herb; the second groweth wild in many of the meadows of this land, and by the hedge-sides and on heaths.

Time.—They flower and seed early, and thereupon are sown again in the end of summer.

Government and Virtues.—The garden chervil being eaten, doth moderately warm the stomach, and is a certain remedy (saith Tragus) to dissolve congealed or clotted blood in the body, or that which is clotted by bruises, falls, &c.: the juice or distilled water thereof being drunk, and the bruised leaves laid to the place, being taken either in meat or drink, it is good to help to provoke urine, or expel the stone in the kidneys, to send down women's courses, and to help the pleurisy and pricking of the sides.

The wild chervil bruised and applied dissolveth swellings in any part, or the marks of congealed blood by bruises or blows in a little space.

CHERVIL (SWEET.)—(*Scandix Odorata.*)

Descrip.—This groweth very like the great hemlock, having large spread leaves cut into divers parts, but of a fresher green colour than the hemlock, tasting as sweet as the aniseed. The stalks rise up a yard high, or better, being cressed or hollow, having leaves at the joints, but lesser; and at the tops of the branched stalks, umbels or tufts of white flowers; after which come large and long crested black shining seed, pointed at both ends, tasting quick, yet sweet and pleasant. The root is great and white, growing deep in the ground, and spreading sundry long branches therein, in taste and smell stronger than the leaves or seeds, and continuing many years.

Place.—This groweth in gardens.

Government and Virtues.—These are all three of them of the nature of Jupiter, and under his dominion. This whole plant, besides its pleasantness in salads, hath its physical virtue. The roots boiled and eaten with oil and vinegar, or without oil, does much please and warm old and cold stomachs oppressed with wind and phlegm, or those that have the phthisis or consumption of the lungs; the same drank with wine is a preservation from the plague: it provoketh women's courses and expelleth the after-birth; procureth an appetite to meat, and expelleth wind: the juice is good to heal the ulcers of the head and face: the candied roots hereof are held as effectual as angelica to preserve from infection in the time of a plague, and to warm and comfort a cold weak stomach. It is so harmless you cannot use it amiss.

CHESTNUT TREE.—(*Castanea Vesca.*)

It were as needless to describe a tree so commonly known as to tell a man he had gotten a mouth; therefore take the government and virtues of them thus:

The tree is abundantly under the dominion of Jupiter, and therefore the fruit must needs breed good blood, and yield commendable nourishment to the body; yet if eaten over much, they make the blood thick, procure headache, and bind the body; the inner skin that covereth the nut is of so binding a quality, that a scruple of it being taken by a man, or ten grains by a child, soon stops any flux whatsoever: the whole nut being dried and beat into powder, and a dram taken at a time, is a good remedy to stop the terms in women. If you dry chestnuts, (only the kernels I mean) both the barks being taken away, beat them into powder, and make the powder up into an electuary with honey, so have you an admirable remedy for the cough and spitting of blood.

CHESTNUTS (EARTH.)—(*Bunium Flexuosum.*)

They are called Earth Nuts, Earth Chestnuts, Ground Nuts, Ciper Nuts, and in Sussex, Pig Nuts. A description of them were needless, for every child knows them.

Government and Virtues.—They are something hot and dry in quality, under the dominion of Venus they provoke lust exceedingly, and stir up these sports she is mistress of; the seed is excellent good to provoke urine: and so also the root, but it doth not perform it so forcibly as the seed doth. The root being dried and beaten into a powder, and the powder made into an electuary, is as singular a remedy for spitting blood and voiding of bloody urine as the former chestnut was for coughs.

CHICKWEED.—(*Alsine Media.*)

It is so generally known to most people, that I shall not trouble you with the description thereof, nor myself with setting forth the several kinds, since but only two or three are considerable for their usefulness.

Place.—They are usually found in moist and watery places, by wood sides and elsewhere.

Time.—They flower about June, and their seed is ripe in July.

Government and Virtues.—It is a fine soft pleasing herb under the dominion of the Moon. It is found to be as effectual as purslain to all the purposes whereunto it serveth, except for meat only. The herb bruised or the juice applied with cloths or sponges dipped therein to the region of the liver, and as they dry to have it fresh applied, doth wonderfully temperate the heat of the liver, and is effectual for all imposthumes, and swellings whatsoever, for all redness in the face, wheals, pushes, itch, scabs: the juice either simply used or boiled with hog's grease applied, helpeth cramps, convulsions, and palsy. The juice, or distilled water, is of much good use for all heats and redness in the eyes, to drop some thereof into them; and is of good effect to ease pains from the heat and sharpness of the blood in the piles, and generally all pains in the body that arise from heat. It is used also in hot and virulent ulcers and sores in the privy parts of men and women, or on the legs or elsewhere. The leaves boiled with marsh-mallows, and made into a poultice with fenugreek and linseed, applied to swellings and imposthumes, ripen and break them, or assuage the swellings and ease the pains. It helpeth the sinews when they are shrunk by cramp or otherwise, and to extend and make them pliable again by this medicine. Boil a handful of chickweed and a handful of red rose leaves dried in a quart of muscadine until a fourth part be consumed, then put to them a pint of oil of trotters or sheep's feet; let them boil a good while still stirring them well, which being strained, anoint the grieved part therewith warm against the fire, rubbing it well with one hand; and bind also some of the herb, if you will, to the place, and with God's blessing it will help in three times dressing.

CHICK-PEASE, OR CICERS.—(*Cicer Aristinum.*)

Descrip.—The garden sorts, whether red, black, or white, bring forth stalks a yard long, whereon do grow many smaller round leaves dented about the edges, set on both sides of a middle rib; at the joints come forth one or two flowers upon sharp foot-stalks, pease fashion, either white or whitish, or purplish red, lighter or deeper, according as the pease that follow will be, that are contained in small thick and short pods, wherein lie one or two pease, more usually pointed at the lower end, and almost round at the head, yet a little cornered or sharp. The root is small, and perisheth yearly.

Place and Time.—They are sown in gardens or fields as pease, being sown later than pease, and gathered at the same time with them, or presently after.

Government and Virtues.—They are both under the dominion of Venus. They are less windy than beans, but nourish more; they provoke urine, and are thought to increase sperm; they have a cleansing faculty, whereby they break the stone in the kidneys; to drink the cream of them being boiled in water is the best way. It moves the belly downwards, provokes women's courses and urine, and increases both milk and seed. One ounce of cicers, two ounces of French barley, and a small handful of marsh-mallow roots clean washed and cut, being boiled in the broth of a chicken, and four ounces taken in the morning, and fasting two hours after, is a good medicine for a pain in the sides. The white cicers are used more for meat than medicine, yet have the same effects, and are thought more powerful to increase milk and seed. The wild cicers are so much more powerful than the garden kind, by how much they exceed them in heat and dryness; whereby they do more open obstructions, break the stone, and have all the properties of cutting, opening, digesting, and dissolving; and this more speedily and certainly than the former.

CINQUEFOIL, OR FIVE-LEAVED GRASS, CALLED ALSO FIVE-FINGERED GRASS.—(*Potentilla.*)

Descrip.—It spreads and creeps far upon the ground with long slender strings like strawberries, which take root again and shoot forth many leaves made of five parts, and sometimes seven, dented about the edges and somewhat hard. The stalks are slender, leaning downwards, and bear many small yellow flowers thereon, with some yellow threads in the middle standing about a smooth green head, which, when it is ripe, is a little rough, and containeth small brownish seeds. The root is of a blackish brown colour, as big as one's little finger, but growing long with some threads thereat; and by the small strings it quickly spreadeth over the ground.

Place.—It groweth by wood sides, hedge sides, the pathway in fields, and in borders and corners of them, almost through all the land.

Time.—It flowereth in summer, some sooner, some later.

Government and Virtues.—This is an herb of Jupiter, and therefore strengthens the part of the body it rules; let Jupiter be angular and strong when gathered; and if you give but a scruple (which is but twenty grains) of it at a time, either in white wine or white wine vinegar, you shall seldom miss the cure of an ague, be it what ague soever, in three fits, as I have often proved to the admiration both of myself and others: let no man despise it because it is plain and easy, the ways of God are all such. It is an especial herb used in all inflammations and fevers, whether infectious or pestilential, or among other herbs to cool and temper the blood and humours in the body; as also for all lotions, gargles, infections, and the like; for sore mouths, ulcers, cancers, fistulas, and other corrupt, foul, or running sores. The juice hereof drunk, about four ounces at a time for certain days together, cureth the quinsey and yellow jaundice; and taken for thirty days together, cureth the falling sickness. The roots boiled in milk and drunk, is a most effectual remedy for all fluxes in man or woman, whether the white or red, as also the bloody flux. The roots boiled in vinegar, and the decoction thereof held in the mouth, easeth the pains of the tooth-ache. The juice or decoction taken with a little honey helpeth the hoarseness of the throat, and is very good for the cough of the lungs. The distilled water of both roots and leaves is also effectual to all the purposes aforesaid; and if the hands be often washed therein, and suffered at every time to dry of itself without wiping, it will in a short time help the palsy or shaking in them. The root boiled in vinegar helpeth all knots, kernels, hard swellings, and lumps growing in any part of the flesh, being thereunto applied; as also inflammations and St. Anthony's fire; all imposthumes and painful sores with heat and putrefaction; the shingles also, and all other sorts of running and foul scabs, sores, and itch. The same also boiled in wine, and applied to any joint full of pain, ache, or the gout in the hands or feet, or the hip gout, called the sciatica, and the decoction thereof drunk the while, doth cure them, and easeth much pain in the bowels. The roots are likewise effectual to help ruptures or burstings, being used with other things available to that purpose, taken either inwardly or outwardly, or both; as also bruises or hurts by blows, falls, or the like, and to stay the bleeding of wounds in any part inward or outward.

Some one holds that one leaf cures a quotidian, three a tertian, and four a quartian ague, and a hundred to one if it be not Dioscorides, for he is full of whimsies. The truth is I never stood so much upon the number of the leaves, or whether I give it in powder or decoction: if Jupiter were strong, and the Moon applied to him, and his good aspect at the gathering I never knew it miss the desired effect.

CIVES.—(*Allium Schœnoprasum.*)

Called also rush leeks, chives, civet, and sweth.

Temperature and Virtues.—I confess I had not added these had it not been for a country gentleman, who by a letter certified to me that amongst other herbs I had left these out. They are indeed a kind of leeks, hot and dry in the fourth degree, and so under the dominion of Mars. If they be eaten raw (I do not mean raw opposite to roasted or boiled, but raw opposite to chemical preparation) they send up very hurtful vapours to the brain, causing troublesome sleep and spoiling the eyesight; yet of them, prepared by the act of the alchymist, may be made an excellent remedy for the stoppage of urine.

CLARY.—(*Salvia Solarea.*)

Descrip.—Our ordinary garden clary hath four square stalks, with broad, rough, wrinkled, whitish, or hoary green leaves, somewhat evenly cut in on the edges, and of a strong sweet scent, growing some near the ground, and some by couples upon stalks. The flowers grow at certain distances, with two small leaves at the joints under them, somewhat like unto flowers of sage, but smaller and of a whitish blue colour. The seed is brownish and somewhat flat, or not so round as the wild. The roots are blackish and spread not far, and perish after seed time. It is usually sown, for it seldom rises of its own sowing.

Place.—This groweth in gardens.

Time.—It flowereth in June and July, some a little later than others, and their seed is ripe in August or thereabouts.

Government and Virtues.—It is under the dominion of the Moon. The seed put into the eyes clears them from motes and such like things gotten within the lids to offend them, and it also clears them from any white and red spots which may be on them. The mucilage of the seed made with water, and applied to tumours or swellings, disperseth and taketh them away. It also draweth forth splinters, thorns, or other things got into the flesh. The leaves used with vinegar, either by itself or with a little honey, doth help boils, felons, and the hot inflammations that are gathered by their pains, if applied before it be grown too great. The powder of the dried root put into the nose provoketh sneezing, and thereby purgeth the head and brain of much rheum and corruption. The seeds or leaves taken in wine provoketh to venery. It is of much use both for men and women that have weak backs, and helpeth to strengthen the reins ; used either by itself or with other herbs conduces to the same effect, and in tansies often. The fresh leaves dipped in a batter of flour, eggs, and a little milk, and fried in butter and served to the table, is not unpleasant to any, but exceedingly profitable for those that are troubled with weak backs, and the effects thereof. The juice of the herb put into ale or beer, and then drunk, bringeth down women's courses and expelleth the after-birth.

It is a usual course with many men, when they have got the running of the reins, or women the whites, to run to the bush of clary, exclaiming—Maid, bring hither the frying-pan, and fetch me some butter quickly. Then they will eat fried clary just as hogs eat acorns, and this they think will cure their disease, forsooth ! Whereas, when they have devoured as much clary as will grow upon an acre of ground, their backs are as much the better as though they had never touched it—nay, perhaps, very much worse.

We will grant that clary strengthens the back ; but this we do deny, that the cause of the running of the reins in men, or the whites in women, lies in the back, though it be sometimes weakened by them ; and therefore for medicine is as proper as for me, when my toe is sore, to lay a plaster on my nose.

CLARY (WILD).—(*Salvia Horminum.*)

WILD clary is most blasphemously called Christ's eye, because it cures diseases of the eyes. I could wish from my soul that blasphemy, ignorance, and tyranny were ceased among physicians, that they might be happy and I joyful.

Descrip.—It is like the other clary, but lesser, with many stalks about a foot and a half high. The stalks are square and somewhat hairy; the flowers are of a bush colour. He that knows the common clary cannot be ignorant of this.

Place.—It grows commonly in this nation in barren places. You may find it plentifully if you look in the fields near Gray's Inn, and the fields near Chelsea, and other such places.

Time.—They flower from the beginning of June until the latter end of August.

Government and Virtue.—It is something hotter and drier than the garden clary is, yet, nevertheless, it is under the dominion of the Moon as well as that. The seeds of it beaten to powder, and drunk with wine, is an admirable help to provoke lust. A decoction of the leaves being drunk warms the stomach, and it would be a wonder if it did not, the stomach being under Cancer, the house of the Moon. It also helps digestion, and scatters congealed blood in any part of the body. The distilled water cleanseth the eyes of redness, waterishness, and heat. It is a capital remedy for dimness of sight, to take one of its seeds and put it into the eye, and there let it remain till it drops out of itself. The pain will be nothing to speak of; it will cleanse the eyes of all filthy and putrefied matter, and in often repeating it, will take off a film which covereth the sight—a handsomer, safer, and easier remedy by a great deal than to tear it off with a needle.

CLEAVERS.—(*Galium Aparine.*)

Descrip.—This plant has many common names, as *Goose-grass, Catchweed, Bed straw, etc.* It is an annual succulent plant, with a weak, procumbent, quadrangular, retrosely-prickled stem, which grows from two to six feet high and is hairy at the joints. The leaves are one or two inches in length, and two or three lines in breadth, rough on the margin and tapering to the base. The flowers are white, small and scattered.

Place.—It groweth by the hedge and ditch-sides, in many places of this land, and is so troublesome an inhabitant in gardens, that it rampeth upon and is ready to choke whatever grows near it.

Time.—It flowereth in June or July, and the seed is ripe and falleth again in the end of July or August, from whence it springeth up again, and not from the old roots.

Government and Virtues.—It is under the dominion of the Moon. The juice of the herb and the seed together taken in wine, helpeth those bitten with an adder, by preserving the heart from the venom. It is familiarly taken in broth, to keep them lean and lank that are apt to grow fat. The distilled water drunk twice a day helpeth the yellow jaundice; and the decoction of the herb, in experience, is found to do the same, and stayeth laxes and bloody fluxes. The juice of the leaves, or they a little bruised and applied to any bleeding wound, stayeth the bleeding. The juice also is very good to close up the lips of green wounds, and the powder of the dried herb strewed thereupon doth the same, and likewise helpeth old ulcers. Being boiled in hog's grease, it helpeth all sorts of hard swellings or kernels in the throat, being anointed therewith. The juice dropped into the ears taketh away the pain of them.

It is a good remedy in the spring, eaten (being first chopped small and boiled well) in water gruel, to cleanse the blood and strengthen the liver, thereby to keep the body in healh, and fitting it for that change of season that is coming.

CLOWN'S WOUNDWORT.—(*Panax Coloni.*)

Descrip.—It groweth up sometimes to two or three feet high, but usually about two feet, with square, green, rough stalks, but slender, joined somewhat far asunder, and two very long, somewhat narrow dark green leaves bluntly dented about the edges thereof, ending in a long point. The flowers stand towards the tops, compassing the stalks at the joints with the leaves, and end likewise in a spiked top, having long and much gaping hoods of a purplish red colour, with whitish spots in them, standing in somewhat round husks, wherein afterwards stand blackish round seeds. The root is composed of many long strings with some tuberous long knobs growing among them, of a pale yellowish or whitish colour; yet some times of the year these knobby roots in many places are not seen in this plant. The plant smelleth somewhat strong.

Place.—It groweth in sundry counties in this land both north and west, and frequently by path sides in the fields near London, and within three or four miles distant about it; yet it usually grows in or near ditches.

Time.—It flowereth in June or July, and the seed is ripe soon after.

Government and Virtues.—It is under the dominion of the planet Saturn. It is singularly effectual in all fresh and green wounds, and therefore beareth not this name for nothing. It is very available in staunching of blood, and to dry up the fluxes of humours in old fretting ulcers, cankers, &c., that hinder the healing of them.

A syrup made of the juice of it is inferior to none for inward wounds, ruptures of veins, bloody flux, vessels broken, spitting, making too much water, or vomiting blood. Ruptures are excellently and speedily, even to admiration, cured by taking now and then a little of the syrup, and applying an ointment or plaster of this herb to the place. Also, if any vein or muscle be swelled, apply a plaster of this herb to it, and if you add a little comfrey it will not do amiss. The herb deserves commendation, though it has received such a clownish name, and whoever reads this, if he try as I have done, will commend it; only take notice that it is of a dry earthly quality.

COCK'S HEAD, RED FITCHLING, OR MEDICK FITCH.—(*Onobrychis.*)

Descrip.—This hath divers weak but rough stalks half a yard long, leaning downwards, but set with winged leaves longer and more pointed than those of lintels, and whitish underneath; from the tops of these stalks arise up other slender stalks, naked without leaves unto the tops, where there grow many small flowers in the manner of a spike, of a pale reddish colour, with a little blue among them; after which rise up in their places round, rough, and somewhat flat heads. The root is tough, and somewhat woody, yet liveth and shooteth anew every year.

Place.—It groweth under hedges, and sometimes in the open fields in divers places of this land.

Time.—They flower all the months of July and August, and the seed ripeneth in the meanwhile.

Government and Virtues.—It is under the dominion of Venus, it hath power to rarify and digest, and therefore the green leaves bruised, and applied as a plaster, disperse knots, nodes, or kernels in the flesh; and if when dry it be taken in wine, it helpeth the strangury; and being anointed with oil it provoketh sweat. It is a singular food for cattle, to cause them to give store of milk; and why then may it not do the like, being boiled in ordinary drink for nurses?

COLUMBINES.—(*Aquilegia.*)

These are so well known, growing almost in every garden, that I think I may save the expense of time in writing a description of them.

Time.—They flower in May, and abide not for the most part when June is past, perfecting their seed in the mean time.

Government and Virtues.—It is also an herb of Venus. The leaves of columbines are generally used in lotions with good success for sore mouths and throats. Tragus saith that a dram of the seed taken in wine with a little saffron openeth obstructions of the liver, and is good for the yellow jaundice, if the person after the taking thereof be laid to sweat well in bed. The seed also taken in wine causeth a speedy delivery of women in childbirth; if one draught suffice not let her drink a second, and it will be found effectual. The Spaniards used to eat a piece of the root thereof in a morning fasting, many days together, to help them when troubled with stone in the reins or kidneys.

COLT'S FOOT (COMMON.)—*(Tussilago Farfara.)*

CALLED also Cough-wort, Foal's-wort, Horse-hoof, and Bull's foot.

Descrip.—This shooteth up a tender stalk, with small yellowish flowers somewhat earlier, which fall away quickly, and after they are past come up somewhat round leaves, sometimes dented about the edges, much lesser, thicker, and greener than those of butter-bur, with a little down or frieze over the green leaf on the upper side, which may be rubbed away, and whitish or mealy underneath. The root is small and white, spreading much underground, so that where it taketh root it will hardly be driven away again, if any little piece be abiding therein; and from thence spring fresh leaves.

Place.—It groweth as well in wet grounds as in drier places.

Time.—And flowereth in the end of February; the leaves begin to appear in March.

Government and Virtues.—The plant is under Venus: the fresh leaves, or juice, or syrup thereof, is good for a hot, dry cough, or wheezing, and shortness of breath. The dry leaves are best for those who have thin rheums and distillations upon their lungs, causing a cough; for which also the dried leaves taken as tobacco, or the root, is very good. The distilled water hereof simply, or with elder-flowers and night-shade, is a singular good remedy against all hot agues, to drink two ounces at a time, and apply cloths wet therein to the head and stomach, which also does much good being applied to any hot swellings or inflammations. It helpeth St. Anthony's fire, and burnings, and is singular good to take away wheals and small pushes that arise through heat; as also the burning heat of the piles, or privy parts, cloths wet therein being thereunto applied.

COMFREY.—*(Symphytum Officinale.)*

Descrip.—The common great comfrey hath divers very large hairy green leaves lying on the ground, so hairy or prickly, that if they touch any tender part of the hands, face, or body, it will cause it to itch: the stalk that riseth from among them being two or three feet high, hollow and cornered, is very hairy also, having many such like leaves as grow below, but lesser and lesser up to the top; at the joints of the stalks it is divided into many branches with some leaves thereon, and at the end stand many flowers in order one above another, which are somewhat long and hollow like the finger of a glove, of a pale whitish colour, after which come small black seeds. The roots are great and long, spreading great thick branches under-ground, black on the outside and whitish within, short and easy to break, and full of glutinous or clammy juice, of little or no taste at all.

There is another sort in all things like this, only somewhat less, and beareth flowers of a pale purple colour.

Place.—They grow by ditches and water-sides, and in divers fields that are moist, for therein they chiefly delight to grow; the first generally through all the land, and the other but in some places. By the leave of my authors, I know the first grows in dry places.

Time.—They flower in June or July, and give their seed in August.

Government and Virtues.—This is an herb of Saturn, and I suppose under the sign Capricorn; cold, dry, and earthy in quality. What was spoken of clown's woundwort may be said of this. The great comfrey helpeth those that spit blood, or make a bloody urine. The root boiled in water or wine, and the decoction drank, helps all inward hurts, bruises, wounds, and ulcers of the lungs, and causes the phlegm that oppresses him to be easily spit forth. It helpeth the defluction of rheum from the head upon the lungs, the fluxes of blood or humours by the belly, women's immoderate courses, as well the reds as the whites, and the running of the reins, happening by what cause soever. A syrup made thereof is very effectual for all those inward griefs and hurts, and the distilled water for the same purposes also, and for outward wounds or sores in the fleshy or sinewy part of the body whatsoever; as also take the fits of agues, and to allay the sharpness of humours. A decoction of the leaves hereof is available to all the purposes, though not so effectual as the roots. The roots being outwardly applied, help fresh wounds or cuts immediately, being bruised and laid thereto: and is special good for ruptures and broken bones; yea, it is said to be so powerful to consolidate and knit together, that if they be boiled with dissevered pieces of flesh in a pot, it will join them together again. It is good to be applied unto women's breasts that grow sore by the abundance of milk coming into them; also to repress the overmuch bleeding of the hemorrhoids, to cool the inflammation of the parts thereabouts, and to give ease of pains. The roots of comfrey taken fresh, beaten small, and spread upon leather, and laid upon any place troubled with the gout, doth presently give ease of the pains; and applied in the same manner giveth ease to pained joints, and profiteth very much for running and moist ulcers, gangrenes, mortifications, and the like, for which it hath by often experience been found helpful.

CORALWORT.—(*Dentaria.*)

It is also called by some Toothwort, Tooth Violet, Dog-teeth Violet, and Dentaris.

Descrip.—Of the many sorts of this herb, two of them may be found growing in this nation; the first of which shooteth forth one or two winged leaves upon long brownish foot-stalks, which are doubled down at their first coming out of the ground; when they are fully opened, they consist of seven leaves, most commonly of a sad green colour, dented about the edges, set on both sides the middle rib one against another, as the leaves of the ash-tree: the stalk beareth no leaves on the lower half of it: the upper half beareth sometimes three or four, each consisting of five leaves, sometimes of three; on the top stands four or five flowers upon short foot-stalks, with long husks; the flowers are very like the flowers of stock gilliflowers, of a pale purplish colour, consisting of four leaves a-piece, after which come small pods which contain the seed; the root is very small, white, and shining; it doth not grow downwards, but creeping along under the upper crust of the ground, and consisteth of divers small round knobs set together; towards the top of the stalk there grows some single leaves, by each of which cometh a small cloven bulb, which when it is ripe, if it be set in the ground, will grow to be a root.

As for the other coralwort which groweth in this nation, it is more scarce than this, being a very small plant much like crowfoot. I know not where to direct you to it, therefore I shall forbear the description.

Place.—The first groweth in Mayfield in Sussex, in a wood called Highread, and in another wood there also called Foxholes.

Time.—They flower from the latter end of April to the middle of May, and before the middle of July they are gone, and not to be found.

Government and Virtues.—It is under the dominion of the Moon. It cleanseth the bladder and provoketh urine, expels gravel and the stone : it easeth pains in the sides and bowels, is excellent good for inward wounds, especially such as are made in the breast or lungs, by taking a dram of the powder of the root every morning in wine ; the same is excellent good for ruptures, as also to stop fluxes: an ointment made of it is excellent good for wounds and ulcers, for it soon dries up the watery humours which hinder the cure.

COSTMARY.—*(Balsamita Vulgaris.)*

CALLED also Alecost, Balsam Herb, or Tanzy. This is so frequently known to be an inhabitant in almost every garden, that I suppose it is needless to write a description thereof.

Time.—It flowereth in June and July.

Government and Virtues.—It is under the dominion of Jupiter. The ordinary costmary, as well as maudlin, provoketh urine abundantly, and moisteneth the hardness of the mother ; it gently purgeth choler and phlegm, extenuating that which is gross, and cutting that which is tough and glutinous, cleanseth that which is foul, and hindereth putrefaction and corruption ; it dissolveth without attraction, openeth obstructions and helpeth their evil effects, and it is a wonderful help to all sorts of dry agues. It is astringent to the stomach, and strengtheneth the liver and all the other inward parts : and taken in whey, worketh more effectually. Taken fasting in the morning, it is very profitable for pains in the head, that are continual ; and to stay, dry up, and consume all thin rheums or distillations from the head into the stomach, and helpeth much to digest raw humours that are gathered therein. It is very profitable for those that are fallen into a continual evil disposition of the body, called cachexia, but especially in the beginning of the disease. It is an especial friend and help to evil, weak, and cold livers. The seed is familiarly given to children for the worms, and so is the infusion of flowers in white wine given them to the quantity of two ounces at a time: it maketh an excellent salve to cleanse and heal old ulcers, being boiled with oil of olive, and adder's tongue with it; and after it is strained, put a little wax, rosin, and turpentine to bring it to a convenient body.

COWSLIPS, OR PEAGLES.—(*Primula veris.*)

BOTH the wild and garden cowslips are so well known, that I will neither trouble myself nor the reader with a description of them.

Time.—They flower in April and May.

Government and Virtues.—Venus lays claim to this herb as her own, and it is under the sign Aries, and our city dames know well enough the ointment or distilled water of it adds to beauty, or at least restores it when it is lost. The flowers are held to be more effectual than the leaves, and the roots of little use. An ointment being made with them, taketh away spots and wrinkles of the skin, sun-burnings and freckles, and adds beauty exceedingly; they remedy all infirmities of the head coming of heat and wind, as vertigo, ephialtes, false apparitions, frenzies, falling sickness, palsies, convulsions, cramps, pains in the nerves; the roots ease pains in the back and bladder, and open the passages of the urine. The leaves are good in wounds, and the flowers take away trembling. If the flowers be not well dried and kept in a warm place, they will soon putrefy and look green: have a special eye over them. If you let them see the sun once a month, it will do neither the sun nor them harm.

Because they strengthen the brain and nerves, and remedy palsies, the Greeks gave them the name *paralysis.* The flowers preserved or conserved, and the quantity of a nutmeg taken every morning, is a sufficient dose for inward diseases, but for wound spots, wrinkles, and sunburnings, an ointment is made of the leaves and hog's grease.

CRAB'S CLAWS.—(*Semper vivum Aquatica.*)

CALLED also Water Seagreen, Knight's Pond Water, Water Houseleek, Pondweed, and Fresh-water Soldier.

Descrip.—It hath sundry long narrow leaves, with sharp prickles on the edges of them, also very sharp-pointed; the stalks which bear flowers seldom grow so high as the leaves, bearing a forked head like a crab's claw, out of which comes a white flower, consisting of three leaves, with yellowish hairy threads in the middle : it taketh root in the mud in the bottom of the water.

Place.—It groweth plentifully in the fens in Lincolnshire.

Time.—It flowereth in June, and usually from thence till August.

Government and Virtues.—It is a plant under the dominion of Venus, and therefore a great strengthener of the reins : it is excellent good in that inflammation which is commonly called St. Anthony's fire : it assuageth all inflammations and swellings in wounds, and an ointment made of it is excellent good to heal them : there is scarce a better remedy growing than this is for such as have bruised their kidneys, and on that account evacuating blood : a dram of the powder of the herb taken every morning, is a very good remedy to stop the terms.

CRESSES (BLACK).—*(Sisymbrium Nigra.)*

Descrip.—It hath long leaves deeply cut and jagged on both sides, not much unlike wild mustard ; the stalk small, very limber, though very tough : you may twist them round as you may a willow before they break. The stones are very small and yellow, after which come small pods which contain the seed.

Place.—It is a common herb growing usually by the wayside, and sometimes upon mud walls in the neighbourhood of London ; but it delights most to grow among stones and rubbish.

Time.—It flowers in June and July, and the seed is ripe in August and September.

Government and Virtues.—It is a plant of a hot and biting nature, under the dominion of Mars. The seed of black cresses strengthens the brain exceedingly, being, in performing that office, little inferior to mustard seed, if at all ; they are excellent good to stay these rheums which may fall down from the head upon the lungs ; you may beat the seed into powder if you please, and make it up into an electuary with honey ; so you have an excellent remedy by you, not only for the premises, but also for the cough, yellow jaundice, and sciatica. The herb boiled into a poultice is an excellent remedy for inflammations, both in women's breasts and in men's testicles.

CRESSES (SCIATICA.)—*(Iberis Sisymbrium.)*

Descrip.—These are of two kinds; the first riseth up with a round stalk about two feet high, spread into divers branches, whose lower leaves are somewhat larger than the upper, yet all of them cut or torn on the edges, somewhat like garden cresses, but smaller; the flowers are small and white, growing at the tops of branches, where afterwards grow husks with small brownish seeds therein, very strong and sharp in taste, more than the cresses of the garden: the root is long, white, and woody.

The other hath the lower leaves whole, somewhat long and broad, not torn at all, but only somewhat deeply dented about the edges towards the ends; but those that grow up higher are lesser. The flowers and seeds are like the former, and so is the root likewise, and both root and seeds as sharp as it.

Place.—They grow by the way-sides in untilled places, and by the sides of old walls.

Time.—They flower in the end of June, and their seed is ripe in July.

Government and Virtues.—It is a Saturnine plant. The leaves, but especially the root, taken fresh in summer time, beaten or made into a poultice or salve with old hog's grease, and applied to the places pained with the sciatica, to continue thereon four hours if it be on a man, and two hours on a woman; the place afterwards bathed with wine and oil mixed together and then wrapped with wool or skins after they have sweat a little, will assuredly not only cure the same disease in hips, huckle-bone, or other of the joints, as gout in the hands or feet, but all other old griefs of the head, (as inveterate rheums) and other parts of the body that are hard to be cured; and if of the former griefs any parts remain, the same medicine after twenty days is to be applied again. The same is also effectual in the diseases of the spleen; and applied to the skin it taketh away the blemishes thereof, whether they be scars, leprosy, scabs, or scurf, which, although it ulcerate the part, that is to be helped afterwards with a salve made of oil and wax. Esteem this as another secret.

CRESSES (WATER.)—(*Sisymbrium Nasturtium Aquatica.*

Descrip.—Our ordinary water cresses spread forth with many weak, hollow, sappy stalks, shooting out fibres at the joints, and upwards long winged leaves made of sundry broad sappy almost round leaves, of a brownish colour. The flowers are many and white, standing on long footstalks, after which come small yellow seed, contained in small long pods like horns. The whole plant abideth green in the winter, and tasteth somewhat hot and sharp.

Place.—They grow for the most part in small standing waters, yet sometimes in small rivulets of running water.

Time.—They flower and seed in the beginning of the summer.

Government and Virtues.—It is an herb under the dominion of the Moon. They are more powerful against the scurvy and to cleanse the blood and humours, than brooklime is, and serve in all the other uses in which brooklime is available, as to break the stone, and provoke urine and women's courses. The decoction thereof cleanseth ulcers by washing them therewith. The leaves bruised, or the juice, is good to be applied to the face or other parts troubled with freckles, pimples, spots, or the like, at night, and washed away in the morning. The juice mixed with vinegar, is very good for those that are dull and drowsy, or have the lethargy.

Water-cress pottage is a good remedy to cleanse the blood in the spring, and helps head-aches, and consumes the gross humours winter hath left behind: those that would live in health may use it if they please, if they will not, I cannot help it. If any fancy not pottage, they may eat the herb as a salad.

CROSSWORT.—(*Valantia Cruciata.*)

Descrip.—Common crosswort groweth up with square hairy brown stalks, a little above a foot high, having four small broad and pointed, hairy, yet smooth thin leaves growing at every joint, each against the other crossway, which has caused the name. Towards the tops of the stalks at the joints, with the leaves in three or four rows downwards, stand small, pale, yellow flowers, after which come small blackish round seeds, four for the most part set in every husk.

The root is very small, and full of fibres, or threads, taking good hold of the ground, and spreading with the branches a great deal of ground, which perish not in winter, although the leaves die every year, and spring again anew.

Place.—It groweth in many moist grounds, as well in meadows as untilled places about London, in Hampstead churchyard, at Wye in Kent, and sundry other places.

Time.—It flowers from May all the summer long, in one place or another, as they are more open to the sun: the seed ripeneth soon after.

Government and Virtues.—It is under the dominion of Saturn. This is a singular good wound herb, and is used inwardly not only to stay bleeding of wounds, but to consolidate them, as it doth outwardly any green wound, which it quickly soldereth up and healeth. The decoction of the herb in wine helpeth to expectorate phlegm out of the chest, and is good for obstructions in the breast, stomach, or bowels, and helpeth a decayed appetite. It is also good to wash any wound or sore with, to cleanse and heal it. The herb bruised and then boiled, applied outwardly for certain days together, renewing it often; and in the mean time the decoction of the herb in wine, taken inwardly every day, doth certainly cure the rupture in any, so as it be not too inveterate; but very speedily, if it be fresh and lately taken.

CROWFOOT.—*(Ranunculus Auricomus.)*

MANY are the names this furious biting herb hath obtained; for it is called Frog's-foot from the Greek name *barrakion;* Crowfoot, Goldknobs, Gold-cups, King's Knobs, Baffiners, Troil Flowers, Polts, Locket-gouleons, and Butter-flowers.

Abundant are the sorts of this herb, that to describe them all would tire the patience of Socrates himself; but because I have not yet attained to the spirits of Socrates, I shall but describe the most usual.

Descrip.—The most common crowfoot hath many thin green leaves cut into divers parts, in taste biting and sharp, biting and blistering the tongue; it bears many flowers of a bright resplendent yellow colour; I do not remember that I ever saw anything yellower—virgins in ancient times used to make powder of them to furrow bride-beds—after which flowers come small heads, some spiked and rugged like a pine-apple.

Place.—They grow very common every where; unless you turn your head into a hedge you cannot but see them as you walk.

Time.—They flower in May and June, even until September.

Government and Virtues.—This fiery and hot-spirited herb of Mars is no way fit to be given inwardly, but an ointment of the leaves or flowers will draw a blister, and may be so fitly applied to the nape of the neck to draw back rheum from the eyes. The herb being bruised and mixed with a little mustard, draws a blister as well, and as perfectly as cantharides, and with far less danger to the vessels of urine, which cantharides naturally delight to wrong. I knew the herb once applied to a pestilential rising that was fallen down, and it saved life even beyond hope: it were good to keep an ointment and plaster of it, if it were but for that.

CUCKOO-PINT.—*(Arum Vulgare.)*

It is called Alron, Janus, Barba-aron, Calve's-foot, Ramp, Starchwort, Cuckoo-pintle, Priest's-pintle, and Wake Robin.

Descrip.—This shooteth forth three, four or five leaves at the most from one root, every one whereof is somewhat large and long, broad at the bottom next the stalk, and forked but ending in a point, without a cut on the edge, of a full green colour, each standing upon a thick round stalk, of a hand-breadth long or more, among which, after two or three months that they begin to wither, riseth up a bare, round, whitish green stalk, spotted and streaked with purple, somewhat higher than the leaves; at the top whereof standeth a long hollow husk close at the bottom, but open from the middle upwards, ending in a point; in the middle whereof stands the small, long pestle or clapper, smaller at the bottom than at the top, of a dark purple colour, as the husk is on the inside, though green without, which after it hath so abided for some time, the husk with the clapper decayeth, and the foot or bottom thereof groweth to be a small long bunch of berries, green at the first, and of a yellowish colour when they are ripe, of the bigness of a hazel-nut kernel, which abideth thereon almost until winter; the root is round and somewhat long, for the most part lying along, the leaves shooting forth at the largest end, which, when it beareth its berries, are somewhat wrinkled and loose, another growing under it which is solid and firm, with many small threads hanging thereat. The whole plant is of a very sharp bitter taste, pricking the tongue as nettles do the hands, and so abideth for a great while without alteration. The root thereof was anciently used instead of starch to starch linen with.

There is another sort of cuckoo-point with lesser leaves than the former, and sometimes harder, having blackish spots upon them, which for the most part abide longer green in summer than the former, and both leaves and roots are more sharp and fierce than it ; in all things else it is like the former.

Place.—These two sorts grow frequently almost under every hedge-side in many places of this land.

Time.—They shoot forth leaves in the spring, and continue but until the middle of summer or somewhat later : their husks appearing before they fall away, and their fruit showing in April.

Government and Virtues.—It is under the dominion of Mars. Tragus reporteth that a dram weight, or more if need be, of the spotted wake-robin either fresh and green, or dried, being beaten and taken, is a present and sure remedy for poison and the plague. The juice of the herb taken to the quantity of a spoonful hath the same effect ; but if there be a little vinegar added thereto, as well as to the root aforesaid, it somewhat allayeth the sharp biting taste thereof upon the tongue. The green leaves bruised and laid upon any boil or plague-sore, doth wonderfully help to draw forth the poison. A dram of the powder of the dried root taken with twice so much sugar in the form of a licking electuary, or the green root, doth wonderfully help those that are pursy and short-winded, as also those that have a cough ; it breaketh, digesteth, and riddeth away phlegm from the stomach, chest, and lungs : the milk wherein the root hath been boiled is effectual also for the same purpose. The said powder taken in wine or other drink, or the juice of the berries, or the powder of them, or the wine wherein they have been boiled provoketh urine, and bringeth down women's courses, and purgeth them effectually after child-bearing, to bring away the after-birth. Taken with sheep's milk it healeth the inward ulcers of the bowels : the distilled water thereof is effectual to all the purposes aforesaid. A spoonful taken at a time healeth the itch : and an ounce or more taken at a time for some days together doth help the rupture. The leaves either green or dry, or the juice of them, doth cleanse all manner of rotten and filthy ulcers, in what part of the body soever ; and healeth the stinging sores in the nose, called polypus. The water wherein the root hath been b oiled, dropped into the eyes, cleanseth them from any film or skin cloud or mist, which begin to hinder the sight, and helpeth the watering and redness of them, or when by some chance they become black and blue. The root mixed with bean flour and applied to the throat or jaws that are inflamed, helpeth them. The juice of the berries boiled in oil of roses, or beaten into powder mixed with the oil, and dropped into the ears, easeth pains in them. The berries or roots beaten with hot ox-dung, and applied, easeth the pains of the gout. The leaves and roots boiled in wine with a little oil and applied to the piles, or the falling down of the fundament, easeth them, and so doth sitting over the hot fumes thereof. The fresh roots bruised and distilled with a little milk, yieldeth a most sovereign water to cleanse the skin from scurf, freckles, spots, or blemishes, whatsoever therein.

Authors have left large commendations of this herb you see, but for my part, I have neither spoken with Dr. Reason nor Dr. Experience about it.

CUCUMBERS.—(*Cucumis Sativus.*)

Government and Virtues.—There is no dispute to be made but that they are under the dominion of the Moon, though they are so much cried out against for their coldness, and if they were but one degree colder they would be poison. The best of Galenists hold them to be cold and moist in the second degree, and then not so hot as either lettuces or purslain : they are excellent good for a hot stomach and hot liver ; the unmeasurable use of them fills the body full of raw humours, and so indeed the unmeasurable use of any thing else doth harm. The face being washed with their juice cleanseth the skin, and is excellent good for hot rheums in the eyes : the seed is excellent good to provoke urine, and cleanseth the passages thereof when they are stopped ; there is not a better remedy growing for ulcers in the bladder than cucumbers are. The usual course is to use the seed in emulsions, as they make almond milk; but a far better way, in my opinion, is this: When the season of the year is, take the cucumbers and bruise them well and distil the water from them, and let such as are troubled with ulcers in the bladder drink no other drink. The face being washed with the same water cureth the reddest face that is; it is also excellent good for sun-burning, freckles, and morphew.

CUDWEED.—(*Gnaphalium Vulgare.*)

Besides Cudweed, it is called Cottonweed, Chaffweed, Dwarf Cotton, and Petty Cotton.

Descrip.—The common Cudweed riseth up with one stalk sometimes, and sometimes with two or three, thick set on all sides, with small, long, and narrow whitish and woody leaves, from the middle of the stalk almost up to the top; with every leaf standeth a small flower of a dun or brownish yellow colour, or not so yellow as others; in which herbs, after the flowers are fallen come small seed wrapped up with the down therein, and is carried away with the wind: the root is small and thready.

There are other sorts hereof, which are somewhat lesser than the former, not much different, save only that the stalks and leaves are shorter, so the flowers are paler and more open.

Place.—They grow in dry, barren, sandy, and gravelly grounds in many places of this land.

Time.—They flower about July, some earlier, some later, and their seed is ripe in August.

Government and Virtues.—Venus is lady of it. The plants are all astringent, binding, or drying, and therefore profitable for all defluctions of rheum from the head, and to stay fluxes of blood wheresoever, the decoction being made into red wine and drunk, or the powder taken therein. It also helpeth the bloody flux, and easeth the torments that come thereby, stayeth the immoderate courses of women, and is also good for inward or outward wounds, hurts, or bruises, and helpeth children both of ruptures and worms; and being drunk or injected for the disease called tenesmus, which is an often provocation to stool without doing any thing. The green leaves bruised and laid to any green wound, stayeth the bleeding and healeth it up quickly. The juice of the herb is, as Pliny saith, a sovereign remedy against the mumps and quinsey: and further saith, that whosoever shall so take it, shall never be troubled with that disease again.

CURRANT-TREE.—(*Ribes Vulgaris.*)

Descrip.—The Currant-tree is well known to be a somewhat taller tree than the goose-berry, with larger leaves, without thorns. The fruit grows in small bunches, of a red colour, and of a sharp sweetish taste.

Place.—It is usually planted in gardens, but is said to grow wild in the north of England.

Time.—It flowers in April, and the fruit is ripe in June.

Government and Virtues.—They are under Jupiter They are cooling to the stomach, quench thirst, and are somewhat restringent; a jelly made with the juice and sugar, is cooling and grateful in fevers.

CYPRESS-TREE.—(*Cupressus.*)

Descrip.—This grows to be a large, tall, high tree, covered all over, almost from the ground, with slender branches growing close together, making the tree have a pyramidal shape, with small, short, sharp, and as it were scaly leaves, which cover over all the young twigs. The flowers are small and staminous, succeeded by cones or nuts, as they are called, which are round, near as big as a wallnut, when ripe opening with several clefts, in which lie brown flattish cornered seeds.

Place.—It is planted in gardens for its pleasant verdure, being a perennial or evergreen, holding its leaves all winter, and shooting out fresh in the spring. We have two species growing in our gardens, whereof the fœmina, or that whose branches grow closer together, is the most common, having somewhat longer nuts than the other, whose branches are more expanded, and cones or nuts rounder.

Time.—The fruit is ripe about the beginning of winter.

Government and Virtues.—This tree is under the government of Saturn. The cones or nuts are mostly used, the leaves but seldom; they are accounted very drying and binding, good to stop fluxes of all kinds, as spitting of blood, diarrhœa, dysentery, the immoderate flux of the menses, involuntary miction; they prevent the bleeding of the gums, and fasten loose teeth: outwardly, they are used in styptic restringent fomentations and cataplasms.

DAFFODILL (COMMON.)—(*Narcissus Pseudo-narcissus.*)

The White Daffodills are also called Primrose Pearls, and the Yellow Daffodills, Lidelillies, and Daffy-downdillies.

Descrip.—There are several kinds of daffodills: some with a crimson or red purple circle in the middle of the flower, and others having a yellow circle, resembling a coronet or cup, in the middle of the flower: there is another kind that is yellow in the middle, and another sort which bears double flowers. The common wild Daffodill grows about a foot high. The leaves are long, narrow, grassy, and of a deep green; and they are nearly as long as the stalk, which is roundish, but somewhat flattish and edged. The flower is large, yellow, and single: it stands at the top of the stalk, and by its weight presses it down a little: the root is round and white.

Place.—It is common in the gardens in its own natural form, and in a great variety of shapes and colours that culture has given it. The yellow Daffodill does not grow naturally in this country, but in gardens where it is planted.

Time.—Daffodills flower in March and April.

Government and Virtues.—Venus governs all the Daffodills, except the yellow, which belongs to Mars. The fresh roots of the former are to be used, and it is very easy to have them always in readiness in a garden; and very useful, for they have great virtues. Given internally, in a small quantity, either in decoction or powder, they act as a vomit, and afterwards purge a little: and are excellent against all obstructions. The best way of giving them is in form of the juice, pressed out with some white-wine; but their principal uses are externally. The fresh roots bruised, and boiled with parched barley-meal, very suddenly heal fresh wounds; mixed with honey, they strengthen sprains, and are good to apply to cuts, and to old aches in the joints. With darnel-meal and honey, they break imposthumes, and help to draw out splinters from the flesh: the juice of the bruised root will allay swellings and inflammations of the breast. The roots of yellow Daffodills boiled, and taken in posset-drink, cause vomiting, and are used with good success at the appearance of approaching agues, especially tertian agues, which are frequently caught in the spring time. A plaster made of these roots, with parched barley-meal, dissolves hard swellings and imposthumes: the juice, mingled with honey, frankincense, wine, and myrrh, and dropped into the ears, is good against all the corrupt filth and running matter in these parts; the roots made hollow, and boiled in oil, help sore kibed heels: the juice of the root is also good for the morphew, and the discolourings of the skin.

DAISIES.—(*Chrysanthemum Leucanthemum.*)

THESE are so well known almost to every child, that I suppose it needless to write any description of them. Take therefore the virtues of them as followeth.

Government and Virtues.—The herb is under the sign Cancer, and under the dominion of Venus, and therefore excellent good for wounds in the breast, and very fitting to be kept both in oils, ointments, and plasters, as also in syrup. The greater wild daisy is a wound herb of good respect, often used in those drinks and salves that are for wounds, either inward or outward. The juice or distilled water of these, or the small daisy, doth much temper the heat of choler, and refresh the liver and the other inward parts. A decoction made of them and drank, helpeth to cure the wounds made in the hollowness of the breast: the same cureth also all ulcers and pustules in the mouth or tongue, or in the secret parts. The leaves bruised and applied to the testicles or any other part that is swollen and hot, doth dissolve it, and temper the heat. A decoction made thereof, of wall-wort and agrimony, and places fomented or bathed therewith warm, giveth great ease to them that are troubled with the palsy, sciatica, or the gout. The same also disperseth and dissolveth the knots or kernels that grow in the flesh of any part of the body, and bruises and hurts that come of falls and blows; they are also used for ruptures and other inward burnings, with very good success. An ointment made thereof doth wonderfully help all wounds that have inflammations about them, or by reason of moist humours having access unto them are kept long from healing, and such are those for the most part that happen to joints of the arms and legs. The juice of them dropped into the running eyes of any, doth much help them.

DAISY LITTLE.—(*Bellis Minor Perennis.*)

Descrip.—The root of the Little common Daisy is a thick bush of fibres, the leaves grow in a circle close to the ground, being thick and fleshy, and are long and narrow at the bottom, ending broad and round, not much bigger than a silver penny, with very few indentings about the edges : the flowers spring immediately from the roots, upon slender stalks three or four inches high, bearing one small single flower at the end, made of a border of white petala, or leaves, set about a yellow thrum ; sometimes the border is edged with a reddish colour, and red underneath. The seed is whitish, slender, and flat.

Place.—Daisies grow every where in the fields and meadows.

Time.—They flower in April and May.

Government and Virtues.—This Daisy is governed by Venus in the sign Cancer. The leaves, and sometimes the roots, are used, and are reckoned among the traumatic and vulnerary plants, being used in wound-drinks, and are accounted good to dissolve congealed and coagulated blood, to help the pleurisy and peripneumonia. In the king's evil the decoction given inwardly, and a cataplasm of the leaves applied outwardly, are esteemed by some extraordinary remedies. This is another herb which nature has made common, because it may be useful. Its leaves taste like those of coltsfoot, but more mucilaginous, and not bitter. An infusion of it just boiled in asses milk, is very effectual in consumptions of the lungs.

DANDELION.—(*Leontodon Taraxacum.*)

1. *Common.* 2. *Rough.* 3. *Branchy.*

VULGARLY called Piss-a-Beds.

Descrip.—It is well known to have many long and deep gashed leaves lying on the ground round about the heads of the roots ; the ends of each gash or jag, on both sides looking downwards towards the roots ; the middle rib being white, which being broken yieldeth abundance of bitter milk, but the root much more ; from among the leaves, which always abide green, arise many slender, weak, naked foot-stalks, every one of them bearing at the top one large yellow flower, consisting of many rows of yellow leaves, broad at the points, and nicked in with deep spots of yellow in the middle, which growing ripe, the green husk wherein the flowers stood turns itself down to the stalk, and the head of down becomes as round as a ball, with long reddish seed underneath, bearing a part of the down on the head of every one, which together is blown away with the wind, or may be at once blown away with one's mouth. The root growing downwards exceeding deep, which being broken off within the ground, will yet shoot forth again, and will hardly be destroyed where it hath once taken deep root in the ground.

Place.—It groweth frequently in all meadows and pasture grounds.

Time.—It flowereth in one place or another almost all the year long.

Government and Virtues.—It is under the dominion of Jupiter. It is of an opening and cleansing quality, and therefore very effectual for the obstructions of the liver, gall, and spleen, and the diseases that arise from them, as the jaundice and hypochondriac; it openeth the passages of the urine both in young and old; powerfully cleanseth imposthumes and inward ulcers in the urinary passages, and by its drying and temperate quality doth afterwards heal them; for which purpose the decoction of the roots or leaves in white wine, or the leaves chopped as pot herbs with a few alisanders, and boiled in their broth, are very effectual. And whoever is drawing towards a consumption, or an evil disposition of the whole body called cachexia, by the use hereof for some time together shall find a wonderful help. It helpeth also to procure rest and sleep to bodies distempered by the heat of ague fits, or otherwise: the distilled water is effectual to drink in pestilenial fevers, and to wash the sores.

You see here what virtues this common herb hath, and that is the reason the French and Dutch so often eat them in the spring; and now if you look a little farther, you may see plainly without a pair of spectacles, that foreign physicians are not so selfish as ours are, but more communicative of the virtues of plants to people.

DARNEL (RED and WHITE.)—(*Lolium, Rubrum et Album.*)

It is called Jura and Wary; in Sussex they call it Crop, it being a pestilent enemy among the corn.

Descrip.—This hath, all the winter long, sundry long, flat, and rough leaves, which, when the stalk riseth, which is slender and jointed, are narrower but rough still; on the top groweth a long spike composed of many heads set one above another, containing two or three husks with sharp but short beards or awns at the ends; the seed is easily shook out of the ear, the husk itself being somewhat rough.

Place.—The country husbandmen do know this too well to grow among their corn, or in the borders and pathways of other fields that are fallow.

Government and Virtues.—It is a malicious part of sullen Saturn. As it is not without some vices, so hath it also many virtues. The meal of darnel is very good to stay gangrenes and other such like fretting and eating canker and putrid sores; it also cleanseth the skin of all leprosies, morphews, ring-worms, and the like, if it be used with salt and raddish roots. And being used with quick brimstone and vinegar, it dissolveth knots and kernels, and breaketh those that are hard to be dissolved, being boiled in wine with pigeon's dung and linseed. A decoction thereof made with water and honey, and the places bathed therewith is profitable for the sciatica. Darnel meal applied in a poultice draweth forth splinters and broken bones in the flesh. The red darnel boiled in red wine and taken, stayeth the lax and all other fluxes and women's bloody issues, and restraineth urine that passeth away too suddenly.

DEVIL'S BIT.—(*Scabiosa Succisa.*)

Descrip.—This riseth up with a round green smooth stalk about two feet high, set with divers long and somewhat narrow, smooth, dark green leaves, somewhat nipped about the edges for the most part, being else all whole and not divided at all, or but very seldom, even at the tops of the branches, which are yet smaller than those below, with one rib only in the middle. At the end of each branch standeth a round head of many flowers set together in the same manner, or more neatly than scabions, and of a more blueish purple colour, which being past, there followeth seed that falleth away. The root somewhat thick, but short and blackish, with many strings, abiding after seed time many years. This root was longer, until the devil (as the friars say) bit away the rest of it for spite, envying its usefulness to mankind: for sure he was not troubled with any disease for which it is proper.

There are two sorts hereof, in nothing unlike the former, save that the one beareth white, and the other blush-coloured flowers.

Place.—The first groweth as well in dry meadows and fields as moist, in many places of this land: but the other two are more rare and hard to be met with, yet they are found growing wild about Appledore, near Rye, in Kent.

Time.—They flower not usually until August.

Government and Virtues.—The plant is venereal, pleasing and harmless. The herb or the root (all that the devil hath left of it) being boiled in wine and drank, is very powerful against the plague, and all pestilential diseases or fevers, poisons also, and the bitings of venomous beasts: it helpeth also all that are inwardly bruised by any casualty, or outwardly by falls or blows, dissolving the clotted blood; and the herb or root beaten and outwardly applied, taketh away the black and blue marks that remain in the skin. The decoction of the herb, with honey of roses put therein, is very effectual to help the inveterate tumours and swellings of the almonds and throat, by often gargling the mouth therewith. It helpeth also to procure women's courses, and easeth all pains of the mother, and to break and discuss wind therein, and in the bowels. The powder of the root taken in drink, driveth forth the worms in the body. The juice or distilled water of the herb, is very effectual for green wounds or old sores, and cleanseth the body inwardly, and the seed outwardly, from sores, scurf, itch, pimples, freckles, morphew, or other deformities thereof, especially if a little vitriol be dissolved therein.

DILL.—(*Anethum Graveolens.*)

Descrip.—The common Dill groweth up with seldom more than one stalk, neither so high nor so great usually as fennel, being round and fewer joints thereon, whose leaves are sadder and somewhat long, and so like fennel that it deceiveth many, but harder in handling, and somewhat thicker, and of a stronger unpleasant scent; the tops of the stalks have four branches, and small umbles of yellow flowers, which turn into small seed, somewhat flatter and thinner than fennel seed. The root is somewhat small and woody, and perisheth every year after it hath borne seed, and is also unprofitable, being never put to any use.

Place.—It is most usually sown in gardens and grounds for the purpose, and is also found wild in many places.

Government and Virtues.—Mercury hath the dominion of this plant, and therefore to be sure it strengthens the brain. The dill boiled and drank, is good to ease both swellings and pains; it also stayeth the belly and stomach from casting. The decoction helpeth women that are troubled with pains and windiness of the mother, if they sit therein. It stayeth the hiccough, being boiled in wine, and but smelled unto, being tied in a cloth. The seed is of more use than the leaves, and more effectual to digest raw and viscous humours, and is used in medicines that serve to expel wind, and the pains proceeding therefrom. The seed being roasted or fried, and used in oils or plaisters, dissolves the imposthumes in the fundament, and drieth up all moist ulcers especially in that part: an oil made of Dill is effectual to warm or dissolve humours or imposthumes, to ease pains, and to procure rest. The decoction of Dill, be it herb or seed, (only if you boil the seed you must bruise it) in white wine, being drunk, it is a gallant expeller of wind and provoker of terms.

DITTANDER.—*(Lepidium Sativum.)*

Called also Pepper-wort.

Descrip.—The common Dittander has a small, white, slender, creeping root, hard to be got out of a garden where it has been once planted. The lower leaves grow on long foot-stalks, are smooth, oblong, sharp pointed and serrated, four or five inches long: the stalks grow to be half a yard high, smooth, and having lesser and narrower leaves growing alternately, sometimes indented about the edges, and sometimes not. The flowers that grow on the top of the stalks are small, white, and four-leaved, and the seed-vessels small and round.

Place.—It grows in moist places, and near rivers.

Time.—It flowers in June and July, The whole plant has a hot and biting taste, like pepper.

Government and Virtues.—It is an herb of Venus. The leaves of Dittander bruised and mixed with hogs-lard, and applied as a cataplasm to the hip, help the sciatica; chewed in the mouth, they cause a great flux of rheum to run out of it, and by that means are said to help scrofulous tumours in the throat: the women in Suffolk give them boiled in ale to hasten the birth.

DITTANY OF CRETE.—(*Origanum Dictamnus.*)

Descrip.—A very pretty plant that grows six or eight inches high; the stalks are square, slender, hard, woody, and branched: the leaves are short, broad, and roundish; they stand two at every joint, and are covered with a white downy matter. The flowers are small and purple: they grow in oblong and slender scaly heads, in the manner of those of origanum: and these heads are themselves very pretty, being elegantly variegated with green and purple. It resembles penny-royal much, only the leaves are larger.

Place.—It originally came from the isle of Candia, but grows with us in gardens.

Time.—It flowers at the latter end of July, and beginning of August.

Government and Virtues.—It is an herb of Venus, and possesses the virtues of penny-royal, but in a superior degree. It is an excellent wound herb, and in much reputation among the ancients, for which Virgil may be quoted. It is good in decoction with wine, to procure speedy and easy deliverance, or with vervain, hyssop, and penny-royal; or boiled in ale, is more effectual for the same purpose. Dittany and milk are good for spitting of blood. Bruised with polipody, and mixed with hogs-lard, it draws splinters out of the flesh, and heals; the roots are cordial and cephalic, resist putrefaction and poison, and are useful in malignant and pestilential distempers. The whole herb is good for diseases of the head, and to open all manner of obstructions. It is a considerable ingredient in the Venice treacle, mithridate, and diascordium.

DITTANY (WHITE.)—(*Dictamnus Albus.*)

Called also Bastard, or False Dittany, or Dictamnum, and Fraxinella.

Descrip.—This species of Dittany resembles in its leaves those of the ash-tree, only smaller, and from whence it derives its name. It grows about three feet high, very much branched, and very beautiful. The stalks are round, thick, firm, and of a green and purple colour, according to its state of forwardness. The leaves stand irregularly, the flowers are large and elegant; they are of a pale red, white, or striped, and sometimes light-blue, and they stand in a kind of spikes at the top of the branches. In the summer months, the whole plant is covered with a kind of inflammable substance, which is glutinous to the touch, and of very fragrant smell; but if it takes fire, it goes off with a flash all over the plant. This does it no harm, and may be repeated after three or four days, a new quantity of the inflammable matter being produced in that time.

Place.—It only grows here in gardens, not being hardy enough to bear the severity of our climate abroad.

Time.—It flowers in June and July.

Government and Virtues.—They are both under the dominion of Venus. The roots of this kind are the only part used; they are cordial, cephalic, resist poison and putrefaction, and are useful in malignant and pestilential distempers; in fevers, and hysteric cases: however, an infusion of the tops of the plant, are a pleasant and efficacious medicine in the gravel; it works powerfully by urine, and gives ease in those colicky pains which frequently attend upon that disorder. The root is a sure remedy for epilepsies, and other diseases of the head, opening obstructions of the womb, and procuring the discharges of the terms.

DOCK (COMMON.)—*(Rumex Obtusifolius.)*

Many kinds of these are so well known, that I shall not trouble you with a description of them.

Government and Virtues.—All Docks are under Jupiter, of which the Red Dock, which is commonly called Bloodwort, cleanseth the blood and strengthens the liver; but the Yellow Dock root is best to be taken when either the blood or liver is affected by choler. All of them have a kind of cooling (but not all alike) drying quality, the sorrel being most cold, and the blood worts most drying. Of the burdock I have spoken already by itself. The seed of most of the other kinds, whether gardens or fields, doth stay laxes and fluxes of all sorts, the loathing of the stomach through choler, and is helpful for those that spit blood. The roots boiled in vinegar helpeth the itch, scabs, and breaking out of the skin, if it be bathed therewith. The distilled water of the herb and roots have the same virtue, and cleanseth the skin from freckles, morphews, and all other spots and discolourings therein.

All Docks being boiled with meat, make it boil the

sooner; besides, Bloodwort is exceeding strengthening to the liver, and procures good blood, being as wholesome a pot herb as any growing in a garden.

DODDER OF THYME.—(*Cuscuta Europæa.*)

Descrip.—This first, from seed, giveth roots in the ground, which shooteth forth threads or strings, grosser or finer as the property of the plant wherein it groweth and the climate doth suffer, creeping and spreading on that plant whereon it fasteneth, be it high or low. The strings have no leaves at all upon them, but wind and interlace themselves so thick upon a small plant, that it taketh away all comfort of the sun from it; and is ready to choke or strangle it. After these strings are risen up to that height, that they may draw nourishment from the plant, they seem to be broken off from the ground, either by the strength of their rising or withered by the heat of the sun. Upon these strings are found clusters of small heads or husks, out of which shoot forth whitish flowers, which afterwards give small pale white-coloured seed, somewhat flat, and twice as big as a poppy-seed. It generally participates of the nature of the plants it climbeth upon; but the Dodder of Thyme is accounted the best, and is the only true one.

Government and Virtues.—All Dodders are under Saturn. Tell me not of physicians crying up Epithymum, or that Dodder which grows upon Thyme, (most of which comes from Hemetius in Greece, or Hybla in Sicily, because those mountains abound with Thyme) he is a physician indeed that hath wit enough to choose his Dodder, according to the nature of the disease and humour peccant. We confess Thyme is the hottest herb it usually grows upon, and therefore that which grows upon Thyme is hotter than that which grows upon colder herbs; for it draws nourishment from what it grows upon, as well as from the earth where its root is, and thus you see old Saturn is wise enough to have two strings to his bow. This is accounted the most effectual for melancholy diseases, and to purge black or burnt choler, which is the cause of many diseases of the head and brain, as also for the trembling of the heart, faintings, and swoonings. It is helpful in all diseases and griefs of the spleen, and melancholy that arises from the windiness of the hypocondria. It purgeth also the reins or kidneys by urine; it openeth obstructions of the gall, whereby it profiteth them that have the jaundice; as also the leaves the spleen; purging the veins of choleric and phlegmatic humours, and helpeth children in agues, a little worm seed being added thereto.

The other Dodders do, as I said before, participate of the nature of those plants whereon they grow: as that which hath been found growing upon nettles in the west country, hath by experience been found very effectual to procure plenty of urine, where it hath been stopped or hindered. And so of the rest.

Sympathy and antipathy are two hinges upon which the whole model of physic turns; and that physician who minds them not, is like a door off from the hooks, more like to do a man mischief than to cure him. Then all the diseases Saturn causes this helps by sympathy, and strengthens all the parts of the body he rules; such has are caused by Sol it helps by antipathy.

DOG'S GRASS.—(*Triticum Repens.*)

CALLED also Couch Grass and Quick Grass.

Descrip.—It is well known that grass creepeth far about under ground, with long white jointed roots, and small fibres almost at every joint, very sweet in taste, as the rest of the herb is, and interlacing one another, from whence shoot forth many fair grassy leaves, small at the ends, and cutting or sharp on the edges. The stalks are jointed like corn, with the like leaves on them, and a large spiked head, with a long husk in them, and hard rough seeds in them. If you know it not by this description, watch the dogs when they are sick, and they will quickly lead you to it.

Place.—It groweth commonly through this land in divers ploughed grounds, to the no small trouble of the husbandmen, as also of the gardener, in gardens, to weed it out if they can; for it is a constant customer to the place it gets footing in.

Government and Virtues.—'Tis under the dominion of Jupiter, and is the most medicinal of all the quick grasses. Being boiled and drunk it openeth obstructions of the liver and gall, and the stoppings of urine, and easeth the griping pains of the belly, and inflammations; wasteth the matter of the stone in the bladder, and the ulcers thereof also. The seed doth more powerfully expel urine, and stayeth laxes and vomiting. The distilled water alone, or with a little worm-seed, killeth the worms in children.

The way of use is to bruise the roots, and having well boiled them in white wine, drink the decoction; it is opening, but not purging, very safe; 'tis a remedy against all diseases coming of stopping, and such are half those that are incident to the body of man; and although a gardener be of another opinion, yet a physician holds an acre of them to be worth five acres of carrots twice told over.

DOG'S MERCURY.—(*Mercurialis Perennis.*)

Descrip.—This is a rank poisonous plant, that grows about a foot high, and has but few leaves, but they are large; the stalk is round, thick, whitish, pointed, and a little hairy: the leaves stand principally towards the top, four, five, or six, seldom more; they are long, and considerably broad, sharp-pointed, notched about the edges, and a little hairy.

Place.—It is most commonly found under hedges.

Government and Danger.—This species of Mercury has been confounded with others of the same name, with which it has been thought to agree in nature. But there is not a more fatal plant, native of our country, than this. The common herbals, as Gerard's and Parkinson's, instead of cautioning their readers against the use of this plant, after some trifling, idle observations, upon the qualities of Mercurys in general, dismiss the article without noticing its baneful effects. Other writers, more accurate, have done this; but they have written in Latin, a language not very likely to inform those who stand most in need of this caution. This is one of the reasons for the compiling of this work; and, among many others, evinces the necessity of placing the Latin name opposite to the English one, to prevent that confusion which similarity of English might unfortunately create.

DOG ROSE.—(*Rosa Canina.*)

CALLED also Wild Rose.

Descrip.—The Dog Rose has winged leaves like garden roses, but smoother and greener; the flowers are single, of five white, and sometimes pale red leaves, and when they are fallen, there succeed roundish red seed-vessels, full of pulp, inclosing white cornered seed, covered with short stiff hairs. On the stalks of this plant grow a green spongy excrescence, made by small flies.

Place.—It grows commonly in the hedges about Cambridge.

Time.—It flowers in May and June, and the seed is ripe at the beginning of September.

Government and Virtues.—It is under the dominion of the Moon. The flowers of the Wild Briar are accounted rather more restringent than the Garden Roses, and by some are reckoned as a specific for the excess of the catamenia. The pulp of the hips has a pleasant grateful acidity, strengthens the stomach, cools the heat of fevers, is pectoral, good for coughs and spitting of blood, and the scurvy. The seed has been known to do great things against the stone and gravel; and the same virtues are attributed to the spongy excrescence which grows upon the stalk. The best way of preserving its virtues is, by keeping it conserved.

DOG'S TOOTH VIOLET.—(*Erythronium dens Canis.*)

Descrip.—A very pretty plant, small, with two broad leaves, and a large drooping flower: it grows five or six inches high. The stalk is round, slender, weak, and greenish towards the top, and often white at the bottom. The leaves stand a little height above ground: they are oblong, somewhat broad, of a beautiful green, not at all dented at the edges, and blunt at the end. They inclose the stalk at the base. The flower is large and white, but with a tinge of reddish: it hangs down, is long, hollow, and very elegant. The root is roundish, and has some fibres growing from its bottom; it is full of a slimy pulp.

Place.—It grows frequently in gardens, but must not be sought for wild.

Time.—It flowers in June, and is in perfection till the fall of the leaf.

Government and Virtues.—This useful plant is governed by the Moon. The fresh gathered roots are the best to be used, for they dry very ill, and generally lose their virtues entirely. They are good against worms in children, and speedily ease the pains of the belly which are produced thereby. The best way of giving them is, in the expressed juice; or if children will not take that, they may be boiled in milk, to which they give very little taste.

It should be remembered it is a very powerful remedy, and a small dose will take effect, especially of the juice, so that it is best to begin with very little; and as that is well borne, to increase the quantity.

DOVE'S-FOOT.—(*Geranium Molle.*)

Descrip.—This hath divers small, round, pale green leaves cut in about the edges, much like mallows, standing upon long, reddish, hairy stalks, lying in a round compass upon the ground, among which rise up two, or three, or more reddish jointed, slender, weak hairy stalks with such like leaves thereon, but smaller, and more cut in up to the tops, where grow many very small, bright, red flowers of five leaves a-piece; after which follow small heads with small short beaks pointed forth, as all other sorts of this herb do.

Place.—It groweth in pasture grounds, and by the path-sides in many places and will also be in gardens.

Time.—It flowereth in June, July, and August, some earlier and some later; and the seed is ripe quickly after.

Government and Virtues.—It is a very gentle, though martial plant. It is found by experience to be singular good for wind colic, as also to expel the stone and gravel in the kidneys. The decoction thereof in wine, is an excellent remedy for those that have inward wounds, hurts, or bruises, both to stay the bleeding, to dissolve and expel the congealed blood, and to heal the parts, as also to cleanse and heal outward sores, ulcers, and fistulas; and for green wounds many do only bruise the herb and apply it to the place, and it healeth them quickly. The same decoction in wine fomented to any place pained with gout, or to joint-ache, or pains of the sinews, giveth much ease. The powder or decoction of the herb taken for some time together, is found by experience to be singular good for ruptures and burstings in people, either young or old.

DOWN, OR COTTON-THISTLE.—(*Carduus Vulgatissimus.*)

Descrip.—This hath large leaves lying on the ground, somewhat cut in, and as it were crumpled on the edges, of a green colour on the upper side, but covered with long hairy wool or cotton down, set with most sharp and cruel pricks, from the middle of whose heads or flowers thrust forth many purplish crimson threads, and sometimes, although very seldom, white ones. The seed that followeth in the heads, lying in a great deal of white down, is somewhat large, long, and round like the seed of Ladies Thistle but somewhat paler. The root is great and thick, spreading much, yet it usually dieth after seed time.

Place.—It groweth in divers ditches, banks, and in corn fields and highways, generally everywhere throughout the land.

Time.—It flowereth and beareth seed about the end of summer, when other thistles do flower and seed.

Government and Virtues.—Mars owns the plant, and manifests to the world, that though it may hurt your finger, it will help your body; for I fancy it much for the ensuing virtues. Pliny and Dioscorides write, that the leaves and roots thereof taken in drink help those that have a crick in their neck, whereby they cannot turn their neck but their whole body must turn also (surely they do not mean those that have got a crick in their neck by being under the hangman's hand.) Galen saith, that the roots and leaves hereof are of a healing quality, and are good for such persons as have their bodies drawn together by some spasm or convulsion, as it is with children that have the rickets, or rather, as the College of Physicians will have it, the rachites; for which name of the disease they have in a particular treatise lately set forth by them, learnedly disputed and put forth to public view, that the world may see they have taken much pains to little purpose.

DRAGON.—(*Dracontium.*)

THEY are so well known to every one that plants them in their gardens, that they need no description; if not, let them look down to the lower end of the stalks, and see how like a snake they look.

Government and Virtues.—The plant is under the dominion of Mars, and therefore it would be a wonder if it should want some obnoxious quality or other: in all herbs of that quality, the safest way is either to distil the herb in alembic, in what vehicle you please, or else to press out the juice and distil that in a glass-still in sand. It scoureth and cleanseth the internal parts of the body mightily, and it cleareth the external parts also, being externally applied, from freckles, morphew, and sun-burnings; your best way to use it externally is to mix it with vinegar: an ointment of it is held to be good in wounds and ulcers; it consumes cankers, and that flesh growing in the nose which they call polypus: also the distilled water being dropped into the eyes takes away spots there, or the pin and web, and mends dimness of sight; it is excellent good against pestilence and poison. Pliny and Dioscorides affirm, that no serpent will meddle with him that carries the herb about him.

DROPWORT.—(*Oenanthe Fistulosa, et Crocata.*)

Descrip.—The roots of Dropwort consist of a great number of oval glandules fastened together by slender strings, from which spring several long, narrow, and as it were pinnated leaves, whose pinnæ are serrated, and not much unlike the smaller burnet saxifrage leaves: the stalks grow to be about a foot high, having but few leaves thereon, but on their tops a pretty many flowers in form of an umbel, which are white within, and reddish on the outside, made of six leaves, with a great number of yellowish stamina in the middle; which are succeeded by several flattish seeds growing in a head together.

Place.—It grows in chalky grounds,

Time.—It flowers in June and July; the root being chiefly used.

Government and Virtues.—Pimpernel Dropwort, (*Spiræa Filipendula,*) which some have described as a lesser species of the filipendula, differs in nothing, according to their own account, from this, but in size, and is evidently a variety. They are accounted under Venus. Dropwort, especially the root, is counted diuretic, and good for the stone, gravel, and stoppage of urine.

DUCK'S-MEAT, OR DUCKWEED.—(*Lens Palustris.*)

Called also Water Lentils.

This is so well known to swim on the tops of standing waters, as ponds, pools, and ditches, that it is needless further to describe it.

Government and Virtues.—Cancer claims the herb, and the Moon will be lady of it: a word is enough to a wise man. It is effectual to help inflammations and St. Anthony's fire, as also the gout, either applied by itself or in a poultice with barley meal. The distilled water is highly esteemed by some against all inward inflammations and pestilential fevers; as also to help the redness of the eyes and swellings of the testicles, and of the breasts before they be grown too much. The fresh herb applied to the forehead, easeth the pains of the head-ache coming of heat.

EGLANTINE.—(*Rosa Rubiginosa.*)

CALLED also Sweet Briar, Wild Briar, and Pimpernel Rose.

Place.—It is cultivated in most gardens and pleasure-grounds, and likewise grows wild in the borders of fields, and in woods.

Time.—It begins to shoot forth its buds early in the spring, and flowers during the time of other roses.

Government and Virtues.—This is under the dominion of Jupiter. The spongy apples or balls which are found upon the Eglantine, if pounded to a paste, and mixed with honey and wood-ashes, are excellent for the alopecia or falling of the hair, and being dried and powdered, and taken in white wine, remove the strangury, and strengthen the kidneys. The same boiled in a strong decoction of the roots, is good for venomous bites. The red berries which succeed the flowers, called hips, if made into a conserve, and eaten occasionally, gently bind the belly, stop defluxions of the head and stomach, help digestion, sharpen the appetite, and dry up the moisture of cold rheum and phlegm upon the stomach. The powder of the dried pulp is good for the whites, and if mixed with the powder of the balls, and given in small quantities, is also good for the colic, and to destroy worms.

ELDER.—(*Sambucus Nigra.*)

Descrip.—The Elder-Tree is a common hedge-tree, whose spreading branches have a spongy pith in the middle; the outside bark is of an ash-colour, under which is another that is green. The leaves are pinnated, of two or three pair of pinnæ, with an odd one at the end, which is larger than the rest; they are oval, sharp-pointed, and serrated about the edges. The flowers grow in large flat umbels; they are small, of one leaf, cut into five sections, with as many small stamina; and are succeeded by small round deep purple berries, full of a purple juice.

Place.—The Elder-tree grows frequently in hedges, especially in moist places.

Time.—It flowers in May, and the berries are ripe in September. The bark, leaves, flowers, and berries are used.

Government and Virtues.—This is under the dominion of Venus. The first shoots of the Common Elder boiled like asparagus, and the young leaves and stalks boiled in fat broth, do mightily carry forth phlegm and choler. The middle or inward bark boiled in water, and given in drink works much more violently ; and the berries, either green or dry, expel the same humour, and are often given with good success to help the dropsy ; the bark of the root boiled in wine, or the juice thereof drank, works the same effects, but more powerfully than either the leaves or fruit. The juice of the root taken, mightily procures vomitings, and purges the watery humours of the dropsy. The decoction of the root taken, cures the bite of an adder, and bites of mad-dogs. It mollifies the hardness of the mother, if women sit thereon, and opens their veins, and brings down their courses : the berries boiled in wine, perform the same effect : and the hair of the head washed therewith, is made black. The juice of the green leaves applied to the hot inflammations of the eyes assuages them ; the juice of the leaves snuffed up into the nostrils, purges the tunicles of the brain ; the juice of the berries boiled with honey, and dropped into the ears, helps the pains of them ; the decoction of the berries in wine being drunk, provokes urine ; the distilled water of the flowers is of much use to clean the skin from sun-burning, freckles, morphew, or the like ; and takes away the head-ache, coming of a cold cause, the head being bathed therewith. The leaves or flowers distilled in the month of May, and the legs often washed with the said distilled water, takes away the ulcers and sores of them. The eyes washed therewith, it takes away the redness and blood-shot ; and the hands washed morning and evening therewith, helps the palsy, and shaking of them.

ELDER (DWARF.)—(*Sambucus Humilis.*)

Descrip.—This is a pretty looking low plant, sending up various spreading stalks, which fall down every year, and rise again in the spring ; on the top of these grow umbels of white flowers, having frequently a dash of purple, each of one small leaf, divided into five segments ; which are succeeded by round berries, when ripe, of a deep purple, or black colour, and full of a purplish juice.

The root is thick, and creeping on the surface of the earth.

Place.—The Dwarf Elder grows wild in many places of England.

Time.—Most of the Elder trees flower in June, and their fruit is ripe for the most part in August. But the Dwarf Elder, or Wallwort, flowers somewhat later, and its fruit is not ripe until September.

Government and Virtues.—The Dwarf Elder is also under Venus, and is more powerful than the Common Elder in opening and purging choler, phlegm, and water, in helping the gout, piles, and women's diseases; colours the hair black, helps the inflammations of the eyes, and pains in the ears, the bite of serpents, or mad dogs, burnings and scaldings, the wind colic, colic and stone, the difficulty of urine, the cure of old sores, and fistulous ulcers.

Of the Dwarf Elder, the bark and seeds are in most repute, for the jaundice and dropsy; in the same intention a decoction of the root and seeds is commended, but should be joined with proper correctors, they being very violent in their operation without. The expressed oil of the seed is by some outwardly used to assuage the pain of the gout.

The inner bark of the Common Elder decocted, operates both by vomit and stool. The same effect is observed but in a milder degree, of the young buds, if in the spring, eaten as young salad, and these in pottage gently relax the bowels. The inner bark outwardly applied, is commended in burns.

The flowers are sudorific and anodyne; infused in sharp vinegar, with the addition of some spices, they make a more reviving liquor to smell to, and to rub the temples with in faintings of women in labour, and after delivery, than all the volatile salts put together.

Take of Elder flowers, half a pound, the flowers of red roses, rosemary, and lavender, each four ounces, of nutmeg and cloves each two drams, of cinnamon three drams, pour upon them five pints of the sharpest white wine vinegar, let all infuse a month or six weeks, and after having pressed it out well, and the liquor is settled, put it into bottles and keep it well stopped for use.

The berries are likewise sudorific, and of admirable use in recent colds, and beginning feverish heats, in which cases nothing is so proper as the juice, without any addition, boiled over a very gentle fire to the consistence of an extract; this is commonly called the Rob of Elder, but is rarely made by apothecaries, though vastly superior to the syrup which is constantly kept in the shops. To make this Rob still more useful in the abovementioned disorders, I would recommend to the patient to take half a dram of fine levigated crabs' eyes, mixed up with half a spoonful of water, and immediately after six drams or an ounce of the said Rob, and to lie down and cover himself well. This will excite a gentle fermentation in the stomach, throw the person into a beneficial sweat, and produce a wonderful amendment. The truth of this has been so generally experienced by the Germans, that one shall hardly travel through a town or village where the inhabitants are unprovided with this Rob.

The juice of the Elder berries mixed with one third part in weight of the genuine powder of liquorice, with a few drops of oil of aniseeds, and boiled to a proper consistence, is a far better remedy on account of its acidity, for cutting the phlegm, and taking off the irritation to cough, than the juice of our liquorice, or the Spanish juice alone. A wine made of the juice of these berries is very wholesome.

ELECAMPANE, OR ELFWORT.—(*Inula Helenium.*)

Descrip.—This is a robust and stately plant; a perennial, with an upright handsome appearance. The leaves are of a dull faint green; and the root, which is long and large, contains the virtues of the plant.

Place.—It grows in moist grounds and shadowy places, almost in every county in England.

Time.—It flowers in the end of June and July, and the seed is ripe in August. The roots are gathered for use, as well in the spring before the leaves come forth, as in autumn or winter.

Government and Virtues.—It is under Mercury. One of the most beneficial roots nature affords for the help of the consumptive. It has a fragrant, very agreeable smell; and a spicy, sharp, and somewhat bitterish taste. It is good for all diseases of the breast, and has great virtues in malignant fevers; in strengthening the stomach, and assisting digestion, not like a bitter, but as a warm, invigorating, animating medicine; and it has not its equal in the cure of the hooping-cough in children, when all other medicines fail. The fresh roots of Elecampane preserved with sugar, or made into a syrup or conserve, are very effectual to warm a cold windy stomach, or the pricking therein, and stitches in the sides caused by the spleen; and to help the cough, shortness of breath, and wheezing in the lungs. The dried root made into powder, and mixed with sugar, and taken, serves to the same purpose; and is also profitable for those who have their urine stopped, or the stopping of women's courses, the pains of the mother, and of the stone in the reins, kidneys, or bladder; it resists poison, and stays the spreading of the venom of serpents, as also putrid and pestilential fevers, and the plague itself.

ELM-TREE.—(*Ulmus.*)

Descrip.—The Elm is one of the commonest trees we have; it has a rough thick bark, and the branches are clothed with somewhat rough, crenated, green leaves. The flowers are small and staminous, coming out early in the spring before the leaves. The seed is round and foliaceous.

Place.—It is common in the fields, and all over the country.

Government and Virtues.—It is a cold and Saturnine plant. The leaves thereof bruised and applied, heal green wounds, being bound thereon with its own bark; the leaves or the bark used with vinegar, cure scurf and leprosy very effectually: the decoction of the leaves, bark, or root, being bathed, heals broken bones. The water that is found in the bladders on the leaves, while it is fresh, is very effectual to cleanse the skin, and make it fair; and if cloths be often wet therein, and applied to the ruptures of children, it heals them, if they be well bound up with a truss. The said water put into a glass, and set into the ground, or else in dung for twenty-five days, the mouth thereof being close stopped, and the bottom set upon a lay of ordinary salt, that the fæces may settle and water become clear, is a singular and sovereign balm for green wounds, being used with soft tents: the decoction of the bark of the root fomented, mollifies hard tumours, and the shrinking of the sinews.

ENDIVE.—(*Cichorium Endivia.*)

Descrip.—Common garden Endive bears a longer and larger leaf than succory, and abides but one year, quickly running up to stalk and seed, and then perishing. It has blue flowers, and the seed is so much like that of succory, that it is hard to distinguish it.

Place.—It is chiefly cultivated in gardens.

Time.—The first sowing should be in May.

Government and Virtues.—It is an herb of Jupiter, and is a fine cooling cleansing plant: the decoction of the leaves, or the juice, or the distilled water of Endive, serves to cool the excessive heat of the liver and stomach, as also the hot fits of agues, and all other inflammations. It cools the heat and sharpness of the urine, and the excoriations into the uritory parts. The seeds have the same properties, though rather more powerful, and besides, are available for faintings, swoonings, and the passions of the heart. Outwardly applied, they serve to temper the sharp humours of fretting ulcers, hot tumours and swellings, and pestilential sores; they greatly assist not only the redness and inflammation of the eyes, but the dimness of sight, and also allay the pains of the gout.

ERINGO, OR SEA HOLLY.—(*Eryngium Maritimum.*)

Descrip.—Common Eryngo has pretty large, white, and long roots, which spread much in the earth, and run deep in the same. The leaves are hard, stiff, and veiny, narrow at bottom, and broad and roundish at the end, with several laciniæ terminating in sharp prickles; the stalk arises not to any great height, being smooth, crested, and channelled; the leaves on the stalks are less, and rather stiffer, set on without foot-stalks, with prickly edges. At the ends of the branches come forth round, somewhat prickly, heads, beset with stiff narrow leaves, growing like a star under them; the flowers are set in these heads, of a greenish white colour, each in a separate calyx, like the teasel, succeeded by flattish seed.

Place.—It grows by the sea-side, in many places, in sandy ground.

Time.—It flowers in June and July. The roots only are used.

Government and Virtues.—The plant is venereal, and breeds seed exceedingly, and strengthens the spirit procreative; it is hot and moist, and under the celestial balance. The decoction of the root hereof in wine, is very effectual to open obstructions of the spleen and liver, and helps yellow jaundice, dropsy, pains of the loins, wind colic, provokes urine, expels the stone, and procures women's courses. The continued use of the decoction for fifteen days, taken fasting, and next to bedward, helps the strangury, the voiding of urine by drops, the stopping of urine, and stone, and all defects of the reins and kidneys: if the said drink be continued longer, it is said that it cures the stone. It is found good against the venereal. The roots bruised and applied outwardly, helps the kernels of the throat, commonly called the king's-evil; or taken inwardly, and applied to the place stung or bitten by any serpent, heals it speedily. If the roots be bruised, and boiled inhog's grease, or salted lard, and applied to broken bones, thorns, &c. remaining in the flesh, they not only draw them forth, but heal up the place again, gathering new flesh where it was consumed. The juice of the leaves dropped into the ear, helps imposthumes therein.

EVEWEED, OR DOUBLE ROCKET.)—(*Hesperis Matronalis.*)

Descrip.—This grows with a round, upright firm stalk, but the top of it usually droops. The leaves are placed irregularly on it, and are oblong and broad at the base: they are dented along the edges, and sharp at the point; their colour is a dusky green at the bottom, but the upper ones grow lighter. The flowers are large, sometimes white and blue, or purple.

Place.—It is a native of our northern counties, Cumberland and Westmoreland.

Time.—It flowers in May.

Government and Virtues.—It is a plant of Mars, yet it is accounted a good wound herb. Some eat it with bread and butter on account of its taste, which resembles garlick. Its juice, taken a spoonful at a time, is excellent against obstructions of the viscera: it works by urine. In some places it is a constant ingredient in clysters.

EYEBRIGHT.—(*Euphrasia Officinalis.*)

Descrip.—Common Eyebright is a small low herb, rising up usually but with one blackish green stalk a span high, or not much more, spread from the bottom into sundry branches, whereon are small and almost round, yet pointed, dark green leaves, finely snipped about the edges, two always set together, and very thick : at the joints with the leaves, from the middle upward, come forth small white flowers, steeped with purple and yellow spots, or stripes ; after which follow small round heads, with very small seed therein. The root is long, small, and thready at the end.

Place.—It grows in meadows and grassy places in this country.

Time.—It flowers in July.

Government and Virtues.—It is under the sign of the Lion, and Sol claims dominion over it. The juice, or distilled water of Eyebright, taken inwardly in white wine or broth, or dropped into the eyes, for divers days together, helps all infirmities of the eyes that cause dimness of sight. Some make conserve of the flowers to the same effect. Being used any of these ways, it also helps a weak brain, or memory.

FAVEREL (WOOLLY.)—(*Draba Incana.*)

Descrip.—The root is composed of many long and thick fibres, and the leaves grow in tufts at the bottom of the stalk ; they are of a deep green, oblong pointed, and very rough and harsh to the touch. The stalk is upright, slender, and green ; there are no leaves on it, but towards the top grow small star-like pale green flowers, with yellow threads in the centre. The seed vessel is small, and the seeds are numerous and brown.

Place.—They are common in Yorkshire and Westmoreland, and other northern counties.

Time.—They sometimes flower as early as April, and, according to their situation, may not come out till June.

Government and Virtues.—They are under the dominion of the Moon. The leaves and roots are commended by the ancients against the sciatica, being beaten into a cataplasm with hog's lard, and applied to the part affected, and kept on four hours to a man, and two to a woman, and the place afterwards washed with wine and oil.

FELWORT.—(*Swertia Perennis.*)

Descrip.—A species approaching gentian, for which it is often taken by the common herbalists. The root is small, long, brown, and divided, and has a bitter taste.

The stalks are of a brownish colour, rigid, firm, straight, a little branched, and from three to eight or ten inches high. The leaves are of a dusky green, and the flowers are blue. The seed is small and brown.

Place.—It is common in hilly pastures.

Time.—It flowers in April and May.

Government and Virtues.—It is like gentian under the dominion of Mars, and a very good stomachic, but inferior to that great kind, the foreign gentian. The country people use it as an ingredient in making bitters, mixing it with orange peel, steeped in wine.

FENNEL (COMMON.)—(*Arethum Fæniculum.*)

Descrip.—It has large, thick, white roots, which run deep into the ground, much dividing, beset with small fibres. It has large winged leaves, of a dark green, divided into many segments, of long, slender, very fine, capilaceous parts. The stalk grows to four feet in height, much divided, and full of whitish pith. The flowers are found at the top in flat umbels, of small yellow five-leaved flowers, each of which is succeeded by a couple of roundish, somewhat flat, striated brown seed. The whole plant has a very strong, but not unpleasant smell.

Place.—It is generally planted in gardens, but it grows wild in several parts, towards the sea-coast, and in the northern counties.

Time.—It flowers in June and July.

Government and Virtues.—Fennel is good to break wind, to provoke urine, and ease the pains of the stone, and helps to break it. The leaves or seed, boiled in barley water, and drunk, are good for nurses, to increase their milk, and make it more wholesome for the child. The leaves, or rather the seeds, boiled in water, stays the hiccough, and takes away the loathings, which oftentimes happen to the stomachs of sick and feverish persons, and allays the heat thereof. The seed boiled in wine and drunk, is good for those that are bit with serpents, or have eat poisonous herbs, or mushrooms. The seed, and the roots much more, help to open obstructions of the liver, spleen, and gall, and thereby ease the painful and windy swellings of the spleen, and the yellow jaundice; as also the gout and cramps. The seed is of good use in medicines, to help shortness of breath and wheezing, by stopping of the lungs. It assists also to bring down the courses, and to cleanse the parts after delivery. The roots are of most use in physic drinks and broths, that are taken to cleanse the blood, to open obstructions in the liver, to provoke urine, and amend the ill colour in the face after sickness, and to cause a good habit through the body. Both leaves, seeds, and roots thereof, are much used in drink or broth, to make people lean that are too fat. The distilled water of the whole herb, or the condensed juice dissolved, but especially the natural juice, that in some counties issues out of its own accord, dropped into the eyes cleanses them from mists and films that hinder the sight.

FENNEL (SOW OR HOG'S.)—(*Peucedanum Officinale.*)

CALLED also Hoar-strange, Hoar-strong, Sulphur-wort, and Brimstone-wort.

Descrip.—The common Sow-Fennel has divers branched stalks of thick and somewhat long leaves, three for the most part joined together at a place, among which arises a crested straight stalk, less than Fennel, with some joints thereon, and leaves growing thereat, and towards the tops some branches issuing from thence; likewise on the tops of the stalks and branches stand divers tufts of yellow flowers, whereafter grows somewhat flat, thin, and yellowish seed, bigger than Fennel seed.

Place.—It grows plentifully in the salt low marshes near Faversham in Kent.

Time.—It flowers plentifully in July and August.

Government and Virtues.—This is also an herb of Mercury. The juice of Sow-Fennel, says Dioscorides, and Galen, used with vinegar and rose water, or the juice with a little Euphorbium put to the nose, helps those that are troubled with the lethargy, frenzy, giddiness of the head, the falling sickness, long and inveterate head-ache, the palsy, sciatica, and the cramp, and generally all the diseases of the sinews, used with oil and vinegar. The juice dissolved in wine, or put into an egg, is good for a cough, or shortness of breath, and for those that are troubled with wind in the body. It purges the belly gently, expels the hardness of the spleen, gives ease to women that have sore travail in child-birth, and easeth the pains of the reins and bladder, and also the womb. A little of the juice dissolved in wine, and dropped into the ears, eases much of the pains in them, and put into a hollow tooth, easeth the pains thereof.

FENNEL FLOWER.—*Nigella Sativa.*

Descrip.—This plant has a small sticky root, which perishes ever year, after ripening the seed. The stalk rises to be a foot and a half, or two feet high, hollow, branched and channelled, having several finely lacinated leaves, pretty much resembling those of lark-spurs, set alternately on them. The flowers grow on the end of the branches, of five small, white, sharp-pointed leaves a-piece, with several stamina in the middle, and are succeeded by oblong round tumid heads, having on their tops five or six crooked horns; the seed is black and somewhat sweet.

Place.—It is sown in gardens.

Time.—It flowers in June and July.

Government and Virtues.—This is also under Mercury. The seed only is used. It is accounted heating and drying, and is said likewise to provoke urine, and to help tertian and quartan agues; but is seldom used.

FENUGREEK.—(*Trigonella Fœnum Græcum.*)

CALLED also Greek Hayes.

Descrip.—It grows up with tender stalks, round, blackish, hollow, and full of branches: the leaves are divided into three parts, like those of trefoil: the flowers are pale or whitish, not much unlike the blossoms of lupines, but smaller. After these are fallen away, there follow long husks, crooked and sharp pointed, wherein is contained the seed, which is of a yellowish colour. The root is full of small hanging hairs.

Place.—It is a native of France, and is found here in the gardens of the curious.

Time.—It blossoms in July, and the seed is ripe in August.

Government vnd Virtues.—It is under the influence of Mercury, hot in the second degree, and dry in the first. The seed which is sold by druggists and apothecaries, is only used in medicine. The decoction, or broth of the seed, drank with a little vinegar, expels and purges all superfluous humours which cleave to the bowels: the same decoction, first made with dates, and afterwards made into a syrup with honey, cleanses the breast, chest, and lungs, and may be taken with success for any complaint thereof, provided the patient be not afflicted with a fever or head-ache, as this syrup being hurtful to the head, would rather increase than alleviate those disorders. It is of a softening and dissolving nature, therefore the meal thereof being boiled in mead, or honey-water, consumes, softens, and dissolves hard swellings and imposthumes: also a paste thereof, with saltpetre and vinegar, softens and wastes the hardness and swellings of the spleen. It is good for women who are afflicted with an imposthume, ulcer, or stoppage in the matrix, to bathe and sit in a decoction thereof; also a suppository made of the juice of this plant, and conveyed to the neck of the matrix, will mollify and soften all hardness thereof.

FERN (BRAKE OR BRACKEN).—*(Pteris Aquilina.)*

Descrip.—Of this there are two kinds principally to be treated of, viz. the Male and Female. The Female grows higher than the Male, but the leaves thereof are lesser, and more divided or dented, and of as strong a smell as the Male: the virtues of them are both alike.

Place.—They grow but too frequently upon commons and heaths.

Time.—They flower and seed at Midsummer.

Government and Virtues.—They are under the dominion of Mercury, both Male and Female. The roots of both those sorts of Fern being bruised and boiled in mead, or honeyed water, and drunk, kills both the broad and long worms in the body, and abates the swelling and hardness of the spleen. The green leaves eaten, purge the belly, and expel choleric and waterish humours that trouble the stomach. They are dangerous for women with child to meddle with by reason they cause abortions. The roots bruised and boiled in oil, or hog's grease, make a very profitable ointment to heal wounds, or pricks gotten in the flesh. The powder of them used in foul ulcers, dries up their malignant moisture, and causes their speedier healing.

FERN (OSMOND ROYAL, OR WATER.)—*(Osmunda Regalis.)*

Descrip.—This is the biggest of our English Ferns, sending forth several large branched leaves, whose long broad pinnulæ are not at all indented about the edges like the other Ferns; they are of a light yellow colour; among these arise several stalks, which have the like leaves growing on them, set one against another, longer, narrower, and not nicked on the edges as the former.

Place.—It grows on moors, bogs, and watery places, in many parts of this country.

Time.—It is green all the summer, and the root only abides in winter.

Government and Virtues.—Saturn owns the plant. This has all the virtues mentioned in the former Ferns, and is much more effectual than they, both for inward and outward uses ; and is accounted singularly good in wounds, bruises, or the like ; the decoction to be drunk, or boiled into an ointment of oil, as a balsam or balm, and so it is singularly good against bruises, and bones broken, or out of joint, and gives much ease to the colic and splenetic diseases ; as also ruptures and burstings.

FEVERFEW, OR FEATHERFEW.—(*Pyrethrum*, or *Matricaria Parthenium.*)

Descrip.—Common Featherfew has large, fresh, green leaves, much torn or cut on the edges. The stalks are hard and round, set with many such like leaves, but smaller ; and at the tops stand many single flowers, upon small foot-stalks, consisting of many small white leaves, standing round about a yellow thrum in the middle. The root is somewhat hard and short, with many strong fibres about it. The scent of the whole plant is very strong, and the taste is very bitter.

Place.—This grows mild in many places of the country, but is for the most part nourished in gardens.

Time.—It flowers in the months of June and July.

Government and Virtues.—Venus commands this herb, and has commended it to succour her sisters (women,) to be a general strengthener of their wombs, and to remedy such infirmities as a careless midwife has there caused ; if they will be pleased to make use of her herb boiled in white wine, and drink the decoction, it cleanses the womb, expels the afterbirth, and does a woman all the good she can desire of an herb. And if any grumble because they cannot get the herb in winter, tell them, if they please, they may make a syrup of it in summer: it is chiefly used for the disease of the mother, whether it be the strangling or rising of the mother, or hardness or inflammations of the same, applied outwardly thereunto. Or a decoction of the flowers in wine, with a little nutmeg or mace put there, and drank often in a day, is an approved remedy to bring down women's courses speedily, and helps to expel the dead-birth and after-birth. For a woman to sit over the hot fumes of the decoction of the herb made in water or wine, is effectual for the same ; and in some cases, to apply the boiled herb warm to the privy parts. The decoction thereof, made with some sugar or honey put thereto, is used by many with good success to help the cough and stuffing of the chest, by colds ; as also to cleanse the reins and bladder, and helps to expel the stone in them. The powder of the herb taken in wine, with some oxymel, purges both choler and phlegm, and is available for those that are short-winded, and are troubled with melancholy and heaviness, or sadness of spirits. It is very effectual for all pains in the head coming of a cold cause, the herb being bruised and applied to the crown of the head : as also for the vertigo, that is, a running or swimming of the head. The decoction thereof drank warm, and the herb bruised, with a few corns of bay-salt, and applied to the wrists before the coming of the ague fits, does take them away.

FEVERFEW (CORN.)—*Pyrethrum*, or *Matricaria-Chamomilla.*

Descrip.—This is an hateful weed to farmers ; but yet it possess virtues that may recompense all the damage it can do among the corn. It sometimes grows to a foot and a half high, with a pale, slender, branchy stalk : the leaves are of a pale green, and they have no smell. The flowers are large and white, with a high yellow disc in the middle, and the leaves are cut into many parts as fine as threads.

Place.—They are found commonly in corn-fields.

Time.—They bloom in July.

Government and Virtues.—These have the virtues of the flowers of camomile, but with more cordial warmth. For those who have cold and weak stomachs, scarcely any thing equals them. They are best taken by way of infusion like tea.

FEVERFEW (SEA.)—(*Pyrethrum*, or *Matricaria Maritima.*)

Descrip.—This grows about eight inches high, upright, and branchy. The stalk is thick and ruddy ; and the leaves are of a dull green, thick, swelled up, hollow underneath, and composed of many parts, which are again cut down to the rib. The flowers are white, with a low yellowish disc.

Place.—This is a sea-side perennial plant, frequently found in Cornwall.

Time.—They bloom in August.

Government and Virtues.—This is a weed of our waste marshes, where it grows in its greatest perfection. Some curious physic gardeners have produced it, but it is not then so full of virtue as when found wild. The virtues of Feverfew are very great. It is an excellent deobstruent. It is, as observed before, a great promoter of the menses, and cures those hysteric complaints which rise from their obstruction. It also destroys worms. In short, the virtues of any sorts of Feverfew are beyond all praise, and above all value.

FEVERFEW (SWEET.)—(*Pyrethrum*, or *Matricaria Suaveolens.*)

Descrip.—The leaves of these Feverfews are stringy and very narrow, but the flower indicates the species. The stalks are stiff, round, or striated, two feet high or more, clothed with smaller leaves, and pretty much branched towards the top, on which grow large flat umbels of flowers, made of several white petals, broader and shorter than those of camomile, set about a yellow thrum. The root is thick at the head, having many fibres under it; the whole plant has a very strong, and, to most, an unpleasant smell.

Place.—They grow in hedges and lanes.

Time.—They flower in June and July. The leaves and flowers are used.

Government and Virtues.—The virtues of Feverfew are very great; it is an herb particularly appropriated to the female sex, being of great service in all cold flatulent disorders of the womb, and hysteric affections; procuring the catamenia, and expelling the birth and secundines. The juice to the quantity of two ounces, given an hour before the fit, is good for all kinds of agues. It likewise destroys worms, provokes urine, and is good for the dropsy and jaundice.

FIG-TREE.—(*Ficus Carica.*)

Descrip.—The Fig-tree seldom grows to be a tree of any great bigness in our parts, being clothed with large leaves bigger than vine-leaves, full of high veins, and divided for the most part into five blunt-pointed segments, yielding a thin milky juice when broken. It bears no visible flowers.

Place.—They prosper very well in our English gardens, yet are fitter for medicine than for any other profit that is gotten by the fruit of them.

Government and Virtues.—The tree is under the dominion of Jupiter. The milk that issues out from the leaves or branches where they are broken off, being dropped upon warts, takes them away. The decoction of the leaves is excellent good to wash foreheads with. It clears the face also of morphew, and the body of white scurf, scabs, and running sores. If it be dropped into old fretting ulcers, it cleanses out the moisture, and brings up the flesh ; because you cannot have the leaves green all the year, you may make an ointment of them whilst you can. A decoction of the leaves being drunk inwardly, or rather a syrup made of them, dissolves congealed blood caused by bruises or falls, and helps the bloody flux. The ashes of the wood made into an ointment with hog's grease, helps kibes and chilblains. The juice being put into a hollow tooth, eases pain ; as also deafness and pain and noises in the ears, being dropped into them. An ointment made of the juice and hogs' grease, is as excellent a remedy for the biting of mad dogs, or other venomous beasts, as most are ; a syrup made of the leaves, or green fruits, is excellent for coughs, hoarseness, or shortness of breath, and all diseases of the breast and lungs : it is very good for the dropsy and falling-sickness.

FIG-WORT, OR THROATWORT.—(*Scrophularia Nodosa.*)

Descrip.—Common Great Figwort sends divers great, strong, hard, square, brown stalks, three or four feet high, whereon grow large, hard, and dark green leaves, two at a joint, harder and larger than nettle leaves, but not stinging ; at the tops of the stalks stand many purple flowers set in husks, which are sometimes gaping and open, somewhat like those of water betony ; after which come hard round heads, with a small point in the middle, wherein lie small brownish seed. The root is great, white, and thick, with many branches at it, growing aslope under the upper crust of the ground, which abides many years, but keeps not its green leaves in winter.

Place.—It grows frequently in moist and shadowy woods, and in the lower parts of the fields and meadows.

Time.—It flowers about July, and the seed will be ripe about a month after the flowers are fallen

Government and Virtues.—Some Latin authors call it Cervicaria, because it is appropriated to the neck; and we Throat-wort, because it is appropriated to the throat. Venus owns the herb, and the Celestial Bull will not deny it; therefore a better remedy cannot be for the king's-evil, because the Moon that rules the disease is exalted there. The decoction of the herb taken inwardly, and the bruised herb applied outwardly, dissolves clotted and congealed blood within the body, coming by any wounds, bruise, or fall; and is no less effectual for the king's-evil, or any other knobs, kernels, bunches, or wens growing in the flesh wheresoever; and for the hæmorrhoids, or piles.

FIGWORT (WATER.)—(*Scrophularia Aquatica.*)

Descrip.—This has larger and taller stalks than the former, less branched, having larger leaves, round-pointed, and in shape like betony, growing on longer foot-stalks. The flowers are in shape like the former, but a little larger, and of a redder colour; the seed-vessel and seed much alike. But the root has none of the knots or tubercles.

Place.—It grows by watery-places, and ditch sides.

Time.—It flowers in June. The root is used.

Government and Virtues.—It is much of the nature of the former, and where that is not to be had, it may supply its place; it is likewise detersive and vulnerary, and is commended by some as good against the itch.

FILIPENDULA.—(*Spirea Filipendula.*)

Called also Dropwort.

Descrip.—It shoots forth many leaves of various sizes, growing on each side of a rib, and much dented on the edges, somewhat resembling wild tansy or agrimony, but feel much harder: among these rise up one or more stalks, two or three feet high, spreading itself into many branches, each bearing several white sweet-smelling flowers consisting of five leaves a-piece, with small threads in the middle: they stand together in a tuft or umbel, each upon a small foot-stalk, and are succeeded by round chaffy heads, like buttons, which contain the seed.

Place.—It grows in many places of this kingdom, in the corners of dry fields and meadows, and also by hedge-sides.

Time.—They flower in June and July, and their seed is ripe in August.

Government and Virtues.—It is under the dominion of Venus, and is very serviceable to open the urinary passages, to help the strangury, and all other pains of the bladder and reins, and to expel the stone and gravel, by taking the root in powder, or a decoction of these in white wine, sweetened with sugar: the same also helps to expel the after-birth. The root made into powder, and mixed with honey, after the manner of an electuary, is good for those whose stomachs are swollen (breaking and expelling the wind which was the cause thereof) as also for all diseases of the lungs, for the shortness of breath, wheezings, hoarseness, coughs, and to expectorate cold phlegm. It is called Dropwort, because it gives ease to those who evacuate their water by drops.

FIR-TREE.—)*Pinus Picea.*)

Descrip.—There are two sorts of Fir; one called the Silver or Yew-leaves, which is reckoned an exotic, coming originally from Germany, and only planted in gardens; but the common pitch-tree, or picea, which is a native with us, differs from it only in that the leaves are smaller and slenderer, sharp and prickly at the ends, standing thicker together, and encompassing the stalk without any order. The cones are longer than those of the Yew-leaved, and hang downwards.

Place.—It grows wild in the northern parts of England, but the Scotch Fir is another distinct species from both these: it is the wild pine. The leaves are long and blueish.

Government and Virtues.—Jupiter owns this tree. The leaves and tops of both sorts are used in diet-drinks for the scurvy, for which they are highly commended by the inhabitants of the northern countries. From this tree, of which there grow great numbers in several parts of Germany, is gotten the Strasburg turpentine, which is clearer, of a pale colour, and of a thinner consistence than Venice turpentine, of a bitterish taste, and of a pleasant smell, a little like lemon-peel. It is of a mollifying, healing, and cleansing nature; and, besides its uses outwardly in wounds and ulcers, is a good diuretic, and of great use in a gonorrhæa and the fluor albus; given in clysters mixed with the yolk of an egg, it is very serviceable against the stone and gravel. It is likewise a good pectoral, and often given in affections of the breast and lungs.

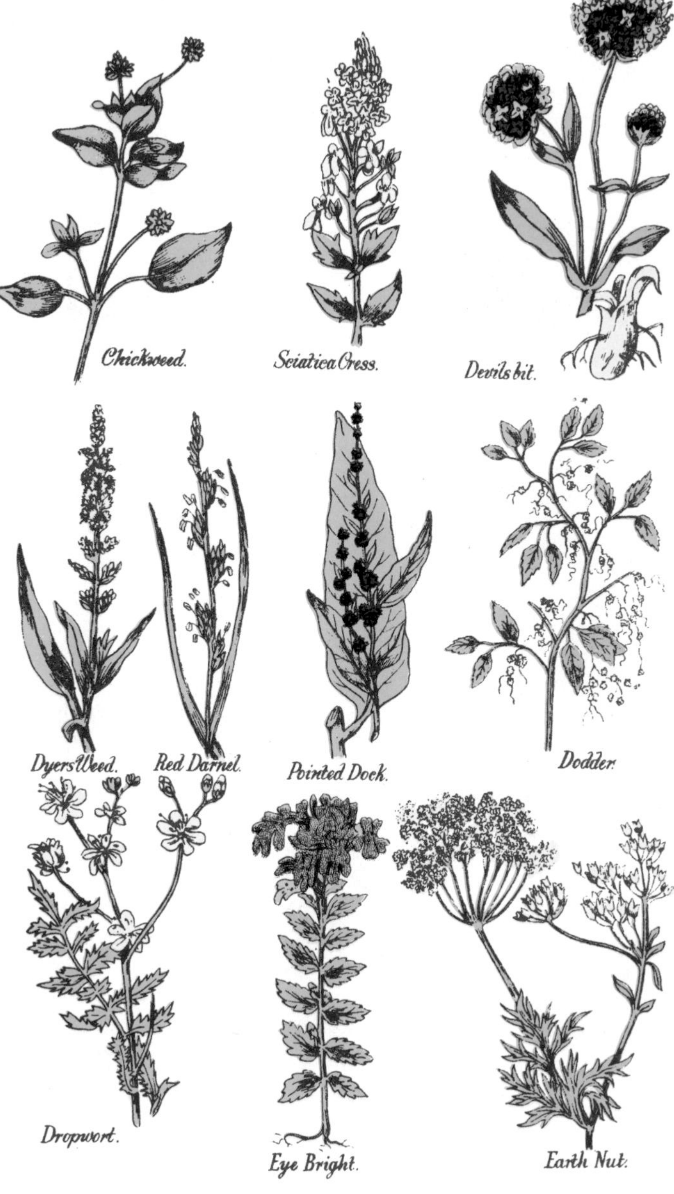
Chickweed.
Sciatica Cress.
Devils bit.
Dyers Weed.
Red Darnel.
Pointed Dock.
Dodder.
Dropwort.
Eye Bright.
Earth Nut.

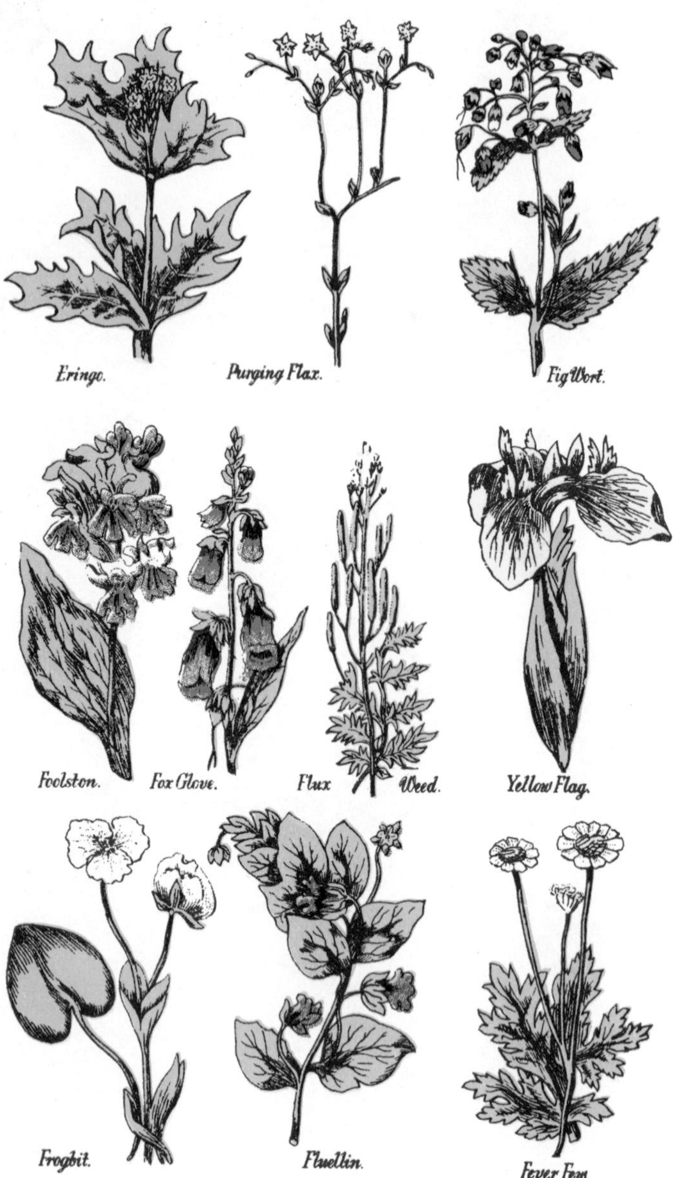
Eringo.
Purging Flax.
Fig Wort.
Foolston.
Fox Glove.
Flux
Weed.
Yellow Flag.
Frogbit.
Fluellin.
Fever Few.

Tar is likewise the product of these trees, which is by some accounted a good pectoral medicine, and used for obstructions of the lungs, and shortness of breath.

From the young branches of the *Pinus Abies* is produced the famous spruce beer; and the juice which runs from the trunk, upon its being tapped, is what is sold in the shops here under the name of the Balm of Gilead. The young tops of this tree make an excellent antiscorbutic either infused or boiled in beer or wine; experience has sufficiently confirmed their efficacy in that distemper in our American plantations, where the inhabitants used to be severely afflicted with it, who since they have taken to brewing a kind of liquor or molasses, in which they boil the young Fir-tops in the room of hops, they are very little troubled with the scurvy; and many of our sailors whose diet on board of ships makes them subject to it, have had reason to commend that liquor. This tree yields two resinous substances; a thin liquid sort, which comes forth from the young Firs, and is known in the shops by the name of Strasburg turpentine; and a dry substance resembling frankincense, to which it is not unlike in quality.

FLAG (YELLOW,) OR FLEUR-DE-LYS.—(*Iris Pseudacorus.*)

CALLED also Myrtle Flag, and Myrtle Grass.

Descrip.—This plant is distinguished from all others, in that, among its leaves, which are much longer and narrower than the Garden Fleur-de-Lys, there arises one or two like the rest, only somewhat narrower, thicker and rounder towards the top, near to which come forth single juli, rarely two, in shape like the catkin of the hazel, or like long pepper, but ending more taper, and standing up obliquely from the leaf. The root is thick, full of joints, and spreads itself on the upper part of the earth, transversely, and not sinking deep in it, being full of large white fibres, increasing much, and soon taking a great deal of ground. It has a strong smell, not so pleasant while green, but growing more grateful and aromatic as it dries.

Place.—It grows in several rivulets, and watery places in England, as about Norwich, and in Cheshire and Surrey, according to Mr. Ray; but what is used in the shops, is mostly imported from abroad.

Time.—It produces its catkins in July and August.

Government and Virtues.—Flags are under Lunar dominion. The roots, which only are used, are hot and dry, opening and attenuating, and good for the obstructions of the liver and spleen ; provoke urine and the menses, help the colic, resist putrefaction, are useful against pestilential contagions and corrupt noxious air ; are an ingredient in the theriaca and mithridate, and are outwardly used in sweet bags and perfumes.

FLAG (BASTARD WATER.)—(*Acorus Adulterinus.*)

Descrip.—This iris, that grows so common in ditches and watery places, bears leaves like the common Fleur-de-Lys, only somewhat longer and narrower ; the stalk rises higher, on the top of which grow three or four flowers, one above another, flowering gradually in shape like an ordinary Fleur-de-Lys, only that they want the upright leaves, instead of which they have only small pieces of leaves in their places. The flowers are succeeded by large triangular seed-vessels, containing three rows of flat seed.

Government and Virtues.—It is under the dominion of the Moon. The spicy bitterness of the root of this plant bespeaks it a strengthener of the stomach and head, and therefore may fitly be put into any composition of that intention. The root preserved may with good success be used by itself, and both the Germans and Turks are very fond of it, and reckon it a great preservative against infectious air, which makes them commonly eat a piece of the preserved root fasting. The leaves having a very grateful flavour, are, by some nice cooks, put into sauce for fish.

FLAX.—(*Linum Usitatissimum.*)

Descrip.—Flax has round slender unbranched stalks, a yard or more high, clothed with many long, narrow, sharp-pointed, glaucous leaves ; on the tops of the stalks grow a pretty many small five-leaved blue flowers, soon falling off ; and are followed by round heads, or seed-vessels, each divided into about ten partitions, containing as many oblong, flattish, shining brown seed. The root is small and woody, and dies as soon as the seed is ripe. Of the bark of the stalks of this plant, which is tough, and made up of a great many slender filaments, is made linen cloth.

Place.—It is sown in fields.

Time.—It flowers in June, the seed only is used.

Government and Virtues.—Mercury owns this useful plant. The seed, which is usually called linseed, is emollient, digesting, and ripening ; of great use against inflammations, tumours, and imposthumes, and is frequently put into fomentations and cataplasms, for those purposes. Cold-drawn linseed oil is of great service in all diseases of the breast and lungs, as pleurisies and peripneuemonia, coughs, asthma and consumption. It likewise helps the colic and stone, both taken at the mouth, and given in clysters. The oil, by expression, is the only officinal preparation.

FLAX-WEED.—(*Linaria vulgaris.*)

CALLED also Toad-Flax.

Descrip.—Our common Flaxweed has divers stalks full fraught with long and narrow ash-coloured leaves, and from the middle of them almost upward, stored with a number of pale yellow flowers, of a strong unpleasant scent, with deeper yellow mouths, and blackish flat seed in round heads. The root is somewhat woody and white, especially the main downright one, with many fibres, abiding many years, shooting forth roots every way round about, and new branches every year.

Place.—This grows by the way-sides and in meadows, as also by hedge-sides and upon the sides of banks, and borders of fields.

Time.—It flowers in summer, and the seed is ripe usually before the end of August.

Government and Virtues.—Mars owns the herb. In Sussex we call it gallwort, and lay it in our chickens' water to cure them of the gall ; it relieves them when they are drooping. This is frequently used to spend the abundance of those watery humours by urine, which cause the dropsy. The decoction of the herb, both leaves and flowers, in wine taken and drunk, does somewhat move the belly downwards, opens obstructions of the liver, and helps the yellow jaundice ; expels poison, provokes women's courses, drives forth the dead child, and after-birth. The distilled water of the herb and flowers is effectual for all the same purposes ; being drunk with a dram of the powder of the seeds of bark or the roots of wall-wort, and a little cinnamon. for certain days together, it is held a singular remedy for the dropsy. The juice of the herb, or the distilled water, dropped into the eyes, is a certain remedy for all heat, inflammation, and redness in them. The juice or water put into foul ulcers, whether they be cancerous or fistulous, with tents rolled therein, or the parts washed and injected therewith, cleanses them thoroughly from the bottom, and heals them up safely. The same juice or water also cleanses the skin wonderfully of all sorts of deformity, as leprosy, morphew, scurf, wheals, pimples, or spots, applied of itself, or used with some powder of lupines.

(FLEABANE (CANADA.)—*Erigeron Canadense.*)

CALLED also Simson.

Descrip.—The stalk is of a dusky green, tinged with brown, and the lower leaves are broad, and rudely dented; the upper narrow and undivided, and all of a dead green. The flowers are white, but of no beauty.

Place.—This is an annual, that grows on our dry banks, and among rubbish: sometimes it is found not six inches high, sometimes two feet or more.

Time.—They bloom in August and September.

Government and Virtues.—It is under Venus. The juice of this, as well as the sweet Fleabane, or *Erigeron Acre*, is an excellent pectoral; but being unpleasant is not often used; however, if the decoction or infusion be sweetened with capilary or syrup of Maidenhair, it may be used with success in consumptive cases.

FLEABANE (MARSH.)—*(Senecio vulgaris.)*

CALLED also Common Rag-wort or Rag-weed, Groundsel, St. James's-wort, Stagger-wort, Hammer-wort, and by some confounded with Segrum.

Descrip.—This has many large and long leaves, of a fresh green, very smooth and delicate, lying on the ground; the leaves are deeply cut at the edges, from which rise up sometimes but one, and sometimes two or three square or crested blackish or brownish stalks, three or four feet high, sometimes branched, bearing divers such-like leaves upon them, at several distances unto the top, where it branches forth into many stalks bearing yellow flowers, consisting of divers leaves, set as a pale or border, with a dark yellow thrum in the middle, which abides a great while, but at last are turned into down, and, with the small blackish grey seed, are carried away with the wind. The root is made of many fibres, whereby it is firmly fastened into the ground, and abides many years.

Place.—They grow wild in pastures, and untilled grounds.

Time.—They flower in June and July, and the seed is ripe in August.

Government and Virtues.—Fleabane or Ragweed is under the command of Dame Venus ; and cleanses, digests, and discusses. The decoction of the herb is good to wash the mouth or throat that has ulcers or sores therein ; and for swellings, hardness, or imposthumations, for it thoroughly cleanses and heals them ; as also the quinsey, and the king's-evil. It helps to stay catarrhs, thin rheums, and defluxions from the head into the eyes, nose, or lungs. The juice is found by experience to be singularly good to heal green wounds, and to cleanse and heal all old filthy ulcers in the privities, and in other parts of the body, as also inward wounds and ulcers ; stays the malignity of fretting and running cankers, and hollow fistulas, not suffering them to spread farther. It is also much commended to help aches and pains either in the fleshy part, or in the nerves and sinews ; as also the sciatica, or pain of the hips or huckle-bone, to bathe the places with the decoction of the herb, or to anoint them with an ointment made of the herb, bruised and boiled in hog's-suet, with some mastic and olibanum in powder added to it after it is strained forth.

FLEABANE (MARSH.)—(*Erigeron viscosum.*)

CALLED also Bird's Tongue.

Descrip.—This is the Pulicaria of Lobel, and so called, because by its smell it drives away and destroys fleas and gnats, has a small stringy root full of fibres, from which spring round, succulent, striated stalks, which are shorter or taller, according to the soil it grows in, and frequently of a reddish colour, the lower leaves are about two inches long, and half an inch broad ; the flowers grow on the tops of the branches, without any petals or border, consisting only of fistular yellow flowers, growing in a green striated calyx, which afterwards turns into down.

Place.—It grows in moist places, and where water has stood all winter.

Time.—It flowers in August and September.

Government and Virtues.—The juice of this herb taken in ale, is accounted by some a gentle vomit, and of use to help pains in the stomach, and evacuate choler, and to help the jaundice ; it likewise destroys worms. Outwardly applied it is useful in scrofulous tumors and inflammations of the breast, and helps scald-heads. It is under Venus. The juice provokes urine, and expels gravel in the reins or kidneys, a dram thereof being given in oxymel, after walking or stirring of the body. It helps also the sciatica, griping of the belly, the colic, defects of the liver, and provokes women's courses. The fresh herb boiled, and made into a poultice, applied to the breasts of women that are swollen with pain and heat, as also the privy parts of man or woman, the seat or fundament, or the arteries, joints, and sinews, when they are inflamed and swollen, does much ease them ; and used with some salt, helps to dissolve knots or kernels in any part of the body. The leaves and flowers, with some fine frankincense in powder, used in wounds of the body, nerves or sinews, do singularly help to heal them. The distilled water of the herb performs well all the aforesaid cures, but especially for inflammations or watering of the eyes, by reason of the defluxions of rheum into them.

FLEABANE (MOUNTAIN.)—(*Senecio Jacobæa.*)

CALLED also Mountain Rag-wort, or Brag-weed.

Descrip.—This is a weed of our high pasture ground, but not common ; its height never exceeds a foot ; it is found to grow upright, and has no branches. The leaves are pale, thick, and downy, and the flowers are of a light yellow: they grow in a cluster at the top of the stalk, and have a circle of narrow leaves under them.

Time.—They bloom in June and July ; and the seed is ripe in August.

Government and Virtues.—This is also under Venus. Taken inwardly it is an acrid and dangerous purge, but its juice applied outwardly, is of good effect. It is injurious to sheep, as their wool grows loose on eating it.

FLEABANE (SMALL.)—(*Pulicaria Dysenterica.*)

Descrip.—This is another ill-looking annual weed, frequent in our waste places. The rays of the flower are very short and waved: it grows to eight inches high, but commonly lies in part upon the ground. The stalk is of a ruddy brown; the leaves are short, small, and of a dull dead green; the flowers are small, very poor, and of a dirty yellow.

Time.—They bloom in August.

Government and Virtues.—The smell of this and the former is supposed delightful to insects, and the juice destructive to them, for they never leave it till the season of their deaths.

FLEA-WORT.—(*Erigeron viscosum.*)

Descrip.—Ordinary Flea-wort rises up with a stalk two feet high or more, full of joints and branches on every side up to the top, and at every joint two small, long, and narrow whitish green leaves somewhat hairy: at the top of every branch stand divers small, short, scaly, or chaffy heads, out of which come forth small whitish yellow threads, like those of the plantain herbs, which are the bloomings of flowers. The seed inclosed in these heads is small and shining while it is fresh, very like unto fleas both for colour and bigness, but turning black when it grows old. The root is not long, but white, hard, and woody, perishing every year, and rising again of its own seed for divers years, if it be suffered to shed: the whole plant is somewhat whitish and hairy, smelling like rosin.

There is another sort hereof, differing not from the former in the manner of growing, but only that this stalk and branches being somewhat greater, do a little more bow down to the ground: the leaves are somewhat greater, the heads somewhat lesser, the seed alike; and the root and leaves abide all winter, and perish not as the former

Place.—The first grows only in gardens, the second plentifully in fields that are near the sea.

Time.—They flower in July, or thereabouts.

Government and Virtues.—The herb is cold, dry, and Saturnine. I suppose it obtained the name of Flea-wort, because the seeds are so like fleas. The seed dried, and taken, stays the flux or lax of the belly, and the corrosions that come by reason of hot choleric, or sharp and malignant humours, or by too much purging of any violent medicine, as scammony, or the like. The mucilage of the seed made with rose water, and a little sugar-candy put thereto, is very good in all hot agues and burning fevers, and other inflammations, to cool thirst, and lenify the dryness and roughness of the tongue and throat. It helps all hoarseness of the voice, and diseases of the breast and lungs, caused by heat, or sharp salt humours, and the pleursy also. The mucilage of the seed made with plantain-water, whereunto the yoke of an egg or two, and a little populcon are put, is a most safe and sure remedy to ease the sharpness, pricking, and pains of the hemorrhoids or piles, if it be laid on a cloth and bound thereto. It helps all inflammations in any part of the body, and the pains that come thereby, as the headache and vapours, and all hot imposthumes, swellings, and breaking out of the skin, as blains, wheals, pushes, purples, and the like; as also the joints of those that are out of joint, the pains of the gout and sciatica, the bursting of young children, and the swellings of the navel, applied thereunto. The juice of the herb with a little honey put into the ears, helps the running of them, and the worms breeding in them: the same also mixed with hog's grease, and applied to corrupt and filthy ulcers, cleanses and heals them.

FLIXWEED, OR FLUXWEED.—*(Sisymbrium Sophia.)*

Descrip.—Flixweed, or Fluxweed, has a white hard woody root full of small fibres at the bottom, perishing after having ripened seed; the stalks rise to be about two feet high, more or less, beset with many long, winged, and very finely and neatly divided green leaves, pretty much resembling those of the true Roman wormwood, beset with very short fine hairs. The flowers grow at the end of the branches, being small, yellow, and four-leaved and are succeeded by very slender seed-vessels, about an inch or thereabout in length, full of very small reddish seed.

Place.—It grows frequently in sandy ground, and among rubbish.

Time.—It flowers in June.

Government and Virtues.—This herb is Saturnine. Both the herb and seed of Flixweed is of excellent use to stay the flux and lax of the belly, being drunk in water wherein gads of steel heated have been often quenched; and is no less effectual for the same purpose than plantain and comfrey, and to restrain any other flux of blood in man or woman; as also to consolidate bones broken or out of joint. The juice thereof drank in wine, or the decoction of the herb drank, does kill the worms in the stomach or belly, or the worms that grow in putrid and filthy ulcers; and made into a salve does quickly heal all old sores, how foul and malignant soever they be. The distilled water of the herbs works the same effects, although somewhat weaker; yet it is a fair medicine, and more acceptable to be taken. It is called Fluxweed because it cures the flux; and for its uniting broken bones, &c. Paracelsus extols it to the skies. It is fitting that syrup, ointment, and plasters of it, were kept in all houses. There is another sort, differing in nothing save only that it has somewhat broader leaves, a strong evil savour, and of a drying taste.

FLEUR-DE-LYS (GARDEN OR BLUE.—(*Iris.*)

Descrip.—The roots of Common Fleur-de-Lys spread themselves pretty much on the surface of the earth, being of a reddish brown colour on the outside, and whitish within; round, an inch and more in thickness, with several transverse rings or circles, and shooting out long fibres. The leaves are nervous, broad and flat, thickest in the middle, with thin edges like a sword: they grow in thick clumps together; the flowers are made of nine leaves like the former, of a purplish blue colour, and have the like seed-vessels, which are full of angular seed.

Place.—It grows with us only in gardens.

Time.—It flowers in May and June.

Government and Virtues.—This herb is Lunar. The juice of the root, which is the only part used, is a strong errhine; being snuffed up the nostrils, it purges the head, and clears the brain of thin serous phlegmatic humours. The same likewise, or a strong decoction of the root, given inwardly, is a strong vomit, and accounted good for the dropsy, jaundice and agues; but by reason it very much vellicates and offends the stomach, it is rarely used without honey and spikenard. The same being drunk, does ease the pains and torments of the belly and sides, the shaking of agues, the diseases of the liver and spleen, the worms of the belly, the stone in the reins, convulsions and cramps that come of old humours; it also helps those whose seed pass from them unawares: it is a remedy against the bitings and stingings of venomous creatures, being boiled in water and vinegar, and drunk: boiled in water, and druuk, it provokes urine, helps the colic, brings down women's courses; and made up into a pessary with honey, and put up into the body, draws forth the dead child. It is much commended against the cough, to expectorate tough phlegm; it much eases pains in the head, and procures sleep; being put into the nostrils it procures sneezing, and thereby purges the head of phlegm: the juice of the root applied to the piles or hemorrhoids, give much ease. The decoction of the roots gargled in the mouth, eases the tooth-ache, and helps a stinking breath. Oil called oleum irinum, if it be rightly made of the great broad flag Fleur-de-Lys, (and not of the great bulbous blue Fleur-de-Lys, as is used by some apothecaries) and roots of the same of the flaggy kinds, is very effectual to warm and comfort all cold joints and sinews; as also the gout and sciatica; and mollifies, dissolves and consumes tumours and swellings in any part of the body, as also of the matrix; it helps the cramp, or convulsions of the sinews: the head and temples anointed therewith, helps the catarrh of thin rheum distilled from thence; and used upon the breast or stomach, helps to extenuate the cold tough phlegm; it helps also the pains and noises in the ears, and the stench of the nostrils. The root itself, either green or in powder, helps to cleanse, heal, and incarnate wounds, and to cover the naked bones with flesh again, that ulcers have made bare; and is also very good to cleanse and heal up fistulas and cankers that are hard to be cured.

FLUELLEIN, LLUELLIN SPEEDWELL, OR PAUL'S BETONY.—(*Veronica Officinalis.*)

Descrip.—It shoots forth many long branches, partly lying upon the ground, and partly standing upright, set with almost red leaves, yet a little pointed, and sometimes more long than round, without order thereon, somewhat hairy, and of an evil greenish white colour; at the joints all along the stalks, and with the leaves, come forth small flowers, one at a place, upon a very small, short foot-stalk, gaping somewhat like snap-dragons, or rather like toad-flax, with the upper jaw of a yellow colour, and the lower of a purplish, with a small heel or spur behind; after which come forth small round heads, containing small black seed. The root is small and thready, dying every year, and raises itself again of its own sowing.

There is another sort of Fluellein which has longer branches wholly trailing upon the ground, two or three feet long, and somewhat more thin, set with leaves thereon, upon small foot-stalks. The leaves are a little larger, somewhat round, and cornered sometimes in some places on the edges; but the lower part of them being the broadest, has on each side a small point, making it seem as if they were ears, sometimes hairy, but not hoary, and of a better green colour than the former. The flowers come forth like the former, but the colours therein are more white than yellow, and the purple not so far: it is a large flower, and so are the seed and seed-vessels. The root is like the other, and perishes ever year.

Place.—They grow in divers corn-fields, and in borders about them, and abundantly in other fertile grounds about Southfleet in Kent; at Buchrite, Hamerton, and Rickmansworth in Huntingdonshire, and in divers other places.

Time.—They are in flower about June and July, and the whole plant is dry and withered before August is over.

Government and Virtues.—It is a Lunar herb. The leaves bruised and applied with barley-meal to watering eyes, that are hot and inflamed by defluxions from the head, very much help them; as also the fluxes of blood or humours, as the lax, bloody-flux, women's courses, and stay all manner of bleeding at nose, mouth, or any other place, or that comes by any bruise or hurt, or bursting a vein: it wonderfully helps all those inward parts that need consolidating or strengthening; and is no less effectual both to heal and close green wounds, than to cleanse and heal all foul or old ulcers, fretting or spreading cankers or the like. Fluellein is a vulnerary plant, and accounted good for fluxes and hemorrhages of all sorts.

FOX-GLOVE.—*(Digitalis Purpurea.)*

Descrip.—It has many long and broad leaves, lying upon the ground, dented upon the edges, a little soft or woolly, and of a hoary green colour, among which rise up sometime sundry stalks, but one very often, bearing such leaves thereon from the bottom to the middle, from whence to the top it is stored with large and long hollow reddish purple flowers, a little more long at the lower edge, with some white spots within them, one above another, with small green leaves at every one, but all of them turning their heads one way, and hanging downwards, having some threads also in the middle, from whence rise round heads, pointed sharp at the ends, wherein small brown seed lies. The roots are so many small fibres, and some greater strings among them; the flowers have no scent, but the leaves have a bitter hot taste.

Place.—It grows on dry sandy ground for the most part, and as well on the higher as the lower places under hedge-sides in almost every county of England.

Time.—It seldom flowers before July, and the seed is ripe in August.

Government and Virtues.—The plant is under the dominion of Venus, being of a gentle cleansing quality, and withal very friendly to nature. The herb is familiarly and frequently used by the Italians to heal any fresh or green wound, the leaves being but bruised and bound thereon; and the juice thereof is also used in old sores, to cleanse, dry, and heal them. The decoction hereof made up with some sugar or honey, is available to cleanse and purge the body both upwards and downwards, sometimes of tough phlegm and clammy humours, and to open obstructions of the liver and spleen. It has been found by experience to be available for the king's-evil, the herb bruised and applied, or an ointment made with the juice thereof, and so used; and a decoction of two handfuls thereof, with four ounces of polypody in ale, has been found by late experience to cure divers of the falling sickness, that have been troubled with it above twenty years. I am confident that an ointment thereof is one of the best remedies for a scabby head.

FUMITORY.—*(Fumaria Officinalis.)*

Descrip.—The Common Fumitory is a tender sappy herb; it sends forth from one square—a slender weak stalk, and leaning downwards on all sides—many branches two or three feet long, with finely cut and jagged leaves of whitish, or rather bluish, sea-green colour: at the tops of the branches stand many small flowers, as it were, in a long spike one above another, made like little birds, of a reddish purple colour, with whitish bellies; after which come small round husks, containing small black seeds. The root is yellow, small, and not very long, full of juice while it is green, but quickly perishes with the ripe seed. In the corn-fields of Cornwall, it bears white flowers.

Place.—It grows in corn-fields almost every where, as well as in gardens.

Time.—It flowers in May, for the most part; and the seed ripens shortly after.

Government and Virtues.—Saturn owns the herb, and presents it to the world as a cure for his own disease, and strengthener of the parts of the body he rules. The juice or syrup made thereof, or the decoction made in whey by itself, with some other purging or opening herbs and roots to cause it to work the better (itself being but weak) is very effectual for the liver and spleen, opening the obstructions thereof, and clarifying the blood from saltish, choleric, and adust humours, which cause leprosy, scabs, tetters, and itches, and such like breakings out of the skin; and, after the purgings, strengthens all the inward parts. It is also good against the yellow jaundice, eradicating it by urine, which it procures in abundance. The powder of the dried herb, given for some time together, cures melancholy, but the seed is strongest in operation for all the former diseases. The distilled water of the herb is also of good effect in the former diseases, and conduces much against the plague and pestilence, being taken with good treacle. The distilled water also, with a little water and honey of roses, helps all the sores of the mouth or throat, being gargled often therewith. The juice dropped into the eyes, clears the sight, and takes away redness and other defects in them, although it procures some pain for the present, and causes tears. Dioscorides says, it hinders any fresh springing of hairs on the eyelids (after they are pulled away) if the eyelids be anointed with the juice hereof with gum arabic dissolved therein. The juice of the Fumitory and docks mingled with vinegar, and the places gently washed or wet therewith, cures all sorts of scabs, pimples, blotches, wheals, and pushes which rise on the face or hands, or any other parts of the body.

FURZE-BUSH.—(*Ulex Europeus.*)

Called also Gorze and Whins.

Descrip.—A common shrub, four or five feet high, and very spreading. The leaves are very small, oblong, of a bluish green, and fall soon after their appearance in spring. The branches are all the year clothed with innumerable green thorns, and the flowers are large and yellow. The lesser and the Needle Furze are two other species of the same genus.

Place.—They are known to grow on dry barren heaths, and other waste, gravelly, or sandy grounds, in all counties of England.

Time.—They also flower in the summer months.

Government and Virtues.—Mars owns the herbs. They are hot and dry, and open obstructions of the liver and spleen. A decoction made with the flowers thereof has been found effectual against the jaundice; as also to provoke urine, and cleanse the kidneys from gravel or stone engendered in them. Mars does this also by sympathy.

GALINGALE.—(*Cyperus Longus.*)

Descrip.—The English Galingale has a great many narrow graffy leaves, rough and hard in handling, among which rises a triangular stalk about two feet high, on the top of which grows a tuft, or pannicle, consisting of small brown scaly spikes, with a few short leaves set on at their bottom. The root is long and slender, of a dark brown colour on the outside, and lighter within, of a pleasant scent, and a little hot and bitter in taste.

Place.—It grows in some parts of England, in the marshes; but we have it generally brought from Italy.

Time.—It flowers in June and July.

Government and Virtues.—This is a martial plant, being heating and drying, expelling wind, and strengthening the bowels; they help the colic, provoke urine, and the terms, and prevent the dropsy: they are cephalic, and good for the swimming of the head and giddiness; and are sometimes in abstersive gargarisms for ulcers in the mouth and gums.

GALL-OAK.—(*Quercus Infectoria.*)

Descrip.—The strong Gall-Oak, so called from the fruit it bears, does not grow so large or high as other oaks, but shorter, and very crooked, with fair spreading branches, and produces long leaves very much cut in on the edges, and hoary underneath. This tree flowers and bears acorns, as also a round woody substances, which are called galls, and the timber is very hard. There are other kinds, much shorter, bearing leaves more or less cut or jagged on the edges, and producing a great quantity of galls, and no acorns: some bear large galls, others small; some knobbed or bunched, and others smooth:

they are of different colours white, red, yellow, and green.

Place.—They chiefly grow in hot countries, Italy, Spain, &c.

Time.—They shoot forth their long catkins or blossoms early in spring, which fall away for the most part before the leaves appear. The acorns are very seldom ripe before October.

Government and Virtues.—The acorns differ but little from those produced in our own country. The small gall is Saturnine, of a sour harsh nature, dry in the third degree, and cold in the second. It is effectual in drawing together and fastening loose and faint parts, as the overgrowing of the flesh : it expels and dries up rheums and other fluxes, especially those that fall upon the gums, almonds of the throat, and other places of the mouth. The other whiter gall also binds and dries, but not so much as the former, having a less quantity of that sour harshness in it : it is good against the dysentry and bloody flux. The decoction of them in water, is of a mean astriction, but more powerful in harsh red wine. Being sat over, it remedies the falling of the mother, or the galls being boiled and bruised, and applied to the fundament when fallen, or to any swelling or inflammation will prove a certain cure. The pods of burned galls being quenched in wine and vinegar, are good to staunch bleeding in any place. They will dye hair black, and are one of the chief ingredients for making ink : it is also used by dyers for colouring black.

The oak apple is much of the nature of galls, though inferior in quality, but may be substituted for them with success to help rheums, fluxes, and other such like painful distempers.

GARLIC.—(*Allium Ampeloprasum.*)

Descrip.—The root consists of several cloves, or small bulbs of a reddish white colour, set together in a round compass, and enclosed in one common skinny coat or cover, having several small fibres at the bottom ; the leaves are broad and long, like those of leeks ; on the top of the stalk, which grows two or three feet high, stands an umbel of small white five-leaved flowers. The whole plant, especially the root, is of a very strong and offensive smell.

Place.—It is a native of the East. but for its use is cultivated every where in gardens.

Time.—It flowers in June and July.

Government and Virtues.—Mars owns this herb. This was anciently accounted the poor man's treacle, it being a remedy for all diseases and hurts (except those which itself breeds.) It provokes urine and women's courses, helps the biting of mad dogs, and other venomous creatures; kills the worms in children, cuts and voids tough phlegm, purges the head, helps the lethargy, is a good preservative against, and a remedy for, any plague, sore, or foul ulcer; takes away spots and blemishes in the skin, eases pains in the ears, ripens and breaks imposthumes, or other swellings; and for all those diseases the onions are as effectual. But the Garlic has some more peculiar virtues besides the former, viz. it has a special quality to discuss inconveniences, coming by corrupt agues or mineral vapours, or by drinking corrupt and stinking waters; as also by taking wolf-bane, hen-bane, hemlock, or other poisonous and dangerous herbs. It is also held good in hydropic diseases, the jaundice, falling-sickness, cramps, convulsions, the piles or hemorrhoids, or other cold diseases. Authors quote many other diseases this is good for; but conceal its vices. Its heat is very vehement; and all vehement hot things send up but ill-savoured vapours to the brain. In choleric men it will add fuel to the fire; in men oppressed by melancholy, it will attenuate the humour, and send up strong fancies, and as many strange visions to the head; therefore let it be taken inwardly with great moderation; outwardly you may make more bold with it.

GARLIC.—(BROAD-LEAVED WILD.)—*(Allium Ampeloprasum.)*

Descrip.—The root of this is round and whitish; the leaves are oblong, very broad, of a fine deep green. The stalk of a pale green, three square, and ten inches high, whereon grow small white flowers.

Place.—It is common in damp grounds in the western counties.

Time.—It flowers in April.

Government and Virtues.—It is under Mars as well as the former. The root is only known in physic; it is a powerful opener, and on account of its subtle parts, in which it abounds, discussive: it seldom agrees with dry constitutions, but it performs almost miracles in phlegmatic habits of body. It wonderfully opens the lungs, and gives relief in asthmas; nor is it without its merit in wind colics; and is a good diuretic, which appears by the smell it communicates to the urine. It is very useful in obstructions of the kidneys, and dropsies, especially in that which is called anasarca. It may be taken in a morning fasting, or else the conserve of Garlic which is kept in the shops may be used.

GENTIAN.—(*Swertia Perennis.*)

CALLED also Baldmony, and Felwort.

It is confessed that Gentian, which is most used among us, was brought from beyond the sea, yet we have several sorts of it growing frequently in this country, which, besides the reasons so often alleged, why English herbs should be fittest for English bodies, has been proved, by the experience of divers physicians, not to be a whit inferior in virtue to that which comes from beyond sea; therefore be pleased to take the description of them as follows:—

Descrip.—There are two sorts, the greater of which has many small long roots thrust deep down into the ground, and abides all the winter. The stalks are sometimes more, sometimes fewer, of a brownish green colour, and frequently two feet high, if the ground be fruitful, having many long, narrow, dark green leaves, set by couples up to the top: the flowers are long and hollow, of a purple colour, ending in fine corners. The smaller sort, which is to be found in this country, grows up sundry stalks, not a foot high, parted into several smaller branches, whereon grow divers small leaves together, very like those of the lesser centuary, of a whitish green colour; on the top of these stalks grow divers perfect blue flowers, standing in long husks, but not so big as the other: the root is very small and full of threads. Autumnal Gentian, or Lung-flower, with large bell-shaped blue flowers; Perfoliate Gentian, and Centaury Gentian, with small blue flowers, constitute all the species natives of Britain; and their difference has occasioned some to divide them into several imaginary sorts; but their virtues are alike, and their flowers declare them of the same genus.

Place.—They are common on hilly pastures, but are kept in botanic gardens

Time.—They flower in August.

Government and Virtues.—They are under the dominion of Mars, and one of the principal herbs he is ruler of. These resist putrefactions and poison; a more sure remedy cannot be found to prevent the pestilence than it is; it strengthens the stomach exceedingly, helps digestion, comforts the heart, and preserves it against faintings and swoonings: the powder of the dry root helps the biting of mad dogs and venomous beasts; opens obstructions of the liver, and restores the appetite. The herb steeped in wine, takes away weariness and cold lodging in the joints, if drank; it helps stitches and griping pains in the sides; it is an excellent remedy for such as are bruised by falls. It provokes urine and the terms exceedingly, therefore let it not be given to women with child: the same is very profitable for such as are troubled with cramps and convulsions, to drink the decoction: also they say it breaks the stone, and helps ruptures most certainly. It is excellent in all cold diseases, and such as are troubled with tough phlegm, scabs, itch, or the fretting sores and ulcers; it is an admirable remedy to kill the worms, by taking half a dram of the powder in a morning in any convenient liquor; the same is exceedingly good to be taken inwardly for king's-evil. It helps agues of all sorts, and the yellow-jaundice: as also the bots in cattle: when kine are bitten on the udder by any venomous beast, stroke the place with the decoction of any of these, and it will instantly heal it.

GERMANDER.—(*Teucrium Marum.*)

Descrip.—Germander has a spreading creeping root, which sends forth several square hairy branches, scarce a foot high, having two small leaves at every joint, on short foot-stalks, about an inch long, and half an inch broad, cut in with several sections, something resembling in shape the leaves of on oak, somewhat hard and crumpled, green above, and hoary white underneath. The flowers grow towards the tops of the branches among the leaves, whorle-fashion, of a purplish red colour; they are labiated, the lip turned upward; but they want the galea, having in its place several stamina standing erect. The seeds grow four together in the hairy five-pointed calyces.

Place.—It grows with us only in gardens.

Time.—It flowers in June and July. The leaves and tops are used.

Government and Virtues.—Germander is an herb of warm thin parts, under Mars, opening obstructions of the liver, spleen, and kidneys: and of use in the jaundice, dropsy, and stoppage of urine. It is a good emmenagogue; and is commended by some as a specific for the gout, rheumatism, and pains in the limbs. It is undoubtedly a good vulnerary, both detersive and healing; and is a proper ingredient in pectoral decoctions. Some extol it for a great antiscorbutic, but the brook-limes exceed it in this particular, which abound in subtle pungent parts, and therefore are better suited to cut those viscidities which are the cause of scorbutic blotches. The juice is very justly recommended among the rest of the antiscorbutic juices to be taken in the spring for some time.

GLADIOLE (WATER.)—*(Butomus Umbellatus.)*

CALLED also Flowering Rush.

Descrip.—This marshy plant has a thick bulbous root, with many short fibres. The stem is round and upright, and the leaves are long and upright also, springing from the root. The flowers grow at the top of the stalk in a very stately manner, in the umbellous form, and they are yellow, and sometimes of a greenish white.

Place and Time.—We find Gladiole growing on the sides of our ditches issuing from the Thames, and on the sides of the Thames itself, it is also found in the marshes near Rotherhithe, Deptford, and Blackwall. It flowers from July to September.

Government and Virtues.—Gladiole is under Saturn, as all rushes are. It is seldom used in medicine. The flowers are of a cooling nature, good for hot humours, inflammations, imposthumes, and green wounds.

GLADWIN.—*(Iris Fœtidissima.)*

Descrip.—This is one of the kinds of fleur-de-lys, having divers leaves rising from the roots, very like fleur-de-lys, but that they are sharp-edged on both sides and thicker in the middle, of a deep green colour, narrower and sharper pointed, and of strong scent, if they be bruised between the fingers. In the middle rises up a strong stalk, a yard high at the least, bearing three or four flowers at the top, resembling the flowers of the fleur-de-lys, with three upright leaves, of a dead purplish ash-colour, with some veins discoloured in them: the other three do not fall down, nor are the three other small ones so arched, nor cover the lower leaves as the fleur-de-lys does, but stand loose or asunder from them. After they are passed, there come up three square hard husks, opening wide into three parts when they are ripe, wherein lieth reddish seed, turning back when it has abode long. The root is like that of the fleur-de-lys, but reddish on the outside, and whitish within, very sharp and hot in the taste, of as evil scent as the leaves.

Place.—This grows well in upland grounds as in moist places, woods, and shadowy spots by the sea-side in many places of this country, and is usually nursed up in gardens.

Time.—It flowers not until July, and the seed is ripe in August or September ; yet the husks, after they are ripe, opening themselves, will hold their seed with them for two or three months, and not shed them.

Government and Virtues.—It is supposed to be under the dominion of Saturn. It is used by many country-people to purge corrupt phlegm and choler, by drinking a decoction of the roots ; the sliced roots and leaves in ale serve well for weak stomachs. The juice of the root snuffed up the nose causes sneezing, and draws corruption from the head. The powder drank in wine helps those troubled with cramp and convulsions, or with gout and sciatica; and gives ease to the most griping pains of the body and belly, and helps those that have the strangury. It stays fluxes, by cleansing and purging them. The root boiled in wine procures womens' courses ; and, used as a pessary, works the same effect, but causes abortion to women with child. Half a dram of the seed beaten to powder, and taken in wine, speedily relieves those troubled with a stoppage of the urine. The same taken in vinegar, dissolves the hardness and swellings of the spleen. The root used with a little verdigris and honey, and the great centuary root, is very effectual in all wounds, especially in the head : as also to draw forth any splinters or thorns, or any other thing, sticking in the flesh, without causing pain. The same boiled in vinegar, and laid upon any swelling or tumour, very effectually dissolves and consumes them ; it is also good for king's-evil. The juice of the leaves or roots, heals the itch, spreading sores, scabs, blemishes, and scars.

GOAT'S BEARD (YELLOW.)—*(Tragopogon Porrifolius.)*

Descrip.—This grows on a firm, upright stalk, of a light pleasant green, and a foot high. The leaves are flat, grassy, of a pretty bluish green ; tender and milky when broken. The flowers are yellow, large and beautiful ; they close at mid-day, and country-people therefore call it, Go-to-bed-at-Noon.

Place.—This is a handsome biennial ; frequently in our pastures, and very plentiful in the north of England.

Time.—It blooms in July.

Government and Virtues.—This herb is under the dominion of Jupiter. A large double handful of the entire plant, roots, flowers, and all bruised and boiled, and then strained, with a little sweet oil, is an excellent clyster in the most desperate case of strangury or suppression of urine, from whatever cause. A decoction of the roots is good for the heart-burn, loss of appetite, disorders of the breast and liver ; expels sand and gravel, slime, and even small stones. The roots dressed like parsnips, with butter, are good for cold watery stomachs. Boiled or cold, or eaten as a raw salad, they are grateful to the stomach ; strengthen the thin, lean, and consumptive, or the weak after long sickness. The distilled water gives relief to inward imposthumes, pleurisy, stitches, or pains in the sides.

GOAT'S BEARD (PURPLE).—*(Tragopogon Pratensis.)*

Descrip.—Purple Goat's Beard grows on a firm, upright stalk, near a yard high. The leaves are large, long, of a fine fresh green, resembling the leaves of leeks. The flower-stalk grows thick at its top ; the flowers are purple, and their long green cups behind add greatly to their beauty.

Place.—This is a biennal ; a wild plant in our pastures, very stately and beautiful ; and it thrives best where there is some moisture.

Time.—They bloom in June and July, and shut up at noon as the other. There is a beautiful variety of this, with the centre of the flower yellow, the rest purple.

Government and Virtues.—The virtues of this are the same as the other, only less pleasant, therefore more bitter, astringent, detersive, and medicinal. This, however, may be eaten in great quantities ; and so will be useful in chronic complaints. The roots are particularly specific in obstruction of the gall, and the jaundice ; the best way to use them, is stewed like chardoons.

GOAT'S RUE.—*(Galega Officinalis.)*

Descrip.—Goat's Rue has many tall, hollow, striated branches about a yard in height, with long, pinnated leaves growing alternately on the joints, consisting of six or eight pair of long oval pinnæ, smooth and not indented about the edges, which are apt to be folded together. The flowers grow in long spikes, hanging downwards in the shape of pea-blossom, but less, of a pale whitish blue colour; the seed grows in long erect pods: the root is thick, spreading in the earth, and abiding long.

Place.—It is a native of Italy, but grows in our gardens.

Time.—It flowers in June and July.

Government and Virtues.—Goat's-Rue is under Mercury in Leo, and is accounted cordial, sudorific, and alexipharmic, and good against pestilential distempers, expelling the venom through the pores of the skin; and is of use in all kinds of fevers, small-pox and measles; it likewise kills worms, and cures the bites of all kinds of venomous creatures. Some commend a decoction of it for the gout; and a bath made of it is very refreshing to wash the feet of persons tired with overwalking. In the northern countries they use this herb for making their cheeses, instead of Rennet, whence it is called also Cheese-Rennet: the flowers containing an acidity, which may be got by distillation. This plant is seldom used in the shops.

GOAT'S THORN, or TRAGANT.—*(Astragalus Tragacantha.)*

Descrip.—It grows with a woody tough root, the stem is moderately thick, and furnished with branches which are covered with dark green leaves; the flowers are produced in clusters at the tops of the branches, and they are small and white. The blossom, when it appears, is butterfly-shaped; the standard or upper petal, is longer than the rest, reflected on the sides, and notched at the end; the wings, or side petals, are shorter than the standard, and the keel, or lowermost of all, is notched at the end.

Place.—A native of the East, but grows in our gardens.

Time.—It flowers here in August.

Government and Virtues.—It is under the dominion of Mars. A gum, known by the name of gum dragant, or tragacanth, is the produce of this little shrub, and sweats out at the bottom of the stem during the heats of summer. It is good for tickling coughs, arising from sharp acrid humours, and against the strangury and heat of urine: but it is far from being a pleasant medicine.

GOLD OF PLEASURE.—(*Myagrum Sativum.*)

Descrip.—It has a long, slender, white, fibrous root. The stalk is round, firm, upright, a foot and a half high, and divided into a great number of branches. The leaves are numerous ; and they are placed with an agreeable regularity, from the bottom to the top : they are oblong. narrow, and of a pale green ; they adhere to the stalk by a broad base, and are from thence smaller to the extremity, where they terminate in a point. The lower leaves are sharply serrated at the edges. The flowers grow along the tops of the branches, and are of a golden yellow.

Place.—It is found in some of the corn-fields of England.

Time.—It flowers in July.

Government and Virtues.—Jupiter governs this useful but much neglected plant. In some part of this country where they raise flax, it is very common. The seeds pass unnoticed, consequently, it rises with the flax from one year to another. The seeds give a useful oil in great quantity, little inferior to olive oil, and will answer its purpose very well. The seeds are good against gravel, and are of a powerful diuretic quality.

GOLDEN ROD (COMMON).—(*Solidago Fragrans.*)

Descrip.—This rises to two feet high, a very handsome plant, with a small reddish brown upright stalk, turned and bent a little from the joints, and terminated by a long and beautiful spike of flowers. The leaves are of a deep, but not very fine green, and they feel a little harsh. The flowers are gold yellow, and numerous though small, and all turned one way ; when they are ripe, they change into down, and are carried away by the wind. The root consists of many small fibres, which grow near the surface of the ground, but survives the winter, and in spring shoots out new branches.

Place.—This is a perennial, that grows by wood-sides, in copses, in moist as well as dry grounds, and on heaths and among thickets.

Time.—It flowers about the month of July, and lasts till August.

Government and Virtues.—Venus rules this herb. It is a balsamic vulnerary herb, long famous against inward hurts and bruises, for which it is most effectual in a distilled water, and in which shape it is an excellent and safe diuretic ; few things exceed it in the gravel, stone in the reins and kidneys, strangury, and where there are small stones so situated, as to cause heat and soreness, which are too often followed with bloody or purulent urine ; then its balsamic healing virtues co-operate with its diuretic quality, and the parts at the same time are cleansed and healed. It is a sovereign wound-herb, inferior to none, both for inward and outward use. It is good to stay the immoderate flux of womens' courses, the bloody flux, ruptures, ulcers in the mouth or throat, and in lotions to wash the privy parts in venereal cases. No preparation is better than a tea of the herb for this service : and the young leaves, green or dry, have the most virtue.

GOLDEN ROD (NARROW-LEAVED.)—*(Solidago Angustifolia.)*

Descrip.—This is another species of the same plant; same in height, but has few or no branches. The stalk is very weak, tender, of a dark green colour, tinged with a ruddy brown. The leaves are of a bright grassy green, smooth, and prettily dented at the edges : the flowers are of a pale yellow, and stand in a loose spike.

Place.—This is a perennial, native of Ireland, and seldom found with us ; there it adorns the rocky hills.

Time.—The flowers bloom in July and August.

Government and Virtues.—It resembles the preceding in virtues as in form. Venus claims the herb, and applied outwardly it is good for green wounds, old ulcers and sores. As a lotion it is effectual in curing ulcers in the mouth and throat, and privy parts of man or woman. The decoction helps to fasten the teeth that are loose.

GOLDEN ROD (WELSH.)—*(Solidago Cambrica.)*

Descrip.—This grows upon a simple upright brown stalk, six or seven inches high. Its leaves are long, narrow, pale, and a little downy ; the flowers are of a gold yellow, and numerous.

Place.—This is a pretty perennial, a native of the Welsh mountains, and a favourite food for the goats.

Time.—The flowers bloom in August, and last till September.

Government and Virtues.—It possesses the same virtues as the first kind, though in an inferior degree. The leaves and tops are the parts used. It is accounted one of our best vulnerary plants, much used in apozems, and wound-drinks; and outwardly in cataplasms and fomentations. It is somewhat astringent, and useful in spitting of blood, and is of great service against the stone.

GOLDEN SAMPHIRE.—(*Inula Crithmifolia.*)

Descrip.—This is a perennial, and grows to a yard high, with many branches. The leaves are three-pointed, of a blue green, thick and juicy, the flowers of a gold colour.

Descrip.—It grows on the margin of our sea marshes.

Time.—It blooms in June and July.

Government and Virtues.—The leaves of the flowers make an excellent and agreeable antiscorbutic. An infusion of the whole plant, sweetened with sugar, is good after a drunken surfeit. It is under the dominion of Jupiter in Libra. The flowers are cooling, moistening, and laxative, good in affections of the breast and lungs, helping coughs and pleuritic pains. The syrup is given to children to open and cool their bodies. The flowers are cooling and opening, and frequently put into clysters, as well as into ointments against inflammations. The seed is reckoned good for the stone and gravel

GOOSEBERRY-BUSH.—(*Ribes Grossularia*).

Descrip.—The Gooseberry-Bush is well known to every body. I need not describe it, the leaves are little and jagged, the flowers small and green, and the berries round or oval, including several seeds in a juicy pulp, sourish when green, but when ripe of a sweet pleasant taste.

Place.—It grows in gardens.

Time.—It flowers early, the berries are ripe in July.

Government and Virtues.—These berries, which are the only parts used, are cooling and astringent, creating an appetite, and quenching thirst. They are under the dominion of Venus. While they are unripe, being scalded or baked, they are good to stir up a fainting or decayed appetite, especially where the stomach is afflicted by choleric humours: they are excellent good to stay the longings of women with child. The decoction of the leaves cool hot swellings and inflammations, and St. Anthony's fire. The ripe Gooseberries are excellent to allay the violent heat of both the stomach and liver. The young leaves break the stone, and expel gravel both from the kidneys and bladder. All the evils they do to the body of man is, they are supposed to breed crudities, and, by crudities, worms.

GOSMORE (LONG-ROOTED).—(*Hypochæris Radicata.*)

CALLED also Hawkweed

Descrip.—This rises from a moderately thick and long brown root, with leaves in a cluster at the bottom; they are oblong, broad, and of a deep green, widely notched at the edges, rather rough to the touch. The stalks are slender, tough, and branched, a foot and a half high, and of a pale green; they have rarely any leaf upon them. The flowers are of a gold colour, and grow on the tops of the branches.

Place.—It is common in pastures, and hilly situations.

Time.—It flowers in June.

Government and Virtues.—This Gosmore, as well as the following, is an herb of Venus, and very useful to the ladies. They are good for stone and stoppage of urine, and promote the menstrual flux, and to that end are frequently mixed with chalybeates; they are likewise good for the gout and sciatica; outwardly they are used for the itch, either the juice or powder mixed with a proper ointment.

GOSMORE (SMOOTH).—(*Hypochæris Glabra.*)

Descrip.—The stalk is hard, leafless, and of a pale green; the leaves a bright shining green; the flowers a pale yellow, their cups having a pretty appearance.

Place.—This is a biennial little plant on high grounds, but not common. It is mostly found in Warwickshire, and about Bristol and Denham.

Time.—It blooms in August.

Government and Virtues.—It has the taste of the former, but faint and unpromising; is seldom used; it is warming, aperient, and useful in disorders of the kidneys, as stone and strangury, provoking urine; it expedites the birth, and brings away the after-birth. It is likewise accounted alexipharmic, and good against the bites and stings of venomous creatures.

GOSMORE (SPOTTED.)—(*Hypochæris Maculata.*)

Descrip.—The stalk is greyish, and naked like the former; has slight films, and a single branch; the leaves are oblong or oval, undivided, of a pale green, and spotted with black. The flowers are of a fine light yellow.

Place.—This is a biennial, native of our heaths; a small, but singular plant; it grows upon Newmarket heath, but it is not common.

Time.—It blooms in August.

Government and Virtues.—This plant is very useful to the ladies, and ought to be found upon their toilets. Its decoction will take away freckles which are brought on by the heat of the sun. It is so innocent, that no harm need be feared from its application.

GOAT-HERB, GOUTWEED, or GOUTWORT.—(*Ægopodium Podagraria*).

Called also Ground-Ash, Herb Guard, and Ashweed.

Descrip.—It is a low herb, seldom rising half a yard, having sundry leaves standing on brownish green stalks by threes, snipped about, and of a strong unpleasant savour: the umbels of the flowers are white, and the seed blackish, the root runs broadly in the ground.

Place.—It grows by hedge and wall-sides, and often in the borders and corners of fields, and in gardens also.

Time.—It flowers and seeds about the end of July.

Government and Virtues.—Saturn rules it. Neither is it to be supposed that Goutwort has its name for nothing, but upon experiment it heals the gout and sciatica; as also joint-aches, and other cold pains.

GREEN (WINTER.)—(*Trientalis Europæa.*)

Descrip.—The stalk is round, thick, upright, and ten inches high. The leaves somewhat resemble those of the pear-tree, but scarcely so large; they all grow from the root, for the stalk is naked. The flowers are small, and of a very bright white; they stand in a kind of loose spike on the tops of the stalk, and are composed of five leaves, which are succeeded by cornered seed-vessels, full of very small seed. The root is small, slender and fibrous.

Place.—It grows wild in some parts of England, but is no where common.

Time.—It flowers in July.

Government and Virtues.—Winter-Green is under the dominion of Saturn, and is a singular good wound-herb, and an especial remedy to heal green wounds speedily, the green leaves being bruised and applied, or the juice of them. A salve made of the green herb stamped, or the juice boiled with hog's-lard, and turpentine added to it, is a sovereign salve. The herb boiled in wine and water, and given to them that have any inward ulcers in their kidreys, or neck of the bladder, does wonderfully help them. It stays all fluxes, as the lax, bloody flux, womens' courses, and bleeding of wounds, and takes away inflammations rising upon pains of the heart; it is no less helpful for foul ulcers hard to be cured; as also for cankers or fistulas. The distilled water effectually performs the same things.

GROUND PINE (COMMON.)—*(Ajuga Chamæpitys.)*

Descrip.—The root is long, slender, and divided. The stalks are numerous, weak, and three inches high; they are or a greyish colour, much branched, and covered thick with leaves. These stand in pairs at small distances, and they have numerous young ones in their bosoms; they are of a pale yellowish green, oblong, narrow, and at the end divided into three points. The flowers rise from the blossoms of the leaves, and are small and yellow; but the upper lip is spotted with purple on the inside.

Place.—It grows in fallow fields and chalky grounds, particularly in Kent, in great plenty.

Time.—It flowers in June and July.

Government and Virtues.—Ground Pine is a martial plant, hot and dry, warming and strengthening the nerves; helps the palsy, gout, sciatica and rheumatism, the scurvy, and all pains of the limbs. It is a strong diuretic, opens obstructions of the womb, and powerfully promotes the menses, it ought not to be given to pregnant women.

GROUNDSEL (COMMON.)—*(Senecio Vulgaris.)*

Descrip.—The stalk is of a round green, rather brownish colour, spreading towards the top into branches, set with long and somewhat narrow leaves, cut with deep irregular notches about the edges. The stalk is tender, juicy, weak, and about eight inches high. At the tops of the branches stand many small green heads, out of which grow many small yellow threads, or thrums, which are the flowers, and are poor and numerous. These continue many days blown in this manner, before they pass into down, and, with the seed are carried away by the wind. The root is small and stringy, and soon perishes, and as soon rises up again of its own sowing, so that it is seen often in one year, both green, in flower, and in seed.

Place.—This annual weed grows everywhere in fields and gardens, both in tilled and untilled ground.

Time.—It flowers all the summer round.

Government and Virtues.—Groundsel is under the dominion of Venus ; and, though common has many virtues. It is cooling and digesting in inflammations ; it is an easy emetic when made like tea. Taken in ale, it acts against the pains of the stomach, strangury, and jaundice ; it destroys worms, and is useful in scrofulous tumours and inflammations of the breasts and scald head. Its juice is a good purgative, but the dose should not exceed two ounces. The leaves bruised and applied outwardly to the stomach, produces the like effect, and there is no better application for the gripes and colic of infants. For the sore breasts of women, pick a handful of the fresh juicy leaves, bruise them, and make a poultice with a little bread boiled in milk, then lay the poultice on, and repeat as often as needful, and an effectual cure will be the result. The juice also provokes urine, and expels the gravel in the reins and kidneys, when taken in wine. A dram of the juice is sufficient to be taken inwardly, and caution should be used so that it may not work mischief. A poultice of it, with a little salt, dissolves knots and kernels in any part of the body. The leaves and flowers, with frankincense in powder, is a good vulnery ; the distilled water performs every thing that can be expected from its virtues, especially for inflammations or watering of the eyes, when proceeding from defluctions of rheum into them. An infusion of it taken inwardly cures staggers and bot-worms in horses.

GROUNDSEL (COTTON OR STINKING.)—(*Senecio Viscosus.*)

Descrip.—This is another sort, like the former, except that it grows not so tall, the leaves are not so finely jagged, nor of so dark a green colour, but rather whitish, soft, woolly, thick and clammy to the touch, and the flowers are usually paler. The whole plant stinks so rankly, that it is called Stinking Groundsel.

Place.—It is an annual, found upon our dry ditch banks.

Time.—It blooms in July, until the end of summer.

Government and Virtues.—This has been praised in fluxes of the belly, and the dysentery; it has the power of ipecacuanha, but in a less degree, and not so agreeable a manner, it is very good in hysteric complaints. The leaves are carminative, and may be used in poultices, fomenta tions, and baths, but more especially the flowers. Inwardly, an infusion will expel wind, strengthen the stomach, and stop vomiting. Two spoonfuls of this herb, with a few drops of the spirit of vitriol given in some broth is said to cure the most violent fit of ague.

GROUNDSEL (HOARY.)—(*Senecio Erucefolius.*)

Descrip.—The stalk is upright, and a yard high, of a pale green, and furnished with many branches. The leaves are of a pale green, and somewhat hoary; the flower is large, handsome, of a light yellow colour, and spreads flat round the thrum.

Place.—This is a perennial plant that loves shade, and is found on the sides of woods, and thrives best in moisture.

Time.—It blooms in July and August.

Government and Virtues.—Its virtues are similar to the others of its kind, and it resembles them in its taste and smell. A strong decoction is an excellent gargle in a sore throat, spitting it out immediately; but its outward uses are considerable. It takes off inflammations, dissolves hard swellings, and assuages pain in old ulcers, whether applied by way of poultice, ointment, or plaster.

GROUNDSEL (MOUNTAIN.)—(*Senecio Sylvaticus.*)

Descrip.—This is a strong tall plant, the stalk is a yard high, of a dull green, tinged with brown. The leaves are smooth, firm to the touch, of a faint green. The flowers are numerous, of light yellow, and their rays turn back.

Place.—This is an annual, common on our ditch banks, and other waste and dry places.

Time.—It blooms in July and August.

Government and Virtues.—It is externally good against pains and swellings. It is detersive, and proper in all glandular obstructions; it is antiscorbutic, and its fresh juice, which is the best, may be taken in broths or medicinal ales. The seeds, which are kept dry, are very light; are met with in the shops, but are not so good as the green herb, for it loses its virtues by drying.

GROUNDSEL (WATER.)—(*Senecio Jacobæa.*)

CALLED also Water Ragwort.

Descrip.—This water plant grows about two feet high, and spreads out wide branches. The root leaves are broad, with a few jags at the base, those on the stalks are deeply divided down almost to the rib, and they are of a lively green, smooth, glossy, sometimes of a reddish colour. The flowers are of a beautiful bright yellow.

Place.—This is a handsome perennial, commonly found at ditch-sides, or where water stands during the winter.

Time.—It blooms in July or August.

Government and Virtues.—There is an acrid sharpness in this plant, but the juice of it is cooling and astringent, and of use in burns, inflammations in the eyes, and also in cancerous ulcers: it takes the pain from the stings of bees, and assuages the pain of the gout, if applied outwardly.

GUM THISTLE.—(*Euphorbia Helioscopia.*)

Descrip.—This plant has no leaves, the root is hung with numerous large fibres, the stem is of dark green colour, thick, upright, and armed all the way with sharp prickles, and from the angles of the stem towards the top proceed the small flowers, which are of a yellowish green colour.

Place.—A native of Africa, but grows in our meadows.

Time.—It is perennial, flowers from June to September.

Government and Virtues.—It is under Mars, and is hot and dry, being a perfect caustic, of thin parts. A plaster made of twelve times as much oil, and a little wax, heals all aches of the joints, lameness, palsies, cramps, and shrinkings of the sinews. Mixed with oil of bay and bears' grease, it cures scurvy and scalds in the head, and restores lost hair; applied with oil to the temples, it heals the lethargy, and by putting it to the nape of the neck, prevents the apoplexy. Mixed with vinegar it removes all blemishes in the skin, or with other ointments, heals the parts that are cold, and heals the sciatica. Taken inwardly, it frets the entrails, and scorches the whole body, for that reason, it must be beaten small, and tempered with something that lubricates and allays its heat, and then it purges water and phlegm. Pills of Gum Thistle greatly help dropsy, pains in the loins and guts by moisture, but should only be given in desperate cases, as it operates violently. The oil of this plant, if snuffed up the nose purges the head of phlegm, and is good in old and cold pains of the joints, liver, and spleen, also cold diseases of the nerves and brain, the head-ache, and pains in the side. It cures cold pains in the kidneys, bladder and womb, by anointing with it. It provokes lust and heals numbness and stiffness of the privities proceeding from cold, by anointing.

HARE'S EAR (SMALL.)—*(Bupleura Rotundifolium.)*

Descrip.—This has a long slender white root; the stalks are numerous, and very small; they are a foot and a half high, and divided toward the top into a few branches: the leaves stand alternately on them; and they are long, narrow, grassy, and of a pale green. The flowers stand on very small umbels at the tops of the stalks, and on the foot-stalks rising at the bosom of the leaves; and they are little and white. The seeds are small and dark-coloured.

Place.—We have it in dry pastures, and by road-sides in Essex, Sussex, and Cambridge

Time.—It flowers in June.

Government and Virtues.—It is somewhat of the nature of Thorough-wax, but of inferior degree. The juice is cathartic and diuretic, good to purge phlegmatic watery humours, and serviceable against dropsy and jaundice, and obstructions of the liver and spleen; it is not often used in England. Venice and Castile Soap are made from its ashes.

HARE'S FOOT.—*(Pes Leporinus.)*

Descrip.—This plant seldom rises very high, but spreads out into many slender branches, having small narrow hairy trefoil leaves set at every joint; on the tops of the branches grow short round heads composed of small papilionaceous pale purple flowers, each set in a soft woolly calyx, making the heads appear soft and downy. The seed is small, lying at the bottom of the calyx; the root is little, and perishes yearly.

Place.—It is frequently found in fallow and corn-fields.

Time.—It flowers in June and July. The whole plant is used, though not very often.

Government and Virtues.—Hare's Foot is a Mercurial herb, drying and binding; accounted good for diarrhœa and dysentery, and to stop the too great flux of the catamenia and the fluor albus. It helps the ulceration of the bladder, and heat and pain in making water. It is a powerful astringent, and recommended in all cases where astringents are safe. The leaves worn in the shoes prevent the feet sweating. It is also a good vulnerary herb.

Sweet Flag.
Male Fern.
Flea Bane.
Hogs Fennel.
Fumitory.
Gladwyn.
Groundpine.
Goutwort.
Glasswort.

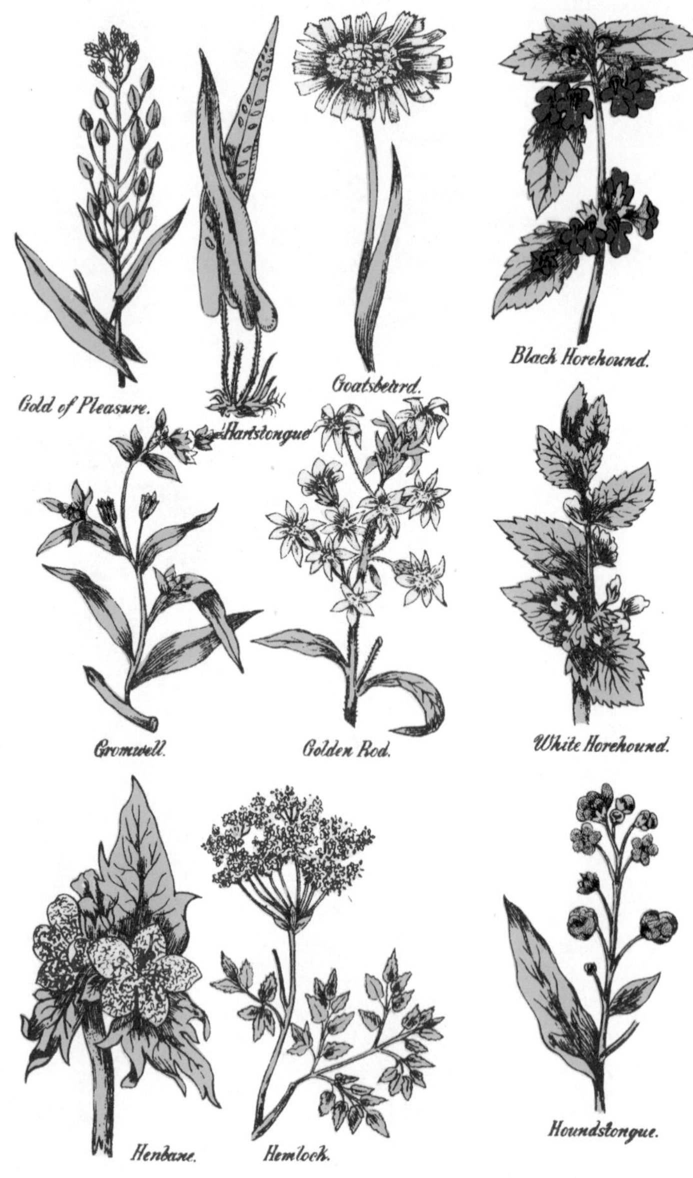
Gold of Pleasure.
Hartstongue
Goatsbeard.
Black Horehound.
Gromwell.
Golden Rod.
White Horehound.
Henbane.
Hemlock.
Houndstongue.

HART'S TONGUE.—(*Asplenium Scolopendrium or Scolopendrium Officinarum.*)

Descrip.—This has divers leaves arising from the root, every one severally; which fold themselves in their first springing and spreading; they are a foot long when full grown, smooth and green above, but hard and with little sap in them, streaked on the back, thwart on both sides of the middle rib, with small and somewhat long and brownish marks; the bottoms of the leaves are a little bowed on each side of the middle rib, somewhat narrow with the length, and a little small at the end. The root is of many black threads, folded or interlaced together.

Time.—Green all winter, but fresh leaves grow yearly.

Government and Virtues.—Jupiter claims dominion over this herb, and it is a good remedy for the liver, both to strengthen it when weak, and ease it when afflicted; a syrup of it should be made, for I think the leaves are not green all the year. It is commended for hardness and stoppings of the spleen and liver, and the heat of the stomach, lax, and the bloody-flux. The distilled water is very good against the passions of the heart, to stay the hiccough, to help the falling of the palate, and to stay the bleeding of the gums, by gargling with it.

HAWK-WEED (COMMON BROAD-LEAVED.)—(*Hyeracia Murorum.*)

Descrip.—It has many large leaves lying upon the ground, much torn on the sides like Dandelion, but with greater parts, more like the smooth Sow-Thistle, from among which rises a hollow, rough stalk, two or three feet high, branched from the middle upward, whereon are set at every joint longer leaves, little or nothing rent or cut, bearing at the top sundry pale ligulated yellow flowers, consisting of many small, narrow leaves, broad pointed, and nicked in at the ends, set in a double row or more, the outermost being larger than the inner, which, from most of the Hawk-weeds, (for there are many kinds) do hold, which turn into down, and, with small brownish seed, is blown away with the wind. The root is long, somewhat greater, and with many fibres thereat. The most common Hawk-weeds are those here represented, viz., the narrow-leaved, with umbeliferous flowers; the Wall Hawk-weed, with hairy stalks and leaves; the Succory-leaved Hawk-weed; the Mouse-ear Hawk-weed, with bare green stalks and fairer yellow flowers; the Auricular narrow-leaved Hawk-weed; the Mountain Hawk-weed, with a rough bare stalk, and fine yellow flowers; and the Scotch Hawk-weed, the largest Hawk-weed of any, with a rough stalk, and small yellow flowers. The virtues are the same in all.

Place.—They grow about field-sides and path-ways in the dry grounds of the hilly-part of Westmoreland.

Time.—They flower and seed late in the summer.

Government and Virtues.—Saturn owns it. Hawk-weed is cooling, somewhat drying and binding, and good for the heat of the stomach, and gnawings therein; for inflammations, and the hot fits of agues. The juice of it in wine helps digestion, dispels wind, hinders crudities abiding in the stomach, and helps the difficulty in making water, it is good against all poisonous bites. A scruple of the dry root given in wine and vinegar, is profitable for dropsy. The decoction of the herb taken in honey digests phlegm, and with hyssop helps the cough. The decoction of the herb and wild succory with wine, helps the wind colic and hardness of the spleen, it procures rest and sleep, hinders venery, cools heat, purges the stomach, increases blood, and helps diseases of the reins and bladder. Outwardly applied, it is good for the defects and diseases of the eyes, used with some womens' milk; it may be used with success for healing spreading ulcers. The green leaves bruised, with a little salt. applied to burns and scalds, greatly helps them: as also St. Anthony's fire, and all pushes and eruptions, and hot and salt phlegm. Applied with meal poultice, it eases and helps cramps and convulsions. The distilled water takes away wrinkles, freckles, spots, &c.

HAWTHORN.—*(Mespilus Oxyacantha.)*

Descrip.—This is well known. The young twigs are reddish, clothed with small leaves, divided into three and sometimes five segments, coming over against the thorns. The flowers grow in clusters, consisting of five white leaves, with reddish apices in the middle; of a pleasant smell, and are succeeded by small, round, and umbelicated berries, of a fine red colour, containing a pretty big stone divided into two, and covered with a little pulp.

Place.—These trees grow in hedges, and flower in May.

Time.—The berries or haws are ripe in September The flowers and fruit are used.

Government and Virtues.—It is a tree of Mars. The

seeds in the berries beaten to powder being drunk in wine, are good against the stone and dropsy. The distilled water of the flowers stays the lax. The seeds cleared of the down and bruised, being boiled in wine, are good for inward pains. If the distilled water be applied to any place pierced with thorns or splinters, it will draw them out.

HAZEL NUT.—(*Corylus Avellana.*)

Descrip.—The Hazel tree is of small magnitude, rising from the root are a number of long, smooth, tough, pliable branches, bearing large, round, rough leaves, indented about the edges, before whose appearing there comes forth on the branches a great many long, loose juli, or catkins. The nuts grow two, three, or four together, on one stalk, covered with a husk, open and jagged at the top; when ripe, the shell is hard and brittle, having a sweet kernel.

Place.—This tree grows in the woods and hedges.

Time.—It flowers in May.

Government and Virtues.—They are under the dominion of Mercury. The parted kernels made into an electuary, or the milk drawn from them with mead or honied water, is good to help an old cough, and a little pepper put in draws rheum from the head. The dried husks and shells, to the weight of two drams, taken in red wine, stays laxness and womens' courses, the skins answer the same purpose.

HEART'S EASE.—(*Viola Tricolor.*)

CALLED also Pansies.

Descrip.—From a long, slender, divided fibrous root, rise numerous weak stalks, of a faint green; they spread upon the ground, and raise themselves up for flowering, and are six or eight inches long, and branched. The lower leaves are short, roundish, and lightly indented; but the upper ones are longer and more deeply cut, and some towards the top divided to the rib by numerous segments. The flowers are of a beautiful purple, variegated with yellow; and there is more or less white or blue, among them. The wild white violet is a species of this genus; many are of a white colour from being starved, and this is the case in respect to the white violet.

Place.—They are found wild in barren places in our fields, and cultivated often in our gardens.

Time.—They flower all the spring and summer long.

Government and Virtues.—The herb is really Saturnine, something cold, viscous, and slimy. A strong decoction or syrup of the herb and flowers, is an excellent cure for the venereal disease. The spirit of it is excellent good for convulsions in children, and a remedy for falling sickness, inflammation of the lungs and breasts, pleurisy, scabs, itch, &c. The flowers are cooling, emollient, and cathartic : it is best to make a syrup, as their virtues are lost by drying.

HEDGEWEEDS.—(*Erysimum Officinale*, and *Erysimum Barbaræa.*)

Descrip.—Common and Winter Hedgeweeds are often taken for Hedge Mustard, as there is a resemblance both in appearance and virtues, it is not of much consequence. The roots of these weeds are long, white, woody, furnished with many fibres. The stalks are round, firm, upright, of a pale green, or purplish ; they grow two feet and a half high, and not much branched. The leaves of the first are long, pointed, and notched at the edges ; but of the Winter Hedgeweed they are broader, thicker, more deeply indented, and rounder. They are of a pale green colour, a bitter taste ; the pith and the stalk have the same taste. The flowers are small and yellow, and the seed-vessels are long, slender, and squared : they stand in a kind of spikes along the upper part of the stalk, when the plant has been some time in flower. Garlic Hedgeweed, or as some call it, Jack by the Hedge (*Alliaria Officinalis,*) has the taste of the former, but the appearance is somewhat different, for this has smaller white flowers and rounder leaves, of a finer green, and not rough at the edges, not so much resembling Wormwood or Southernwood as those do ; but the seed-vessels are the same shaped, and the seed looks the same.

Place.—They are common in waste places, which are overrun with water; the fens in the Isle of Ely, in Cambridgeshire, and in Derbyshire, produce them abundantly.

Time.—They are sometimes in flower in April, and sometimes not till September.

Government and Virtues.—They are martial plants, hot and astringent ; the juice, or a strong decoction, is good to stop effusion of blood in a very safe manner. The seed, which is the best part that is used, is drying and binding, of service in all kinds of fluxes and hemorrhages, either from the bowels or any other part ; they help the incontinence of urine, and the making bloody urine. They are also alexipharmic, and good in pestilential fevers; they resist poison, and the bites and stings of venomous creatures

HELLEBORE (BLACK.)—*(Helleborus Niger.)*

Called also Setter-wort, Setter-grass, Bear's-foot, Christmas herb, and Christmas-flower.

Descrip.—It has sundry fair green leaves rising from the root, each of them standing about a handful high from the earth ; each leaf is divided into seven, eight, or nine parts, dented in the middle of the leaf to the point sides, abiding green all the winter ; about Christmas-time, if the weather be any thing temperate, the flowers appear upon foot-stalks, also consisting of five large, round, white leaves a-piece, which sometimes are purplish towards the edges, with many pale yellow thrumbs in the middle ; the seeds are black, and in form long and round. The root consists of numberless blackish strings all united into one head. There is another species, which grows in the woods very like this, but only the leaves are smaller and narrower, and perish in the winter, which this does not.

Place.—The first grows in gardens. The second is commonly found in the woods in Northamptonshire.

Time.—The first flowers in December or January ; the second in February or March.

Government and Virtues.—It is an herb of Saturn, and therefore no marvel if it has some sullen conditions with it, and would be far safer, being purified by the alchymist than given raw. Goat's milk is an antidote for it, if any one suffers from taking too much. The roots are very effective in quartan agues and madness, they help falling sickness, the leprosy, both the yellow and black jaundice, the gout, sciatica, and convulsions. Used as a pessary, the roots provoke the terms exceedingly ; also being beaten to powder, and strewed upon foul ulcers, it eats away the dead flesh, and instantly heals them : nay, it helps gangrenes in the beginning. Twenty grains taken inwardly is a sufficient dose for one time, and let that be corrected with half as much cinnamon.

HELLEBORE (WHITE,) or INDIAN POKE.—*(Veratrum Viride.)*

Descrip.—The roots are thick at the head, white on the inside, and very full of fibres all round, of a hot nauseous taste. The stalks are numerous, about a foot high ; they are round, green, firm, and upright. The lower leaves are large, of a deep green, divided into several parts, sharp pointed and serrated at the edges. The flowers are umbelliferous, large, and singular ; they have no cup, they are green, but paler than the leaves, and they have a great number of threads, with white buttons in their centre. The seed-vessels appear among these, and afterwards ripen ; the flower not falling, but remaining with them.

Place.—It is a scarce plant. It has been found in woods in Kent and Sussex, and in Buckinghamshire.

Time.—It flowers early in spring.

Government and Virtues.—Like the former it is a cold Saturnine plant, and possesses but in an inferior degree the virtues of Black Hellebore. The leaves dried and powdered, are given to robust habits ; as also the infusion of the leaves, but it is a very harsh medicine, and should be given with caution. The powder of the dried root ought not to be given to pregnant women.

HEMLOCK.—(*Conium Maculatum.*)

Descrip.—The common great Hemlock grows up with a green stalk, four or five feet high, or more, full of red spots sometimes, and at the joints very large winged leaves one set against the other, dented about the edges, of a sad green colour branched towards the top, where it is full of umbels of white flowers, and afterwards with whitish flat seed ; the root is long, white, and sometimes crooked, and hollow within. The whole plant, and every part, has a strong, heady, and ill-favoured scent.

Place.—It grows by walls and hedges throughout all parts of this country.

Time.—It flowers and seeds in July, or thereabouts.

Government and Virtues.—Saturn claims dominion over this herb. Hemlock is exceedingly cold, and very dangorous, especially to be taken inwardly. It may safely be applied to inflammations, tumults, and swellings in any part of the body, as also to St. Anthony's fire, wheals, pushes, and creeping ulcers that arise of hot sharp humours, by cooling and repelling the heat ; the leaves bruised and laid to the brow or forehead, are good for red and swollen eyes ; as also to take away a pin and web growing there ; take a small handful of this herb, and half as much bay-salt, beat together, and applied to the contrary wrist of the hand, removes it in two applications. The root roasted and applied to the hands, helps the gout. Pure wine is the best antidote if too much of this herb is taken

Poisonous Water Hemlock, *Cicuta Virosa*, and Thick Water Hemlock, are but accidental variations which situation and soil naturally produce, they are thought to be poisonous, but there is nothing certain on this head.

HEMP.—(*Cannabis Sativa.*)

Descrip.—The stalks grow to five or six feet high, angular, covered with a strong tough bark : and clothed with many digitated or fingered leaves, each leaf composed of five, six, or seven parts, long and narrow, sharp-pointed, and serrated about the edges, the middlemost being longest, set together upon one long footstalk ; they are green above, hoary underneath, and rough in handling. The flowers grow toward the tops of the stalks, in that they call the male, in small and staminous bunches, which perish without bringing any seed ; that being produced by the female only, without any previous flowers.

Place.—It is cultivated in many counties.

Time.—It is sown at the end of March, or beginning of April ; and is ripe in August or September.

Government and Virtues.—It is a plant of Saturn. The seed expels wind, and too much use of it dries up the seed for procreation ; yet being boiled in milk, and taken, helps such as nave a hot or dry cough. The emulsion of the seed is good for the jaundice, if there be ague accompanying it, for it opens obstructions of the gall, and causes digestion of choler. The emulsion or decoction of the seed stays the lax and continual fluxes, eases the colic, and allays the troublesome humours of the bowels, it also stays bleeding at the mouth, nose, or other places. It is good to kill worms in man or beast ; and the juice dropped into the ears kills worms in them, and draws forth earwigs or other living creatures. The decoction of the root allays inflammations of the head, or any other parts ; the herb or the distilled water of it, does the same. The decoction of the root eases the pains of the gout, the hard humours of knots in the joints, the pains and shrinkings of the sinews, and the pains of the hips. The fresh root mixed with a little oil and butter, is good for burns.

HENBANE (COMMON.)—(*Hyoscyamus Niger.*)

Descrip.—Our Common Henbane has very large, thick, soft, woolly leaves, lying on the ground, much cut in, or torn on the edges, of a dark, ill greyish green colour ;

among which arise up divers thick and short stalks, two or three feet high, spread into divers small branches, with lesser leaves on them, and many hollow flowers, scarce appearing above the husk, and usually torn on one side, ending in five round points, growing one above another, of a deadish yellow colour, paler towards the edges, with many purplish veins therein, and of a dark yellowish purple in the bottom of the flower, with a small point of the same colour in the middle, each of them stand in a hard close husk, which, after the flowers are passed, grows rather sharp at the top points, wherein is contained much small seed, very like poppy seed, but of a dusky greyish colour. The root is great, white, and thick, branching forth divers ways under ground, so like parsnips that it has deceived many. The whole plant, more than the root, has a very heavy, ill, offensive smell.

Place.—It grows by way-sides, and under hedges.

Time.—It flowers annually in May, June and July.

Government and Virtues.—This herb is under the dominion of Saturn. The leaves cool inflammations of the eyes, and any part of the body, and are good for the swellings of the testicles, or womens' breasts, or elsewhere, if they be boiled in wine, and either applied themselves, or the fomentation warm ; it also assuages the pain of the gout, the sciatica, and other pains in the joints which arise from a cold cause, and applied with vinegar to the temples and forehead, helps the head-ache, and want of sleep in hot fevers. The juice of the herb or seed, does the same. The oil of the seed is good for deafness, noise, and worms in the ears, being dropped there ; the juice of the herb or root acts the same. The decoction of the herb or seed, kills lice in man or beast. The fume of the dried herb, stalks and seeds, burned, quickly heals swellings, chilblains or kibes in the hands or feet, by holding them in the fumes thereof. This herb must never be taken inwardly, it is altogether an outward medicine. Goat's milk, Honey water, and Mustard-seed, are amongst the best antidotes when Henbane has been taken inwardly.

HENRY (GOOD.)—*(Mercurialis Annua.)*

CALLED also English Mercury.

Descrip.—This plant has a thick, yellowish, perennial root, with several fibres ; the leaves grow upon long footstalks of a triangular shape, like spinach, of a yellow green colour, feeling greasy or unctuous in handling. The stalks grow about a foot high, with several of the like leaves growing on them; and, on their tops, spikes of small herbaceous flowers, inclosing little round black seeds.

Place.—It grows in waste places, amongst rubbish.

Time.—It flowers in spring.

Government and Virtues.—It is under the dominion of Mercury. This herb is detersive and diuretic, and ought to have a place in vulnerary decoctions and fomentations. It is preferred to spinach, and is much superior in firmness and flavour. The young shoots, the succeeding leaves, and at last the flowery tops, are fit for kitchen purposes. It is good for scurvy, and provokes urine ; outwardly it is much used in clysters, and a cataplasm of the leaves helps the pains of the gout.

HERB CHRISTOPHER.—(*Actæa Spicata.*)

Descrip.—This is a species of the Bane-berry. The root is long and thick, black on the outside, yellow within, and of a disagreeable taste. The first leaves are large, and divided into a great many parts three together ; so that they resemble some of the umbelliferous plants : they are of a dusky green, and of a glossy surface. The stalk is round, green, upright, branched, and a yard high ; the upper leaves resemble those of the root ; they are large, and their separate parts are broad, serrated, and have also a kind of trifid division. The flowers are small and white ; they stand in clusters upon tender foot-stalks, forming a kind of spike, and the berries are large, of a roundish, but somewhat of an oblong figure, and black.

Place.—It is found in woods in our northern counties.

Time.—It flowers in July, the berries ripen in August.

Government and Virtues.—It is under the dominion of Saturn. The berries are poisonous. Outwardly the leaves are good for inflammations, and supply the place of Common Nightshade. They may also be applied with good success to hard tumours or swellings on the breast.

HERB ROBERT.—(*Geranium Robertianum.*)

Descrip.—It rises up with a reddish stalk two feet high, having divers leaves thereon, upon very long and reddish foot-stalks, divided at the ends into three or five divisions, each of them cut in on the edges, some deeper than the others, and all dented likewise about the edges, which sometimes turn reddish. At the tops of the stalks come forth divers flowers made of five leaves, much larger than the dove's-foot, and of a more reddish colour; after which come black heads, as in others: the root is small and thready, and smells as the whole plant, very strong.

Place.—This grows every where, by the way-sides, on ditch banks, and upon waste grounds.

Time.—It flowers in June and July, and the seed is ripe shortly afterwards.

Government and Virtues.--It is under the dominion of Venus, and is commended against the stone, and to stay blood, where or however flowing; it speedily heels all green wounds, and is effectual in old ulcers in the privy parts, or elsewhere. All geraniums are vulnaries, but this herb more particularly so, only rather more detersive and diuretic, which quality is discovered by its strong, soapy smell; it answers very well taken inwardly with wine in powder, and also outwardly applied, for old ruptures. A decoction of it has also been of service in obstructions of the kidneys and in gravel.

HERB TRUE-LOVE.—*(Paris Quadrifolia.)*

CALLED also One-Berry.

Descrip.—True-Love has a small creeping root running under the uppermost crust of the earth, shooting forth stalks with leaves, some of which carry no berries, and others which do; every stalk smooth without joints, and blackish green, about a foot high, if it bear berries, otherwise seldom so high; at the top there are four leaves set directly one against another, in the manner of a cross or ribband tied, in a true-love's knot, which are each of them apart, like the Nightshade leaf, but somewhat broader, having sometimes three, sometimes five, sometimes six, leaves, and those sometimes greater than in others; in the middle of the four leaves rises up one small slender stalk, about an inch high; bearing at the tops one flower spread open like a star, consisting of four small and long narrow pointed leaves of a yellowish green colour, and four others lying between them less than they; in the middle thereof stands a dark round purplish button or head, compassed about with eight small yellow mealy threads with three colours. This button or head becomes a blackish purple berry, full of juice, about the size of a grape, having many white seeds. The whole plant is without taste.

Place.—It grows in woods and copses, and sometimes in the borders of fields and waste grounds, in many parts of this country, and abundantly in the woods about Chislehurst and Maidstone in Kent.

Time.—They spring up in April or May, and flower soon after, and the berries are ripe in May and June.

Government and Virtues.—Venus owns it; the leaves or berries are good as antidotes against all kinds of poison, especially that of aconites, and pestilential disorders. The roots in powder, taken in wine, ease the pains of colic; the leaves are very effectual for green wounds, and to heal filthy old sores and ulcers, and powerful to discuss all tumours and swellings in the privy parts, the groin, or any other part of the body, and to allay all inflammations. The juice of the leaves applied to felons, or those nails of the hands or feet that have sores or imposthumes at the roots of them, heals them in a short time.

HOLLY, HOLM, OR HULVER-BUSH.—(*Ilex Aquifolium.*)

Descrip.—This is a well-known large bush. The bark is whitish on the trunk, but the young shoots are green. The leaves are oblong, irregular at the edges and prickly; the flowers are greenish, and the berries black. Another species has thinner leaves, and yellow berries.

Place.—This is often planted as a garden-hedge.

Time.—It flowers in May.

Government and Virtues.—The tree is Saturnine. The berries expel, and are profitable in the colic. The berries have a strong faculty in them; if you eat a dozen of them in the morning fasting, when they are ripe and not dried, they purge the body of gross and clammy phlegm; but if you dry the berries, and beat them into a powder, they bind the body, and stop fluxes, bloody-fluxes, and the terms in women; the bark and the leaves also are excellent, being used in fomentations for broken bones, and such members as are out of joint.

HOLLY (SEA.)—(*Eryngium Maritimum.*)

CALLED also Sea Eryngo.

Descrip.—The first leaves of our Sea Holly are not so hard and prickly as when they grow old, being almost round, and deeply dented about the edges, hard and sharp pointed, and a little crumpled, of a bluish green colour, every one upon a long foot-stalk ; but those that grow up higher with the stalk, encompass it about. The stalk is round and strong, crested with joints and leaves, divided, sharp and prickly ; the branches rising from thence, which have likewise other small branches, each of them having several round prickly heads, with many small, jagged, prickly leaves under them, standing like a star, and sometimes found greenish or whitish ; the root grows to eight or ten feet in length, set with circles on the upper part, cut smooth, and without joints lower down, brownish on the outside, and very white within, with a pith in the middle, of a pleasant taste, but much more, being artificially preserved, and candied with sugar.

Place.—It is found plentifully about the sea-coast.

Time.—It flowers at the end of summer, and gives ripe seed within a month afterwards.

Government and Virtues.—Sea Holly is under the Moon: the roots are hepatic and diuretic, opening obstructions of the liver, helping the jaundice and dropsy, provoking urine, and easing the strangury. Candied with sugar, the roots are very restorative, good for consumptive persons, and those wasted with long illness and too much venery, they are reckoned strengtheners to the parts of generation, and are recommended for the lues venerea and gonorrhœa.

HOLLYHOCKS (GARDEN.)—*(Althæa Rosea.)*

Descrip.—This is a tall plant, six or seven feet high, with thick round stalks, and large hairy round leaves; the flowers grow upon the stalk, coming forth with the leaves, being very large, of one leaf cut into five segments, of a pale red colour, having a spiked umbo in the middle, full of dusty apices. The roots are branched, white and large.

Place.—It grows only in gardens.

Time.—It flowers in July and August.

Government and Virtues.—This species of mallows is of the nature of Common Marsh-mallows, but less mollifying ; it is mostly used in gargles for the swelling of the tonsils, and the relaxation of the uvula. All the parts of the plant have a rough and austere taste, but more especially the root, which is of a very binding nature, and may be used to advantage both inwardly and outwardly, for incontinence of urine, immoderate menses, bleeding wounds, spitting of blood, the bloody-flux, and other fluxes of the belly. It is also of efficacy in a spongy state of the gums, attended with looseness of the teeth, and soreness in the mouth. Dried and reduced to powder, or boiled in wine, and partaken of freely, it prevents miscarriage, helps ruptures, dissolves coagulated blood from falls, blows, &c., and kills worms in children.

HONEWORT (CORN.)—(*Sison, Segeton,* or *Cryptotænia Canadensis.*)

Descrip.—This rises from a long, thick, white root, the stalks are numerous, round, fleshy, and a foot and a half high, of a pale and bluish colour. The leaves grow at equal distances; they are usually drooping, large, finely cut at the edges, and pointed, sometimes spotted with white, the colour is a bluish green. The flowers are few, and, like the leaves of the plant, hang down; they are yellow in the upper part, and purple at the base, though some are white.

Place.—It grows in corn-fields, and in thick hedges.

Time.—It flowers in July.

Government and Virtues.—It is a flower of the Sun; a great vulnerary. The flowers contain a deal of honey-juice, they are cooling and moistening, good for inflammations of the liver, St. Anthony's fire, redness and pimples in the face, being applied to the parts affected as a cataplasm, or cloths dipped in the juice, laid on, and now and then shifted; made into a poultice with hogs'-lard, it helps hot swellings and tumors.

HONEWORT (SLENDER.)—(*Sison Ammonium.*)

Descrip.—This is a species of stone parsley, a weak plant of two feet and a half in height; the stalk is brown, and very slender, supporting itself by leaning against the bushes: the leaves are of a fine green; the flowers are small and white: and the seeds are of an olive brown.

Place.—It is found in damp thickets, and moist hedges.

Time.—It flowers in July.

Government and Virtues.—This little plant is under the dominion of Venus, in the sign Cancer, and is excellent to allay swellings, which are called Hones. The leaves are to be fresh gathered, and beat in a mortar with a kind of paste. they are then to be laid on a swelling that is red, painful, and threatens bad consequences, which they disperse It is good for disorders of the skin, and even in the king's-evil. The Corn Honewor possesses still more virtue.

HONEY-SUCKLE.—(*Lonicora Caprifolium.*)

CALLED also Woodbine.

Descrip.—The trunk or body of this bush is seldom much thicker than the wrist, shooting out long, twining, slender stalks, which twist about anything they meet with : the leaves grow two together, at a joint, of a long round form, pointed at the end, of a bluish green colour; the flowers are made up of several long slender tubes set together, open at the top, with broad lips, turned back with several stamina in the middle, of a pale red colour, and a pleasant smell, succeeded by small red berries.

Place.—It grows every where in the hedges.

Time.—It flowers nearly all summer

Government and Virtues.—This is a hot martial plant in the sign of Cancer. The leaves are the only parts used, and are put into gargarisms for sore throats. Some recommend a decoction for a cough, and the phthisic, and to open obstructions of the liver and spleen. The oil made by infusion of the leaves, is healing and warming, and good for the cramp and convulsions of the nerves.

HONEY-SUCKLE (DWARF.)—(*Cornus Herbacea.*)

Descrip.—The root is long, slender and spreading, and is furnished with many fibres. The stalk is round, slender, upright, and about five inches high. The leaves are in pairs, large, oblong, broad-pointed at the ends, and marked with high ribs : they have no foot-stalks, and their colour is of a bluish green. The flower is large and white, and stands at the top of the stalk, but there usually rises two little shoots from the same point ; each of which has two or four leaves on it like the others. The fruit consists of several small berries joined together, of a fine red. As this plant decays it becomes more red.

Place.—It grows on hills in the north of England

Time.—It flowers in May.

Government and Virtues.—This is a martial herb. The root is bitterish to the taste, the leaves mildly acid ; boiled up with sugar, the leaves make a very agreeable jelly, which is of great use in hot bilious fevers, and putrid disorders. A decoction of the bark is a good lotion for the itch, and other cutaneous eruptions.

HONEY-WORT.—(*Cerinthe Major.*)

Descrip.—There are several species of the Honey-worts, consisting of the great, small, and the rough, as the greater yellow and red, the greater yellow and purple, and the lesser yellow and white. The greater Honey-wort grows upon a thick green stock to a moderate height, having a number of deep-pointed green leaves, placed one above another: towards the top of each stalk come umbels of very sweet flowers, thick set, and rising up spiral or crested; of a bright yellow colour, though some are red, others purple, and some perfectly white.

Place.—They grow in England in gardens.

Time.—They spring up in April, and flower from May to August, but perish in the winter.

Government and Virtues.—They are under Mercury, and are of a cold quality, and somewhat astringent. They stop bleeding at the mouth and nose, immoderate fluxes of the belly, and womens' courses. The juice of the herb, with a little saffron dissolved in it, is an excellent remedy for weak, watery, bleared eyes, and is used to heal foul ulcers, after they have been cleansed, particularly in tender parts of the body. It is used instead of Bugloss and Borage.

HOPS.—(*Humulus Lupulus.*)

Descrip.—The Hop runs to a great height, climbing up, and twisting round the poles which are placed for its support; the branches are rough and hairy, being large, rough, vine-like leaves, divided into three parts, serrated about the edges. On the tops of the stalks, grow clusters of large, loose, scaly heads, of a pale greenish yellow colour when ripe, and a pretty strong smell.

Place.—The manured hops are cultivated in gardens: the wild are found frequently in hedges.

Time.—They are ripe in September.

Government and Virtues.—It is under the dominion of Mars. This will open obstructions of the liver and spleen, cleanse the blood, loosen the belly, cleanse the reins from gravel, and provoke urine. The decoction of the tops cleanses the blood, cures the venereal disease, and all kinds of scabs, itch, and other breakings out of the body; as also tetters, ringworms, spreading sores, the morphew, and all discolourings of the skin. The decoction of the flowers and tops help to expel poison. Half a dram of the seed in powder, taken in drink, kills worms in the body, brings down womens' courses, and expels urine. A syrup made of the juice and sugar, cures the yellow jaundice, eases the head-ache that comes of heat, and tempers the heat of the liver and stomach, and is profitable given in long and hot agues that arise from choler and blood. The young hop sprouts, which appear in March and April being mild, if boiled and served up like asparagus, are a very wholesome as well as a pleasant tasted spring food. They purify the blood, and keep the body gently open.

HOREHOUND.—*(Marubium Vulgare.)*

Descrip.—Common Horehound grows up with square hairy stalks, half a yard or two feet high, set in the joints with two crumpled rough leaves of a sullen hoary green colour, of a good scent but a bitter taste. The flowers are small, white, and gaping, set in a rough hard prickly husk round about the joints, with the leaves from the middle of the stalk upward, wherein afterward is found small round blackish seed. The root is blackish, hard and woody, with many strings; and abides many years.

Place.—It is found in waste dry grounds in England.

Time.—It flowers in July, the seed is ripe in August.

Government and Virtues.—It is an herb of Mercury. A decoction of the dried herb, with the seed, or the juice of the green herb taken with honey, is a good remedy for a cough, or consumption. It helps to expectorate tough phlegm from the chest, being taken with the roots. It is given to women to bring down their courses, to expel the afterbirth, and to them that have sore and long travails; as also to persons who have taken poison. The leaves used with honey, purge foul ulcers, stay running and creeping sores, and the growing of the flesh over the nails. It also helps pains in the sides. The juice, with wine and honey, helps to clear the eyesight, and snuffed up the nostrils, it purges away the yellow jaundice; and, with oil of roses, dropped into the ears, eases the pains of them. It opens obstructions both of the liver and spleen, and used outwardly it cleanses the chest and lungs. A decoction of Horehound is available for those that have hard livers, or those who have the itch or running tetters. The powder taken, or the decoction, kills worms; the green leaves bruised, and boiled in hog's-grease into an ointment, heals the bites of dogs, abates the swollen part and pains which come by pricking thorns, with vinegar, it cleanses and heals tetters. The syrup of Horehound is excellent for cold rheums in the lungs of old people, and for those who are asthmatical or short-winded.

HOREHOUND (BLACK.)—(*Balota Nigra.*)

Descrip.—The Black Horehound grows taller, and is more branched than the white, with taller darker leaves, of a keen earthy smell. The flowers are found among the leaves, in two clusters on each side of the stalk, towards the fore part of it, each cluster on a common foot-stalk, and every flower in a wide-mouthed five-cornered large calyx of a red colour, being galated and labiated, they appear a little above the calyx : the seeds are in the bottom, small and oblong. The root is long, and spreads much.

Place.—It grows in bye-paths and in hedges.

Time.—It flowers in July.

Government and Virtues.—This is also under Mercury, but has not as much virtue as the former. The leaves and tops only are used. The leaves beaten with salt, and applied to the wound, cures the bites of mad dogs, and the juice, mixed with honey, cleanses foul ulcers. It is recommended as a remedy against hysteric and hypochondriac affections. It is an intense bitter, which bespeaks it to be a strengthener of weak stomachs ; it is endowed with the properties of a balsam, and is a powerful alterative, and capable of opening obstructions of any kind ; it is a promoter of the menses ; some praise it very much as a pectoral in coughs and shortness of breath ; but it is necessary to observe some caution, viz, that it ought only to be administered to gross phlegmatic people, and not to thin plethoric persons. The powder is good to kill worms.

HORSE-TAIL.—(*Equisetum,*)

Descrip.—There are many kinds of this herb, which are but knotted rushes, some with leaves and others without. The great Horse-tail at the first has heads resembling Asparagus, and afterwards grow to be hard, rough, hollow stalks, joined at sundry places at the top, a foot high, so made as if the lower parts were put into the upper, where grow on each side a bush of small long rush-like hard leaves, each part resembling a horse-tail. At the top of the stalks come forth small catkins, like those of trees. The root creeps in the ground, having joints at sundry places.

Place.—This herb grows in wet grounds.

Time.—It springs up in April, and its catkins in July; it seeds in August, and perishes in winter.

Government and Virtues.—This herb belongs to Saturn. It is very powerful to stop bleeding either inward or outward, the juice of the decoction being drunk, or the juice, decoction, or distilled water applied outwardly. It also stays laxes or fluxes in man or woman, and heals the inward ulcers, and the excoriation of the entrails, bladder, &c. It solders together the tops of green wounds, and cures all ruptures in children. The decoction, taken in wine, provokes urine, and helps the stone and strangury; and the distilled water drank two or three times a day, and a small quantity at a time, also eases the entrails or guts, and is effectual in a cough that comes by distillation from the head. The juice or distilled water, used as a warm fomentation is of service in inflammations, pustules or red wheals, and other breakings-out in the skin, and eases the swelling heat and inflammation of the fundament, or privy parts, in men or women.

HORSE-TONGUE.—(*Hippoglossum.*)

Descrip.—The root of this plant has a thick head, from which spring several hard white thready fibres. The stalks are about six or eight inches high, tough and flexible, it has large nervous leaves, pointed at the ends, thick and full of hard veins, rising sometimes alternately, and sometimes two opposite; on the middle of the upper part of each leaf, but in shape or make like the former; at the setting on of this grow one or two small mossy flowers, which are succeeded by round red berries.

Place.—It is cultivated only in botanic gardens.

Time.—It flowers in June and July.

Government and Virtues.—This plant is under Mars in Libra. It is heating and drying; and serviceable in disorders and suffocations of the womb, and hysteric fits, as likewise to hasten the birth, expel the afterbirth, and procure the catamenia: but it is very rarely used. There is a lesser species, more common, but it does not possess as many virtues. They are both very drying and astringent, and good for all sorts of fluxes, hemorrhages and bleedings, both inward and outward, and to strengthen the joints.

HOUND'S-TONGUE.—(*Cynoglossum Officinale.*)

Descrip.—The root of the Common Hound's-Tongue is thick and long, of a dark brown colour on the outside, and whitish within; the lower leaves are near a foot long, and two or three inches broad, pointed at the ends, and soft and woolly to the touch; the stalk rises two or three feet high, with shorter and narrower leaves, and having several flowers growing in clusters on the top, of a sullen red colour, appearing a little above the calyces they stand in; each flower is followed by four flat seeds, standing about the pistillium, like a shield or buckler. The whole plant has a fœtid smell.

Place.—It is found by hedges and road-sides.

Time.—It flowers in June and July, the root only is used.

Government and Virtues.—The plant is governed by Mercury. The root is cold, drying, and binding, it is useful in catarrhous defluxions upon the lungs, and to temper the sharpness of the blood; and, by consequence, excellent for all kinds of fluxes, and hemorrhages, as well as for gonorrhœa. It is likewise reckoned among the vulneraries, and helpful in scrofulous tumours, both taken inwardly and applied outwardly as a cataplasm. The leaves boiled in wine or water, and oil and salt, mollify and open the belly downwards. It also cures the bites of mad dogs, some of the leaves being applied to the wound; the leaves bruised, or the juice of them boiled in hog's-lard and applied, helps the falling away of the hair, which comes of hot and sharp humours; as also for any place that is scalded or burnt; the leaves bruised and laid to any green wound, heals it up quickly: the root baked under the embers, wrapped in paste and a suppository made thereof, and put into or applied to the fundament, does very effectually help the painful piles or hemorrhoids. The distilled water of the herbs and roots is a remedy for all the purposes aforesaid, to be used inwardly to drink, and outwardly to wash any sore place, for it heals all manner of wounds, and all the foul ulcers that arise by the venereal disease.

HOUSELEEK.—(*Sempervivum Tectorum.*)

Called also Sengren.

Descrip.—Houseleek has a great many thick, succulent leaves, set together in a round form, convex on the outside, flattish within, sharp-pointed, with hairy edges. The stalk grows about a foot high, reddish, with a succulent bark, covering a pithy substance, the leaves on the top are thinner and longer than those below ; from the top of these stalks rise reflected spikes of starry flowers made up of several narrow, sharp-pointed, reddish petals, set about a greenish hollow crown, which is afterwards enlarged into small, hollow, horned pods or seed-vessels, which inclose very small seed. The root is long, woody, and full of fibres.

Place.—It grows on the tops of houses in this country.

Time.—It flowers in July.

Government and Virtues.—It is an herb of Jupiter. Our ordinary Houseleek is good for the inward heats as well as outward, and in the eyes or other parts of the body; a posset made of the juice of Houseleek, is good in hot agues, for it cools and tempers the blood and spirits, and quenches thirst, and is also good to stay hot defluctions or sharp and salt rheums in the eyes, the juice being dropped into them, or into the ears, helps them. It helps also other fluxes of humours in the bowels, and the immoderate courses of women. It cools and restrains all violent inflammations, St. Anthony's fire, scalds and burns, the shingles, fretting ulcers, cankers, tetters, ringworms, and the like ; and much eases the pain of the gout proceeding from any hot cause. The juice also takes away warts and corns in the hands or feet, being bathed with it, and the skin and leaves laid on them afterwards. It eases head-ache, and distempered heat of the brain in frenzies, or through want of sleep, if applied to the temples and forehead. The leaves bruised and laid upon the crown of the head, stays bleeding at the nose quickly. The distilled water of the herb is profitable for all the diseases aforementioned. The leaves gently rubbed on the places stung by nettles or bees, will quickly remove the pain.

HOUSELEEK (SMALL.)—(*Sedum Minus.*)

Descrip.—The stalks of this *Sedum*, before they flower, are of a bluish green colour, beset, especially towards the tops, with fat, thick, succulent, blunt-pointed, round leaves; when they rise to flower, they have a few of the like leaves growing alternately on them ; they have on their tops small umbels, of white five-leaved flowers, which are succeeded by as many little horned seed-vessels, full of very small seed. The root is fibrous.

Place.—It grows upon old stone-walls and buildings.

Time.—It flowers in summer.

Government and Virtues.—The leaves and stalks are used, being much of the nature of the *Sempervivum Tectorum*, and, like that, cooling, and good for all kinds of inflammations. It is also under Jupiter.

HOUSELEEK (STONE-CROP.)—(*Sedum Minus Hæmatodes.*)

Descrip.—This *Sedum* in manner of growing is much like the last, the chief difference is, that the leaves are slenderer, sharp-pointed, flattish in the inside, and seeming only stuck on the stalks, the lower parts of them turning up a little. The flowers grow in umbels, being yellow, of six sharp-pointed leaves, with as many stamina and apices in the middle. The seeds grow in horned pods, as the other, and the root much alike; it grows upon old walls, and on the tops of houses, and is much more frequent than the last, flowering at the same time, and may very well supply its place, being cooling, and serviceable in many respects.

Government and Virtues.—The Houseleek is cooling and astringent, though not often given inwardly, yet is recommended by some to quench thirst in fevers, mixed with posset-drink; as also for heat and sharpness of urine. Three ounces of the juice of this and *Persicaria Maculata* boiled to the consistence of a julep, are recommended to allay the heat of inflammations.

HOUSELEEK (WALL PEPPER.)—(*Sedum Acre.*)

Descrip.—Wall-Pepper, or Small Stone-crop, has its stalks four or five inches long, wholly covered with thick, fat, triangular, blunt leaves, and on their tops a few star-like, five-leaved, yellow flowers, with several stamina in the middle. The root is small and fibrous.

Place.—It grows upon walls, and the tops of low houses.

Time.—It flowers in May and June. It has a very hot biting taste, from which it is often called Pepper-wort.

Government and Virtues.—This is sometimes sold for *Sedum Minus*, but its qualities are directly opposite to the other *Sedums*, and more apt to raise inflammations than cure them, it ought not to be put into the *Unguent Populeon*, nor into any other medicine for it. It is good for scurvy, both inwardly in decoctions, and outwardly bathed as a fomentation. It is also commended for king's-evil.

HOUSELEEK (WATER.)—(*Semper vivum Aquatica.*)

CALLED also Water Parsnep, and Crab's Claws.

Descrip.—It has sundry long narrow leaves, with sharp prickles on the edges, very sharp-pointed; the stalks on which the flowers grow do not rise as high as the leaves, but bear a forked head like crab's claws, out of which a white flower comes, consisting of three leaves, with yellowish threads in the middle; it takes root in the mud at the bottom of the water.

Place.—It grows in the fens in Lincolnshire.

Time.—It flowers from June until August.

Government and Virtues.—It is under the dominion of Venus, and is a great strengthener of the reins; it is good against St. Anthony's fire, and assuages swellings and inflammations in wounds; an ointment made of it is good to heal bruised kidneys. A dram of the powdered herb if taken every morning, stops the terms.

HYACINTH.—(*Hyacinthus.*)

CALLED Harebell, (*Campanula Rotundifolia,*) and Bluebell, (*Hyacinthus non Scriptus.*)

Descrip.—There are many species of Hyacinths. The following are reckoned the most beautiful: 1. The Hyacinth with the flowers alternate, and a little drooping; 2. The Hyacinth with irregular flowers, divided into six parts; 3. The campanulated Hyacinth, with the flowers cylindric at the base, and lightly divided at the edge into six segments; 4. The Hyacinth with a clustered conic tuft of flowers, or Peruvian Hyacinth; 5. The Hyacinth with funnel-shaped flowers, lightly divided into six parts at the rim, and swollen at the base; 6. The funnel-flowered Hyacinth, with the flowers swollen at the base, and lightly cut at the edge into six segments; 7. The Hyacinth with a clustered and rounded head of flowers, or grey starry Hyacinth; and 8. The scaly-rooted Hyacinth, or autumnal starry Hyacinth.

Place.—It is common under hedges, and in gardens.

Time.—It flowers in the beginning of May.

Government and Virtues.—The root is full of a slimy juice, a decoction of which operates by urine. Dried and reduced to powder, it is of a balsamic and styptic nature. Its virtues are little known, it will cure the whites. The fresh root is poisonous, and may be made into starch.

HYPOCISTUS.—(*Cytinus Hypocistis.*)

Descrip.—This plant does not derive its nourishment from the earth, but from some other plant to which it attaches itself. It is composed of a single leaf with a cylindric tube, and expanded or spreading border, which is divided into four obtuse coloured segments. It has a great number of broad, short, skinny films, by way of leaves, and the flowers grow at the top intermixed with them, and are large and beautiful.

Place.—It is a native of the Grecian Isle, but it is found on the roots of the Cistus shrub in this country

Time.— It flowers in the middle of summer.

Government and Virtues.—The berries abound with a large quantity of glutinous juice, which being evaporated over the fire till it acquires the consistence of Spanish juice, or liquorice, it is a good medicine in violent purgings, attended with bloody stools; likewise in excessive menstrual evacuations, and other hemorrhages. The best method of giving it is in an electuary made with conserve of roses.

HYSSOP.—(*Hyssopus Officinalis.*)

Descrip.—Our Common Hyssop grows to about a foot high or more, with many stalks which are square at first, but grow round as they come to flower. The leaves are long, narrow, and sharp-pointed, set two at a joint ; the flowers grow in long spikes, made of thin whorles, of pretty large blue leaves disposed all on one side of the stalk. They have a galea cut in two, and the labella divided into four segments ; the seeds are black, growing four together in the calyx. The root is thick, woody, and much divided; the whole plant is of a pretty strong aromatic smell.

Place.—It is sown in gardens, but is a native of Italy.

Time.—It flowers in August. The whole plant is used.

Government and Virtues.—The herb is Jupiter's, and the sign Cancer. It strengthens all the parts of the body under Cancer and Jupiter. Hyssop boiled with honey and rue, and drank, helps those that are troubled with coughs, shortness of breath, wheezing and rheumatic distillations upon the lungs ; taken with oxymel, it purges gross humours by stool ; with honey kills worms in the belly; and with fresh new figs bruised, helps to loosen the belly, and more forcibly if fleur-de-lys and cresses be added thereto. It amends and cherishes the native colour of the body spoiled by the yellow jaundice, and taken with figs and nitre, helps the dropsy and spleen ; being boiled with wine, it is good to wash inflammations, and takes away the blue and black marks that come by strokes, bruises or falls, if applied with warm water. It is an excellent medicine for the quinsy, or swelling in the throat, to wash and gargle it, when boiled with figs ; it helps to cure tooth-ache, if boiled in vinegar, and the mouth rinsed with it. The hot vapours of the decoction taken by a funnel in at the ears, eases the inflammations and singing noise of them. Being bruised with salt, honey, and cumin seed put to it, helps those stung by serpents. The head anointed with the oil, kills lice, takes away the itching of the head. It is good for falling sickness, expectorates tough phlegm, and is effectual in all cold griefs, or diseases of the chest and lungs, when taken as a syrup. The green herb bruised with sugar, quickly heals any cut or green wounds, if properly applied. The pains and discolourings of bruises, blows, and falls may be quickly removed by a cataplasm of the green leaves sewed in a linen cloth, and put on the place.

HYSSOP (HEDGE.)—*(Gratiola Officinalis.)*

Descrip.—Two or three sorts of this herb grow in this country, the description of two I shall give. The first is a smooth, low plant, not a foot high, very bitter in taste, with many square stalks, diversely branched from the top to the bottom, with divers joints, and two small leaves at each joint, broader at the bottom than they are at the end, a little dented at the edges, of a sad green colour, and full of veins. The flowers stand at the joints, of a fair purple colour, with some white spots in them, in fashion like those of dead nettles. The seed is small and yellow, and the roots spread much under ground. The second seldom grows half a foot high, sending up many small branches, whereon grow many small leaves set one against the other, somewhat broad, but very short. The leaves are like the flowers in fashion, but of a pale reddish colour. The seeds are small and yellowish. The root spreads like the other, neither will it yield to its fellow one ace of bitterness.

Place.—They grow in low wet grounds, and by the water-sides ; the last may be found on Hampstead Heath, and in the north of Scotland.

Time.—They flower and seed in June and July.

Government and Virtues.—They are herbs of Mars, and

are most violent purges, especially of choler and phlegm. It is not safe taking them inwardly, unless they be rectified by the art of the alchymist, and only the purity of them given; so used they may be very helpful for the dropsy, gout, and sciatica; outwardly used in ointments, they kill worms, the belly anointed with it; and are excellent to cleanse old and filthy ulcers. The best way is, to powder the root, and give it in small doses; in which form it is excellent against worms; it also removes all the mucous matter from the intestines, which harbours them. It approaches to the nature of the Fox-glove in qualities as well as in form; and should be very moderately used, as its powers are very great.

IVY-TREE.—(*Hedera Helix.*)

Descrip.—The leaves of Ivy run on the ground, and are angular and cornered; but when the stalks rise up, and are fastened to a wall or tree, they become rounder, ending in one point. The leaves of both are of a firm texture, and a dark green colour; those of the first full of small white veins, the branches insinuate themselves by short cirrhi into a wall, or the body of the tree that it climbs on. The flowers grow in corymbi or umbels, consisting of small six-leaved yellowish flowers, followed by round umbellicated berries, black when ripe, bearing several angular seeds.

Place.—It grows in woods upon the trees, and on stone walls of churches, houses, &c, and sometimes it grows alone.

Time.—It flowers in July; and the berries are ripe at Christmas, when they have felt winter frosts.

Government and Virtues.—It is under the dominion of Saturn. A pugil of the flowers, about a dram, drank twice a day in red wine, helps the lax and bloody-flux. It is an enemy to the nerves and sinews, being much taken inwardly, but very helpful to them being outwardly applied. The yellow berries are good against the jaundice, and a drunken surfeit, it helps the spitting of blood; the white berries taken inwardly, or applied outwardly kill worms in the belly. The berries prevent and heal the plague, by drinking the powder in wine, two or three days together, this drink breaks the stone, provokes urine and womens' courses; and the fresh leaves boiled in vinegar, and applied warm to the sides of those that are troubled with the spleen, ache or stitch in the sides, do give much ease; the same applied with rose-water and oil of roses to the temples and forehead, eases the long-standing head-ache. The fresh leaves boiled in wine, will cleanse old ulcers, if washed with it. It also quickly heals green wounds, and is effectual to cure all burns and scalds, and all kinds of exulcerations coming thereby, or by phlegm or humours in other parts of the body; the juice of the berries or leaves snuffed up the nose, purges the head and brain of thin rheum that makes defluxions into the eyes and nose, and cures the ulcers and stench therein; the same dropped into the ears, helps the old and running sores of them.

JESSAMINE.—(*Jasminum Officinale.*)

Descrip.—This tree or shrub shoots out long, slender, green twigs or branches, which must be supported, or else they hang down; they are clothed with long, pinnated leaves, made of several sharp-pointed pinnæ, set opposite to each other, with an odd one at the end, larger than the rest. The flowers come forth among the leaves, several together on a common foot-stalk; but each standing on a slender short one of its own, being longish tubes, spreading out at the top into five broad segments, standing in very short calyces, so that they easily fall off, when full blown: they are of a white colour, and a pleasant agreeable smell; each flower is succeeded by a berry, divided into two parts, but seldom coming to perfection here.

Place.—It is usually planted in gardens.

Time.—It flowers in June and July.

Government and Virtues.—Jessamine is a warm, cordial plant, governed by Jupiter in the sign Cancer. The flowers only are used. It warms the womb, and heals schirrhi therein, and facilitates the birth; it is useful for cough, difficulty of breathing, &c. The oil made by infusion of the flowers, is used for perfumes. It disperses crude humours, and is good for cold and catarrhous constitutions, but not for the hot. The oil is good also for hard and contracted limbs, it opens, warms, and softens the nerves and tendons, if used as a liniment to the parts, or taken in drink, or clysters. It removes diseases of the uterus, and is of service in pituitous colics. A poultice of the leaves, boiled in wine, dissolves cold swelling and hard tumours.

JEW'S-EAR.—(*Exidia Auricula Judæ.*)

Descrip.—A membranaceous fungus which grows in the shape of an ear, it is usually ash-coloured beneath, blackish on the top, and the taste is earthy and flat, but has no smell. It sticks close to the body of the tree, and has little or no pedicle.

Place.—It grows at the bottom of old elder-trees.

Time.—Mild damp weather is the most favourable.

Government and Virtues.—This is under Saturn, in the sign Virgo. It is astringent and drying, but is seldom taken inwardly, as it is dangerous. However, they are good for sore throats, quinsy, and swelling or inflammation of the tonsils.

JOHN'S WORT (ST.)—(*Hypericum Perforatum.*)

Descrip.—Common St. John's Wort shoots forth brownish, upright, hard, round stalks, two feet high, spreading many branches from the sides up to the tops of them, with two small leaves set one against another at every place, which are of a deep green colour, somewhat like the leaves of the lesser centaury, but narrow, and full of small holes in every leaf, which cannot be so well perceived, as when they are held up to the light; at the tops of the stalks and branches stand yellow flowers of five leaves each, with many yellow heads in the middle, which being bruised do yield a reddish juice like blood; after which do come small round heads, which contain small blackish seed, smelling like rosin. The root is hard and woody, with divers strings and fibres, of a brownish colour, which abides in the ground many years, shooting anew every spring.

Place.—This grows in shady woods and copses.

Time.—It flowers about Midsummer, and its seed is ripe in the latter end of July or August.

Government and Virtues.—It is under the celestial sign Leo, and the dominion of the Sun. St. John's Wort is aperative, detersive and diuretic, helpful against tertian and quartan agues, is alexipharmic, and destroys worms; it is an excellent vulnerary plant. A tincture of the flowers in spirit of wine, is commended against melancholy and madness. Outwardly, it is of great service in bruises, contusions, and wounds, especially in the nervous parts, if it be boiled in wine: made into an ointment, it opens obstructions, dissolves swellings, and closes up the lips of wounds. The decoction of the herb and flowers, especially the seed, being drunk in wine, with the juice of knot-gass, helps all manner of vomiting and spitting of blood, it is good also for those who cannot make water, and are bitten or stung by venomous creatures. Two drams of the seed made into powder, and drank in broth, expels choler or congealed blood in the stomach. The seed taken in warm wine, is recommended for sciatica, falling-sickness, and the palsy. It is vulnerary and abstersive, and opens obstructions and scours the urinary passages.

JULY FLOWER.—(*Motthiala Incona.*)

CALLED also Gilly-Flower and Wild-Pink.

Descrip.—This plant grows in almost every garden, and is so well known, that it needs little to be said about it. It has long, narrow, hoary, or whitish leaves, set alternately on the stalks; the flowers are large, of four leaves each, sometimes white, red, and frequently striped, of a pleasant, sweet scent. The seed is flat and round, growing in long hoary pods, divided in two parts in the middle.

Place.—It grows only in gardens.

Time.—It flowers about Midsummer.

Government and Virtues.—It is under Jupiter; all the species of Wild Pinks have the same medicinal virtues, and their quality is principally in the flowers, the purple kind possessing most; they are cordial and cephalic; good in faintings, head-aches, and other nervous disorder. A tincture of the flowers is the best medicine for these disorders.

JUNIPER-TREE.—(*Juniperis Communis.*)

Descrip.—This grows only to the size of a bush or shrub. The branches are thick-set, with narrow stiff leaves, of a bluish green colour, sharp and prickly at the ends; the flowers are small, mossy, and staminous; the berries round, green for the first year, and afterwards of a dark purple or black colour, each containing three-cornered seeds.

Place.—It grows upon the heaths of this country.

Time.—The berries are not ripe the first year, but continue green two summers and one winter before they are ripe, they are black, and ripen with the fall of the leaf.

Government and Virtues.—The berries are hot in the third degree, and dry in the first, being counter-poison, and a resister of the pestilence, and excellent against the bites of venomous beasts; it provokes urine, and is available in dysenteries and strangury. It is a remedy against dropsy, and brings down the terms, helps the fits of the mother, expels the wind, and strengthens the stomach. Indeed there is no better remedy for wind in any part of the body, or the colic, than the chymical oil drawn from the berries. They are good for cough, shortness of breath, consumption, pains in the belly, rupture, cramps, convulsions, and speedy delivery to pregnant women; they strengthen the brain, fortify the sight, by strengthening the nerves, are good for agues, help the gout and sciatica, and strengthen the limbs of the body; it is also a speedy remedy to such as have the scurvy, to rub the gums with; the berries stay all fluxes, help the hemorrhoids or piles, and kill worms in children: a lye made from the ashes of the wood, and the body bathed with it, cures the itch, scabs and leprosy; the berries break the stone, procure appetite when it is lost; and are good for all palsies, and falling-sickness.

KARSE (DITTANDER.)—(*Lepidium Sativum.*)

Descrip.—The root is fibrous, and the first leaves are very large, of a deep green, they stand on long slender foot-stalks; they are oblong, broad, and serrated at the edges: they are large near the base, and sharp-pointed. The stalk is round, firm, upright, considerably branched, and three feet high. The leaves grow at the joints, with long slender foot-stalks, like those from the roots, but are smaller and paler. The flowers stand in great numbers at the tops of numerous branches, and they are small and white. The seed is small and brown.

Place.—It grows in Essex, and the north, on damp plains.

Time.—It flowers in July.

Government and Virtues.—The taste is acrid. This is very successful for the sciatica, gout, and pains in the joints. The leaves bruised, and mixed with hogs' lard, and applied to the places affected will give relief; it also amends deformities or discolourings of the skin, and takes away scars, marks, scabs and burns. The juice is given in ale to procure women a speedy delivery in travail.

KIDNEYWORT.—(*Cotyledon Umbilicus.*)

Called also Wall Pennyroyal, or Penny-wort.

Descrip.—It has many thick, flat, and round leaves, all having a long foot-stalk, fastened underneath, about the middle of it, and a little unevenly weaved about the edges, of a pale green colour, and somewhat yellow on the upper side, from which rise one or more tender, smooth, hollow stalks half a foot high, with two or three small leaves thereon, usually long and divided at the edges; the tops are somewhat divided into long branches, bearing a number of flowers, set round about a long spike one above another, which are hollow and like a little bell, of a whitish green colour, after which come small heads containing very small brownish seed, which falling on the ground, will plentifully spring up before the winter, if it have moisture. The root is round, and most usually smooth, greyish without, and whitish within, having small fibres at the head of the root, and bottom of the stalk.

Place.—It grows plentifully on stone walls, rocks, and in stony places upon the ground, at the bottom of old trees.

Time.—It flowers in the beginning of May, the seed ripens soon afterwards, but the plant dies in winter.

Government and Virtues.—Venus challenges the herb under Libra. The juice or distilled water if drunk is good to cool inflammations and unnatural heats, a hot stomach, a hot liver, or the bowels ; the herb, juice, or distilled water applied outwardly, heals pimples, St. Anthony's fire, and other outward heats. It also helps sore kidneys, torn by the stone, or exulcerated within : it provokes urine, is available for dropsy, and helps to break the stone. Being used as a bath, or made into ointment, it cools the painful piles or hemorrhoidal veins. It gives ease to hot gout, the sciatica, and the inflammations and swellings in the testicles ; it helps the kernels or knots in the throat, called the king's evil ; the juice heals kibes and chilblains, if bathed with it, or anointed with ointment made from it, and some of the skin of the leaf upon them ; it is also used in green wounds to stay the blood, and to heal them quickly.

KNAPWEED (COMMON.)—(*Centaurea Scabiosa.*

Descrip.—It has broad dark green leaves, rising from the root, dented at the edges, sometimes rent on both sides in two or three places, and somewhat hairy ; among which rises a long round stalk, four or five feet high, divided into many branches, at the tops whereof stand great scaly green heads, and from the middle of them thrust forth a number of dark purplish red thrumbs or threads, which after they are withered and past, there are found divers black seeds, lying in a great deal of down, somewhat like unto thistle-seed, but smaller ; the root is white, hard and woody, with fibres, which perish not, but abide with leaves thereon, during winter, shooting afresh in spring.

Place.—It grows in moist places, about borders, hedges and waste grounds in meadows, almost every where.

Time.—It flowers in June, the seed ripens shortly after.

Government and Virtues.—Saturn owns this herb. It is good to stay fluxes of blood both of the mouth and nose, other outward parts, and the veins that are broken inwardly, as also fluxes of the belly; it stays distillation of the thin and sharp humours from the head upon the stomach and lungs; it is good for those who are bruised by any fall, blows, or otherwise, by drinking a decoction of the herb roots in wine, and applying the same outwardly to the place. It is good in all running sores, cancerous and fistulous, drying up the moisture, and healing them up gently, without sharpness; it does the same to running sores or scabs of the head or other parts. It is of especial use for sore throat, swelling of uvula and jaws, and excellently good to stay bleeding, and heal up all green wounds.

KNAPWORT HARSHWEED.—(*Sagmen Jaceoides.*)

Descrip.—This much resembles the last. The root has innumerable thick, long, and brown fibres. The stalk is robust, brown, two and a half feet in height, variously and irregularly branched. The leaves are large, and some of them are entire; others divided to the rib into many parts, of a deep green, and the flowers stand at the tops of the branches; they grow out of green heads; they are large, and of a lively purple. The seeds are large and brown.

Place.—It is common in hilly pastures.

Time.—It flowers in July.

Government and Virtues.—This is under Saturn. It is an astringent, and is best given in decoction; but, as the quantity to have any effect, must be large, it is but seldom used. Inwardly it is opening, attenuating and healing, good to cleanse the lungs of tartareous humours, and helpful against coughs, asthma, difficulty of breathing, and cold distempers; as a cephalic, it is good for diseases of the head and nerves. Outwardly, the bruised herb is famous for taking away black and blue marks out of the skin.

KNOT GRASS.—(*Illecebrum Verticillatum.*)

Descrip.—The stalks of this plant incline pretty much to the earth, being smooth and finely channelled, slender, and branched, full of knots and joints, at which grow long oval sharp-pointed leaves, set alternately on short footstalks. Some are broader and more oval than others. At the joints with the leaves, grow several small staminous blinking flowers; sometimes of a white, and sometimes of a reddish colour; a small black seed grows in each. The root is long and large, and strikes deep in the earth.

Place.—It grows in the way-sides and foot-paths in fields.

Time.—It springs up late in spring, but dies in winter.

Government and Virtues.—Saturn owns this herb. The juice is effectual to stay bleeding at the mouth, if drank in red wine, and the bleeding of the nose, if applied to the forehead or temples. It will allay the heat of the blood and stomach, and stay any flux of blood and humours, as laxes, bloody-flux, womens' courses, and running of the reins. It provokes urine, and helps the strangury; it expels the stone in the kidneys and bladder, a dram of the powdered herb being taken in wine for some days together, boiled in wine and drank, it is profitable for those bitten or stung by venomous creatures, and to stay all defluctions of rheumatic humours upon the stomach, quiets inward pains that arise from heat, sharpness and corruption of blood and choler. The distilled water taken by itself, or with the powdered herb, is effectual for all the purposes beforementioned. It also cleanses foul ulcers, cancers, sores, imposthumes, and green and fresh wounds, and speedily heals them. The juice dropped into the ears, will cleanse all runnings in them. It is very prevalent for the premises; as also for broken joints and ruptures.

LADIES MANTLE.—*(Alchemilla Vulgaris.)*

Descrip.—It has many leaves rising from the root, standing upon long hairy foot-stalks, being almost round, and a little cut on the edges, into eight or ten parts, making it seem like a star, with so many corners and points, and dented round about, of a light green colour, somewhat hard in handling, and as it were folded at first, and then crumpled in divers places, and a little hairy, as the stalk is also, which rises up among them to the height of two or three feet; it is so weak that it cannot stand upright, but bends to the ground, divided at the top into two or three small branches, with yellowish green heads, and flowers of a whitish colour breaking out of them; which being past, there comes a yellowish seed like poppy-seed: the root is long and black, with many strings and fibres thereat.

Place.—It grows in pastures and wood-sides in Hertfordshire, Wiltshire, Kent, and other parts of this country

Time.—It flowers in May and June, and is always green.

Government and Virtues.—Venus claims this herb. It is proper for those wounds that have inflammations, and is effectual to stay bleedings, vomitings, and fluxes of all sorts, bruises by falls or otherwise, and helps ruptures, and women who have over-flagging breasts, causing them to grow less and hard, both when drank and outwardly applied; the distilled water drank for twenty days together, helps conception, and to retain the birth, if the woman do sometimes sit in a bath made of the decoction of the herb. It is also a good wound-herb both inwardly and outwardly, by drinking a decoction, or bathing and fomenting, for it dries up the humidity of the sores, and heals inflammation. It draws the corruption from, and heals green wounds; it cures all old sores, though fistulous and hollow.

LADY'S SMOCK.—(*Cardamine Pratensis.*)

Called also Cuckoo Flower.

Descrip.—The root is composed of many small white threads, from whence spring up divers long stalks of winged leaves, consisting of round, tender, dark green leaves, set one against another upon a middle rib, the greatest being at the end, amongst which rise up divers tender, weak, round, green stalks, somewhat streaked, with longer and smaller leaves upon them; on the tops of which stand flowers, almost like the stock gilliflowers, but rounder, and not so long, of a blushing white colour; the seed is reddish, and grows to small bunches, being of a sharp biting taste, and so is the herb.

Place.—They grow in wet places, on brook-sides.

Time.—They flower in April and May, and the lower leaves continue green all the winter.

Government and Virtues.—They are under the dominion of the Moon, and very little inferior to water-cresses in all their operations; they are good for the scurvy, provoke urine, break the stone, and effectually warm a cold and weak stomach, restore lost appetite, and help digestion.

LANG DE BŒUF.—(*Helminthia Echioides.*)

Called also Ox-Tongue.

Descrip.—A species of the Bugloss and Borage. It rises from a thick brown root, and sends forth large, rough, hairy leaves, half a foot long, narrow and sharp-pointed. The stalks rise to the height of two or three feet, full of short stiff hairs, on which grow long narrow leaves set on without foo t-stalks; the flowers grow several together at the top of the branches, in long rough calyces, of a single leaf cut into five round partitions, of a purple colour at first, and turning to a bright blue as they stand, and are succeeded by four-cornered rough seed.

Place.—It grows in gardens, and wild in the fields.

Time.—It flowers in June and July.

Government and Virtues.—It is under Jupiter. Its virtues are best preserved in a conserve of the flowers. A decoction of the whole plant is deobstruent, and good to purge melancholy, and for that purpose the tops are frequently put into wine and cool tankards; they are likewise alexipharmic, and good in malignant fevers.

LAVENDER.—(*Lavandula Spica.*)

Descrip.—The common Lavender is a shrubby plant, having a great many woody branches, thick-set with long hoary narrow leaves, two at a joint, which are round-pointed and broadest at the end; from among these spring several square stalks, having but few leaves upon them, and those narrower than the lower, bearing long spikes, of blue galeated and labiated flowers, set in hoary calyces.

Place.—It is a native of France and Spain, where it grows wild, but is cultivated with us only in gardens.

Time.—It flowers in July.

Government and Virtues.—Mercury owns this herb. It is of especial use in pains of the head and brain which proceed from cold, apoplexy, falling-sickness, the dropsy, or sluggish malady, cramps, convulsions, palsies, and often faintings. It strengthens the stomach, and frees the liver and spleen from obstructions, provokes womens' courses, and expels the dead child and afterbirth. The flowers if steeped in wine help those to make water that are stopped, or troubled with the wind or colic, if the place be bathed therewith. A decoction made of the flowers of Lavender, Horehound, Fennel and Asparagus-root, and a little Cinnamon is profitable to help falling-sickness, and the giddiness or turning of the brain: to gargle the mouth with a decoction thereof, is good against the tooth-ache. Two spoonfuls of the distilled water of the flowers help them that have lost their voice, the tremblings and passions of the heart, and fainting and swoonings, applied to the temples or nostrils, to be smelt unto, but it is not safe to use it where the body is replete with blood and humours, because of the hot and subtle spirit wherewith it is possessed. The oil used with the Oil of Spike, is of a fierce and piercing quality, and ought to be carefully used, a very few drops being sufficient for inward or outward maladies

LAVENDER (COTTON.)—(*Lavandula Tæmina.*)

Descrip.—This is a shrubby plant, with a roundish leaf, holding its leaves all the winter. It has many woody, brittle, hoary stalks, beset with long, white, hoary leaves, that appear four-square, resembling the leaves of our common heath ; of a strong though not unpleasant scent, and a bitter taste. On the tops of the branches stand long stalks, each bearing a single naked flower, made up only of a thrum of small yellow fistular five-cornered flosculi, without any border of petala; standing together in a scaly calyx. The seed is small, longish, and striated ; the root firm, hard, and durable, divided into several fibrous branches.

Place.—It is a native of Italy, but is planted in our gardens, where it serves for borders and edgings.

Time.—It flowers in July and August.

Government and Virtues.—The leaves, and sometimes the flowers are used ; it destroys worms, the leaves and flowers being boiled in milk, and taken fasting ; it is an antidote for all sorts of poison, and the bites and stings of venomous creatures, and good against obstructions of the liver, the jaundice, and to promote the menses. A dram of the powdered leaves taken every morning fasting, stops the running of the reins in men, and whites in women. The seed beaten into powder, and taken as worm-seed, kills the worms, not only in children, but also in people of riper years; the herb acts the same, being steeped in milk, and the milk drank ; the body bathed with a decoction of it, helps scabs and the itch. It is under Mercury.

LAUREL (EVERGREEN, OR SPURGE.)—(*Daphne Laureola.*)

Descrip.—This is a low shrub, seldom growing above two or three feet high, with a woody stem about a finger thick, covered with an ash-coloured bark ; it is divided towards the top into several branches, clothed with thick, long, smooth, and shining green leaves, which are found at the tops of the branches. The flowers grow among these. They are small, considered singly, of a sad, yellowish green colour, and unpleasant smell. The seed is roundish.

Place.—It grows wild in the woods and hedges.

Time.—It flowers in March, the fruit is ripe in August.

Virtues.—Very happy effects have been produced by the use of this plant in rheumatic fevers. It is a rough purgative, and is an efficacious medicine for worms, but it requires some caution in the administration, and might in unskilful hands, be productive of dangerous consequences. The whole plant has the same qualities, but the bark is the strongest, and a dose of not more than ten grains should be given. An infusion of the leaves is a good emetic and purgative, and cures the dropsy. Dried and reduced to powder, they are useful in the venereal disease.

LENTILS.—*(Ervum Lens.)*

Descrip.—This plant has many long-winged leaves, consisting of many small oval pinnæ, set opposite, with claspers at the end of the leaf. The flowers are small and white, standing for the most part singly on a long foot-stalk, and are succeeded by short flattish pods, containing two round seeds less than tares, and flatter.

Place.—They grow in fields in all parts of England.

Time.—They flower in May, and the seed is ripe in July.

Government and Virtues.—They are under Venus. The flour or meal of them is goood as emollient cataplasms, and stops fluxes. Eaten with their skins they bind the body, and stop looseness, but the liquid they are boiled in loosens the belly; the flower of them may be used outwardly in cataplasms for the same purposes as bean-flower.

LETTUCE (COMMON GARDEN.)—*(Lactuca Sativa.)*

Government and Virtues.—The Moon owns it. The juice mixed or boiled with oil of roses, applied to the forehead and temples, procures sleep, and cures the head-ache proceeding from a hot cause; being eaten boiled, it helps to loosen the belly. It helps digestion, quenches thirst, increases milk in nurses, especially griping pains in the stomach or bowels that come of choler. It abates bodily lust, represses venereous dreams, being outwardly applied to the testicles with a little camphire. Applied in the same manner to the region of the heart, liver or reins, or by bathing the said place with the juice of distilled water, wherein some white sanders, or red roses are put: also it not only represses the heat and inflammations therein, but comforts and strengthens those parts; and also tempers the heat of urine. The seed or distilled water works the same effects in all things; but the use is forbidden to those who spit blood, or are imperfect in their lungs.

LETTUCE (GREAT WILD.)—(*Lactuca Virosa.*)

Descrip.—This plant grows to five or six feet high. The stalk is thick, round, very upright, branched and of a reddish yellow, or rather brown. The leaves at the bottom are very large, a foot long, and five inches broad, of a fresh fine green; those higher up the stalk are smaller, they are deeply indented at the edges; and the innumerable little flowers with which its top and branches are crowned, are perfectly like those of the common Lettuce of the gardens, and are of a light yellow. From whatever the plant is wounded, there flows out a milky juice, which has the smell of opium, and its hot bitter taste.

Place.—It grows in our hedges, and ditch-sides.

Time.—It has the greatest vigour in the month of April.

Government and Virtues.—It is under the government of Mars. The smell and taste is much like opium. A syrup made from a strong infusion of it, is an excellent anodyne; it eases the most violent pains of the colic, and other disorders, and gently disposes the patient to sleep, for it has none of the violent effects of other opiates. The best way of giving it is, to dry the juice which runs from the roots by incision; this dissolves freely in mountain wine, if one ounce be put into a gallon of wine there is produced an excellent quieting medicine, a teaspoonful of which is a dose in a glass of water. This takes off spasms, convulsions, stays fluxes of all kinds proceeding from irritation.

LIGHTWORT (SEA.)—(*Pneumaria Maritima.*)

Descrip.—This is an elegant plant. It is of the Lungwort species, the root is long, thick, and white, and is furnished with many fibres. The first leaves are numerous, and large, broad, and sharp-pointed, rough and of a beautiful green colour, with numerous branches, about a yard high. The flowers are of a beautiful blue, and stand all over the tops of the stalks and branches; the seed is dark.

Place.—It grows in the pastures of Kent and Essex.

Time.—It flowers in July.

Government and Virtues.—It is a plant of Jupiter, and has considerable virtues. It is balsamic and astringent, and is good against coughs. It may be used with success for the whites, and the powdered root is good for restraining bloody stools, and the piles, &c.

LILY OF THE VALLEY.—*(Convalearia Majalis.)*

CALLED also May Lily.

Descrip.—It has a slender creeping root that runs upon the surface of the earth, shooting out two or three leaves, oblong, round, and full of nerves, five or six inches long, from the middle of which rises a stalk about a span high, angular and slender; bearing six or seven flowers in a spike, one above another, and looking all one way; they are small, hollow, and round, of one leaf cut into five parts, of a pleasant grateful scent, which are succeeded by small round red berries, like those of Asparagus.

Place.—It grows on heaths and other open situations.

Time.—It flowers in May, the seed ripens in September.

Government and Virtues.—It is under the dominion of Mercury, and therefore strengthens the brain. The distilled water dropped into the eyes helps inflammation there. The spirit of the flowers distilled in wine, restores speech, helps the palsy, and is good in the apoplexy, and comforts the heart and vital spirits. It is also of service in disorders of the head and nerves, such as epilepsy, vertigo, and convulsions of all kinds, swimming in the head; and are made use of in errhines and cephalic snuff.

LILY (WATER.)—*(Nymphæa Odorata.)*

Descrip.—The white Lily has very large and thick dark green leaves lying on the water, sustained by long and thick foot-stalks, that rise from a great, thick, round, and tuberous black root, spongy or loose, with many knobs thereon, like eyes, and whitish within; from which rise similar stalks, sustaining one great flower thereon, green on the outside, but as white as snow within, consisting of divers rows of long and somewhat thick and narrow leaves, smaller and thinner the more inward they be, encompassing a head with many yellow threads or thrums in the middle; where, after they are past, stand round like poppy-heads, full of broad, oily, bitter seed. The yellow kind is different only in having fewer leaves on the flowers, and greater and more shining seed, and a whitish root, within and without. The roots of both are somewhat sweet.

Place.—They grow in pools, and standing water, and in slow running rivers in different parts of this country.

Time.—They flower mostly about the end of May, and the seed is ripe in August.

Government and Virtues.—It is under the dominion of the Moon, and therefore cools and moistens like the former. The leaves and flowers are cold and moist, but the roots and seeds are cold and dry; the leaves, both inward and outward are good for agues; the syrup of the flowers procures rest, and settles the brain of frantic persons. The seed as well as the root is effectual to stay fluxes of blood or humours, either of wounds or of the belly; but the roots are most used, and are more effectual to restrain all fluxes in man or woman; also running of the reins, and passing away of the seed when one is asleep, but the frequent use extinguishes venereous actions. The root will also cool hot urine if boiled in wine and water, and the decoction drank. The distilled water of the flowers is effectual for all the diseases aforesaid, both inwardly and outwardly; and will also take away freckles, spots, sunburn, and morphew from the face and other parts of the body. The oil of the flowers cools hot tumours, eases pains, and helps sores.

LILLY (WHITE GARDEN.)—(*Lilium Candidum.*)

Descrip.—This is a very common plant, having a round scaly root, and a stalk three or four feet high, with long, narrow, thick leaves, and on the top several large sweet, white flowers, with several yellow apices in the middle.

Place.—It grows in gardens.

Time.—It flowers in June.

Government and Virtues.—The flowers and roots are used, but chiefly in external applications; they are emollient, suppling and anodyne, good to dissolve and ripen hard tumours and swellings, and to break imposthumations. They are under the dominion of the Moon, and are good antidotes for poison; they are excellent in pestilential fevers, the roots being bruised and boiled in wine, and the decoction drank. The juice, being baked with barley-meal, and eaten, is good for the dropsy; and ointment made of the roots and hogs'-grease, is excellent for scald-heads, it unites the sinews when they are cut, and cleanses ulcers. The root boiled in any convenient decoction, gives delivery to women in travail, and expels the afterbirth, roasted, the root mixed with hog's-grease, makes a good poultice to ripen and break plague-sores. This ointment is good for swellings in the privities, and cures burns and scalds without fear, and trimly deck a blank place with hair.

LIME TREE.—(*Tilia.*)

CALLED also Linden Tree.

Descrip.—This tree is well known, having a handsome body with a smooth bark, spreading its branches round in a regular manner; the leaves are broad and roundish, with a sharp point, serrated about the edges, at the foot of these, in the summer, spring out thin leafy ligulas, of a yellow colour, from the middle of the back ribs of which rise stalks about an inch long, divided into four or five shorter ones, each bearing a yellow, five-leaved, sweet flower, full of stamina, after which comes a small fruit as big as a pea.

Place.—It grows in parks and gentlemen's gardens.

Time.—It flowers in July.

Government and Virtues.—Jupiter governs the Lime-tree. The flowers are the only parts used, and are a good cephalic and nervine, excellent for apoplexy, epilepsy, vertigo, and palpitation of the heart. They are put into the *aqua pœon. comp.* and the spirit *lavandulæ.* The *aqua florum tiliæ* takes its name from them.

LIQUORICE.—(*Glycyrrhiza Glabra.*)

Descrip.—Our English Liquorice rises up with divers woody stalks, whereon are set, at several distances, many narrow, long, green leaves, set together on both sides of the stalk, and an odd one at the end, very well resembling a young ash tree, sprung up from the seed. This by many years continuance in a place without removing, and not else, will bring forth flowers, many standing together spike fashion, one above another upon the stalk, of the form of pea-blossoms, but of a very pale blue colour, which turn into long, somewhat flat and smooth pods, wherein is contained the seed, round and hard; the roots run very deep into the ground, with divers other small roots and fibres growing with them, and shoot out suckers from them in roots all about, whereby it is much increased, of a brownish colour on the outside, and yellow within.

Place.—It is planted in gardens and fields and divers places of this country, and a good profit is made from it.

Time.—It flowers in August.

Government and Virtues.—It is under the dominion of Mercury. Boiled in water, with some Maiden-head and figs, makes a good drink for those who have a dry cough or hoarseness, wheezing or shortness of breath, and for all the pains of the breasts and lungs, phthisic or consumptions caused by the distillation of salt humours on them. It is also good for pains of the reins, the strangury, and the heat of urine: the fine powder of the root blown into the eyes through a quill of those that have a pin and web, or rheumatic distillations in them, does cleanse and help them; the juice is effectual in all the diseases of the breast and lungs, the reins and bladder, as the decoction. The juice distilled in rose-water, with some gum tragacanth, is a fine medicine for hoarseness, wheezing, &c. The root of this plant is deservedly in great esteem, and can hardly be said so be an improper ingredient in any composition of whatever intention. It is a great sweetener of the blood, detersive, and at the same time softening and emollient, and therefore balsamic. It is good for dropsy, and allays thirst. It is an excellent pectoral, and the juice prepared to a proper consistence, is the best form, and excels Spanish juice. A strong decoction of the root given to children loosens the bowels, and takes off feverish heats which attend costiveness. It is likewise a corrector of cathartics. The juice, or extract is made by boiling the fresh roots in water, straining the decoction, and when the impurities have subsided, evaporating it over a gentle heat till it will no longer stick to the fingers. It is better to cut the roots into small pieces before boiling them, as the virtues will by that means be better extracted. A pound of Liquorice-root boiled in three pints down to one quart will be found the best for all purposes. The juice is the most effectual, and may be obtained by squeezing the roots between two rollers. When made with due care, it is exceedingly sweet, of a much more agreeable taste than the root itself, and has an agreeable smell. Put into boiling water, it totally dissolves without depositing any sediment.

LIVERWORT (COMMON.)—*(Hepatica.)*

Descrip.—Common Liverwort grows close, and spreads much upon the ground in moist and shady places, with many small green leaves, or rather, as it were, sticking flat to one another, very unevenly cut in on the edges, and crumpled; from among which arise small slender stalks, an inch or two high, bearing small star-like flowers at the top. The roots are very fine and small.

Place.—It grows plentifully in Nottingham-Park, and on Rapford Lings, and in most dry barren places.

Time.—It is in its prime in October and November.

Government and Virtues.—It is under the dominion of Jupiter, and under the sign Cancer. It is a singular good herb for all diseases of the liver, both to cool and cleanse it, and helps inflammations in any part, and the yellow jaundice; being bruised and boiled in small beer, if drank, it cools the heat of the liver and kidneys, and helps the running of the reins in men, and the whites in women, it is a good remedy to stay the spreading of tetters, ringworm, and other fretting or running sores and scabs; and is an excellent remedy for such as have livers that are corrupted by surfeits, which cause their bodies to break out: for it fortifies and strengthens the liver exceedingly. It is recommended for the bites of mad-dogs, if used in the following manner: take nine or ten ounces of blood from the body for four mornings successively, and give the patient the following in warm cow's milk: take ash-coloured Liverwort, half an ounce, black pepper, two drams, both finely powdered, mixed, and divided into four equal parts.

Having first taken the four doses, let the person, for one month, bathe two or three times a day in the sea, and the longer he stays in the better.

LOOSESTRIFE.—(*Lysimachia.*)

CALLED also Yellow Willow Herb.

Descrip.—The Loosestrife has several brown hairy stalks, two feet high or more, having sometimes three or four, but oftener only two leaves at a joint, which are of a yellowish green colour, hairy underneath, and darker, about three inches long, and an inch broad in the middle, growing narrower at both ends. The flowers stand several together on the tops of the branches, consisting of a single leaf divided into five parts, with several stamina in the middle, of a yellow green colour. The seed-vessels are round, and parted in two, containing small seed; the root is long and slender, and creeps upon the surface of the earth.

Place.—It grows in watery places, and by river-sides.

Time.—It flowers from June to August.

Government and Virtues.—This herb is good for all manner of bleeding at the mouth or nose; for wounds, and all fluxes of the belly, and the bloody-flux, given either to drink, or else taken by clyster; it stays also the abundance of womens' courses; it is good for green wounds, to stay the bleeding, and quickly closes up the lips of the wound.

if the herb be bruised and the juice only applied. It is good as a gargle for sore-throats. The smoke drives away flies and gnats, when they are troublesome.

LOVAGE.—(*Ligusticum Levisticum.*)

Descrip.—It has many long and great stalks, of large winged leaves, divided into many parts, every leaf being cut about the edges, broadest forward, and smallest at the stalk, of a sad green colour, smooth, and shining, from among which rise sundry strong, hollow green stalks, five or six, sometimes seven or eight feet hight, full of joints, but lesser leaves set on them than grow below; and with them towards the tops come forth large branches, bearing at their tops large umbels of yellow flowers, and after them flat brownish seed. The root grows thick, great and deep, spreading much, and enduring long, of a brownish colour on the outside, and whitish within. The whole plant and every part of it smells strong and aromatically.

Place.—It is planted in gardens, where it grows large.

Time.—It flowers in July, and seeds in August.

Government and Virtues.—It is an herb of the Sun, under the sign Taurus. It opens, cures, and digests humours, and provokes womens' courses and urine. Half a dram at a time of the dried root in powder taken in wine, warms a cold stomach, helps digestion, and consumes all raw and superfluous moisture therein; eases all inward gripings and pains, dissolves wind, and resists poison and infection. The decoction of the herb is a remedy for ague, and pains of the body and bowels which proceed from cold. The seed is effectual for all the purposes aforesaid, except the last, and works more powerfully. The distilled water helps the quinsy in the throat, if the throat and mouth be gargled with it, and it helps the pleurisy, if drank three or four times. It takes away the redness and dimness of the eyes if dropped into them; it removes spots and freckles from the face. The leaves bruised, and fried in hog's-lard, and laid hot to any blotch or boil, will quickly break it.

LUNGWORT.—(*Pulmonaria Officinalis.*)

Descrip.—This is a kind of moss that grows on oak and beech trees, with broad, greyish, rough leaves, diversely folded, crumpled, and gashed on the edges, some are spotted on the upper side. It never bears any stalk or flower.

Government and Virtues.—Jupiter owns this herb. It

is of great use in diseases of the lungs, and for coughs, wheezings, and shortness of breath, which it cures. It is profitable to put into lotions to stay the moist humours that flow to ulcers, and hinder their healing, as also to wash ulcers in the privy parts. It is drying and binding, good to stop inward bleeding, and the too great flux of the menses. It is good for consumptions and disorders of the breast, boiling it in pectoral drinks, and making syrups of it. It is commended as a remedy against yellow-jaundice.

LUPINE.—*(Lupinus.)*

Descrip.—The white Lupine has a hairy stalk, on which grow digitated leaves, set in a round compass, upon long foot-stalks, consisting of nine parts, narrow near the stalk, and ending in an obtuse point, soft and hairy. The flowers grow in verticillated spikes on the tops of the branches, in shape of pea-blossoms, of a white colour, and are succeeded by upright flat hairy large pods, including three or four flat white seeds. There are several kinds of Lupines: the great white Lupine; the spotted white Lupine; the blue Lupine, because it has blue flowers, and the small blue Lupine.

Place.—They are sown every year in gardens.

Time.—They flower in June, and the seed ripens in July.

Government and Virtues.—They are governed by Mars in Aries. The seeds are somewhat bitter in taste, opening and cleansing, good to destroy worms, to bring down the menses, and expel the birth and secundines. Outwardly they are used against deformities of the skin, scabby ulcers, scald heads, and other cutaneous distempers.

MADDER.—*(Rubia Tinctorum.)*

Descrip.—The roots of Madder are thick, round, and much branched, of a reddish colour, clear and transparent, having a small slender hard tough string in the middle, of a sweetish taste, with a little bitterness; from these spring many square rough weak stalks, full of joints, about which are set five or six long sharp-pointed leaves, that are broadest in the middle, and narrow at both ends, rough almost to prickliness. The flowers grow in long spikes, coming forth at the joints with the leaves, small and yellow, of one leaf cut into four segments, each succeeded by two small moist blackish berries, containing two round umbilicated seeds.

Place.—It is cultivated in many parts of England.

Time.—The flowers appear in July.

Government and Virtues.—It is an herb of Mars. The roots are the only parts used for medicinal purposes, and they have a weak, bitterish, and somewhat astringent taste. A strong decoction is diuretic and good in obstructions of the viscera. It disperses congealed blood, cures the jaundice, and is useful in dropsy. It also cleanses the kidneys and urinary organs from gravel; it is also valuable for the palsy and sciatica, and effectual for bruises inward and outward, and is therefore much used in vulnerary drinks. The root is good for all the aforesaid purposes, if boiled in wine or water, as the case requires, and some honey and sugar put in afterwards. The seed taken in vinegar and honey, helps the swelling and hardness of the spleen. The decoction of the leaves and branches is a good fomentation to bring down the courses. The leaves and roots beaten and applied to any part that is discoloured with freckles, morphew, the white scurf, or any such deformity of the skin, cleanses thoroughly, and takes them away.

MAIDENHAIR (COMMON.)—(*Adiantum Capillus Veneris.*)

Descrip.—From a number of hard black fibres, grow a a number of blackish shining brittle stalks, hardly a span long, in many not half so long; they are set on each side very thick, with small round dark green leaves, and spotted on the back of them like a fern.

Place.—It grows plentifully about rock-holes, and upon stone walls in the western parts, and in Kent. It is also found by the sides of springs and wells; in moist and shady places; and is always green.

Time.—The seed appears in August and September..

Government and Virtues.—This and all other Maidenhairs are under Mercury. This is a good remedy for coughs, asthmas, pleurisy, &c., and on account of its being a gentle diuretic, also, in the jaundice, gravel, and other impurities of the kidneys. All the Maidenhairs should be used green, and in conjunction with other ingredients, because their virtues are weak.

MAIDENHAIR (GOLDEN.)—(*Adiantum Aureum.*)

Descrip.—This is a large kind of moss, with a stalk three or four inches high, whose lower part is covered with small, short, hard, and stiff brown leaves; the upper part is bare to the top, on which grows a seed-vessel, covered with a woolly, pointed reddish-yellow cap, which falls of as the head grows ripe. The root is small and stringy.

Place.—It grows on heathy barren and boggy ground, and frequently on old ant-hills.

Virtues.—This is rarely used, but it is very good to prevent the falling off of the hair, and to make it grow thick, being boiled in water or lye, and the head washed with it.

MAIDENHAIR (WHITE.)—(*Asplenium Ruta Muraria.*)

CALLED also Wall Rue.

Descrip.—This is a small low plant, growing about two or three inches high, its slender stalks being of a whitish colour, whereon grow a few small roundish stiff leaves, crenated a little about the edges, of a whitish-green colour above, covered underneath, when come to its full growth, with brown dusty seed.

Place.—It grows on old stone walls and buildings, its little fibrous root abiding several years.

Virtues.—This is used in pectoral decoctions, and diuretic apozems. The decoction being drunk, helps those that are troubled with cough, shortness of breath, yellow-jaundice, diseases of the spleen, stopping of the urine, and helps to break the stone in the kidneys. It provokes womens' courses, and stays both bleeding and fluxes of the stomach and belly, especially when the herb is dry; for being green it loosens the belly, and voids choler and phlegm from the stomach and liver; it cleanses the lungs, and by rectifying the blood, causes a good colour to the whole body. The herb boiled in oil of camomile, dissolves knots, allays swellings, and drys up moist ulcers. The lye made thereof is singularly good to cleanse the head from scurf, and from dry and running sores; stays the shedding or falling of the hair, and causes it to grow thick, fair, and well-coloured; for which purpose boil it in wine, putting some smallage-seed thereto, and afterwards some oil.

MALLOWS (COMMON.)—(*Malva Sylvestris.*)

Descrip.—The common Mallow grows three or four feet high. The stalk is round, thick, and strong. The leaves are roundish, but indented and divided at the edges; and the flowers are numerous, large, and red. The seeds are flattish and round. The root is long and white, of a firm texture, and has no disagreeable taste.

Place.—It grows every where by way-sides.

Time.—It flowers in May and June.

Government and Virtues.—All the Mallows are under Venus. The whole plant is used, but the root has most virtue. The leaves dried or fresh, are put into decoctions for clysters; the root may be dried, but it is best fresh, if chosen when there are only leaves growing from it, not a stalk. When boiled in water, the strong decoction is good if drank, to provoke urine, take off the strangury, sharp humours of the bowels, and the gravel. Sweetened with syrup of violets, it cures the dysury or pain of making water with heat; for which a conserve of Mallow flowers is good, or a syrup of the juice, or a decoction of turnips, or willow, or lime-tree ashes, or the syrup of ground-ivy. There is a smaller kind of Mallow, with white flowers, which lies flat on the ground. It has a more pleasant taste, with all the virtues of the foregoing. A tea made of the roots and tops is agreeable, and good to promote urine.

MALLOWS (COMMON MARSH.)—(*Althæa Officinalis.*)

Descrip.—Our common Marshmallows have divers soft hairy white stalks, three or four feet high, spreading forth many branches, the leaves are soft and hairy, smaller than the other Mallow leaves, but longer pointed, cut, for the most part, into some few divisions, but deep. The flowers are many, but smaller than other Mallows, and white, or bluish coloured. After which come long, round cases and seeds, as in other Mallows. The roots are many and long, shooting from one head, of the size of a thumb or finger, very pliant, tough, like Liquorice, of a whitish yellow colour on the outside, and white within, full of a slimy juice, which if laid in water will thicken, as if it were a jelly.

Place.—It grows in most of the salt marshes, from Woolwich down to the sea, and in other places.

Time.—It flowers all the summer months.

Government and Virtues.—The leaves and roots boiled in water, with parsley or fennel roots, helps to open the body, cool hot agues, and other distempers of the body, if the leaves be applied warm to the belly. It not only voids hot choleric, and other offensive humours, but eases the pains of the belly coming thereby; and are therefore used in all clysters, and for giving abundance of milk to nurses.

The decoction of the seed made in milk or wine, doth help excoriations, the phthisic, pleurisy, and other diseases of the chest and lungs. The leaves and roots work the same effects. They help also in the excoriations of the bowels, and hardness of the mother, and in all hot and sharp diseases thereof. The juice drank in wine, or the decoction of them therein, helps women to a speedy and easy delivery. The syrup also, and conserve made of the flowers, are very effectual for the same diseases, and to open the body. The leaves bruised, and laid to the eyes with a little honey, takes away the imposthumations of them. The leaves bruised or rubbed upon any place stung with bees, wasps, or the like, takes away the pain, inflammation and swelling ; the decoction of the roots and leaves is an antidote for poison. A poultice made of the leaves, with some bean or barley flour, and oil of roses, is an especial remedy against all hard tumours and inflammations, imposthumes, or swellings of the testicles, or other parts, and eases the pains of them ; as also against the hardness of the liver or spleen, if applied to the places. The juice of Mallows boiled in old oil, takes away roughness of the skin, scurf, or dry scabs in the head, or other parts, if they be anointed with the decoction, and preserves the hair from falling off. It is effectual against scalds and burns, St. Anthony's fire, and all other hot and painful swellings in any part of the body. The flowers boiled in oil or water, and a little honey and alum put in is an excellent gargle to heal sore throat or mouth in a short time. If the feet be washed in the decoction, it will draw the rheum from the head. The green leaves, beaten with nitre and applied, draws thorns from the flesh. The decoction opens the strait passages, and makes them slippery, whereby the stone may descend the more easily, and without pain, out of the reins, kidneys, and bladder, and eases the pains thereof. But the roots are of more special use for those purposes, as well for coughs, hoarseness, shortness of breath, and wheezings, being boiled in wine or honeyed water, and drunk. The roots and seeds being boiled in wine or water, are profitable against ruptures, cramps or convulsions of the sinews, and boiled in white wine, for kernels that rise behind the ears, and inflammations or swellings in womens' breasts. The dried root boiled in milk, and drunk, is good for the chin-cough. The decoction of the roots, or juice, is good to drink for those who are wounded, and ready to faint through loss of blood, and apply the same, mixed with honey and rosin, to the wounds. As also, the roots boiled in wine, for hurts, bruises, falls, blows, sprains, or disjointed limbs, or any swelling pain, or ache in the muscles, sinews, or arteries. The mucilage of the roots, and of linseed and fenugreek put together, is much used in poultices, ointments, and plasters, to mollify and digest hard swellings, and the inflammation of them, and to ease pains in any part of the body. The seed either green or dry, mixed with vinegar, cleanses the skin of morphew, &c.

MANDRAKE.—*(Mandragora.)*

Descrip.—This has a large brown root, sometimes single and sometimes divided into three parts, growing deep, from which spring several large dark green leaves, a foot or more in length, and four or five inches broad, sharp pointed at the ends, of a fœtid smell; from among these spring the flowers, each on a separate footstalk, about the height and size of a primrose, of a whitish colour, and of one bell-fashioned leaf, cut into five segments, standing in a large five-cornered calyx, and are succeeded by smooth round fruit, about as big as a small apple, of a deep yellow colour when ripe, and of a very strong smell.

Place.—It comes from Spain, but grows in our gardens.

Time.—It flowers here in July and August.

Government and Virtues.—It is governed by Mercury. The fruit has been accounted poisonous, but without cause. The leaves are cooling, and are used for ointments, and other external applications. The fresh root operates very powerfully as an emetic and purgative, so that few constitutions can bear it. The bark of the root dried, acts as a rough emetic. The root formerly was supposed to have the human form, but it really resembles a carrot or parsnip.

MAPLE-TREE.—*(Acer.)*

There are many varieties of this tree, according to the place of its growth, and the taste of the planter; but the principal are, the Greater and the Less; Greater striped-leaved Maple; Smaller or Common Maple; another with red seed; Virginian Ash-leaved Maple; Norway Maple, with plane-tree leaves; Striped Norway Maple; Virginian Scarlet-flowering Maple; Sir Charles Wager's Maple; American Sugar Maple; Pennsylvania Mountain Maple;

Italian Maple, or Orpalus; Montpelier Maple; Cretan Ivy-leaved Maple; Tartarian Maple.

Descrip.—It is so well known, that little need be said here about it.

Place.—It grows in hedges, and in gentlemens' parks.

Time.—It blossoms from March to the end of May.

Government and Virtues.—It is under the dominion of Jupiter. The decoction of the leaves or barks strengthens the liver very much. It is good to open obstructions of the liver and spleen, and eases the pain which proceeds from thence. The larger Maple, if tapped, yields a considerable quantity of liquor, of a sweet and pleasant taste, which may be made into wine. The wood boiled as sugar-cane, leaves a salt hardly to be distinguished from sugar.

MARJORAM (COMMON WILD.)—*(Origanum Vulgare.)*

CALLED also Origane, Origanum, Eastward Marjoram, Wild Marjoram, and Grove Marjoram.

Descrip.—Wild or Field Marjoram has a root that creeps much under ground, which continues a long time, sending up sundry brownish, hard, square stalks with small dark green leaves, very like those of Sweet Marjoram, but harder and broader, at the top of the stalk stand tufts of purplish-red flowers. The seed is small, and rather blacker than that of Sweet Marjoram.

Place.—It grows in borders of corn-fields, and in copses.

Time.—It flowers towards the end of the summer.

Government and Virtues.—This is under the dominion of Mercury. It strengthens the stomach and head much; there is scarcely a better herb growing for relieving a sour stomach, loss of appetite, cough, consumption of the lungs; it cleanses the body of choler, expels poison, remedies the infirmities of the spleen, and helps the bites of venomous beasts. It provokes urine and the terms in women, helps the dropsy, scurvy, scabs, itch, and yellow jaundice. The juice dropped into the ears, helps deafness, pain and noise in them. The whole plant is a warm aromatic, and an infusion of the dried leaves is extremely grateful. The essential oil poured on a little lint, and put into the hollow of an aching tooth, removes the pain. It is an excellent medicine in nervous cases. The leaves and tops dried, and given in powder, are good in head-aches. The tops made into a conserve, are good for disorders of the stomach and bowels, such as flatulencies, and indigestion; an infusion of the whole plant is serviceable in obstructions of the viscera, and against the jaundice.

MARJORAM (SWEET.)—*(Origanum Marjorana.)*

Sweet Marjoram is so well known that it is needless to write any description of it, or of either Winter Sweet Marjoram *(Origanum Heracleoticum,)* or Pot Marjoram *(Origanum Onites.)*

Place.—It grows commonly in gardens; some sorts grow wild in the borders of corn-fields and pastures.

Time.—It flowers in the end of summer.

Government and Virtues.—It is an herb of Mercury, and under Aries, and is an excellent remedy for the brain and other parts of the body. Our Common Sweet Marjoram is warming and comforting in cold diseases of the head, stomach, sinews, and other parts, taken inwardly or outwardly applied. The decoction thereof being drunk, helps diseases of the chest, obstructions of the liver and spleen, old griefs of the womb, and the windiness thereof, and the loss of speech, by resolution of the tongue. The decoction, made with some Pellitory of Spain, and long pepper, if drunk, is good for dropsy, for those who cannot make water, and against pains in the belly. It provokes womens' courses, if put up as a pessary. Made into powder, and mixed with honey, it takes away the marks of blows, and bruises; it takes away the inflammation and watering of the eyes, if mixed with fine flour, and laid into them. The juice dropped into the ears, eases the pains and singing noise in them. It is profitably put into ointments and salves that are warm, and comforts the outward parts, as the joints and sinews; for swellings also, and places out of joint. The powder snuffed up into the nose provokes sneezing, and thereby purges the brain; chewed in the mouth, it draws forth much phlegm. The oil is very warm and comforting to the joints that are stiff, and the sinews that are hard, to mollify and supple them.

MARIGOLD (CORN.)—*(Chrysanthemum Segetum.)*

Descrip.—This grows with leaves pretty thick and juicy, of a pale yellow-green colour, broader at the end than at that part next the stalk, somewhat clammy in handling; the stalks grow a foot or more high, beset with smaller leaves. The flowers grow singly at the end of the stalks, consisting of a border of gold yellow petal, set about the middle thrum, of a dark reddish fistular flosculi, of a strong, somewhat resinous smell, standing in green scaly calyces. The seed is large and crooked, of a brownish colour.

Place.—It grows in gardens.

Time.—It flowers in summer : the flowers are frequently double. The leaves and flowers are used.

Government and Virtues.—This plant is hot and dry, therefore under the Sun. It is accounted cordial, alexipharmic, good in all kinds of fevers ; it promotes sweat, and is frequently used to drive out small-pox and measles; it also helps the jaundice. A good quantity of the juice is put into treacle water. The juice is recommended for sore eyes, and to take away warts.

MASTERWORT.—(*Imperatoria Ostruthium.*)

Descrip.—Common Masterwort has divers stalks of winged leaves divided into sundry parts, three for the most part standing together at a small foot-stalk on both sides of the greater, and three likewise at the end of the stalk, somewhat broad, and cut in on the edges into three or more divisions, all of them dented about the brims, of a dark green colour, from smaller leaves near the bottom rise up two or three short stalks about two feet high, and slender, with such like leaves at the joints which grow below, with lesser and fewer divisions, bearing umbels of white flowers, and after them, thin, flat black seeds. The root is somewhat great, growing rather sideways than down deep in the ground, shooting forth sundry heads, which taste sharp, biting the tongue, and is the hottest and sharpest part of the plant, and the seed next unto it being somewhat blackish on the outside, and smelling well.

Place.—It grows in gardens with us in England.

Time.—It flowers and seeds about the end of August.

Government and Virtues.—It is an herb of Mars. The root is hot, and very available in colds and diseases of the head, stomach and body, dissolving very powerfully upwards and downwards. The root is of a cordial sudorific nature, and stands high as a remedy of great efficacy in malignant and pestilential fevers. It is most efficacious when taken out of the ground, and if given in a light infusion. It is also used in a decoction with wine against all cold rheums, distillation upon the lungs, or shortness of breath. It provokes urine, and helps to break the stone, and expel the gravel from the kidneys: provokes womens' courses, and expels the dead-birth ; is singularly good for strangling of the mother, and other such feminine disorders. It is effectual against the dropsy, cramps, and falling sickness ; the decoction in wine being gargled in the mouth, draws down much water and phlegm from the brain, purging and easing it of what oppressed it. It is of a rare quality against all sorts of cold poison, to be taken as there is cause ; it provokes sweat. But lest the taste of the seed should be too offensive, the best way is to take water distilled both from the herb and root. The juice dropped into green wounds or filthy ulcers, and envenomed wounds, does soon cleanse and heal them. The same is also very good to help the gout coming of a cold cause.

MASTIC HERB.—*(Thymus Mastichina.)*

CALLED also Summer Savory.

Descrip.—This is a shrubby plant, full of round slender brown stalks, a foot high or more, having small leaves at a joint. The flowers grow on the tops of the stalks, in soft, downy, verticillated spikes, by which it may be known from the other plants of this kind : they are small, white, and galeated. The whole plant has a pleasant smell.

Place.—It is a native of France, but grows in our gardens.

Time.—It flowers in June and July.

Government and Virtues.—This is a mild but martial plant. The tops when in flower, gathered and dried, are good in disorders of the head and nerves, and against stoppages in the viscera, being of a warm aromatic nature. The resinous concrete substance commonly known by the name of gum-mastic, is the produce of the foreign tree. This mastic is recommended in doses of from half a scruple to half a dram, as a mild corroborant, and restringent medicine in old coughs, spitting of blood, looseness, weakness of the stomach, &c.

MAYWEED (STINKING.)—*(Pyrethrum Parthenium.)*

Descrip.—It grows to a foot high, branched and spreading ; the stalk is ruddy, and the leaves are of a deep and blackish green, and of an ill smell. The flower is white, with a high yellow disk, pointed at top, and the divisions of the leaves swell in the middle.

Place.—This is an annual weed, found in ploughed soil.

Time.—It flowers in May and June.

Virtues.—The flowers have, but in a very inferior degree, some of the virtues of camomile, and are far more disagreeable in taste. The leaves operate by urine, and in some constitutions by stool; but both ways roughly, and should be very cautiously tampered with.

MEADOW-SWEET.—(*Spiræa Ulmaria.*)

Descrip.—It has a long reddish fibrous root, from which spring several pinnated leaves, having two or three pair of opposite, large, serrated pinnæ, with an odd one at the end, cut into three parts; they are hoary underneath, and green above, wrinkled, and full of veins, and having several small pieces between the pinnæ; the stalk is red and angular, growing two or three feet high, beset in an alternate order with the like leaves. The flowers grow upon the tops of the stalks in umbel-fashion, being small, five-leaved, and full of apices, of a white colour, followed by little round heads, screw-fashion, of several seeds together.

Place.—It grows in moist meadows and by river-sides.

Time.—It flowers in June. The leaves and tops are used.

Government and Virtues.—Jupiter is regent of the Meadow-sweet. The flowers are alexipharmic and sudorific, and good in fevers, and all malignant distempers; they are likewise astringent, binding, and useful in fluxes of all sorts. An infusion of the fresh-gathered tops of this plant promotes sweating. It is an excellent medicine in fevers attended with purgings, and may be given to the quantity of a moderate bason full, once in two or three hours. It is a good wound-herb, whether taken inwardly or externally applied. A water distilled from the flowers is good for inflammations of the eyes.

MEDLAR.—(*Mespilus Germanica.*)

Descrip.—The branches grow to a reasonable size, with long and narrow leaves, not dented about the edges. At the end of the sprigs stand the flowers, made of white, great pointed leaves, nicked in the middle with some white threads, after which come the fruit, of a brownish green colour, being ripe, bearing a crown as it were on the top, which were the five green leaves; and being rubbed off, or fallen away, the head of the fruit is seen to be somewhat hollow. The fruit is very harsh before it is mellowed, and hath usually five hard kernels within it.

Place.—It is a native of Germany, and is cultivated in our gardens and orchards for the sake of its fruit.

Time.—Its blossoms appear in April and May, and the fruit ripens in September and October.

Government and Virtues.—The fruit is Saturn's. It stays womens' longings. A plaster made of the fruit dried before they are rotten, and other convenient things, and applied to the reins of the back, stops miscarriage in pregnant women. They are very powerful to stay fluxes of blood or humours in men or women; the leaves also have this quality. The fruit, if eaten by pregnant women, stays their longings for unusual meats. The decoction of the fruit is good to gargle the mouth, throat, and teeth, when there are any defluctions of blood to stay it, or of humours, which causes the pains and swellings. It is a good bath for women to sit over, whose courses flow too abundantly; or for bleeding piles. If a poultice or plaster be made with dried medlars, beaten and mixed with the juice of red roses, whereunto a few cloves and nutmegs may be added, and a little red coral also, and applied to the stomach that is given to loathing of meat, it will effectually help. The dried leaves in powder strewed on fresh wounds, restrains the blood, and heals up quickly. The Medlar-stones made into powder, and drank in wine, wherein some parsley-roots are infused all night, or a little boiled, breaks the stone in the kidneys, and helps to expel it.

MELILOT.—(*Trifolium Melilotus.*)

Called also King's-Clover.

Descrip.—The Melilot has a large, woody, spreading white root, from which spring many slender channelled smooth stalks, two or three feet high, having at every joint three oblong, round-pointed green leaves, set together on one footstalk, serrated about the edges. The flowers grow on long spikes, and are of a yellow colour; succeeded by a rough round pod. The whole plant, but especially the flowers, has a strong pleasant smell.

Place.—It grows frequently among corn, and in hedges.

Time.—It flowers in June and July. The leaves and flowers are used.

Government and Virtues.—Melilot, boiled in wine, and applied, softens all hard tumours and inflammations in the eyes, or other parts of the body, as the fundament and privy parts of men or women; and sometimes the yolk of a roasted egg, or fine flour, or poppy seed, or endive, is added unto it. It helps spreading ulcers in the head if washed with a lye made of it. It helps the pains of the stomach, being carefully applied fresh or boiled with any of the aforenamed things; it will ease pains in the ears, if dropped into them; steeped in vinegar or rose-water, it mitigates the head-ache. The flowers of Melilot and Camomile, are used together in clysters to expel wind, and ease pains; also in poultices for the same purpose, and to assuage swelling tumours in the spleen and other parts, and helps inflammations in any part of the body. The juice dropped into the eyes, is a singular good medicine to take away the film that dims the sight. The head often washed with the distilled water of the herb and flowers is good for those who swoon, also to strengthen the memory, to comfort the head and brain, and to preserve them from pain, and the apoplexy. A plaster made of this herb boiled in mutton-suet, wax and rosin, is drawing, and good for green wounds; the fresh plant makes an excellent poultice for hard swellings and inflammatory tumours, at once ripening them, and taking away the pain.

MERCURY (FRENCH.)—*(Mercurialis Gallium.)*

Descrip.—French Mercury, male and female, grows a foot high, full of smooth angular stalks, beset with narrow leaves, about an inch and a half long, broadest in the middle, and sharper at both ends, indented about the edges, of a pale yellow green colour, growing in spikes, which rise from the bosom of the leaves. Those of the female fall off without any seed. The male has a couple of testiculated seeds at the end of the spike. The root is fibrous, and perishes after it has flowered and given seed.

Place.—It grows among rubbish in waste places.

Time.—It flowers in June.

Government and Virtues.—This plant is under the dominion of the Moon. The leaves and stalks are used, and are aperitive and mollifying; the decoction purges choleric and serous humours: it is also used in clysters. A decoction of the seeds with wormwood, is commended for the yellow jaundice. The juice takes away warts.

MEZEREON SPURGE.—*(Daphne Mezereum.)*

Called also Olive Spurge, Flax or Dwarf Bay.

Descrip.—It has a woody root, tough and spreading, and the stem is shrubby, full of branches, covered with a roughish grey bark, and grows five or six feet high. The leaves grow in clusters from certain small protuberances in the bark; they are oblong, smooth on the surface, entire at the edges, and of a dark green colour. The flowers are so numerous as to make the branches appear almost the whole length, of a beautiful red colour; sometimes, however, they are white. The seed grows single, nearly round, and of a fleshy substance.

Place and Time.—It is found wild in several parts of England and is kept in most gardens for the beautiful appearance it makes in January, February, and March, the months in which it flowers.

Government and Virtues.—It is Saturnine. The whole plant has an exceeding acrid biting taste, and is very corrosive. An ointment prepared from the bark, or the berries is a serviceable application to foul ill-conditioned ulcers. A decoction made of a dram of the bark of the root in three pints of water, till one pint is wasted, and this quantity taken in the course of a day, for a considerable time together, has been found very efficacious in resolving and dispersing venereal swellings and excrescences. The bark of the root, or the inner bark of the branches, is to be used, but it requires caution in the administration, and must only be given to people of robust constitutions, and very sparingly even to those; for if given in too large a dose, or to a weakly person, it will cause bloody stools and vomiting; it is good in dropsy and other stubborn disorders. A light infusion is the best mode of giving it.

GARDEN MINT, OR GARDEN SPEAR.—(*Mentha Viridis.*)

Descrip.—This Mint has many square stalks, which, in good ground, will grow to two or three feet high, having two long sharp-pointed leaves, set opposite at a joint, without footstalks, high-veined underneath, thinly serrated at the edges. The flowers grow in long spikes on the tops of the stalks, set on verticillatim, being small and purplish, having a galea and labella so small, that they are hardly perceiveable, a white, long pontel standing out of their mouths. The root creeps and spreads much in the earth, being long and slender. The leaves, stalks, and flowers, have a pleasant and agreeable smell.

Place.—It is planted in gardens.

Time.—It flowers in July.

Government and Virtues.—It is an herb of Venus, and

has a binding, drying quality; the juice taken in vinegar, stays bleeding, stirs up venery, or bodily lust; two or three branches taken in the juice of four pomegranates, stays the hiccough, vomiting, and allays the choler. It dissolves imposthumes, being laid to with barley-meal. It is good to repress the milk in womens' breasts. Applied with salt, it helps the bites of mad dogs: with mead or honeyed water, it eases the pains of the ears, and takes away the roughness of the tongue, being rubbed thereupon. It suffers not milk to curdle in the stomach, if the leaves be steeped or boiled in it before being drunk; it is very profitable to the stomach. Often using it will stay womens' courses and the whites. Applied to the forehead and temples, it eases the pains in the head, and is good to wash the heads of young children with, against all manner of breakings out, sores or scabs, and heals the chops in the fundament. It is also profitable against the poison of venomous creatures. The distilled water of mint is available for all the purposes aforesaid, yet more weakly. But if a spirit thereof be chemically drawn, it is more powerful than the herb. It helps a cold liver, strengthens the belly, causes digestion, stays vomiting and the hiccough; it is good against the gnawing of the heart, provokes appetite, takes away obstructions of the liver, but too much must not be taken, because it makes the blood thin, and turns it into choler, therefore choleric persons must abstain from it. The dried powder taken after meat, helps digestion, and those that are splenetic. Taken in wine, it helps women in their sore travail in child-bearing. It is good against the gravel and stone in the kidneys, and the strangury. Being smelled unto, it is comforting to the head. The decoction gargled in the mouth, cures the mouth and gums that are sore, and amends an ill-favoured breath. Mint is an herb that is useful in all disorders of the stomach, as weakness, squeamishness, loss of appetite, pain, and vomiting; it is likewise very good to stop gonorrhœa, the fluor albus, and the immoderate flow of the menses; a cataplasm of the green leaves applied to the stomach, stays vomiting, and to womens' breasts, prevents the hardness and curding of the milk. A decoction is good to wash the hands of children when broken out with scabs and blotches.

Officinal preparations of Mint are, a simple water and spirit, a compound spirit, and a distilled oil.

MINT (PEPPER.)—(*Mentha Piperita.*)

Descrip.—The leaves of this Mint are broader and somewhat shorter than Spear-mint, growing on footstalks, half an inch long, sharply serrated about the edges. The stalks are square, about two feet high. The flowers are numerous, and grow in loose oblong spikes on the tops of the branches; they are bigger than those of Spear-mint, but of the same colour, and more thickly set. Both leaves and flowers have a pleasant scent, and a hot biting taste, like pepper. The root is slender and creeping.

Place.—It grows in several places, both on the banks of rivers, and is an inhabitant of almost every garden.

Time.—It blossoms in July and August.

Virtues.—This herb has a strong, agreeable, aromatic smell, and a moderate warm bitterish taste; it is useful for complaints of the stomach, such as wind, vomitiug, &c. for which there are few remedies of greater efficacy. It is good in poultices and fomentations to disperse curdled milk in the breasts, and also to be used with milk diets. All Mints are astringent, and of warm subtle parts; great strengthceners of the stomach. Their fragrance betokens them cephalics; they effectually take off nauseousness and retchings to vomit; they are also of use in looseness. The simple water given to children, removes the gripes; but these virtues more particularly belong to Spear and Pepper-mint.

MINT (WATER).—(*Mentha Aquatica.*)

Descrip.—This Mint has square, hairy, brown stalks, a foot high, or more, with two pretty large leaves at a joint, set on short footstalks, broad at the basis, and narrower at the edges, of a very strong smell. The flowers grow on the tops of the stalks, in round spikes, with one or two of the same a little lower on the stalks, at the setting on of the upper leaves. They are larger than common mint, of a pale purple colour. The root is astringent and fibrous.

Place.—It grows in damp watery places, wild, and is cultivated in most gardens for its medicinal qualities.

Time.—The flowers appear in August.

Virtues.—The distilled water of this plant is well known as a carminative and antispasmodic; it relieves colic, and other disorders of the stomach and bowels most instantaneously; and is good in the gravel. It is a valuable medicine in flatulent colics, hysteric depressions, and other complaints of a similar nature. Water Mint expels wind out of the stomach, opens the obstructions of the womb, and produces catamenia. The juice dropped into the ears, eases pain and helps deafness, though not much used.

MINT (WILD, OR HORSE.)—*(Mentha Sylvestris.)*

Descrip.—This Wild-Mint grows not so tall as Garden Mint, or so much branched, having square hoary stalks, with two long, sharp-pointed leaves, hoary likewise, especially underneath, and serrated about the edges, without any footstalks. The flowers grow at the end of the stalks, in long narrow spikes, being small and purple. The whole plant has a strong but not unpleasant smell.

Virtues.—It is good for wind and colic in the stomach, to procure the menses, and expel the birth and secundines. The juice dropped into the ears eases the pains of them, and destroys the worms that breed therein. The juice laid on warm, helps the king's-evil, or kernels in the throat. The decoction or distilled water helps a stinking breath, proceeding from corruption of the teeth ; and snuffed up the nose, purges the head. It helps the scurf or dandruff of the head used with vinegar.

MISSELTOE.—*(Viscus Quercus.)*

Descrip.—This plant fixes itself and takes root on the branches of trees. It spreads out into large bushes, having many woody branches, covered with a yellow-green bark, of different sizes, being full of joints that easily part asunder, having at each two thick firm leaves, narrowest at the bottom, and broader and round at the ends. It bears several small yellow four leaved flowers, to which succeed round, white, almost pellucid berries, as big as white currants, full of a tough viscid juice, in the middle of which lies one flat heart-fashioned seed. It grows upon several trees, as the apple, the crab, the hazel, the ash, the maple, the lime, the willow, the whitethorn, and the oak; this last is best of all.

Government and Virtues.—This is under the dominion of the Sun, with something of the nature of Jupiter. Both the leaves and berries do heat and dry, and are of subtle parts ; the bird-lime mollifies hard knots, tumours, and imposthumes, ripens and discusses them, and draws forth thick as well as thin humours from the remote parts of the body, digesting and separating them, being mixed with equal parts of rosin and wax, mollifies the hardness of the spleen, and helps old ulcers and sores, mixed also with sanderic and orpiment, it helps to draw off foul nails, and if quick lime and wine lees be added thereto, it works the stronger. Made into powder, and given to drink, it is good for falling-sickness. The fresh wood bruised, and the juice thus extracted dropped into the ears is effectual in curing the imposthumes in them. Misseltoe is a cephalic and nervine medicine, useful for convulsive fist, palsy, and vertigo. The bird-lime which is made of the berries of Misseltoe is a powerful attractive, and is good to ripen hard tumours and swellings.

MONEYWORT.—(*Lysimachia Nummularia.*)

CALLED also Herb Twopence.

Descrip.—The common Moneywort sends forth from a small thready root divers long, weak, and slender branches, running upon the ground two or three feet long, set with leaves one against another at equal distances, which are almost round, but pointed at the ends, smooth, and of a good green colour. At the joints with the leaves from the middle forward come forth at every point sometimes one yellow flower, and sometimes two, standing each on a small footstalk, and made of five leaves, narrow-pointed at the end, with some yellow threads in the middle, which being past, there comes small round heads of seeds.

Place.—It grows plentifully in moist grounds by hedge-sides, and in the middle of grassy fields.

Time.—It flowers in June and July, and the seed is ripe shortly afterwards.

Government and Virtues.—Venus owns it. It is good to stay all fluxes in man or woman, whether they be laxes, bloody-fluxes, or the flowing of women's courses; bleeding inwardly or outwardly; the weakness of the stomach that is given to casting. It is good also for ulcers or excoriations of the lungs, or other inward parts. It will quickly heal green wounds, and old spreading ulcers. The juice of the herb, or the powder drank in water, wherein hot steel has been quenched, will act the same for the aforenamed purposes, as well also a decoction of the green herb, drank in wine or water, or to bathe the outward wounds. The juice is effectual also for overflowings of the menses, and the roots dried and powdered, are good in purgings.

MOONWORT.—(*Osmunda Lunaria.*)

Descrip.—It has one dark, green, thick and flat leaf, standing upon a short footstalk, two fingers in breadth; when it flowers it bears a slender stalk, four or five inches high, having one leaf in the middle, divided on both sides into five or seven parts, each part is small like the middle rib, broader forwards, pointed and round, resembling a half moon, the uppermost parts being bigger than the lowest. The stalks rise above this leaf two or three inches, bearing many branches of smaller tongues, of a brownish colour, which, after continuing a while, resolve into a mealy dust. The root is small and fibrous. This has sometimes divers leaves like those before described, with many branches arising from one stalk, each divided from the other.

Place.—It grows on grassy hills and heaths.

Time.—It is found only in April and May.

Government and Virtues.—The Moon owns this herb. It is cold and drying, and is available for wounds both outward and inward. The leaves boiled in red wine, and drank, stay immoderate courses and the whites. It stays bleeding, vomiting, and other fluxes. It helps all blows and bruises, and consolidates all fractures and dislocations. It is good for ruptures, and is put into oils and balsams to heal fresh and green wounds.

MOSS (GROUND.)—(*Lychen Terrestris.*)

Descrip.—This grows in barren ground, and at the roots of trees. It spreads on the ground, with numerous slender flagellæ, having small triangular leaves set close to the stalks, among which spring reddish stalks an inch long, almost as fine as hairs, bearing on the tops little hollow dusty cups, of a whitish colour.

Place.—It grows in our moist woods, in boggy ground, in shadowy ditches, and such like places.

Government and Virtues.—It is under Saturn, and is good to break the stone, to expel and drive it forth by urine, if boiled in wine, and drank. The herb, bruised and boiled in water, and applied, eases all inflammations and pains from a hot cause; and is useful too to ease the gout. The tree moss is cooling and binding, and partakes of a digesting and mollifying quality. Each moss partakes of the nature of the tree on which it grows, the oak is binding, and of good effect to stay fluxes, vomiting and bleeding, if the powder be taken in wine. The decoction in wine is good to bathe or sit in, to stay the overflowing of the courses. The powder taken in drink is available for dropsy. The oil with the moss steeped in it for a time, and afterwards boiled and applied to the temples and forehead, eases the head-ache coming of a hot cause, and the distillations of hot rheums in the eyes, or other parts.

MOTHERWORT.—(*Leonurus Cardiaca.*)

Descrip.—This has a hard, square, brownish, rough strong stalk, rising three or four feet high, spreading into many branches, whereon grow leaves on each side, with long footstalks, two at every joint, somewhat broad and long, as if it were rough and coupled, with many great veins therein of a sad green colour, deeply dented about the edges, and almost divided. From the middle of the branches up to the tops of them, which are long and small, grow the flowers round them in distances, in sharp pointed, hard rough husks, of a red or purple colour, after which come small, round, blackish seeds in great plenty. The root sends forth a number of long strings and small fibres, taking strong hold in the ground, of a dark yellowish or brownish colour.

Place.—It grows only in gardens with us in England.

Time.—It flowers in July or the beginning of August.

Government and Virtues.—Venus owns the herb, and it is under Leo. There is no better herb to take melancholy vapours from the heart, and to strengthen it. It may be kept in a syrup or conserve; it makes mothers joyful, and settles the womb, therefore is it called Motherwort. It is of use for the trembling of the heart, fainting and swooning. The powder, to the quantity of a spoonful, drank in wine, helps women in sore travail, as also for the suffocating or rising of the mother. It provokes urine and womens' courses, cleanses the chest of cold phlegm, kills the worms in the belly. It is of use to digest and disperse them that settle in the veins, joints, and sinews of the body, and to help cramps and convulsions.

MOUSE-EAR.—(*Cerastium Vulgatum.*)

Descrip.—This is a low herb, creeping on the ground by small strings, whereby it shoots forth small roots, whereat grow many small and short leaves, set in round form together, and very hairy which being broken, give a whitish milk; from among these leaves spring up two or three small hoary stalks a span high, with a few smaller leaves thereon; at the tops whereof stand usually but one flower, consisting of many pale yellow leaves, broad at the point, and a little dented in, set in three or four rows, the greater uppermost, a little reddish underneath about the edges, especially if it grows in a dry ground; which, after they have stood long in flower, do turn into down, which, with the seed, is carried away by the wind.

Place.—It grows in dry ditches, and ditch-banks.

Time.—It flowers in June or July, and is green all winter.

Government and Virtues.—The Moon owns this herb. The juice taken in wine, or the the decoction drank, helps the jaundice, if taken morning and evening. It is a special remedy against the stone, and the pains thereof: and the griping pains of the bowels. The decoction, with succory and centaury, is effectual to help the dropsy, and diseases of the spleen. It stays the fluxes of the blood, either at the mouth or nose; it is good also for inward or outward wounds, and stays bloody-flux and womens' courses. A syrup made of the juice and sugar, is good for coughs or phthisic. The same is good for ruptures or burstings. The green herb bruised, and bound to any cut or wound, quickly solders the lips thereof. And the juice, decoction, or powder of the dried herb, is efficacious to stay spreading and fretting cancers and ulcers in the mouth and secret parts. The distilled water of the plant is available in all the diseases aforesaid, and to wash outward wounds and sores, by applying tents of cloth wet therein.

MUGWORT (COMMON.)—*(Artemisia Vulgaris.)*

Descrip.—Common Mugwort has many leaves lying on the ground, much cut, and divided into many sharp parts, of a dusky green on the upper side, but white and hoary underneath. The stalk is ruddy brown, firm and hard, four feet and a half high, upright, full of branches with spiry tops, whereon grow many chaffy flowers, of a yellow brown colour, like buttons, which, after they are gone, are succeeded by small seeds inclosed in round heads. The root is long and hard, with many small fibres growing from it, whereby it takes firm hold of the ground, spreading much. It survives the winter, and blooms afresh in spring.

Place.—This is a perennial, frequent in waste grounds by the sides of waters and foot-paths.

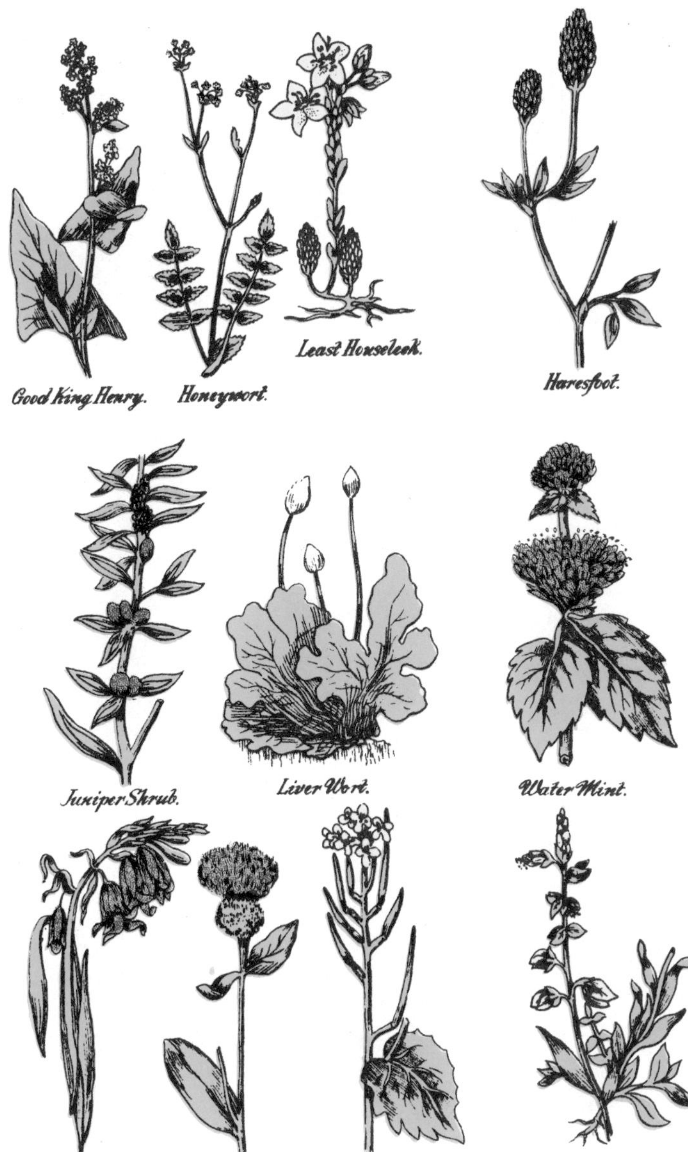
Least Houseleek.
Good King Henry.
Honeywort.
Haresfoot.
Juniper Shrub.
Liver Wort.
Water Mint.
Jacinth.
Knapweed.
Jack by the Hedge.
Milk Wort.

Water Lily.
Ox Eye.
Mother Wort.
T. Mustard.
W. Mullien.
Persicaria.
Mug Wort.
Mother of Thyme.
Meadow Sweet.
Marsh Mallow.

Time.—It flowers in June and July, when it is ready for use ; the seed is ripe at the end of summer.

Government and Virtues.—This is an herb of Venus. Its tops, leaves and flowers are full of virtue ; they are aromatic, and most safe and excellent in female disorders. For this purpose the flowers and buds should be put into a teapot, and boiling water poured over them, and when just cool, be drunk with a little sugar and milk ; this may be repeated twice a day, or oftener, as occasions require. It is boiled among other herbs for drawing down the courses, by sitting over it, and for hastening the delivery, and helps to expel the afterbirth, and is good for the obstructions and inflammations of the mother. It breaks the stone and provokes water. The juice made up with myrrh, and put under as a pessary, works the same effects, and so does the root. Made up with hog's-grease into an ointment, it takes away wens, hard knots and kernels that grow about the neck, more effectually if some daisies be put with it. The herb itself being fresh, or the juice, is a special remedy upon the over-much taking of opium. Three drams of the powder of the dried leaves taken in wine, is a speedy and certain help for the sciatica. A decoction made with camomile and agrimony, and the place bathed therewith while it is warm, takes away the pains of the sinews, and the cramp. The moxa, so famous in the eastern countries for curing the gout by burning the part affected, is the down which grows upon the under side of this herb.

MULBERRY-TREE.—*(Morus Nigra.)*

Descrip.—There are two kinds of mulberries, the common black, and the white. It grows to a large tree, with a brown rugged bark, shooting out its leaves very late in the spring, which are large, and rough or scabious, broad at the base, and growing narrower towards the end, serrated about the edges, and set on short footstalks. The flowers stick close to the branches, each composed of four small leaves, growing in clusters. The fruit is oblong, consisting of a great number of acini, set together in a round form, of a dark purple, almost black when ripe, full of a sweet, pleasant, purple juice.

Place.—It grows in gardens.

Time.—The fruit is ripe in August and September. The bark of the root, and the fruit are used.

Government and Virtues.—Mercury rules the tree. It is

of different parts; the ripe berries open the body, and the unripe bind it, especially when they are dried, and then they are good to stay fluxes, laxes, and womens' courses. The bark of the root kills the broad worms in the belly. The juice, or syrup made of the juice of the berries, helps all inflammations or sores in the mouth or throat. The juice of the leaves is a remedy against the bites of serpents, and for those that have taken aconite. A decoction made of the bark and leaves, is good to wash the teeth when they ache. The leaves stay the bleeding at the mouth or nose, or the bleeding of the piles, or of a wound, if bound unto the places.

MULLEIN (BLACK.)—(*Verbascum Nigrum.*)

Descrip.—The stalk is round and hoary, arising usually single, about as tall as a man. The lower leaves are large, a foot long, and three or four inches broad, sharp pointed at the end, slightly indented about the edges, covered with a hoary down. Those which grow on the stalk, have their middle ribs affixed to it for half their length, which make the stalk appear winged. The flowers grow in a long spike, set thick and close, each consisting of one leaf cut into five segments, of a yellow colour, with as many woolly stamina, having purple apices. The seed-vessels are oblong and pointed, opening in two when ripe, and showing a small brownish seed. The root is single, and small.

Place.—It grows in highways, and by hedge-sides.

Time.—It flowers in July. The leaves are used.

Virtues.—They are accounted pectoral, and good for coughs, spitting of blood, and other affections of the breast; they are likewise good for griping and colic pains, arising from sharp humours ; outwardly used in fomentations or fumigations, they are reckoned a specific against the pains and swelling of the hemorrhoids, or piles.

MULLEIN (WHITE.)—(*Verbascum Lychnitis.*)

Descrip.—This has many fair, large, woolly white leaves, lying next the ground, somewhat larger than broad, pointed at the end, and dented about the edges. The stalk rises to four or five feet high, covered over with such like leaves, but less, so that no stalk can be seen for the number of leaves set thereon up to the flowers, which come forth on all sides of the stalk, without any branches for the most part, and are many set together in a long spike, in some of a yellow colour, in others more pale, consisting of five round pointed leaves, which afterwards have small round heads, which contain small brownish seed. The root is long, white, and woody, perishing after it hath borne seed.

Place.—It grows by way-sides and lanes, in many places in the west of England.

Time.—It flowers in July, or thereabouts.

Government and Virtues.—It is under the dominion of Saturn. A small quantity of the root is commended against laxes and fluxes of the body. The decoction, if drunk, is profitable for those that are bursten, and for cramps, convulsions, and old coughs. The decoction gargled, eases tooth-ache, and the oil made by infusion of the flowers, is of good effect for the piles. The decoction of the root in red wine or water, is good for ague; when red-hot steel has been quenched in it, if drank it will stay bloody-flux, and open obstruction of the bladder and reins. A decoction of the leaves, with sage, marjoram, and camomile flowers, and the places bathed therewith, is good for colds, stiff sinews, and cramps. Three ounces of the distilled water of the flowers drank morning and evening is a remedy for the gout. The juice of the leaves and flowers laid on rough warts, as also the powder of the dried roots rubbed on, takes them away. The powder of the dried flowers is a remedy for bowel complaint, or the pains of the colic. The decoction of the root and the leaves, is of great effect to dissolve the tumours, swellings, or inflammations of the throat. The seed and leaves boiled in wine, draw forth speedily thorns or splinters from the flesh, eases the pains, and heals them. The seed bruised and boiled in wine, and laid on any member that has been out of joint, and newly set again, takes away all swelling and pain.

MUSHROOM (GARDEN.)—(*Agaricus Campestris.*)

Descrip.—This is much better than that which grows in the field, which is often unwholesome and pernicious. It is a fungous plant, without the least appearance of leaves, flowers, or seed. It rises from the ground in its perfect form, with a straight stem, an inch or more high, covered with a round, high, thick, soft white head; underneath it is of a reddish flesh-colour, and when the plant has arrived at its full growth, the head is expanded almost flat, forming a large flap, which, if not gathered, falls to the ground, shedding what is supposed to be the seed. This

Mushroom is distinguishable from the others, by its imparting an agreeable smell. As it increases in size, the fleshy colour underneath turns redder, and the edges become a blackish red, but without losing or changing its fleshy colour within.

Place.—In the field it owes its origin to the putrefaction of earth or dung. From this beginning they discover themselves under the form of a white, mouldy substance, called spawn, which produces numerous white knots, or embryo plants, gradually increasing to the perfect Mushroom.

Time.—In fields it is of very short duration and growth at particular times; but in gardens it is propagated from rotten horse dung and putrid moist litter all the year.

Government and Virtues.—Mushrooms are under Mercury in Aries. Roasted and applied in a poultice, or boiled with white lily roots, and linseed, in milk, they ripen boils and abscesses better than any preparation that can be made. Their poultices are of service in quinsies, and inflammatory swellings. Inwardly, they are unwholesome, and unfit for the strongest constitutions.

MUSTARD (BLACK.)—*(Sinapis Nigra.)*

Descrip.—The lower leaves are large and rough; the stalk grows four or five feet high, smooth, branched, and with smaller leaves than those below, thick, smooth, and less cut in, a little serrated about the edges, and hanging down on long footstalks. The flowers are small and yellow, of four leaves each, set many together, and flowering by degrees; before they have done flowering, the spike of the seed-vessel is extended to a great length; they are squarish, clasping close to the stalks, and sharp-pointed at the end, full of round, dark, brown seed, of a hot biting taste. The root is whitish, branched, and full of fibres.

Place.—It grows frequently in waste places, and among rubbish; and is frequently sown in gardens.

Time.—It flowers in June.

Government and Virtues.—It is an excellent sauce for clarifying the blood, and for weak stomachs, being an herb of Mars, but unfit for choleric people; it also strengthens the heart and resists poison. Let such as have weak stomachs take of Mustard-seed and Cinnamon, one dram each, beaten into powder, with half a dram of powdered mastic and gum-arabic dissolved in rose-water, made into troches of half a dram each in weight, one of these troches to be taken an hour or two before meals. Old people may take much of this medicine with advantage. Mustard-seed has the virtue of heat, discussing, ratifying, and drawing out splinters of bones, and other things of the flesh. It is good to bring down the courses, for falling-sickness or lethargy, to use it both inwardly and outwardly, to rub the nostrils, forehead, and temples, to warm and quicken the spirits; it purges the brain by sneezing, and draws down rheum and other viscous humours, and with some honey added it is good for old coughs. The decoction of the seed made in wine and drank, resists poison, the malignity of mushrooms, and the bites of venomous creatures, if taken in time. The seed taken either in an electuary or drink, stirs up lust, and helps the spleen and pains in the sides, and gnawings of the bowels; used as a gargle it draws up the palate of the mouth, if fallen; and it dissolves swellings about the throat, if outwardly applied. Chewed in the mouth, it helps the tooth-ache. The outward application upon the pained place of the sciatica, discusses the humours, and eases the pain; as also the gout and other joint-aches and is often used to ease the pains in the sides or loins, the shoulders, or other parts of the body, upon the applying thereof to raise blisters, and cures the disease by drawing it to the outward parts of the body. It is also used to help the falling off of the hair. The seed bruised, with honey, and applied, or made up with wax, takes away marks, spots, or bruises, the roughness or scabbiness of the skin, as also the leprosy, or lousy evil. The distilled water of the herb, when in flower, is drank to help in any of the diseases beforenamed, either inwardly, or outwardly for scabs, itch, or such like infirmities, and it cleanses the face from spots, freckles, and other deformities.

MUSTARD (HEDGE.)—(*Sisymbrium Officinale.*)

Descrip.—This grows up with one blackish green stalk, easy to bend, but tough, branched into divers parts, and sometimes with divers stalks, set full of branches, whereon grow long, rough, or hard rugged leaves, much torn on the edges in many parts, some large, and some small, of a dirty green colour. The flowers are small and yellow, that grow on the tops of the branches in long spikes, flowering by degrees; so that continuing long in flower, the stalk will have small round cods at the bottom growing upright and close to the stalk, while the top flowers yet show themselves, in which are contained small yellow seed, sharp and strong, as the herb is also. The root grows down slender and woody, yet abiding and springing again every year.

Place.—It grows by way and hedge-sides, and sometimes in open fields. It is common in the Isle of Ely.

Time.—It flowers most usually about July.

Government and Virtues.—Mars owns this herb also. It is good in diseases of the chest and lungs, and hoarseness; by the use of the decoction lost voice has been recovered. The juice made into a syrup with honey and sugar, is effectual for the same purpose, and for coughs, wheezing, and shortness of breath. The same is profitable for the jaundice, pleurisy, pains in the back and loins, and colic, if used in clysters. The seed is a remedy against poison and venom, and worms in children. It is good for the sciatica, and in joint-aches, ulcers and cankers in the mouth, throat, or behind the ears, and for hardness and swelling of the testicles, or of womens' breasts.

MUSTARD (WHITE.)—(*Sinapis Alba.*)

Descrip.—This does not grow tall, but is branched ; its branches bear leaves, which are rough, hairy, and divided. The flowers are larger than other mustards, of a deep yellow colour, the seed-vessels stand from the stalks, hairy, ending in a long, empty point, containing four or five white seed, larger than the common, which make the seed-vessel appear knotted : they are not quite so hot as the other.

Place.—It grows wild in several places, but is scarce.

Time.—It flowers about July.

Government and Virtues.—It is like Black Mustard in its virtues, which are considerable. The young shoots are eaten with other salads, and this way it is very wholesome. The seed bruised and infused in wine or ale, is of service against the scurvy and dropsy, provoking urine and the menses. Mustard outwardly applied is very drawing and ripening: and laid on paralytic members it recalls the natural heat. Poultices made with Mustard-flower, crumbs of bread, and vinegar, are frequently applied to the soles of the feet in fevers, and may be used to advantage in old rheumatic and sciatic pains. In short, whenever a strong stimulating medicine is wanted to act upon the nerves, and not excite heat, there is none preferable to Mustard-seed.

MYRRH (ENGLISH.)—(*Cicufaria Odorata.*)

Descrip.—The leaves of English Myrrh are large and winged, with several long pinnæ on each side; of a pleasant aromatic smell; the stalks are somewhat hairy and channelled, beset with the like leaves, but smaller, bearing on their tops umbels of white five-leaved flowers, which are succeeded by pretty large long seed, deeply furrowed, and having five sharp ridges. The root is thick and spreading, with many fibres.

Place.—It is sown in gardens.

Time.—It flowers in May and June. The leaves and seed are used.

Government and Virtues.—This plant is of a hot nature, it is of fine aromatic parts, and under Jupiter. A large spoonful of the unbruised seeds taken every morning, is excellent against rheumatic complaints and falling sickness. They operate by urine, and promote the menstrual discharge; and while they are producing these good effects, they strengthen the stomach, expel wind and create appetite. Eaten as a salad, it is an excellent antiscorbutic.

MYRTLE TREE.—(*Myrtus Communis.*)

Descrip.—This is a little tree or bush, shooting forth many slender tough branches, sometimes brown and sometimes of a reddish colour, on which grow small, oblong, sharp-pointed, green leaves, set alternately on the stalks, of a pleasant aromatic smell, among these come forth the flowers, each singly on short footstalks, consisting of five white round leaves, full of a great many white stamina, which being fallen, the calyx becomes a small, round, black berry, with a small crown on the top, full of white seeds.

Place.—It grows wild in the south of Europe; but with us is an ornament of our gardens.

Time.—It flowers in August.

Government and Virtues.—This tree is under Mercury. The leaves sometimes, but chiefly the berries are used. They are both of them drying and binding, good for diarrhœa and dysentery, spitting of blood, and catarrhous defluctions upon the breast, the fluor albus, the falling down of the womb or fundament, both taken inwardly, and used outwardly, in powders and injections.

NAILWORT, OR WHITLOW GRASS.—(*Draba Verna.*)

Descrip.—This has no roots, save a few strings, and grows only about a hand-breadth high; the leaves are small and long, among which rise up divers slender stalks, bearing white flowers one above another, which are small; after which come small flat pouches containing the seed, which is very small, but of a sharp taste.

Place.—It grows on old stone and brick walls, and in sheltered gravelly grounds, where there is grass or moss.

Time.—It flowers early in January, and in February; and perishes immediately afterwards.

Government and Virtues.—It is good for imposthumes in the joints and under the nails, called whitlows, felons, andicons, and nailwheals. It is an excellent wound herb, and under Jupiter. Inwardly taken, it is a balsamic medicine, a remedy for the whites, and weaknesses occasioned by venereal disorders. It operates by urine, brings away gravel, and is good in disorders of the lungs.

NAVELWORT.—(*Cotyledon Umbilicus.*)

Descrip.—This plant has a thick knobbed root, with fibres at the bottom; from which spring several fat succulent leaves, the lowermost of which have their footstalks set on upon the side of the leaf, which is roundish and crenated about the edges: but the upper leaves have the footstalk inserted in the middle, they are round and somewhat hollow; the flowers grow on the tops of the branches in long spikes, of a whitish green colour, hollow, and of an oblong cylindrical shape; each of which is succeeded by two little horned vessels, which contain many small seeds.

Place.—It grows upon old stone walls and buildings, in divers parts of England.

Time.—It flowers in May. The leaves only are used.

Government and Virtues.—Saturn owns this plant. It is cooling and moistening, useful in hot distempers of the liver; it provokes urine, and takes off the heat and sharpness thereof. The juice outwardly applied, helps the shingles, St. Anthony's fire, the pain and inflammation of the piles. it is likewise useful against kibes and chilblains. It is an ingredient of the *Unguentum Populeon*

NAVEW.—(*Brassica Campestris.*

Descrip.—The first leaves are moderately broad and long, of a pale green. The stalks grow two or three feet high, set with smaller leaves, smooth as well as the stalk, a little torn, especially those which grow high upon the branches, which are round and broad at the bottom, and encompass the stalk, ending in a narrow point, of a bluish green colour. The flowers grow on the tops of the stalks, of four bright yellow leaves, succeeded by long cylindrical pods, containing small round black seed, the root is white, long, and slender.

Place.—It is sown in gardens.

Time.—It flowers in April. The seed is used in medicine.

Government and Virtues.—This is a plant of Venus. The seed is good against all kinds of poison, and the bites of venomous creatures, to provoke urine, and the terms. It is extolled against all kinds of infectious distempers, and to expel the malignity, and drive out the small-pox and measles. It is an ingredient in the *Theriaca Andromachi.*

NEP.—*(Nepeta Cataria.)*

Called also Cat-Mint.

Descrip.—It shoots forth hard, foot-square stalks, with a hoariness on them, about a yard high, full of branches, bearing at every point two broad leaves, soft, white, and hoary, nicked about the edges, and of a strong sweet scent. The flowers grow in long tufts at the tops of the branches, and underneath them likewise on the stalks many together, of a purplish white colour. The roots are composed of many long strings or fibres, fastened firmly in the ground, and abide with green leaves thereon all the winter.

Place.—It is only nursed up in our gardens.

Time.—It flowers in July, or thereabouts.

Government and Virtues.—It is an herb of Venus, and is generally used to procure womens' courses, taken outwardly or inwardly, either alone, or with other convenient herbs in a decoction to bathe them, or sit over the hot fumes ; and by frequent use it takes away barrenness, the wind and pains of the mother. It is used in pains of the head coming of any cold cause, catarrhs, rheums, and swimming and giddiness ; and is of use for wind in the stomach and belly. It is effectual for cramp or cold aches, and is used for colds, coughs, and shortness of breath. The juice drunk in wine, is profitable for bruises by accidents. The green herb bruised and applied, eases the piles ; the juice made up into an ointment, is effectual for the same purpose. The head washed with the decoction, takes away scabs. and will do the same for other parts of the body

NETTLE (COMMON.)—(*Urtica Dioica.*)

Descrip.—The root is creeping, the stalk is ridged, and grows a yard or more high, beset with little prickles or stings, with a perforation at the point, and a bag at the base; when the sting is pressed, it readily enters the skin, and the same pressure forces an acrid liquor from the bag into the wound, which produces a burning tingling sensation. The leaves are large, broad, oblong, sharp-pointed, serrated, and covered with the same prickles. The flowers are greenish and inconsiderable.

Place.—It is common by way-sides, and in hedges.

Time.—It flowers in July.

Government and Virtues.—This is an herb of Mars. It consumes the phlegmatic superfluities in the body of man, that the coldness and moisture of winter has left behind. The roots or leaves boiled, or the juice of either of them, or both, made into an electuary with honey and sugar, is a safe and sure medicine to open the passages of the lungs, which is the cause of wheezing and shortness of breath, and helps to expectorate phlegm, also to raise the imposthumed pleurisy; it likewise helps the swelling of both the mouth and throat if they be gargled with it. The juice is effectual to settle the palate of the mouth to its place, and heal the inflammations and soreness of the mouth and throat. If the decoction of the leaves be drunk in wine, it will provoke the courses, settle the suffocation and strangling of the mother, and all other diseases thereof; as also, applied outwardly, with a little myrrh. The same, or the seed, provokes urine, and expels the gravel and stone. It kills the worms in children, eases pains in the sides, and dissolves the windiness in the spleen, as also the body. The juice of the leaves taken two or three days together, stays bleeding at the mouth. The seed being drunk, is a remedy against the bites of mad dogs, the poisonous qualities of hemlock, henbane, nightshade, mandrake, or such herbs as stupify the senses; as also the lethargy, especially if used outwardly, to rub the forehead or temples in that disease. The distilled water is effectual, though not so powerful, for the diseases aforementioned; as for outward wounds or sores to wash them, and to cleanse the skin from morphew, and other discolourings thereof. The seed or leaves bruised, and put into the nostrils, stays the bleeding of them, and takes away the polypus. The juice of the leaves, or the decoction of the root, is good to wash either old, rotten, or stinking sores or fistulas, and gangrenes, and such as fretting, eating, or corroding scabs, manginess, and itch, in any part of the body ; as also green wounds, by washing them therewith, or applying the green herb bruised thereto. It eases the pains, and dries or dissolves the defluctions. An ointment made of the juice, oil, and a little wax, is good to rub cold and benumbed members. One handful of the leaves of green nettles, and another of Wallwort, or Deanwort, bruised and applied simply themselves to the gout, sciatica, or joint aches in any part, hath been found an admirable help thereunto.

NIGHTSHADE (COMMON.)—(*Solanum.*)

Descrip.—This has an upright, round, green, hollow stalk, about a foot high, with many branches, whereon grow several green leaves, somewhat broad and pointed at the ends, soft and full of juice, and unevenly dented at the edges. At the tops of the stalk and branches come forth three or four, or more, white flowers, consisting of five small pointed leaves each, standing on a stalk together, one above another, with yellow pointels in the middle, composed of four or five yellow threads set together, which afterwards run into as many pendulous green berries, of the size of small peas, full of green juice, and small, whitish, round flat seeds. The root is white, and a little woody after the flower and fruit are past, and has many small fibres in it. The whole plant is of a waterish, insipid taste, but the juice of the berries is somewhat viscous, and of a cooling and binding quality. There are two varieties of this, which are found growing in England; the most common is an upright plant, with oval acute pointed smooth leaves, and black berries (*Solanum Nigrum*:) the other is a low branching plant, with indented leaves, and greenish yellow berries (*Solanum Nigrum baccis viridis.*)

Place.—It grows wild under our walls, and in rubbish, the common paths, and sides of hedges and fields ; also in gardens, where it becomes a very troublesome weed.

Time.—It dies every year, and rises again in the latter end of April ; and its berries are ripe in October.

Government and Virtues.—It is a cool Saturnine plant. It is used to cool hot inflammations, either inwardly or outwardly, being in no way dangerous, as most of the Nightshades are ; yet it must be used moderately. The distilled water of the whole herb is safest to be taken inwardly; the juice also clarified and taken, being mingled with a little vinegar, is good for an inflamed mouth and throat; but outwardly, the juice of the herb or berries, with oil of roses, and a little vinegar and ceruse beat together in a lead mortar, is good to anoint all hot inflammations in the eyes. It also does good for the shingles, ringworms, and in all running, fretting, and corroding ulcers, if applied thereto. A pessary dipped in the juice, and dropped into the matrix, stays the immoderate flow of the courses; a cloth wet therein, and applied to the testicles, upon any swelling therein, gives ease; also to the gout, if it comes of hot and sharp humours. The juice dropped into the ears, eases pains that arise from heat or inflammation: it is good for hot swellings under the throat. Be sure you do not mistake the Deadly Nightshade for this.

NIGHTSHADE (DEADLY.)—(*Atropa Belladonna.*)

CALLED also the Dwale.

Descrip.—This is the largest of the Nightshades. It is five feet high, having several long spreading roots, that shoot many long angulated stalks of a deep green, beset with dull green leaves, shaped like common Nightshade, but larger. The flowers are set on among the leaves, growing singly on long footstalks arising from the bosom of the leaves, and have a dismal aspect. They are large, hollow, and hang down like bells. On the outside they are of a dusky colour, between brown and green, and within they are purple. They are succeeded by berries of the size of cherries, black and shining when ripe, and full of a purplish juicy pulp, of a sweetish and mawkish taste.

Place.—It is seldom found wild, but often in gardens.

Time.—It flowers in July.

Government and Virtues.—Only a part of this plant has its uses. This Nightshade bears a very bad character as being of a poisonous nature. It is not good at all for inward uses; but both leaves and root may with good success be applied outwardly, by way of poultice, to inflammatory swellings. An ointment made of the juice evaporated to the consistence of an extract, does wonders in old sharp ulcers, even of a cancerous nature. The leaves applied to the breasts of women, will dissipate any hard swellings of those parts. A poultice made of the roots boiled in milk, has been found serviceable in hard ill-conditioned tumours, and foul ulcers. Sometimes even the outward application is dangerous as the following instance proves:—A lady, troubled with a small ulcer a little below one of her eyes, which was supposed to be of a cancerous nature, applied a small piece of the green leaf to it at night, and the next morning the uvea of that eye was affected in so frightful a manner, that the pupil would not contract in the brightest light, while the other eye retained its usual powers. The leaf being removed, the eye was gradually restored to its original state, and this effect could not be accidental, for the experiment was repeated three different times, and the application was always attended with the same results.

OAK TREE.—(*Quercus Robur.*)

Descrip.—This tree grows to a vast height, spreading out into innumerable and irregular branches. The leaves are oblong, obtuse, deeply finulated, and of a dark green. The flowers are both barren and fertile on the same tree ; the former are collected into loose catkins ; the latter are seated in the buds, and both sorts are small and inconsiderable. The seed is oval-formed, of a leather-like coat, which appears as if rasped at the base, and is fixed to a short cup.

Place.—It is too common to require a particular specification of the place of its growth.

Time.—The flowers appear in April, and the acorns are ripe in October and November.

Government and Virtues.—Jupiter owns the tree. The leaves and bark, and the acorn cups, bind and dry much. The inner bark and the thin skin that covers the acorn, are used to stay the spitting of blood, and the flux. The decoction of that bark, and the powder of the cups, stay vomiting, spitting of blood, bleeding at the mouth, or other flux of blood in man or woman ; laxes also, and the involuntary flux of natural seed. The acorn in powder taken in wine, provokes urine, and resists the poison of venomous creatures. The decoction of acorns and bark made in milk, and taken, resists the force of poisonous herbs and medicines ; as also the virulence of cantharides, when the bladder becomes ulcerated by taking them, and voids bloody urine. The distilled water of the buds, before they break out into leaves, is good to be used either inwardly or outwardly, to assuage inflammations, and to stop all manner of fluxes in man or woman. The same is singularly good in pestilential and hot burning fevers; for it resists the force of the infection, and allays heat ; it cools the heat of the liver, breaks the stone, and stays women's courses. The decoction of the leaves work the same effects. The water that is found in the hollow places of Oaks, is very effectual against any foul or spreading scabs. The distilled water of the leaves is one of the best remedies for the whites.

OATS.—*(Avena Sativa.)*

Descrip.—The root is fibrous, the stalk hollow, jointed a yard high; the leaves are long, narrow, and of a pale green. The flowers are in a loose panicle, and terminate the stalk.

Place.—It grows wild from seed, but is cultivated.

Time.—It is reaped early in harvest.

Government and Virtues.—Oats fried with bay salt, and applied to the sides, take away the pains of stitches and wind in the sides of the belly. A poultice made of the meal of oats, and some oil of bays added, helps the itch and leprosy; as also the fistulas of the fundament, and dissolves hard imposthumes. The meal of oats boiled with vinegar and applied, takes away freckles and spots in the face, and other parts of the body.

ONION.—*(Allium Cepa.)*

This plant is so common and well known that it needs no description.

Place.—It is not a native of this country, but is largely cultivated in our gardens, for esculent purposes.

Time.—The flowers appear early in Summer.

Government and Virtues.—Mars owns them. They are flatulent, or windy, and provoke appetite, increase thirst, ease the bowels, provoke the courses, help the bites of mad dogs, and of other venomous creatures, used with honey and rue; increase sperm, especially the seed: they kill worms in children, if they drink the water fasting wherein they have been steeped all night. Being roasted under the embers, and eaten with honey, or sugar and oil, they much conduce to help an inveterate cough, and expectorate tough phlegm. The juice being snuffed up the nostrils, purges the head, and helps the lethargy, yet often eaten is said to procure pains in the head. The juice is good for either scalds or burns. Used with vinegar it takes away all blemishes, spots, and marks in the skin; and dropped into the ears, eases the pains and noise in them. Applied also with figs beaten together, helps to ripen and break imposthumes, and other sores. Leeks *(Allium Porrum)* are like them in quality; they are a remedy against a surfeit of mushrooms, if baked under the embers and taken ; and being boiled and applied warm, help the piles. Though leeks possess the quality of onions, they are not so powerful. A syrup made of the juice of onions and honey, is an excellent medicine in asthmatical complaints. Onions are good for cold watery humours, but injurious to persons of bilious habit, affecting the head, eyes, and stomach. When plentifully eaten, they procure sleep, help digestion, cure acid belchings, remove obstructions of the viscera, increase the urinary secretions, and promote insensible perspiration. Steeped all night in spring water, and the infusion given to children to drink in the morning fasting, kills worms. Onion bruised, with the addition of a little salt, and laid on fresh burns, draws out the fire, and prevents them blistering. The use is fittest for cold weather, and for aged, phlegmatic people, whose lungs are stuffed, and breathing short.

ORACH.—(*Atriplex Patula.*

Descrip.—Under the article Arrach, *Atriplex*, is described a species of this herb. It grows to four feet high ; the stalks are whitish, the leaves of a faint green, and the flowers of a greenish white. The seeds are olive-coloured.

Place.—It grows wild on waste land, but the seeds of the manured kind are the best for use.

Time.—It flowers in July ; the seed is ripe soon after.

Government and Virtues.—It is under Venus. It may be eaten soon after as salad ; but the virtues lie in the seed. These are to be gathered when just ripe; for, if suffered to stand longer, they lose part of their virtue. A pound of these bruised, and put into three quarts of spirit, of moderate strength, after standing six weeks, afford a light and not unpleasant tincture ; a tablespoonful of which, taken in a cup of water-gruel, has the same effect as a dose of ipecacuanha, only that its operation is milder, and does not bind the bowels afterwards. The patient should go to bed after taking the dose, and a gentle sweat will follow, carrying off whatever offending matter the motions have dislodged ; and thus preventing long disease. It cures headaches, wandering pains, and the first attacks of rheumatism. As some stomachs are harder to move than others, if the first dose does not perform its office, a second tablespoonful may be taken without fear.

ORCHIS.—*(Satyrium.)*

CALLED also Dog-stones, Goat-stones, Fool-stones, Fox-stones, Satirion, Cullians, &c., &c.

Descrip.—To describe all the several sorts of it would be an endless piece of work. The roots are the only parts used, and a description of them will be sufficient. The roots of each sort are double within, some of them round, in others like a hand ; these roots alter every year by course, when one rises and waxes full, the other waxes lank and perishes : now, that which is full is to be used in medicines, the other being either of no use at all, or else it destroys the virtue of the other, quite undoing what the other does

Place.—It grows in meadows.

Time.—One or other may be found in flower from the beginning of April to the latter end of August.

Government and Virtues.—They are hot and moist in operation, under the dominion of Venus, and provoke lust, which the dried and withered roots do restrain. They kill worms in children; if bruised and applied to the place they heal the king's-evil. There is another sort, called the Female Orchis. It is a less plant than the former, having no spots on the leaves ; the spike of the flowers is less, of a purplish colour ; it grows in the same places, rather later. The root has the same virtues and shape. They all provoke venery, strengthen the genital parts, and help conception. Applied outwardly in the form of a cataplasm, they dissolve hard tumours and swellings. Salep is a preparation of the roots, of which there are many species, according to the soil they grow in. It is one of the most valuable plants growing. The best way to use it is, to wash the new root in water ; separate it from the brown skin which covers it, by dipping it in hot water, and rubbing it with a coarse linen cloth. When a sufficient number of roots have been thus cleaned, they are to be spread on a tin plate, and placed in an oven heated to the usual degree, where they are to remain five or six minutes, in which time they will have lost their milky whiteness, and acquired a transparency like horn without any diminution in bulk. When arrived at this state, they are to be removed in order to be dried and hardened in the air, which will require several days to effect ; or by using a gentle heat, they may be finished in a few hours. This Salep contains the greatest quantity of nourishment in the smallest bulk, and will support the system in privation and during famine, it is good for those who travel long distances and are compelled to endure exposure without food.

ORPINE.—(*Sedum Telephium.*)

Descrip.—Common Orpine grows with divers round brittle stalks, thick set with flat and flesh leaves, without order, and a little dented about the edges, of a green colour. The flowers are whitish, growing in tufts, after which come small chaffy husks, with seed like dust in them. The roots are thick, round, white tuberous clogs; and the plant grows less in some places than in others where it is found.

Place.—It grows wild in shadowy fields and woods in almost every county, and is cultivated in gardens, where it rises greater than the wild.

Time.—It flowers about July, the seed ripens in August.

Government and Virtues.—The Moon owns this herb. It is seldom used in inward medicines. The distilled water is profitable for gnawings or excoriations in the stomach and bowels, or for ulcers in the lungs, liver, or other inward parts; and in the matrix, it helps all those diseases, if drank for some days together. It stays the bloody flux, and other fluxes in the body or in wounds. The root acts with the like effect. Outwardly it cools any inflammation upon any hurt or wound, and eases the pain; it also cures burns or scalds, if the juice be beaten with some green salad-oil, and anointed. The leaves bruised, and laid to any green wound in the legs or hands, heals them quickly, and if bound to the throat, helps the quinsey; it helps also ruptures. It is of a styptic astringent nature, and the roots contain the principal virtues. Bruised and applied externally they are serviceable in wounds, burns, and bruises. The leaves boiled in milk, and the decoction, and a large teacupful taken taken three or four times a-day, promotes the urinary discharge, and is serviceable for piles and other hemorrhages.

PARSLEY (COMMON.)—(*Petroselinum Sativum.*)

Descrip.—The roots are long, thick, and white, having a wrinkled bark; from which spring many shining, green, winged leaves, growing on long footstalks; which are divided into three sections, and each of those subdivided into three more, which are triangular and cut in at the ends. The stalks grow to be two feet high, much branched and divided: they are smooth and striated, beset with smaller and finer leaves; and on their tops have small umbels of little, five-leaved, white flowers, which are succeeded by small, round, striated, brown seed.

Place.—It is sown in gardens.

Time.—It flowers in summer. The roots, leaves, and seeds are used.

Government and Virtues.—It is under the dominion of Mercury; is very comforting to the stomach; helps to provoke urine and the courses, to break wind, both in the stomach and bowels, and opens the body, but the root much more. It opens obstructions both of liver and spleen, it is good against falling-sickness, and to provoke urine, especially if the roots be boiled, and eaten like parsnips. The seed provokes urine, and women's courses, expels wind, breaks the stone, and eases the pains thereof; it is effectual in the lethargy, and good against coughs. The distilled water is a familiar medicine with nurses to give children when troubled with wind in the stomach or belly, and it is also of service to upgrown persons. The leaves laid to the eyes inflamed with heat, or swollen, helps them, if used with bread or meal, or fried with butter, and applied to womens' breasts that are hard through the curding of their milk, it abates the hardness, and takes away black and blue marks coming of bruises or falls. The juice dropped into the ears with a little wine, eases the pains. It helps the jaundice, falling-sickness, the dropsy, and stone in the kidneys in this manner: Take of Parsley seed, fennel, annise, and carraways, of each one ounce, of the roots of Parsley, burnet, saxifrage, and carraways, of each an ounce and a half; let the seeds be bruised, and the roots washed and cut small, let them lie all night and steep in a bottle of white wine; and in the morning be boiled in a close earthen vessel to a third of the quantity; of which being strained and cleared, take four ounces night and morning fasting. This opens obstructions of the liver and spleen, and expels the dropsy and jaundice by urine.

PARSLEY PIERT, OR PARSLEY BREAKSTONE.—(*Alchemilla Arvensis.*)

Descrip.—The root is very small and thready, yet it continues many years, from whence arise many leaves lying along the ground, each standing upon a long small foot-stalk, the leaves are as broad as a man's nail, very deeply dented on the edges, of a dusky green colour The stalks are weak and slender, three or four fingers in length, set so full of leaves that they can hardly be seen, either having no footstalk at all, or but a very short one, the flowers are so small that they can hardly be seen, and the seed is very small also.

Place.—It is found in barren, sandy, moist places. It grows plentifully about Hampstead-Heath, Hyde Park, and in Tothill-fields.

Time.—It may be found all the summer-time, even from the beginning of April, to the end of October.

Government and Virtues.—In its operation it provokes urine, and breaks the stone. It is a good salad herb. The whole plant is to be used, and is best when gathered fresh. A strong infusion is good against the gravel, for it operates by urine, and cleanses the kidneys and urinary passages of all concretions. It is good in jaundice, and other complaints arising from obstructions of the liver or any other viscera. This herb may be dried, or a syrup made of it for use. If a dram of the powder be taken in white wine it will bring away gravel from the kidneys, without much pain. It also helps the strangury.

PARSLEY (ROCK.)—*(Peucedanum Officinale.)*

CALLED also Hog's Fennel.

Descrip.—This has a long striated stalk, with small grassy leaves, of a pale green, and they are in a very elegant manner divided into narrow and pointed segments. It grows about a foot high, upright, and much branched. The flowers stand at the tops of the branches, so that the plant appears to be covered with them ; they are small and yellow. The seed is brown, and the root long and slender, and hung about with several fibres.

Place.—It is frequent upon the hills and exposed parts of the north of England, and St. Vincent's rock at Bristol.

Time.—It flowers in August.

Virtues.—The seeds are the only parts used in medicine. They are mild and gentle in their operation, and are therefore given in powder. This powder increases the secretion by the kidneys, promotes the menstrual discharge, and is good in the colic and gravel. It is likewise recommended for the dropsy and jaundice.

PARSLEY (COMMON STONE)—*(Sison Amomum;)* PARSLEY (SMALL STONE)—*(Caucalis Arvensis;)* & PARSLEY (SMOOTH STONE.)—*(Caucalis Leptophylla.)*

Descrip.—These plants have the flower umbelliferous, on a few branches, with numerous subdivisions; there are some narrow leaves, both at the base of the larger branches and of the smaller. The first has white flowers, but the other two are pale purple; the leaves are of a good green, and deeply notched; the three plants grow to about a foot long, and the seeds are oblong, rough, small, and brown.

Place.—They grow near Aylesbury and Kingston.

Time.—They flower in June, the seed is ripe soon after.

Government and Virtues.—All the Parsleys are under Mars. The seeds contain an essential oil, and will cure intermitting fevers or agues. A strong decoction of the roots is a powerful diuretic, and assists in removing obstructions of the viscera. They are good against the jaundice and gravel, and moderately promote the menses.

PARSNIP (COW.)—*(Heracleum Sphondylium.)*

Descrip.—This grows with three or four large, spread-winged, rough leaves, lying often on the ground, or raised a little from it, with long, round, hairy footstalks under them, parted usually into five divisions, the two couples standing each against the other; and one at the end, and each leaf being almost round, yet somewhat deeply cut in on the edges in some leaves, and not so deep in others, of a whitish green colour, smelling somewhat strongly; among which rises up a round, crested, hairy stalk, two or three feet high, with a few joints and leaves thereon, and branched at the top, where stand large umbels of white, and, sometimes reddish flowers; and after them flat, whitish, thin, winged seed, two always joined together. The root is long and white, with two or three long strings growing into the ground, smelling likewise strongly and unpleasant.

Place.—It grows in moist meadows, and the borders and corners of fields, and near ditches, throughout this land.

Time.—It flowers in July, and seeds in August.

Government and Virtues.—Mercury has dominion over it. The seed is of a sharp cutting quality, and is a fit medicine for a cough and shortness of breath, the falling-sickness and jaundice. The root is available for all the purposes aforesaid, and is of use to take away the hard skin that grows on a fistula, if it be but scraped upon it. The seed being drunk, cleanses the belly from tough phlegmatic matter, eases those who have overgrown liver, as well if drank as by receiving the fumes underneath, and likewise raises such as are fallen into a deep sleep, or have the lethargy, by burning it under their nose. The seed and root boiled in oil, and the head rubbed therewith, helps not only those that are fallen into a frenzy, but also the lethargy or drowsy evil, and those that have been long troubled with the head-ache, if it be likewise used with rue. It helps also the running scab and the shingles. The juice of the flowers dropped into the ears that run and are full of matter, cleanses and heals them.

PARSNIP (UPRIGHT WATER.)—*(Sium Angustifolium.)*

Descrip.—This water plant has large, deep, green leaves consisting of several longish pinnæ, broad at the bottom, narrow, and sharp-pointed at the end, much cut in about the edges. The stalks are tall, hollow, and channelled, having several small leaves growing on them; and on the tops large umbels of white flowers, succeeded by small striated seed. The root is large, having several long stringy fibres.

Place.—It grows in rivers and large waters.

Time.—It flowers in May and June. The leaves are used.

There are other varieties of growth, as that distinguished by the name Creeping Water Parsnip, *Sium Nodiflorum*, with white flowers, which grows also in watery places, and flowers in June ; and the Great Water Parsnip, *Sium Latifolium*, common about ditches, with white flowers, blowing in July. Of these latter, the seeds only are used.

Virtues.—They are accounted opening and attenuating, useful for obstructions of the liver and spleen, and the womb; help the stone and strangury, and scorbutic affections; outwardly applied, they are commended against cancerous tumours in the breasts. Reduced to powder and taken in doses of about a scruple, it stops purging, and is good in all kinds of hemorrhages, but particularly in excessive menstrual discharges, and spitting of blood. Taken in larger doses, it cures intermitting fevers and agues. A strong decoction is good for sore mouths. The leaves infused in the manner of tea allays the heat in burning fevers. The roots boiled in vinegar, and applied in the form of a poultice, disperses swellings or inflammations in any part of the body; and applied to old putrid sores, cleanses and disposes them for healing. The juice is good to bath inflamed and sore eyes with, and drank to the amount of four ounces a day for several days together, is a certain cure for the jaundice. It is of service in the whites and other female disorders.

PEACH-TREE.—(*Amygdalus Persica.*)

Descrip.—The Peach-tree spreads branches reasonably well, from which spring small reddish twigs, whereon are set long and narrow green leaves dented about the edges. The blossoms are large, of a light purple colour ; the fruit is russet, red or yellow, waterish or firm, with a frieze or cotton all over, with a cleft therein like an apricot, and a large rough stone, with a bitter kernel therein.

Place.—It is a native of the East, but flourishes with us, and in warm seasons its fruit ripens without artificial heat.

Time.—It flowers in Spring, and fructifies in Autumn.

Government and Virtues.—Venus owns this tree. For children and young people, nothing is better to purge choler and the jaundice, than the leaves or flowers of this tree, being made into a syrup or conserve ; the fruit provokes lust. The leaves bruised and laid on the belly, kill worms ; and boiled in ale and drank, they open the belly ; and if dried it is a safe medicine to discuss humours. The powder, if strewed upon fresh wounds stays their bleeding, and closes them up. The flowers steeped all night in a little warm wine, strained in the morning, and drank fasting, gently opens the belly, and purges. A syrup made as the syrup of roses is made, works forcibly to provoke vomiting, and spends waterish and dropsical humours by the continuance. The flowers made into a conserve, work the same effect. The liquor that drops from the wounded tree, is given with a decoction of colt's foot, to those who are troubled with a cough or shortness of breath, by adding thereto some sweet wine and saffron. It is good for hoarseness, loss of voice, and helps defects of the lungs, vomiting and spitting of blood. Two drams given in the juice of lemons or radish, is good for the stone. The kernels of the stones ease the pains of the belly, through wind or sharp humours, and help to make an excellent medicine for the stone. The milk or cream of the kernels if drawn forth with some vervain water, and applied to the forehead and temples, helps to procure rest and sleep to sick persons. The oil drawn from the kernels, the temples being therewith anointed, does the same. This oil put into clysters, eases the pains of the wind colic · and anointing the lower part of the belly does the like. Anointing the forehead and temples with it, helps the megrim, and all other parts of the head. If the kernels be bruised and boiled in vinegar, until they become thick, and applied to the head, it marvellously makes the hair to grow again upon bald places, or where it is too thin.

PEAR-TREE.—(*Pyrus Sativa.*)

PEAR-TREES are so well known that they need no description.

Government and Virtues.—This tree is under Venus. For their medicinal use, they are best discerned by their taste. All the sweet and luscious sorts, whether cultivated or wild, help to move the belly downwards, more or less. Those that are hard and sour, do, on the contrary, bind the belly as much, and the leaves do so also: those that are moist in some sort cool, but harsh and wild sorts much more, and are very good in repelling medicines; and if the wild sorts be boiled with mushrooms, it makes them less dangerous. If boiled with a little honey, they help much the oppressed stomach, as all sorts of them do, some more, some less; but the harsher sorts do more cool and bind, serving well to be bound to green wounds, to cool and stay the blood, and to heal up the wound without further trouble, or inflammation. Wild Pears sooner close the lips of green wounds than others.

PELLITORY OF SPAIN.—(*Anthemis Pyrethrum.*)

THERE are two sorts, one is cultivated, the other is wild.

Descrip.—Common Pellitory is a very common plant, but it needs great care and attention in our gardens. The root goes down right into the ground bearing leaves, is long and finely cut upon the stalk, lying on the soil. At the top it has but one large flower at a place, with a border of many leaves, white on the upper side, and reddish underneath, with a yellow thrum in the middle.

The other Common Pellitory which grows here, has a root of a sharp biting taste, scarcely discernible by the taste from that before described, from whence arise divers brittle stalks, about a yard high, with narrow leaves, finely dented about the edges, standing one above another to the tops. The flowers are many and white, standing in tufts, with a small yellowish thrum in the middle. The seed is small.

Place.—The last grows in fields by hedge-sides and paths, almost every where.

Time.—It flowers at the latter end of June and July.

Government and Virtues.—It is under Mercury, and is

one of the best purgers of the brain that grows. An ounce of the juice taken in muscadel an hour before the fit of the ague comes, will effectually drive away the ague at the second or third dose at the furthest. Either the herb or dried root chewed in the mouth, purges the brain of phlegmatic humours; thereby not only eases pains in the head and teeth, but also hinders the distillation of the brain upon the lungs and eyes, preventing coughs, phthisics and consumption, the apoplexy and falling-sickness. It is an excellent remedy in the lethargy. The powder of the herb or root if snuffed up the nostrils, produces sneezing, and eases headache; made into an ointment with hogs' grease, it takes away black and blue spots, and helps both the gout and sciatica. The roots have a hot pungent taste when chewed in the mouth, which, by stimulating the salival glands, promotes a flow of viscid humours from the head and the adjacent parts, and by this means relieves the tooth-ache, head-ache, lethargy, palsy of the tongue, &c. Internally it is taken in small doses, for paralysis and rheumatism.

PELLITORY OF THE WALL.—(*Parietaria Officinalis.*)

Descrip.—It rises with brownish, red, tender, weak, clear, and almost transparent stalks, about two feet high, upon which grow at the joints two leaves somewhat broad and long, of a dark green colour, which afterwards turn brownish, smooth on the edges, but rough and hairy, as the stalks are also. At the joints with the leaves from the middle of the stalk upwards, where it spreads into branches, stand many small, pale, purplish flowers in hairy, rough heads, or husks, after which come small, black, rough seed, which will stick to any cloth or garment that it touches. The root is long, with small fibres, of a dark reddish colour, which abides all winter, although the stalks and leaves perish and spring every year.

Place.—It grows wild about the borders of fields, by the sides of walls, and among rubbish. It can be brought up in gardens, if planted on the shady side.

Time.—It flowers in June and July; and the seed is ripe soon after.

Government and Virtues.—It is under Mercury. The dried herb made up into an electuary with honey, or the juice of the herb, or the decoction made up with honey and sugar, is a singular remedy for an old and dry cough, the shortness of breath and wheezing in the throat. Three ounces of the juice taken at a time, wonderfully helps stopping of the urine, and expels the stone or gravel in the kidneys or bladder, and is put among other herbs used in clysters to mitigate pains in the back, sides, or bowels, proceeding from wind. If the bruised herb, sprinkled with some muscadel, be warmed upon a few quick coals in a chafing-dish, and applied to the belly, it works the same effect. The decoction, if drunk, eases pains of the mother, brings down the courses, and griefs from obstructions of the liver, spleen, and reins. With a little honey added, the decoction is also good to gargle a sore throat. The juice held in the mouth, eases the pains of the teeth. The distilled water, if drunk with sugar, works the same effect, and cleanses the skin from spots, freckles,. pimples, wheals, sunburn, morphew, &c. The juice dropped into the ears, eases the noise in them, and takes away the prickling and shooting pains therein; the same, or the distilled water, assuages hot and swelling imposthumes, burns and scalds, and all hot tumours and inflammations, and breakings out of heat, if often bathed with it ; the juice made into a liniment with ceruse, and oil of roses, and anointed therewith, cleanses foul rotten ulcers, stays spreading ulcers, and running scabs or sores in childrens' heads ; and helps to stay the hair from falling off. The said ointment, or the herb applied to the fundament, opens the piles, and eases the pains ; mixed with goat's tallow, it helps the gout ; the juice is very effectual to cleanse fistulas, and to heal them ; or the herb bruised, and applied with a little salt. It is effectual to heal green wounds, if bruised and bound thereto three days. A poultice made with mallows, and boiled in wine and wheat bran and bean-flour, and some oil put thereto, and applied warm to any bruised sinew, tendon, or muscle, in a short time restores them, taking away the pains of the bruises or blows. The juice clarified and boiled in a syrup with honey, and a spoonful drank every morning is good for the dropsy ; by taking the dose once a week, that disease will be cured.

PENNY-ROYAL.—(*Mentha Pulegium.*)

Descrip.—It has many creeping fibrous roots, from which spring many smooth roundish stalks, slender, leaning to the ground, sending out small fibres, by which it roots itself in the ground. It bears two small, round, pointed leaves, at a joint ; the flowers grow towards the upper part of the branches, coming forth just above the leaves in thick close whorles; they are of a pale purple colour, small and galated, set in small downy calices, in which are small seeds. The whole plant has a strong smell, and a hot aromatic taste.

Place.—It grows on moist commons and dried pools. It is cultivated in gardens, where it grows tall and large.

There is a greater kind than that found wild with us, but it differs from it only in the largeness of the leaves and stalks, in rising higher, and not creeping on the ground so much. The flowers are purple, growing in rundles about the stalks like the others. It is found wild by the highways from London to Colchester, and in other counties, and is planted in gardens in Essex.

Place.—They flower about August.

Government and Virtues.—This herb is under Venus. It makes thin, tough phlegm, warms any part to which it is applied, and digests corrupt matter; if boiled and drank, it provokes womens' courses, and expels the dead child and afterbirth, and stays the disposition to vomit, if taken in water and vinegar mingled together. Being mingled with honey and salt, it voids phlegm out of the lungs, and purges by stool. Drank with wine, it is good for venomous bites, and applied to the nostrils with vinegar, revives those who faint and swoon. Dried and burnt, it strengthens the gums, helps the gout, if applied of itself to the place until it is red; and applied in a plaster, it takes away spots or marks on the face; applied with salt, it profits those who are splenetic, or liver-grown. The decoction helps the itch, if washed therewith: it helps the swellings and hardness of the mother, if the patient bathe by sitting therein. The green herb bruised and put into vinegar, cleanses foul ulcers, and takes away the marks of bruises and blows about the eyes, and burns in the face, and the leprosy, if drank, and applied outwardly; boiled in wine with honey and salt, it helps the tooth-ache. It helps the cold griefs of the joints, taking away the pains, and warming the cold part, being safe bound to the place, after a bathing or sweating in a hot-house. Penny-Royal and mints together, help those who swoon and faint, if smelled at, or put into the mouth. It eases head-ache, pains of the breast and belly, and gnawing of the stomach: applied with honey, salt, and vinegar, it helps cramps or convulsions of the sinews; boiled in milk, and drank, it is effectual for coughs, and for ulcers and sores in the mouth; the decoction if drank, helps the jaundice and dropsy, and clears the eye-sight. It helps the lethargy, and put into the ears, eases the pains of them. It is of subtle, warm, and penetrating parts; it is also opening, discussive, and carminative ; it promotes the menses, and loche, and prevents the fluor albus. In asthmatic disorders it must be sweetened with honey. One spoonful of the juice sweetened with sugar-candy, is a cure for the hooping-cough.

PENNYWORT (COMMON MARSH.)—(*Hydrocotyle Vulgaris.*)

Descrip.—The root is round, tuberous, and furnished with fibres at the bottom. The leaves rise in thick and regular clusters, and are supported on footstalks of three inches long, and these are in the centre, the leaf spreading every way into roundness from them. These leaves are of a bluish green, prettily notched round the edges, of a watery taste. The stalk is eight inches, and is round and firm; toward the top it divides into two or three branches, and on these hang numerous flowers in long spikes, small, greenish, and dented at the rim. The seeds are numerous and small.

Place.—It frequently grows upon walls in Somersetshire.

Time.—It flowers in July.

Government and Virtues.—It is under Venus, and is good to break the stone and void it; also the gravel in the reins or bladder. It helps suppression of urine and the strangury.

PEONY (MALE.)—(*Pæonia.*)

Descrip.—It rises up with a brownish stalk, whereon grow green and reddish leaves, without any particular division in the leaf. The flowers stand at the top of the stalks, consisting of five or six broad leaves, of a purplish red colour, with many yellow threads in the middle, standing about the head, which rises up to be the seed-vessels, divided into two, three, or four crooked pods like horns, which, being full ripe, open and turn themselves down backward, shewing within them divers round, black, shining seeds, having also many crimson grains intermixed with black. The roots are great, thick, and long, spreading and running down deep in the ground.

Place.—It grows in gardens.

Time.—It flowers usually about May.

Government and Virtues.—It is an herb of the Sun, and under the Lion. The roots are held to be of more virtue than the seed ; next the flowers; and last of all, the leaves. The root, fresh gathered, cures the falling-sickness ; take the root, washed clean and stamped small, and infuse in sack for twenty-four hours at the least, afterwards strain it, and take a good draught morning and evening for days together, this will cure old persons as well as young ones if the disease be not of too long standing and past cure, especially if the body be prepared by taking a drink-posset made of betony, &c. The root is effectual for cleansing the womb after child-birth, and easing the mother. The seed beaten to powder, and given in wine, will answer the same purpose. The black seed taken morning and evening, is effectual for night-mare. It is also good against melancholy dreams. The distilled water or syrup made of the flowers, works the same effects that the root and seed do, although more weakly.

PEPPER.—(*Piper.*)

THERE are three sorts, black, white, and long, which all grow alike, and the last differs from the other two only in the fruit.

Place.—It is a native of Java, Sumatra, Malabar, &c.

Government and Virtues.—All the peppers are under the dominion of Mars, and of temperature hot and dry, almost to the fourth degree ; but the white is the hottest. It comforts and warms a cold stomach, consumes crude and moist humours, and stirs up the appetite. It dissolves wind in the stomach or bowels, provokes urine, helps the cough, and other diseases of the breast, and is an ingredient in the great antidotes ; but the white pepper is more sharp and aromatical, and is more effectual in medicine, and so is the long, being used for agues, to warm the stomach before the coming of the fit. All are used against the quinsey, being mixed with honey and taken inwardly and applied outwardly, to disperse the kernels in the throat, and other places.

PEPPER (GUINEA.)—(*Capsicum Frutescens.*)

CALLED also Cayenne Pepper and Bird Pepper.

Descrip.—There are several kinds. It grows with an upright, firm, round stalk, with a certain pith within it, about two or three feet high, spreading into many branches on all sides, from the very bottom, which divide themselves again into other smaller branches, at each joint come two long leaves upon short footstalks, with several veins, not dented about the edges, and of a dark green colour: the flowers stand severally at the joints, consisting usually of five, and sometimes six, white, small-pointed leaves, standing open like a star, with yellow threads in the middle, after which come the fruit, either great or small, long or short, round or square, as the kind is, either standing upright or hanging down, as their flowers show themselves ; the seeds are numerous, kidney-shaped, and a little compressed ; the root annual and fibrous spreading plentifully in the ground, but perishing after it has ripened all its fruit.

Place.—It is a native of India, but will bear our climate, and ripen its fruit if brought forward in a hot bed in spring, and afterwards planted out in the open ground.

Time.—In India it flowers in August, and the seed-pods ripen in November, where it lives throughout the year, but in this country the seed-pods ripen in the hottest part of summer, and perish with the first frost if not housed.

Government and Virtues.—All kinds of Guinea Pepper are under Mars, and are of a fiery, sharp, biting taste, and of a temperature hot and dry ; they are so hot that they raise a ind of blister in the mouth and throat, or other part of the skin if the seed or husks be used alone ; the vapour from them occasions sneezing, coughing, and even vomiting, and if the hands touch the nose or eyes after handling them, inflammation of those parts will follow : but though dangerous, they have great medicinal properties. Take the husks, dry them with flour in an oven, cleanse them from the flour and beat them very small, to every ounce put a pound of flour, with yeast, bake them into cakes, then beat the cakes to a fine powder, and sift ; this powder is good to season meat, broth, soup, stew, &c. Put in the diet it drives away wind and helps flatulency, taken into a cold stomach with the meat, it gives great relief, causing phlegm to be voided ; it helps digestion, gives appetite, provokes urine ; if taken with saxifrage water it expels the stone in the kidneys and the phlegm that breeds it, and takes away dimness of the sight if used in meats. Taken with *Pillulæ Aleophanginæ*, it helps dropsy ; the powder, taken for three days together in the decoction of penny-royal expels the dead-birth, the powder, taken fasting, for three or four days, with a little fennel seed, will ease all the pains of the mother. If made up with a little powder of gentian and oil of bays, into a pessary, with some cotton wool, it will bring down the courses ; the same mixed with an electuary will help an inveterate cough ; mixed with honey it helps quinsey, if applied to the throat ; and made up with turpentine, and laid on hard knots or kernels in any part of the body, it will dissolve them; applied with nitre it takes away freckles, spots, morphew, marks and discolourings of the skin: along with hen's grease, it dissolves cold imposthumes and carbuncles; mixed with vinegar it dissolves the hardness of the skin: rubbed upon the back with *Unguentum de Albastro*, it will take away the ague: a plaster made with tobacco, will heal venomous stings and bites. The decoction of the husks is a good gargle for the tooth-ache, and preserves the teeth from rottenness; the ashes rubbed on the teeth will clean them. The decoction helps watery ruptures, if applied morning and evening. If steeped in *aqua vitæ*, it helps the palsy, if the place be bathed with it; steeped in wine, and two spoonfuls drunk every morning, fasting, makes stinking breath sweet. It is a stimulant in phlegmatic disorders, paralytic complaints, and relaxations of the stomach, and is put into aloetic and nervous medicines for all female disorders. It is good for the quinsey, if put into bread poultice, and applied to the part which is affected.

PEPPER (WATER.)—(*Polygonum Hydropiper.*)

Descrip.—It sends forth long broad leaves, finely dented on the edges, pointed at the ends, of a light bluish-green colour, standing upon round hard stalks, three or four feet high, spreading many branches on all sides, having many small white flowers at the tops, after which come small seeds in small heads. The root is slender, spreads much under ground, shooting up again in many places; and both leaves and roots are of a very hot and sharp taste.

Place.—It grows naturally in many parts of this country.

Time.—It flowers in the end of June, and in July.

Virtues.—It is good for sciatica, gout, or pains in the joints, or any other inveterate disease, if the leaves are bruised and mixed with hog's-grease, and applied to the place, and kept on four hours in men, and two hours in women, the place being afterwards bathed with wine and oil mixed together, and then wrapped up with wool or skins, after which they sweat a little. It amends the deformities or discolourings of the skin, and helps to take away marks, scars, or scabs, produced by burns.

PERIWINKLE (GREAT.)—(*Vinca Major.*)

Descrip.—It has many branches running on the ground, shooting out small fibres, taking hold of the ground, and roots in divers places. At the joints of these branches stand two small, dark, green, shining leaves, and with them come forth the flowers, one at a joint, standing upon a tender footstalk, long and hollow, parted at the brims, sometimes into four, sometimes into five leaves; the most ordinary sorts are of a pale blue colour, some of a pure white, and some of a dark reddish purple colour.

Place.—Those with the pale blue, and those with the white flowers, grow in woods and orchards, by the hedge-sides, in divers parts of this country; but those with the purple flowers in gardens only.

Time.—They flower in March and April.

Government and Virtues.—Venus own this herb. It is a great binder, and stays bleeding at the mouth and nose, if it be chewed. It is a good female medicine, and may be used with advantage in hysteric and other fits. An infusion is good to stay the menses; a two ounce dose will have the same effect. It is good in nervous disorders; the young tops made into a conserve is good for the night-mare. The small Periwinkle (*Vinca Minor*) possesses all the virtues of the othre kind, and may very properly supply its place.

PETER'S WORT. (ST.)—(*Ascyrum Stans.*)

Descrip.—It rises up with square, large, brown, upright stalks, having leaves at every joint, round pointed, with few or no holes to be seen thereon, and sometimes smaller leaves rising from the bosom of the greater, with a little hair thereon. At the tops of the two stalks stand many star-like flowers, with yellow threads in the middle, larger than those of St. John's wort, the seed being like it. The root abides long, sending forth new shoots every year.

Place.—It grows in small low woods, in divers places of this country, also near water-courses.

Time.—It flowers in June and July; and the seed is ripe in August.

Government and Virtues.—Two drams of the seed taken at a time in honied water, purges choleric humours, and helps the sciatica. The leaves bruised are good for burns.

PILEWORT (COMMON.)—(*Ficaria Verna.*)

Descrip.—This small plant, besides the slender, white, fibrous root, has several small, oval, whitish tubercles, resembling the piles. The leaves grow on long footstalks, smooth and shining, sometimes spotted white. The flowers grow on pretty long stalks, inclining to the earth, with a leaf or two on them more angular, sharper-pointed, and smaller than the other ; they consist of eight or nine narrow, sharp-pointed petals of shining yellow colour, with a few yellow stamina in the middle, set about a green head that is composed of small naked seeds.

Place.—It grows in moist pastures and by hedge-sides.

Time.—It flowers in April.

Government and Virtues.—This herb is good for the piles, to ease their pain and swelling, and stop their bleeding ; the roots being taken inwardly, and an ointment being made of the leaves and roots, is cooling and good for inflamed sores and ulcers. The expressed juice of the plant is used to cure internal wounds, bruises, and spitting of blood, with good success. The leaves bruised and boiled in hog's-lard, until they become crisp, and then strained, affords an excellent cooling ointment.

PIMPERNEL (WATER.)—(*Anagallis Aquatica.*)

Descrip.—It has divers weak square stalks lying on the ground, beset with two small and almost round leaves at every joint, one against another, but no footstalks; for the leaves, as it were, compass the stalk, consisting of five small round-pointed leaves, of a pale red colour, tending to an orange, with many threads in the middle, in whose places succeed smooth round heads, wherein is contained small seed. The root is small and fibrous, perishing every year.

Place.—It is found only in brooks and running waters.

Government and Virtues.—This plant is warm and dry, with a little stypticity, and is a good vulnerary. The juice mixed with cow's milk, is useful in consumptions and distempers of the lungs ; it is put into cordial waters, as an alexipharmic, and good against malignant distempers. It helps bites and stings of venomous creatures, being applied either inwardly or outwardly. It also opens obstructions of the liver, and is available against the infirmities of the reins: it provokes urine, and helps to expel the stone and gravel out of the kidneys and bladder, and helps inward pains and ulcers. The decoction or distilled water is effectual if applied to green wounds, or old, filthy, fretting, and running ulcers, which it speedily cures. A little mixed with the juice, and dropped into the eyes, cleanses them from cloudy mists, or thick films which grow over them. It helps tooth-ache, being dropped into the ear on the contrary side of the pain. It is also effectual to ease the piles. This herb is a good deobstruent and antiscor

Mouse Ear.
Wild Parsnip.
Purple Loosestrife.
Wood Sage.
Scurvy Grass.
Sneeze Wort.
Pelitory of the Wall.

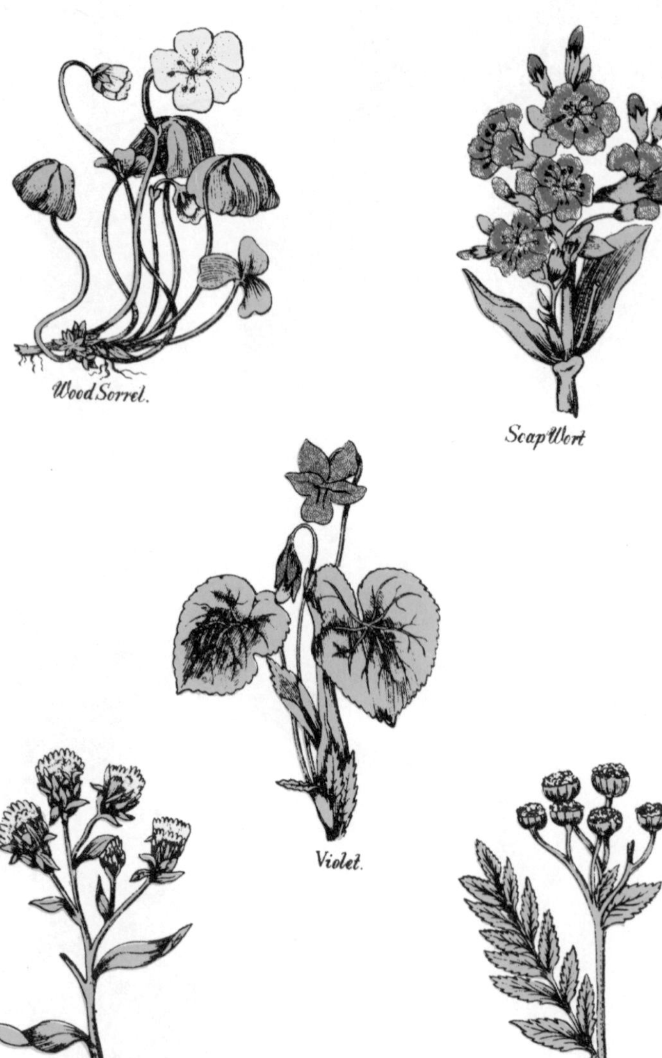
Wood Sorrel.
Soap Wort
Violet.
Spikenard.
Tansy.

butic, abounding with volatile parts, good for the scurvy, and is an ingredient of the antiscorbutic juices and diet drinks for that distemper. It is likewise detersive and cleansing, and useful in many inward obstructions.

PINE-TREE.—(*Pinus Sylvestris.*)

Descrip.—On the continent it grows to a great height, but with us not so tall. It is found in parks and inclosures. The leaves are short and slender, and the cones are sharp-pointed, including small kernels.

Place.—It ows its existence in this country to the curious, who plant it for its beauty and ornament.

Government and Virtues.—It is a tree of Mars. From it common turpentine, which is thick, whitish, and opaque, is obtained. It has a strong smell, and is used by farriers from this the distilled oil, sometimes called the spirit of turpentine, is extracted ; what is left at the bottom of the still is the common rosin, which, if taken out before it is drawn too high, and then washed in water, is called white, or yellow rosin. The black is more evaporated, and not washed at all, they are the same in nature, being used in ointments and plasters. The kernels are excellent restoratives in consumptions, and after long illness. The best way of giving them is in an emulsion beat up with barley-water, which is also very good for heat of urine, and other disorders of the urinary passages.

PLANTAIN.—(*Plantago Major.*)

Descrip.—The root is thick at the head, having whitish fibres growing from it. The leaves are broad, large, and oval, waved at the edges, with seven large nerves running through the whole length of them, and even the broad hollow footstalks into the root. The flowers grow in long spikes, above half the length of the footstalks, small and staminous, cut into four parts, which are succeeded by two small, oblong, shining brown seeds, hollow on the one side, growing in little roundish capsulæ, which open horizontally when the seed is ripe.

Place.—It is every where by the way-side.

Time.—It flowers in May. The whole plant is used.

Government and Virtues.—This is under Venus, and it cures the head by its antipathy to Mars, and the privities by its sympathy to Venus ; neither is there a martial disease but it cures. The juice, clarified and drank for days together, either by itself, or with other drink, helps excoriations or pains in the bowels, the distillations of rheum from the head, and it stays all manner of fluxes, even womens' courses, when too abundant. It is good to stay spitting of blood and bleedings at the mouth, or the making of foul and bloody water, by reason of any ulcer in the reins or bladder ; and staunches the too free bleeding of wounds. The seed is profitable against dropsy, falling-sickness, yellow-jaundice, and stoppings of the liver and reins. The roots, and Pellitory of Spain, beaten into powder, and put into hollow teeth, takes away the pains of them. The juice, or distilled water, dropped into the eyes, cools the inflammations in them, and takes away the pin and web. If the juice be mixed with oil of roses, and the temples and forehead be anointed therewith, it eases the pains of the head proceeding from heat. The same also is profitably applied to all hot gouts in the hands and feet. It is good if applied to bones out of joint, to hinder inflammations, swellings, and pains that presently rise thereupon. The powder of the dried leaves taken in drink, kills worms of the belly ; boiled in wine, it kills worms which breed in old and foul ulcers. One part of the herb water and two parts of the brine of powdered beef, boiled together and clarified, is a remedy for all scabs and itch in the head and body, all manner of tetters, ringworms, the shingles, and all other running and fretting sores. All the Plantains are good wound herbs to heal fresh or old wounds, or sores, either inward or outward.

PLANTAIN (BUCK'S-HORN.)—(*Plantago Coronopus.*)

Descrip.—Like the other, this Plaintain has a slender, fibrous root. The leaves are numerous and beautiful; like a star lying on the ground, and spreading every way from the head of the root ; they are long, narrow, and deeply jagged at the edges, like the horn of a buck, pale green and hairy. The stalks are upright, and like other Plantains, with small, irregular, four-leaved flowers, growing on hoary stalks three or four inches long. The seed is small, of a dark brown shining colour.

Place.—It grows in sandy grounds, and upon heaths.

Time.—It flowers in June.

Government and Virtues.—This has the nature of other Plantains, moderately drying and binding, and is a good wound herb, both inwardly and outwardly; it is commended against venomous bites, especially those of a mad dog.

PLANTAIN (GRASS.)—*(Plantago Uniflora.)*

Descrip.—This is a grassy and apparently weedy herb. The leaves are green, curling, entwined with each other in a curious manner, like Sea Grass. The flowers are single, consisting of four white leaves each, with long threads growing out of each centre, at the top are small white buttons. The whole plant grows about four inches high.

Place.—It is common in the Isle of Sheppy, and in other parts about the sea-coasts.

Time.—It flowers in June.

Virtues.—The expressed juice is good against spitting of blood, immoderate flow of the menses, and piles. The seeds reduced to powder, and taken, stop the whites. The fresh leaves bruised, and applied to fresh cuts, soon heal them, and are good to cleanse and heal ulcers. This is astringent, cooling, and healing. A decoction is excellent in all urethral and uterine disorders.

PLANTAIN (RIBWORT.)—*(Plantago Lanceolata.)*

Descrip.—The leaves are narrower than the former, sharp-pointed, having five ribs, or nerves, running quite through them to the root, which is less and more stringy than the former: the flowers grow at the end of long slender stalks in oblong spikes, an inch long; they are small and staminous, with white apices. The seeds grow like the others, but are somewhat larger.

Place.—It grows in fields and hedges.

Time.—The flowers appear in May and June.

Virtues.—The leaves are astringent and vulnerary, and are useful for the same purposes as the former. The juice of it is commended for the ague, to lessen its effects.

PLOUGHMAN'S SPIKENARD.—(*Conyza Squarrosa.*)

Descrip.—This is a biennial, a coarse, but ill-looking plant. The stalk is two feet and a half high, of a ruddy brown, dry, brittle, branchy towards the top. The leaves are broad lanced, rugged on the surface, of a coarse dead green, and a little dented about the edges. The flowers are of a dull yellow, and stand in a close tuft, at the tops of the stalk; they grow out of an oblong and rugged cup; the scales are sharp-pointed, stand wide and are bent out.

Place.—It is found by road sides, and in waste places.

Time.—The flowers bloom in August.

Government and Virtues.—It is under the government of Venus. The leaves, when bruised, emit a quick and aromatic smell. They are bitterish to the taste, with some sharpness. A weak tea made of this herb is good to promote the menses, and much preferable to any mineral.

PLUMS.—*(Prunus Domestica.)*

THEY are so well known that they need no description.

Government and Virtues.—All Plums are under Venus. There is great diversity of kinds, some that are sweet moisten the stomach, and make the belly soluble, those that are sour quench thirst more, and bind the belly; the moist and waterish corrupt the stomach, but the firm do nourish more, and offend less. The dried fruit, under the name of damask Prunes, somewhat loosen the belly, and when stewed, are used, both in health and sickness, to relish the mouth and stomach, to procure appetite, and to open the body, allay choler, and cool the stomach. Plum-tree leaves boiled in wine, are good to wash and gargle the mouth and throat, to dry the flux of rheum coming to the palate, gums, or almonds of the ears. The gum of the tree is good to break the stone. The gum or leaves boiled in vinegar, and applied, kills tetters and ringworms.

POLEY (MOUNTAIN.)—*(Teucrium Polium.)*

Descrip.—This grows about a foot high, much branched, with squarish woolly husks, having two small white woolly leaves at a joint, not above half an inch long, and scarcely half so broad, blunt pointed, and indented about the edges towards the end. The flowers grow at the ends of the branches, in round woolly thick spikes, small, and of a white colour, labiated, but having no galea, being set in white, hoary, five-pointed calices; both leaves and flowers have a pleasant aromatic scent.

Place.—It is a native of Italy, but will bear the cold of our country, if taken care of in a green-house in winter.

Time.—It flowers in July and August.

Government and Virtues.—It is under the dominion of Venus. It is opening and attenuating, good for obstructions of the liver and spleen; it is good in dropsy and jaundice ; it provokes urine and the menses, and is serviceable in venomous bites. Outwardly applied, it is emollient, xlpening and dissolving, good for hard tumours and swellings, and is put into ointments and plasters for that object.

POLYPODY.—(*Polypodium Vulgare.*)

Descrip.—This is a perennial herb of the fern tribe, distinguishable by the seeds being in roundish spots, distributed on the under surface of the leaf. The root is shagged with hairs, and of the thickness of one's little finger, and, when broken, is found to be green within; and to the taste at once austere and sweet.

Place.—It is common among mossy stones, upon the joints of old walls which are in the shade, and upon the stumps of trees; but the best sort grows upon the decayed parts of old oak trees.

Time.—It is in perfection in October and November.

Government and Virtues.—It is under Jupiter in Leo. With laxatives it gently carries off the contents of the bowels without irritation. By itself it is a very mild and useful purge: but being very slow, it is generally mixed by infusion or decoction with other ingredients, or in broths with beets, parsley, mallow, cummin, ginger, fennel and anise. The best form to take it for a complaint in the intestines, is as follows: To an ounce of the fresh root bruised, add an ounce and a half of the fresh roots of white beets, and a handful of wild mallow; pour upon these a pint and a quarter of water, boiling hot, and let it stand till next day, then strain it off. A quarter of a pint of this liquor contains the infusion of two drams of this root. It should be sweetened with sugar-candy, or honey.

POMEGRANATE-TREE.—(*Punica Granatum.*)

Descrip.—This is a shrubby plant, covered with a brownish bark, and divided into a number of branches, which spread in an irregular manner, and are armed with sharpish spines, and have their upper end pretty thick set with long narrow smooth leaves, two inches in length, to half an inch in breadth; among these come forth the flowers, of a bright scarlet colour, consisting of five leaves set in a tough brown calyx, which in time enlarging itself becomes the bark or covering of the fruit, having a crown on its upper part, in shape and size like an orange, but with a broader and harder peel, in the inside of which grow a great number of cornered acini or kernels, compacted together in regular order, containing each a sweet vinous juice, or one more acid, with a small stone in the middle.

Place.—It is a native of Italy and Spain, and needs the shelter of a green-house in this country.

Government and Virtues.—This tree is under Mercury. Both the flowers and bark of the fruit are strongly astringent; a decoction of them stops bleedings and purgings of all kinds, and is good for the whites. The pulp of the fruit, when in perfection, is very grateful, and has the same general qualities with the other acid fruits. A strong infusion cures ulcers in the mouth and throat, and fastens teeth.

PUMPKIN.—*(Cucurbita Pepo.)*

Descrip.—This takes up a great compass of ground, with its large, thick, creeping stalks, furnished with large claspers: its leaves are large and rough, like those of melons. The flowers are large, like a yellow lily in colour. The fruit is large, having large, white, oval, flattish seeds.

Place.—It is sown on dunghills.

Time.—It is ripe in September and October.

Government and Virtues.—It is a moist plant under the dominion of the Moon. The seed is cooling, of the nature of the melon and other cold seeds, and may serve very well to make emulsions. It is rarely used in medicine.

POPLAR (BLACK.)—*(Populus Nigra.)*

Descrip.—This tree grows higher and straighter than the white, with a greyish bark, bearing broad green leaves, like ivy leaves, not cut on the edges, but whole and dented, ending in a point, and not white underneath, hanging by slender long footstalks, which are continually shaking. The catkins are greater than those of the white, composed of round green berries, as if set together in a long cluster, containing much downy matter, which being ripe is blown away with the wind. The clammy heads hereof, before they spread into leaves, are of a yellowish green colour, and small, somewhat sweet, but strong.

Place.—It grows in moist woods, and by water-sides in sundry places in England.

Time.—The catkins come out before the leaves in summer.

Government and Virtues.—Saturn has dominion over both White and Black Poplars. The White is of a cleansing property; one ounce of the powdered bark drunk, is a remedy for the sciatica, or the strangury. The juice of the leaves dropped into the ears, eases the pains in them. The young clammy buds or eyes, before they break out into leaves, bruised, and a little honey put to them, is a good medicine for dull sight. The Black is more cooling than the White ; the leaves bruised, and applied with vinegar, help the gout. The seed drank in vinegar, is good against falling-sickness. The water that drops from the hollows of this tree, takes away warts, pushes, wheals, and breakings-out of the body. The leaves and buds are used to make the *Unguent Populeon ;* but as the Black is hot, the ointment cannot receive virtue from its leaves or buds, but from the other ingredients which are put in it.

POPLAR (WHITE.)—*(Populus Alba.)*

Descrip.—This kind grows great and high, covered with thick, smooth, white bark, especially the branches, having long leaves cut into several divisions almost like the vine leaf, but not so deep green on the upper side, and hoary white underneath, of a reasonable good scent, the whole representing the form of coltsfoot. The catkins which it brings forth before the leaves, are long, and of a faint reddish colour, which fall away, bearing seldom good seed with them. The wood is smooth, soft, and white, very finely waved, whereby it is much esteemed.

POPPY (BLACK.)—*(Papaver Nigrum.)*

Descrip.—This does not grow so high as the White, but in other respects it is much like it. The chief difference is in the flower, which in this is of a purplish colour, with a black bottom ; and in the heads which do not grow the same size, and contain black seed. The roots of both are sticky, and perish when the seed is ripe.

Place.—It is sown in gardens.

Time.—It flowers in June and July.

Virtues.—The heads are rarely used, being left alone with the other. The flowers are however of a gentle sudorific nature, and are peculiarly good in pleurisies, quinsies, and all disorders of the breast.

POPPY (CROWFOOT.)—*(Papaver Ranunculus Latifolius.)*

Descrip.—The stalk is thick and naked, round and fleshy. The leaves are irregular and few, stripped into many divided segments, and of a pale green colour. The flower is large and single, growing at the top of the stalk; the usual colour of it is bright scarlet, but it is sometimes yellow or white. In the middle is a tuft of yellow threads.

Place.—It is sown only in gardens.

Time.—It flowers in June.

Government and Virtues.—It is under Saturn, and good to remove warts. The expressed juice is used to make way for the instruments of surgery; and the whole plant bruised has been applied to remove head-ache, but care must be taken to keep it from the eyes, or it will inflame them.

POPPY (VIOLET HORNED.)—(*Chelidonium Corniculatum.*)

Descrip.—This differs from the others, only the leaves are divided into numerous fine segments, in a double pinnated manner. The stalk is four or five feet high, having no branches at the top, and but two or three at most below, bearing every one but one head wrapped up in a thin skin, which bows down before it is ready to bloom, and then rising, and being broken, the flower within it spreads itself open, consisting of very large white round leaves, with many whitish round threads in the middle, set about a small, round, green head, having a horn or star-like point shooting out at the head, which, growing ripe, becomes as large as a great apple, wherein are contained a great number of small round seeds in several partitions next to the shell, the middle thereof remaining hollow and empty.

Place.—It is common in corn-fields.

Time.—It flowers in July.

Virtues.—An infusion of the flowers boiled into a syrup, partakes slightly of the nature of opium. The juice is of the same acrid and bitter taste with the other species.

POPPY (WHITE, OR OPIUM.)—(*Papaver Somniferum.*)

Descrip.—This is cultivated for its medicinal uses. It has many large, long, whitish green leaves, much torn and cut in on the edges. The stalk is smooth and round, growing five or six feet high; towards the top it is divided into three or four branches, having at the end of each a round head, hanging down at first, but as the flower comes on to open, it grows erect. The flower consists of four large leaves, inclosed in a couple of green skinny husks, which soon drop off when the flower opens; when the flowers are fallen, the seed-vessel grow as big as a large orange, having a denticillated crown on the head ; it is divided into membraneous partitions, to the sides of which grow the small white seed. The whole plant is full of a bitter milk, of a strong, virose, unpleasant smell.

Place.—It grows wild in Ireland, but it is cultivated in the gardens in England.

Time.—It flowers during the months of Summer.

Government and Virtues.—It is under the dominion of the Moon. The seed-vessels are the parts to use. Syrup of diacodium is a strong decoction of them, boiled to a consistence with sugar. The syrup is a gentle narcotic, easing pain, and causing sleep; half an ounce is a full dose for an upgrown person, for younger it must be diminished accordingly. The seeds, beaten into an emulsion, with barley-water, are good for the strangury, and heat of the urine; but they have none of the sleepy virtues of the syrup, nor of the other parts of the preparations of the poppy. Opium is nothing more than the milky juice of this plant, concreted into a solid form. It is procured by wounding the heads, when they are almost ripe, with a five-edged instrument, which makes as many parallel incisions from top to bottom; and the juice which flows from these wounds is the next day scraped off, and the other side of the head wounded in like manner. When a quantity of this juice is collected, it is worked together with a little water, till it acquires the consistence and colour of pitch, when it is fit for use. Opium has a faint disagreeable smell, and a bitterish, hot, biting taste; taken in proper doses, it procures sleep, and a short respite from pain, but great caution is required in administering it, for it is a very powerful, and, consequently, a very dangerous medicine in unskilful hands. It relaxes the nerves, abates cramps, and spasmodic complaints; but it increases paralytic disorders, and such as proceed from weakness of the nervous system. It incrassates thin serous acrid humours, and thus proves a speedy cure for catarrhs and tickling coughs, but must never be given in phthisical or inflammatory complaints; for it dangerously checks perspiration, unless its effects are counteracted by the addition of ammoniac or squills, and by producing a fulness and distention of the whole habit, it exasperates all inflammatory symptoms, whether internal or external. It promotes perspiration, but checks all evacuations, and is good for stopping purgings and vomitings; and this is effected by small doses, judiciously given. With regard to the dose, half a grain, or at most, a grain, in all common cases is sufficient: and even when larger doses are required, it is more advisable to repeat them more frequently, than to give a larger quantity. An over-dose causes immoderate mirth or stupidity, redness of the face, swelling of the lips, relaxation of the joints, giddiness of the head, deep sleep, accompanied with turbulent dreams and convulsive starting, cold sweats, and frequently death.

POPPY (WILD.)—(*Papaver Rhœas.*)

CALLED also Corn Rose.

Descrip.—This has long narrow leaves, very much cut in on the edges into many divisions, of a light green colour, sometimes hairy; the stalk is blackish and hairy, but not so tall as the garden-kind, having such like leaves as grow below, whereon grow small hairy heads bowing down before the skin breaks, wherein the flower is inclosed, which, when it is full blown, is of a fair yellowish red or crimson colour, and in some much paler, without any spots at the bottom of the leaves, having many black soft threads in the middle, compassing a small green head, which, when ripe, is not bigger than one's little finger's end, wherein is contained much black seed, smaller than that of the garden. The root perishes every year, and springs again of its own sowing. Of this kind there is one lesser in all the parts thereof and differs in nothing else. This is called the Welsh Poppy, or *Papaver Cambricum.*

Place.—They are sown in gardens.

The Wild Poppy, or Corn Rose, is plentiful in the corn-fields in all parts of this country, upon ditch-banks, and by hedge-sides. The smaller wild kind is also found in corn-fields and other places, but is not so plentiful.

Time.—The garden kinds are sown in Spring, and flower in May. The wild ones flower from May until July; and the seed of them is ripe soon after the flowering.

Government and Virtues.—The herb is Lunar; and a syrup is made of the seed and flowers, which is useful to give sleep and rest to invalids, and to stay catarrhs and defluxions of rheums from the head into the stomach and lungs, which causes a continual cough, the forerunner of consumption; it helps hoarseness of the throat, and loss of voice, which the oil of the seed does likewise. The black seed boiled in wine, and drank, stays the flux of the belly, and womens' courses. The poppy-heads are usually boiled in water, and given to procure rest and sleep; so do the leaves in the same manner; if the head and temples be bathed with the warm decoction, or with the oil, the green leaves or heads bruised, and applied with a little vinegar, or made into a poultice with barley-water, or hog's-grease, cools and tempers all inflammations, and St. Anthony's fire. It is generally used in treacle and mithridate, and in all other medicines that are made to procure sleep and rest, and to ease pains in the head as well as in other parts. It cools inflammations, and agues. It is put in hollow teeth, to ease the pain; it is also good for the gout.

POPPY (YELLOW HORNED.)—*(Glaucium Luteum.)*

Descrip.—The root is long and thick at the head, divided into branches which fix themselves deep in the earth, from which spring blueish-green winged leaves divided generally into five parts, the section at the end being the largest. The stalk grows to be a foot or more high, full of thick joints, having two smaller leaves at each joint; the flowers grow together upon a footstalk three or four inches long, each having a shorter of its own; they consist of four small yellow leaves, included in calyces of two hollow parts; and after they are fallen, they are followed by long, narrow pods, full of small, round, shining black seed. Every part of the plant, when broken, emits a yellow, bitter, acrid juice.

Place.—It grows among waste grounds and rubbish, upon walls and buildings.

Time.—It flowers in May.

Government and Virtues.—It is under the Sun in Leo; and is aperative and cleansing, opening obstructions of the spleen and liver, and of great use in curing the jaundice and scurvy. Outwardly it is used for sore eyes, to dry up the rheum, and take away specks and films, as also against tetters and ringworms, and the breakings-out of scurvy. The root dried and powdered, is balsamic and sub-astringent. It is given against bloody-fluxes, and in other hemorrhages, half a dram for a dose.

PRIMROSE.—*(Primula Vulgaris.)*

Descrip.—This has a perennial root consisting of a short thick head, furnished with a great number of thick and long fibres. The leaves arising from the root make a large tuft; they are large, oblong, without leaf-stalks, wrinkled on the surface, entire at the edges, of a deep green colour. The flowers are supported singly on long slender hairy stalks: which rise immediately from the root; they are large, and of a white or pale yellow colour. The seeds are small, numerous, and of a roundish figure.

Place.—It is common in woods, hedges, and thickets, particularly in a clayey soil.

Time.—The flowers appear in March and April.

Government and Virtues.—It is under the dominion of Venus. The roots are used as a sternutatory to the head: the best way of using them is to bruise them, and express the juice, which, being snuffed up the nose, occasions violent sneezing, and brings away a great deal of water, but without being productive of any bad effect. Dried and reduced to powder, it will produce the same effect, but not so powerfully. In this state it is good for nervous disorders, but the dose must be small. A dram and a half of the dried roots, taken in autumn, is a strong, but safe emetic.

PRIVET.—*(Ligustrum Vulgare.)*

Descrip.—This bush does not grow large, it has many smooth, tough, pliant branches, clothed with small oblong leaves, broadest in the middle, and sharp-pointed at the end. It bears long and narrow green leaves by the couples, and sweet-smelling white flowers in tufts at the ends of the branches, which turn into small black berries that have a purplish juice in them, and some seeds that are flat on the one side, with a hole or dent therein.

Place.—It grows in this country, in divers woods.

Time.—It flowers in June and July; and the berries are ripe in August and September.

Government and Virtues.—The Moon owns this herb. It is used more especially in lotions to wash sores, and sore mouths, to cool inflammations, and dry up fluxes. The sweet water distilled from the flowers, is good to heal all those diseases that need cooling and drying, and helps all fluxes of the belly and stomach, bloody-fluxes, and womens' courses, if drunk or applied; as the voiding of blood at the mouth, or any other place, for distilling rheum from the eyes, especially if it be used with Tutia.

PURSLANE.—*(Portulaca Oleracea.)*

Descrip.—This plant is so well known that a short description may serve, it having round, smooth, reddish, and succulent brittle stalks, with fat thick leaves, and broader at the end than next the stalk. The flowers grow on the tops of the stalks among the leaves, being small, five-leaved and yellow, succeeded by roundish seed-vessels, including small, black, rugged seed. The root is small and fibrous.

Place.—It is sown in gardens ; the leaves and seeds are used. The seed is one of the lesser cold seeds.

Government and Virtues.—It is an herb of the Moon. It is good to allay the heat of the liver, blood, reins, stomach, and hot agues : it stays hot and choleric fluxes of the belly, womens' courses, the whites, and gonorrhœa, the distillation from the head, and pains therein proceeding from heat, want of sleep, or the frenzy. The seed is more effectual than the herb, and is good to cool the heat and sharpness of urine. The seed bruised and boiled in wine, and given to children, expels the worms. The juice of the herb is effectual to all the purposes aforenamed ; also to stay vomitings, and taken with sugar and honey, helps an old and dry cough, shortness of breath, and the phthisic, and stays immoderate thirst. The distilled water is preferred by many, and it works the same effects. The juice is good for inflammations and ulcers in the secret parts, as well as in the bowels, and hemorrhoids, when they have excoriations in them ; the herb bruised and applied to the forehead and temples, allays excessive heat therein, that hinders rest and sleep ; and applied to the eyes it takes away inflammation in them, those other parts where pushes, wheals, pimples, St. Anthony's fire, and the like, break forth; if a little vinegar be put to it, and laid to the neck, with as much of gall and linseed together, it takes away the pains therein, and the crick in the neck. Applied to the gout, it eases the pains, and helps the hardness of the sinews, if it come not of the cramp or a cold cause.

QUICK GRASS.—*(Agrostis.)*

Descrip.—There are several sorts. 1. Common Quick Grass *(A. Vulgaris,)* which creeps about under ground, with long white jointed roots, and small fibres almost at every joint. 2. Quick Grass *(A. Plumosa,)* with a more spreading penicle. 3. Smaller Quick Grass *(A. Canina,)* with a spreading tuft. 4. Low-bending Quick Grass *(A. Alba.)* 5. Quick Grass *(A. Mutica,)* with a penicle that does not spread. 6. Small Sweet Grass *(A. Pumila,)* with many low creeping branches.

Place.—The first is common in ploughed grounds and gardens; the second and third are more scarce, and delight in sandy or chalky grounds; the three next are also found in ploughed fields.

Time.—They flourish in the beginning of summer.

Government and Virtues.—These are plants of Mercury. The Quick Grass, the root of which is of temperature cold and dry, and has a little mordacity in it and some tenuity of parts, is the most medicinal of all other sorts: a decoction thereof drank, opens obstructions of the spleen and liver, stoppings of urine, to ease the griping pains in the belly and inflammations, and to waste the excrementitious matter of the stone in the bladder and the ulcers thereof: the root being bruised and applied, knits together and consolidates wounds. The seed more powerfully expels wind, binds the belly, and stays vomiting. The distilled water is good to be given to children for worms.

QUINCE TREE.—*(Pyrus (Cydonia.)*

Descrip.—This tree grows to the height of a good-sized apple-tree, crooked, with a rough bark, spreading branches far abroad. The leaves resemble those of the apple-tree, but thicker, broader, and fuller of veins, and whiter on the under-side, not dented about the edges. The flowers are large and white, somewhat dashed over with a blush. The fruit is yellow, being near ripe, and covered with a white frieze; thick set on the younger, growing less as they get nearer ripe, bunched out oftentimes in some places: some being like an apple, some like a pear, of a strong heady scent, and not durable to keep; it is sour, harsh, and of an unpleasant taste to eat fresh; but being scalded, roasted, baked, or preserved, becomes more pleasant.

Place.—It grows plentifully near ponds and water sides.

Time.—It flowers not until the leaves come forth. The fruit is ripe in September or October.

Government and Virtues.—Saturn owns this tree. The fruit has a strong, very pleasant smell, and acid taste. Its expressed juice, taken in small quantities, is a mild, astringent stomachic medicine, and is of efficacy, in sickness, vomiting, eructations, and purgings. A grateful cordial, and lightly restringent syrup, is made by digesting three pints of the clarified juice, with a dram of cinnamon, half a dram of ginger, the same of cloves, in warm ashes, for six hours, then adding a pint of red port, and dissolving nine pounds of sugar in liquor, and straining it. And a useful jelly is made by boiling the juice with a sufficient quantity of sugar, till it attains a due consistence. The seeds abound with a soft mucilaginous substance, which they readily impart to boiling water, making it like the white of an egg. This is excellent for sore mouths, and useful to soften and moisten the mouth and throat in fevers, and other diseases. The green fruit helps all sorts of fluxes in man or woman, and in choleric laxes. The crude juice is preservative against the force of poison. The oil is useful to bind and cool outwardly hot fluxes; it strengthens the stomach and belly by anointing, and the sinews that are loosened by sharp humours falling on them, and restrains immoderate sweatings. The mucilage taken from the seeds, and boiled in water, is good to cool the heat, and heal the sore breasts of women. The same, with a little sugar is good to lenify the harshness and soreness of the throat, and the roughness of the tongue. The cotton or down boiled, and applied to plague sores, heals them up; and laid as a plaster, made up with wax, it brings hair to those who are bald, and keeps it from falling off, if it be ready to shed.

RADISH (COMMON GARDEN.)—(*Raphanus Sativus.*)

THIS plant is so well known that it needs no description.

Place.—It is planted in gardens.

Time.—It flowers in May.

Government and Virtues.—It is under Mars, and is opening, attenuating, and antiscorbutic ; it does not give much nourishment, and is very windy ; it provokes urine and is good for the stone and gravel. The expressed juice of the root, with the addition of a little wine, is an admirable remedy for gravel. The roots eaten plentifully sweeten the blood and juices, and are good against the scurvy.

RADISH (WILD, OR HORSE.)—(*Cochlearia Armoracia.*)

Descrip.—The first leaves rise before winter, a foot and a half long, cut on the edges in many parts, of a dark green colour, with a white rib in the middle ; after these have been up a while, others follow, which are taller, rougher, broader, and longer, whole and not divided at first, dented about the edges. The root is great, white, and rough, sending up divers heads of leaves, which may be parted for increase, but it doth not creep in the ground, nor run above, it is of a strong, sharp taste, almost like mustard.

Place.—It is found wild in some places, but is chiefly planted in gardens, in moist and shady places.

Time.—It seldom flowers, but when it does, it is in July.

Government and Virtues.—It is under Mars. The juice

of the root drank, is effectual for scurvy. It kills worms in children, if given to drink. The bruised root laid to the part affected with the sciatica, joint-ache, or the hard swellings of the liver and spleen, helps them all. The distilled water of the herb and root is more familiar to be taken with a little sugar for all the purposes aforesaid.

RAMPION (HORNED.)—*(Phyteuma Obiculare.)*

Descrip.—This rises from a long, thick, white, and fibrous root. The lower leaves are short, and almost round, but pointed at the end, and some few of them at times oval, or oblong: they have long footstalks, and are serrated at the edges. The stalk is tender, striated, or hollow, about a foot high. The leaves stand irregularly on it, and are altogether unlike those from the root: they are long, narrow, and sharp-pointed, serrated at the edges, and of a pale green; those towards the bottom have long footstalks, but those towards the upper parts have none. The flowers stand at the top of the stalk in a round thick head; they are small and purple, close together, and curled round like a horn, from which the plant derives its name.

Place.—It is a perennial plant, and not uncommon in the hilly pastures of Kent and Sussex.

Time.—It flowers in August.

Government and Virtues.—There are several species of this plant, but this possesses most virtue. The roots of any of them may be eaten as a salad in spring, they are well tasted, and full of a milky juice. They are under Venus. The root, if eaten in due quantity, operates by urine, and may be good to create an appetite.

RAMPION (SHEEP'S.)—*(Jasione Montana.)*

Descrip.—The root, from a small head, shoots out many fibres. The stalk is upright, of a pale green, and rises to about three feet in height. The leaves are of a faint green, divided at the edges into small segments. The flowers grow in a large head like scabious, and are of a fine blue; but they are sometimes found of a reddish or white colour.

Place.—It is a biennial; common on high pastures.

Time.—It flowers in August.

Government and Virtues.—It is under the dominion of Mercury, and of a bitter, light, astringent quality, excellent against disorders of the breast, such as coughs, asthmatic affections, difficulty of breathing, &c., for which purpose an infusion of the flowers is the best preparation. The flowers are good against feverish complaints; the juice applied externally heals foulness and discolourings of the skin.

RAMPION (HAIRY SHEEP'S.)—*(Phyteuma Spicatum.)*

Descrip.—Grows upon a dry, brittle stock, slender, and of a pale green. The leaves are of a pale dead green, and a little hairy; milk runs from them when broken, and pressed. The flowers are a beautiful blue, pale, and elegant.

Place.—Most found on heaths and dry upland grounds.

Time.—It flowers in August.

Government and Virtues.—This is under Venus, and is cooling and diuretic. The leaves are an excellent diuretic, useful in gravel and the stone : boiled in milk, and sweetened with sugar, they cure the heat of urine. They help the jaundice, by opening the obstructions of the liver and gall bladder : and the dropsy, by carrying off the water.

RATTLE GRASS.—*(Rhinanthus.)*

Of this there are two kinds, which I shall speak of, viz., the red and yellow.

Descrip.—The common Red Rattle *(Pedicularis Sylvatica)* has reddish, hollow stalks, sometimes green, rising from the root, lying mostly on the ground, some spring more upright, with many small reddish or green leaves, set on both sides of a middle rib finely dented about the edges : the flowers stand on the tops of the stalks and branches, of a purplish red colour ; after which come blackish seed in small husks, which lying loosely, will rattle with shaking. The root consists of two or three small whitish strings with some fibres thereat.

The common Yellow Rattle *(Rhinanthus Crista Galli)* has seldom above one round great stalk, rising from the foot, about a yard or two feet high, with but few branches, having two long broad leaves set at a joint, deeply cut in on the edges, broadest next to the stalk, and smaller to the end. The flowers grow at the tops of the stalks, with some shorter leaves with them, hooded after the manner that the others are, but of a fair, yellow colour, some paler, and others more white. The seed is contained in husks, and when ripe, rattle same as the red kind does. The root is small and slender, perishing yearly.

Place.—They grow in the meadows and woods throughout this country.

Time.—They flower from Midsummer until August is past, sometimes.

Government and Virtues.—They are both under the dominion of the Moon. The Red Rattle is profitable to heal fistulas and hollow ulcers, and to stay the flux of humours in them, and the abundance of womens' courses, or other fluxes of blood, if boiled in wine, and drank.

The Yellow Rattle is good for cough, or dimness of sight, if the herb boiled with beans, and some honey put thereto, be drunk, or dropped into their eyes. The whole seed being put into the eyes, draws forth any skin, dimness of film, from the sight, without pain or trouble.

RASPBERRY.—*(Rubus Idæus Hortensis.)*

CALLED also Hindberry.

Descrip.—This cannot properly be called a fruit-tree, yet, as the fruit is valuable, something is expected of the shrub that produces it. Besides the small flowering sort, the common small red and white, there are other sorts much larger of the same colour, called Rombullions ; the former has the richest flavour, but in dry seasons they are apt to wither. It is so well known that it needs no further description.

Place.—It grows wild in woods in England and Wales, and is plentifully cultivated in fruit-gardens.

Time.—It flowers in May, and the fruit is ripe in June and July.

Government and Virtues.—Venus owns this shrub. The fruit, which is the only part used, has a pleasant grateful smell and taste, is cordial and strengthens the stomach, stays vomiting, is somewhat astringent, and good to prevent miscarriage. The fruit is very grateful as nature presents it, but made into a sweetmeat with sugar, or fermented with wine, the flavour is improved. It is fragrant, a little acid, and of a cooling nature. It dissolves the tartarous concretions on the teeth, but is inferior to strawberries for that purpose. The juice of the ripe fruit boiled into a syrup, with refined sugar, is pleasant and agreeable to the stomach, and prevents sickness and retchings.

REST HARROW.—*(Ononis.)*

CALLED also Cammock.

Descrip.—Common Rest Harrow rises up with divers woody twigs, half a yard or a yard high, set at the joints without order, having little roundish leaves, sometimes more than two or three at a place ; of a dark green colour, without thorns when they are young, but afterwards armed in sundry places with short and sharp thorns. The flowers come forth at the tops of the twigs and branches, like peas and broom blossoms, but lesser, flatter, and somewhat closer, of a faint purplish colour; after which come small pods, containing small, flat, round seed ; the root is blackish on the outside, and whitish within, very rough, and hard to break when it is fresh and green, and as hard as horn when it is dried.

Place.—It grows in many places in this land, as well in the arable as waste ground.

Time.—It flowers in July, the seed is ripe in August.

Government and Virtues.—It is under the dominion of Mars. It is excellent to provoke urine, and to break and expel the stone, which the bark of the root taken in wine performs effectually. The decoction with some vinegar used to wash out the mouth, eases tooth-ache, especially when it comes of rheum; it is powerful to open obstructions of the liver and spleen, and other parts. The powder of the root made into an electuary, or lozenges, with sugar, as also the bark of the fresh roots boiled tender, and afterwards beaten to a conserve with sugar, works the like effect. The powder of the roots strewed upon the brims of ulcers, or mixed with any other convenient thing, and applied, consumes the hardness, and causes them to heal the better.

RHUBARB.—*(Rheum Palmatum.)*

Descrip.—This has a long, thick, perennial root, of a yellow colour on the outside, and marbled within, full of reddish veins ; firm, but not too hard or heavy, of a pretty strong smell, of a bitterish, somewhat styptic taste, tinging the spittle of a yellow saffron colour.

Place.—The roots are brought from China, Turkey, Russia, and Siberia ; but as good rhubarb plants now grows in our botanic gardens as any that come from abroad.

Time.—It flowers in June and July.

Government and Virtues.—It is a mild purgative, and also a mild astringent. It strengthens the intestines, and generally leaves the belly costive, for which reason it is preferred to other purgatives, in obstinate purgings, and bloody flux. It is given more as a strengthener than as a purgative. That of a bright, or light texture, moist, fragrant, and sound, should be chosen, as being milder in its operation, more grateful to the stomach, and more likely to answer the purpose of an astringent, a diuretic, or an alterative.

In acute fevers, where it is dangerous to take purgatives, rhubarb may be safely given. In bloody flux, and those loosenesses occasioned by acrid matter remaining in the intestines, this root is very useful. There is a spirituous tincture sold in the shops, intended as a strengthener and purgative ; for the first of these purposes, two or three spoonfuls is a sufficient dose at a time; but for the latter, two or three ounces is frequently necessary.

RHUBARB (CULINARY, OR TART.)—(*Rheum Rhaponticum.*)

Descrip.—This has a large root, thick at the head, and divided into many branches, of a dark brown on the outside, and a deep yellow colour within, of a bitterish taste. From the root arise several large, somewhat crumpled, green leaves; roundish, but pointed at the end, of a sourish taste, growing on reddish footstalks, from among these arises a thick stalk three or four feet high, having small leaves, and a numerous company of white staminous six-leaved flowers, succeeded by large, shining, triangular, brown seed.

Place.—It is a native of Scythia, but grows in our gardens.

Time.—It flowers in the middle of summer.

Government and Virtues.—It is under the dominion of Mars. As to its purgative quality, it is much weaker than Rhubarb, but is more astringent, and good in fluxes, and weakness of the stomach, spitting of blood, and making bloody urine. It is good against venomous bites.

RHUBARB (GREAT MONK'S.)—(*Rumex Alpinus*

CALLED also Great Garden Patience.

Descrip.—At its first appearance, when the winter is past, it hath a great round brownish head, rising from the middle or sides of the root, which opens itself into sundry leaves one after another, very much crumpled or folded together at the first, and brownish ; but afterwards it spreads itself, and becomes smooth, very large and almost round, every one standing on a brownish stalk of the thickness of a man's thumb, when they are grown to their fulness, and most of them two feet or more in length, especially when they grow in any moist or good ground; and the stalk of the leaf, from the bottom thereof to the leaf itself, being also two feet, the breadth thereof from edge to edge, in the broadest place, being two feet, of a sad or dark green colour, of a fine tart or sourish taste, much more pleasant than the garden or wood sorrel. The root grows very great, with divers great spreading branches from it, of a dark brownish or reddish colour on the outside, with a pale yellow skin under it, which covers the inner substance or root, which rind and skin being pared away, the root appears of so fresh and lively a colour, with fresh coloured veins running through it, that the choicest of the Rhubarb that is brought from beyond the seas cannot excel it, which root, if it be dried carefully, by the gentle heat of a fire, and every piece kept from touching one another, will hold its colour almost as well as when it is fresh, and hath been approved of and commended by those who have oftentimes used it.

Place.—It grows in gardens, and flowers in June; the seed is ripe in July.

Time.—The roots that are to be dried and kept all the year following, are not to be taken up until the stalk and leaves are quite withered and gone, and that is not until the middle or end of October; and if they be taken a little before the leaves spring, or when they are sprung up, the roots will not have half so good a colour in them.

Government and Virtues.—Mars claims dominion over all these wholesome herbs. A dram of the dried root, with a scruple of ginger made into powder, and taken fasting in a draught of warm broth, purges choler and phlegm downwards very gently and safely, without danger. The seed thereof binds the belly, and helps to stay bloody-flux. The distilled water heals foul ulcerous sores, and allays inflammation of them; the juice of the leaves or roots, or the decoction of them in vinegar, is used as a most effectual remedy to heal running sores. The Culinary Rhubarb has all the properties of Monk's Rhubarb, but is more effectual both for inward and outward diseases. The decoction without vinegar dropped into the ears, takes away the pains; gargled in the mouth, takes away the tooth-ache; and if drank, heals the jaundice. The seed taken, eases the griping pains of the stomach, and takes away the loathing unto meat. The root helps the ruggedness of the nails; and if boiled in wine, helps the swelling of the throat, called king's-evil, as well as the swellings of the kernels of the ears. It expels the stone, provokes urine, and helps the dimness of sight. The Culinary Rhubarb purges the choler and phlegm, taken either by itself, made into powder, and drank in a draught of white wine, or steeped therein all night, and taken fasting, or put into other purgatives, as shall be convenient, cleansing the stomach, liver, and blood, it opens obstructions, and helps those diseases that come thereof, as the jaundice, dropsy, swelling of the spleen, tertian and daily agues, and pains in the sides. It also stays spitting of blood. The powder taken with cassia dissolved, and washed Venice turpentine, cleanses the reins, and strengthens them, and is effectual to stay gonorrhœa. It is also taken for pains and swellings in the head, and melancholy, and helps the sciatica, gout, and cramp. The powder taken with a little mummia and madder roots in red wine, dissolves clotted blood in the body, which comes by falls or bruises, and helps all burstings and broken parts, as well inward as outward. It is useful to heal those ulcers that happen in the eyes or eyelids, if steeped and strained; as also to lessen the swellings and inflammations; and applied with honey, boiled in wine, it takes away all blue spots or marks that happen therein. Whey or white wine are the best liquors to steep it in, and thereby it more effectually opens obstructions and purges the stomach. Indian spikenard is the best corrector of it.

RICE.—(*Oryza Sativa.*)

THE foreign plant which produces this useful grain has no medicinal virtues, a description of it is therefore unnecessary.

Place.—It grows very plentifully in the East Indies, all through Ethiopia, Africa, Syria, Egypt, Italy, &c.

Time.—It is ripe about the middle of autumn ; in some places it yields two crops a year.

Government and Virtues.—It is a Solar grain, and it stays laxes and fluxes of the stomach and belly, especially if it be parched before it is used, and hot steel quenched in the milk wherein it is boiled, being somewhat drying and binding. The flour of the rice has the same property, and is put into cataplasms to repel humours from flowing to the place, and also to womens' breasts to stay inflammations.

ROCKET CRESS (ANNUAL.)—(*Hesperis Matronalis.*)

Descrip.—This plant is sometimes improperly called Cresling. The root is slender, long, hard, furnished with many fibres : the first leaves are numerous, long, and irregularly divided in the pinnated manner, with a pointed odd segment at the end. The stalks are numerous, round, upright, and the leaves stand on them irregularly ; they resemble those from the root, but they are more deeply divided, and of a lighter green. The flowers stand in a loose spike at the top of the stalks, of a faint yellow, with streaks of black.

Place.—It has been found upon Salisbury Plain.

Time.—It is an annual, and blooms in July.

Government and Virtues.—This species is under Venus, and the juice is excellent in asthmas, and all diseases of the lungs. The best way of using it is in the form of a syrup; it will relieve oppression and obstructions of the breast, and cure inveterate coughs and severe colds in the stomach.

ROCKET CRESS (DWARF.)—(*Iberis Nudicaulus.*)

Descrip.—This is a small plant, with pale leaves, which grow near the bottom, they grow in a thick tuft, without footstalk, but are narrowest at the base, and broadest towards the end; they are notched at the edges. The stalk is round, upright, and divided into many branches. It is of a pale green colour, and about ten inches high. The flowers stand in great numbers on the tops of the branches, and they are small and white.

Place.—It is an annual, and grows upon commons. It is found about Putney and Barnes Common.

Place.—It flowers in May.

Government and Virtues.—This is under the Moon. All these Cresses are celebrated as remedies for all the diseases of the urinary passage. The expressed juice, or the infusion of the whole plant, is the best way of taking it.

ROCKET (GARDEN.)—(*Eruca Sativa.*)

Descrip.—This has a slender, white woody root, of a hot taste; the leaves are shaped like mustard, but smoother; the stalks grow two or three feet high, clothed with lesser leaves, having on their tops many flowers of a whitish yellow colour, full of dark purple veins; the seed-vessels are long, slender, and smooth, parted in two by a thin membrane, and open at the sides when the seed is ripe.

Place.—It is sown in gardens.

Time.—It flowers here in August.

Government and Virtues.—All this kind of Rockets are martial plants. This species is celebrated against diseases of the lungs. The juice is excellent in asthmas, and a syrup of it in all oppressions and obstructions of the breast; as also against inveterate coughs.

ROCKET (PURPLE SEA.)—(*Cakile Maritima.*)

CALLED also Red Bunny.

Descrip.—This is a tall plant, with long leaves deeply divided into segments; they have large veins, and are of a deep green. The stalk is thick, tough, and of a pale green. The flowers are purple, and grow in spikes on the tops of the stalks. It has a very disagreeable smell.

Place.—It is an annual, frequent in salt-marshes, and about the sea-coast in Cornwall, and the Isle of Man.

Time.—It flowers in July.

Government and Virtues.—It is a martial plant, of a hot nature, and bitterish taste, opening and attenuating, good to cleanse the lungs of tough viscid phlegm, and of great service in asthmas, and difficulty of breathing; and is often used as an emetic, and to help the jaundice and dropsy.

ROCKET (WILD.)—(*Eruca Sylvestris.*)

Descrip.—This has long narrow leaves, divided into slender cuts and jags on both sides of the middle rib more than the garden kinds; of a sad green colour, from among which rise stalks two or three feet high, set with the like yellow leaves, but smaller upwards, branched in the middle into stiff stalks, bearing yellow flowers on them, made of four leaves each, as the others are, which afterwards yield small reddish seed, in small long pods, of a more bitter and hot taste than the garden kinds, as the leaves are also.

Place.—It is found wild in several parts of this country.

Time.—It flowers about June or July, and the seed is ripe in August.

Government and Virtues.—This plant is forbidden to be used alone, because its sharpness strikes into the head, causing aches and pains therein. It serves to help digestion, and provokes urine abundantly. The seed cures the bites of venomous reptiles, and other poisons, and expels worms and other noisome creatures that breed in the belly. The herb boiled or stewed, and sugar added, helps the cough in children, if taken often. The seed taken in drink, carries away the ill-scent of the arm-pits, increases milk in nurses, and wastes the spleen. The seed mixed with honey, and used on the face, cleanses the skin from morphew, and used with vinegar takes away freckles and redness of the face, and other parts; and with the gall of an ox, it amends foul scars. black and blue spots, and the marks of the small-pox.

ROCKET (WINTER.)—(*Eruca Brumalis.*)

CALLED also Winter Cresses.

Descrip.—This plant has large sad green leaves lying on the ground, torn in different parts, like turnip-leaves, with smaller pieces next the bottom, and broad at the ends, from which rise up small round stalks, full of branchos, bearing many small yellow flowers of four leaves each, after which come small pods with reddish seed in them; the root is rather stringy, and perishes every year after the seed is ripe.

Place.—It grows of its own accord in gardens and fields, by the way-sides, in many places.

Time.—It flowers in May, seeds in June, and then dies.

Government and Virtues.—This is profitable to provoke urine, to help strangury, and expel gravel and the stone. It is good for the scurvy, and serviceable to cleanse all inward wounds; if the juice or decoction be drunk, or outwardly applied to wash foul ulcers and sores, cleanses them by sharpness, hinders and abates the dead flesh from growing therein, and heals them by a drying quality.

ROOT OF SCARCITY.—(*Beta Altissima.*)

Descrip.—This is a species of the beet-root, and grows in the same manner. In Germany, it is called Dick Reuben, (the Great Turnip); Dick Wurzel, (the Great Root); and Mangel Wurzel, (the Root of Scarcity). It is known by the name of Mangel Wurzel in this country.

Government and Virtues.—This root is under Saturn. It is easy to cultivate it, and its nourishing qualities are so many that it ought to be cultivated every where. Insects and vermin which destroy other roots and plants, will not touch or injure it: it is not affected by mildew, or blasted by drought. It not only does not draw the virtues from the soil, but the better prepares it for the reception of corn or other seed which may be put in. Cattle, sheep, and horses will readily eat the leaves, and poultry may be fed upon the roots if cut small and mixed with bran. When the crops have failed, or provender is scarce, this plant will be found one of the cheapest, most valuable and wholesome roots that has ever been introduced into this country, and is preferable to either turnips, carrots, or beet-root.

A very agreeable dish may be prepared for the table, by taking the root and dressing it as spinach.

ROSE (DAMASK.)—(*Rosa Damascena.*)

Descrip.—This does not grow tall or large as the white, but yet taller and fuller of prickles than the red, especially about the stalk. The leaves are whiter and more hairy. The flowers are less double than the Provence Rose, the beards prickly. They are a pale red colour, and of a pleasant scent.

Place.—A native of France, but is common in our gardens.

Time.—It blooms in June and July.

Government and Virtues.—It is under the dominion of Venus. Botanists describe a vast number of roses, but this, and the common red rose, and the dog rose, or hip, are the only kinds regarded in medicine. There is a syrup made from the flowers of the damask rose, by infusing them twenty-four hours in boiling-water, and then straining off the liquor, adding twice the weight of refined sugar to it. This syrup is an excellent purge for children and grown people of a costive habit ; a small quantity taken every night will keep the bowels regular. There is a conserve made of the unripe flowers, which has the same properties as the syrup; there is likewise a conserve made of the fruit of the wild or dog rose, which is very pleasant, and of considerable efficacy for common colds and coughs. The flowers of the common red rose dried, are given in infusions, and sometimes in powder, against overflowings of the menses, spitting of blood, and other hemorrhages. There is likewise an excellent tincture made from them by pouring a pint of boiling water on an ounce of the dried petals, and adding fifteen drops of oil of vitriol, and three or four drams of the finest sugar in powder, after which they are to be stirred together, and left to cool. This tincture, when strained, is of a beautiful red colour. It may be taken to the amount of three or four spoonfuls, twice or three times a day, for strengthening the stomach, and preventing vomiting. It is a powerful and pleasant remedy in immoderate discharges of the menses, and all other fluxes and hemorrhages. The damask rose, on account of its fragrance, belongs to the cephaltics ; but the next valuable virtue it possesses, consists in its cathartic quality. After the water, which is a good cordial, is drawn off in a hot still, the remaining liquor, strained, will make a very good purging syrup from two drams to two ounces. An infusion made of half a dram to two drams of the dried leaves, answers the same purpose.

ROSE (HIP.)—(*Rosa Canina.*)

CALLED also Wild Briar.

Descrip.—This grows in the hedges, has winged leaves like garden roses, but smoother and greener; the flowers are single, of five white, and sometimes pale red leaves, when they fall, they are followed by red seed-vessels, full of pulp, inclosing white, cornered seed, covered with short stiff hairs.

Place.—It grows every where in the hedges.

Time.—It flowers in June, and the hips are fit to be gathered about the end of September.

Government and Virtues.—This is under Jupiter. The flowers are accounted more astringent than the garden roses, and are a specific for the excess of the catamenia. The pulp of the hips has a grateful acidity, strengthens the stomach, cools the heat of fevers, is pectoral, good for coughs and spitting of blood, and in cases where astringents are safe; they are a good ingredient in compositions for the whites, and too great a discharge of the menses. The hips are grateful to the taste, and a considerable restorative, fitly given to consumptive persons; the conserve is proper in all distempers of the breast, and in coughs and tickling rheums. The white and red roses are cooling and drying; the bitterness in the roses when they are fresh, especially the juice, purges choler, and watery humours; but being dried, and that heat which caused the bitterness being consumed, they have then a binding and astringent quality: those also that are not full blown, do both cool and bind more than those that are full blown, and the white rose more than the red. The decoction of red roses made with wine and used, is very good for head-ache, and pains in the eyes, ears, throat and gums; as also for the fundament, and the lower parts of the belly and the matrix, being bathed or put into them. The same decoction, with the roses remaining in it, is applied to the region of the heart to ease the inflammation therein, as also St. Anthony's fire, and other diseases of the stomach. Being dried and beaten to powder, and taken in steeled beer or water, it helps to stay womens' courses. The yellow threads in the middle of the roses being powdered, and drunk, in the distilled water of quinces, stays the overflowing of womens' courses, and stays the defluxions of rheum upon the gums and teeth, preserving them from corruption, and fastening them if they be loose, if washed therewith, and some vinegar of squills added. The heads with the seed being used in powder, or in a decoction, stays the lax and spitting of blood. Red roses strengthen the heart, the stomach, the liver, and the retentive faculty ; they mitigate the pains that arise from heat, cool inflammations, procure rest and sleep, stay both the whites and reds in women, the gonorrhœa, or running of the reins, and fluxes of the belly; the juice purges and cleanses the body from choler and phlegm. The husks, with the beards and nails of the roses, are binding and cooling, and the distilled water is good for the heat and redness in the eyes, and to stay and dry up the rheums and watering of them. The electuary of roses is purging ; two or three drams taken by itself, or in some convenient liquor, is a purge sufficient for a weak constitution, but may be increased to six drams, according to the strength of the patient. It purges choler without trouble, and is good in hot fevers, and pains in the head, which arise from hot choleric humours, and heat of the eyes; the jaundice also, and joint-aches proceeding of hot humour. The moist conserve is of much use, both binding and cordial, for until it is about two years old, it is more binding than cordial, and after that more cordial than binding. Some of the younger conserve taken with mithridate, is good for those troubled with defluxions of rheum in the eyes, and mixed with the powder of mastic, is good for gonorrhœa, and looseness of humours in the body. The old conserve mixed with *aromaticum rosarum*, is a remedy for those who faint, swoon, or are troubled with weakness and tremblings of the heart, it strengthens both it and a weak stomach, helps digestion, stays casting, and is a preservative in the time of infection. The dry conserve, which is called the sugar of roses, strengthens the heart and spirits, and stays defluxions. The syrup of dried roses strengthens a stomach given to casting, cools an overheated liver, and the blood in agues, comforts the heart, and resists putrefaction and infection, and helps to stay laxes and fluxes. Honey of roses is used in gargles and lotions to wash sores, either in the mouth, throat, or other parts, both to cleanse and heal them, and stay the fluxes of humours that fall upon them. It is used in clysters both to cool and cleanse. The cordial powders, called *diarrhodon abbatis* and *aromaticum rosarum*, comfort and strengthen the heart and stomach, procure an appetite, help digestion, stay vomiting, and are very good for those that have slippery bowels, to strengthen them, and to dry up their moisture : red rose-water is well known, and of a similar use on all occasions, and better than the damask rose-water, it is cooling, cordial, refreshing, quickening the weak and faint spirits, used either in meats or broths, to wash the temples, to smell at the nose, or to smell the sweet vapours out of a perfume pot, or cast into a hot fire-shovel. It is of much use against the redness and inflammations of the eyes to bathe therewith, and the temples of the head. The ointment of roses is much used against heat and inflammations of the head, to anoint the forehead and temples, and if mixed with the *Unguentum Populeon* procures rest; it is also used for the heat of the liver, the back, and reins, and to cool and heal pushes, wheals, and other red pimples rising in the face and other parts. Oil of roses is used by itself to cool hot inflammation or swellings, and to bind and stay fluxes of humours to sores, and is also put into ointments and plasters that are cooling and binding, and restraining the flux of humours. The dried leaves of the red roses are used both outwardly and inwardly; they cool, bind, and are cordial, for of them are made *aromaticum rosarum*, *diarrhodon abbatis*, and *saccharum rosarum*. Rose-leaves and mint, heated and applied outwardly to the stomach, stay castings, strengthen a weak stomach, and, applied as a fomentation to the region of the liver and heart, greatly cool and temper them; quiet the over-heated spirits, and cause rest and sleep. The syrup of damask-roses, is both simple and compound, and made with agaric. The simple solusive syrup is a familiar, safe, gentle, and easy medicine, purging choler, taken from one ounce to three or four. The conserve and preserved leaves of those roses operate by mildly opening the belly. The hips of wild roses, when ripe, are made into a conserve with sugar, of a pleasant taste, it binds the belly, and stays defluxions from the head upon the stomach, and dries up the moisture, and helps digestion. The pulp of the hips dried to a hard consistence, that it may be powdered, and this powder taken in drink, speedily stays the whites. It is often used in drink, to break the stone, provoke urine when it is stopped, and ease and help the colic; some persons burn it and then take it for the same purpose.

ROSE (RED.)—(*Rosa Rubra.*)

Descrip.—This has lower bushes than the former; the flowers have few prickles on the stalks, and the calyx, or beards, are shorter and smoother; they are less double than either the damask or white, having a great many yellow anthera in the middle.

Virtues.—This binds more and is more restringent than any of the other species, good against all kinds of fluxes; it strengthens the stomach, prevents vomiting, stops tickling coughs, by preventing the defluxion of the rheum; and is of service in consumptions; the anthera, or apices, are accounted cordial. The conserve of the red buds is excellent in consumptive cases, especially in spitting of blood. The distilled water, made of the full-blown flower, is cooling, of good use in recent inflammations of the eyes, if it be dissolved in a small quantity of rock saltpetre. Some apply the conserve for that purpose. A strong tincture, drawn from the dried red roses, makes a pleasant julep, and helps the bark in its operations.

ROSE (WHITE.)—*(Rosa Alba.)*

Descrip.—This tree grows taller than most other kinds of roses, having fewer prickles on the branches, and those pretty large; the leaves are of a dark green colour; the flowers white and more double, or fuller of leaves than the damask or red, having a less fragrant scent than either of them.

Government and Virtues.—This is under the Moon. The flowers only are used, being drying, binding, and cooling; the water distilled from them is used in collyriums for sore inflamed eyes, it is the only officinal preparation from them.

ROSEMARY.—*(Rosmarinus Officinalis.)*

Descrip.—This rises from a long woody divided root, a little fibrous. The shrub is covered with a brown tough bark; and the youug shoots are of a greyish green. The leaves are numerous, and of a firm substance; they are oblong, narrow, sharp-pointed, not at all indented at the edges, and of a very fragrant smell: they are of a beautiful green on the upper side, and silvery grey underneath. The flowers rise in great numbers from the bosom of the leaves toward the upper part of the branches; they are large, and of a pale blue, variegated with white. The seeds are small and oblong. The whole plant has a fragrant and aromatic smell; it is lighter and more delicate in the flower, and stronger in the leaves. The taste is pleasant, warm, and aromatic.

Place.—It is cultivated plentifully in gardens.

Time.—It flowers in April and May, sometimes in August.

Government and Virtues.—The Sun claims dominion over it. The decoction of Rosemary in wine, helps the cold distillations of rheums into the eyes, and other cold diseases of the head and brain, as the giddiness and swimmings therein, drowsiness or dulness, the dumb palsy, or loss of speech, the lethargy, the falling-sickness, to be both drunk and the temples bathed therewith. It helps the pains in the gums and teeth, by rheum falling into them, not by putrefaction, causing an evil smell from them, or stinking breath. It helps a weak memory, and quickens the senses. It is very comfortable to the stomach in all the cold maladies thereof; helps both the retention of meat, and digestion, the decoction of the powder being taken in wine. It is a remedy for the windiness in the stomach, bowels, and spleen, and expels it powerfully. It helps those that are liver-grown, by opening the obstructions thereof. It helps dim eyes, and procures a clear sight, the flowers thereof if taken all the while it is flowering, every morning fasting, with bread and salt. Both the flowers and leaves are very profitable for the whites, if they be taken daily. The dried leaves shred small, and smoked as tobacco, helps those that have any cough, phthisis, or consumption, by warming and drying the thin distillations which cause those diseases. The leaves are very much used in bathings; and made into ointments or oil, are good to help cold benumbed joints, sinews, or members. The chymical oil drawn from the leaves and flowers, is a sovereign help for all the diseases aforesaid, to touch the temples and nostrils with two or three drops for all the diseases of the head and brain spoken of before; as also to take one drop, two or three, as the case requires, for the inward diseases; yet it must be done with discretion, for it is very quick and piercing, and therefore but a little must be taken at a time. There is also another oil made by insolation in this manner:—Take what quantity you will of the flowers, and put them into a strong glass close stopped, tie a fine linen cloth over the mouth, and turn the mouth down into another strong glass, which being set in the sun, an oil will distil down into the lower glass, to be preserved as precious for divers uses, both inward and outward, as a sovereign balsam to heal the diseases before mentioned, to clear dim sight, and take away spots, marks, and scars in the skin. Hungary water is made by distilling a pure spirit from the tops of this plant; or in a coarser way, by mixing a few drops of its oil in such a spirit.

ROSEMARY (MARSH.)—(*Andromeda Polifolia.*)

CALLED also Wild Cestus.

Descrip.—This is a smaller plant than the former, but in general appearance it is somewhat like. The stalk is woody and brown without. The leaves of a firm consistence : they are oblong, narrow, sharp-pointed, not indented, and of a beautiful green. The flowers are of a pale blue, variegated with white and purple.

Place.—This is perennial, but not common. It is sometimes found in low damp woods, and near waters.

Time.—It flowers in April.

Government and Virtues.—This is under Mars. It is very restringent, drying, and binding, good for diarrhœas and dysenteries, spitting of blood, and all kinds of hemorrhages; it fastens loose teeth, stops the bleeding of the gums, and helps the scurvy in them.

RUE (GARDEN.)—(*Ruta Graveolens.*)

Descrip.—This is a shrubby plant, whose elder branches are tough and woody, having smooth blueish green leaves, divided into a certain number of small oval sections, which are somewhat thick and fat, and round-pointed at the end, abiding all winter. The flowers grow on the tops of the younger shoots, consisting usually of four yellow, hollow, scoop-like leaves, torn in about the edges, and having eight yellow stamina encompassing a roundish green head, cut as it were into four parts, growing large, and seemingly punched full of holes, containing small black rough seed. The root is woody, having many fibres.

Place.—It is planted in gardens ; the leaves and seed are used. The whole plant has a very strong scent.

Time.—It generally flowers in August.

Government and Virtues.—It is an herb of the Sun, and under Leo. It provokes urine and womens' courses, if taken in meat or drink. The seed taken in wine, is an antidote against all dangerous medicines or deadly poisons. A decoction made with some dried dill-leaves and flowers, eases all inward pains and torments, if drunk, and outwardly applied warm to the part affected. The same if drunk, helps the pains of the chest and sides, coughs and hardness of breathing, inflammations of the lungs, and the tormenting pains of the sciatica and the joints, if anointed, or laid to the places ; as also the shaking fits of agues, to take a draught before the fit comes on; being boiled in oil, it is good to help the wind colic, the hardness and windiness of the mother, and frees women from the strangling or suffocation thereof, if the parts be anointed with it ; it kills and drives forth the worms of the belly, if it be drunk after it has been boiled in wine to the half, with a little honey ; it helps the gout or pains in the joints, hands, feet or knees, applied thereto ; and with figs it helps the dropsy, if bathed therewith ; being bruised and put into the nostrils, it stays the bleeding; it helps the swelling of the testicles, if bathed with the decoction and bay leaves. It takes away wheals and pimples, if bruised with a few myrtle leaves it be made up with wax, and applied. It cures the morphew, and takes away all sorts of warts, if boiled in wine with some pepper and nitre, and the place rubbed therewith ; and with almond and honey, helps the dry scabs, or any tetter or ringworm. The juice warmed in a pomegranate shell or rind, and dropped into the ears, helps the pains of them. An ointment made of the juice with oil of roses, ceruse, and a little vinegar, and anointed, cures St. Anthony's fire, and all running sores in the head. It helps disorders in the head, nerves, and womb, convulsions and hysteric fits, the colic, and weakness of the stomach and bowels ; it resists poison, and cures venomous bites.

RUE (MEADOW OR WILD.)—(*Thalictum Flavum.*)

Descrip.—This rises up with a yellow stringy root, much spreading in the ground, shooting forth new sprouts round about, with many herby green stalks, two feet high, crested all the length of them, set with joints here and there, and many large leaves on them, being divided into smaller leaves, nicked or dented in the fore part of them, of a red green colour on the upper side, and pale green underneath : toward the top of the stalk there shoots forth divers short branches, on every one whereof stand two, three, or four small heads, which breaking the skin that incloses them, shoot forth a tuft of pale greenish yellow threads, which falling away, there comes in their places small three-cornered pods, containing small, long, and round seed. The whole plant has a strong unpleasant scent.

Place.—It grows in many places of this country, in the borders of moist meadows, and ditch-sides.

Time.—It flowers about July, or beginning of August.

Government and Virtues.—This herb bruised and applied, perfectly heals old sores, and the distilled water of the herb and flowers does the like. It is used among other pot-herbs to open the body, and make it soluble; but the roots washed clean, and boiled in ale and drank, provoke to stool more than the leaves, but yet very gently.

RUGGEDWORT.—(*Jacobea Hibernica.*)

Descrip.—Its flowers grow large and yellow in some, in others paler and moderate small. The stalk is two feet high, upright, and divided into many branches.

Place.—It is common on salt-marshes in Lincolnshire

Time.—It flowers in July.

Government and Virtues.—It is under the Moon. The juice taken in wine, or the decoction drank morning and evening, helps the jaundice, but all other drink must be avoided for three hours after the dose is taken. Added to centaury and succory, it helps the dropsy and the diseases of the spleen. It is also good for inward bleeding and the bloody-flux, and it is a good wound-herb.

RUPTURE-WORT.—(*Herniaria Vulgaris.*)

Descrip.—This spreads very many thready branches round about on the ground, about a span long, divided into many other smaller parts full of small joints set very thick together, whereon come two very small leaves of a French yellow, and green coloured branches, where grow forth also a number of exceeding small yellowish flowers, scarce to be discerned from the stalks and leaves, which turn into seeds as small as dust. The root is very long and small, thrusting deep into the ground. This has neither smell or taste at first, afterwards it has an astringent taste, without any manifest heat, yet a little bitter and sharp withal.

Place.—It grows in dry, sandy, and rocky places.

Time.—It is green all summer, but flowers in July.

Government and Virtues.—It is Saturn's own, and is a noble anti-venerean, found by experience to cure rupture also, not only in children, but older persons, if the disease be not too inveterate, by taking a dram of the powder of the dried herb, every day in wine, or a decoction made and drank for some days together. The juice or distilled water of the green herb, taken in the same manner, helps all other fluxes either in man or woman; vomitings also, and the gonorrhœa, being taken any of the ways aforesaid. It helps those that have the strangury, or are troubled with the stone or gravel in the reins or bladder. The same also helps stitches in the sides, griping pains of the stomach or belly, the obstructions of the liver, and cures the yellow-jaundice ; it likewise kills worms in children. Being outwardly applied, it conglutinates wounds notably, and helps much to stay defluxions of rheum from the head to the eyes, nose, and teeth, being bruised green, and bound thereto ; or the forehead, temples, or the nape of the neck behind, bathed with the decoction of the dried herb. It also dries up the fistulous ulcers or any other that are foul and spreading.

RUSH (SQUINANTH.)—*(Juncus Odoratus.)*

Descrip.—Though this is commonly called a Rush, yet it is a species of grass, whose leaves grow thick together, inclosing one another, having a small fibrous root; they are long and narrow, of a pleasant sweet smell. The stalks grow a foot or more high, bearing pannicles of short woolly spikes, set opposite to one another. It grows in Arabia, and other eastern countries. The flowers only are used.

Government and Virtues.—All rushes are under Saturn. This is heating and drying, opening obstructions of the liver and spleen, and provoking the catamenia; it eases the pain of the womb after child-bearing, provokes urine, cleanses the reins, and helps the hiccough, occasioned by wind in the stomach. It is an ingredient in the two great compositions, *Theriaca Andromachi*, and *Mithridate.*

RUSHES.—*(Juncus.)*

ALTHOUGH there are several kinds, yet those which have most medicinal virtues, and are best known, such as the Bulrushes, and some of the smoother sorts, ought to be selected. These grow commonly in almost every part of this country, and a description of them is needless.

Place.—They grow by the sides of watery ditches issuing from the Thames, and in the marshes near Blackwall.

Time.—They flower from July to September.

Virtues.—The seed of the soft kind, if drank in wine and water, stays laxes and womens' courses, when they come down abundantly ; but it causes head-ache, and provokes sleep, and must be given with caution. The root boiled in water, to the consumption of one third, helps the cough.

RUSHY GLONDE, OR AWL-WORT.—(*Subularia Aquatica.*)

Descrip.—This grows from a root composed of long and thick fibres. The leaves are long, slender, and sharp-pointed; they stand upright, and are of a deep green, and very rough and harsh to the touch: they are rounded on the back, and flat on the upper side, biggest at the bottom, and smallest at the extremity. The stalk is slender and green, there are no leaves on it, but single white flowers at distances, four-leaved, greenish white, seldom quite open.

Place.—It is found at the bottom of fish-ponds in the northern parts of England and Wales.

Time.—It flowers in August.

Government and Virtues.—This is a Lunar plant. The flowers are seldom used, but the leaves are put in cooling ointments, being good for burns, inflammations, and hot swellings, and are an ingredient in the *Unguentum Populeon.*

RYE.—(*Secale Cereale.*)

Descrip.—Farmers cultivate the Winter Rye, which has the largest grain. In many of the northern counties rye and wheat are often mixed and sown together.

Place.—It is generally sown and thrives best in poor, limestone, dry, gravelly, and sandy soils.

Time.—It is sown in autumn, and rises in a much shorter time than wheat.

Virtues.—It is more digesting than wheat; the bread and the leaven of it ripens and breaks imposthumes, boils, and other swellings; the meal put between a double cloth, and moistened with a little vinegar, and heated in a pewter-dish, set over a chafing-dish of coals, and bound fast to the head while it is hot, eases continual pains therein.

SAFFRON.—(*Crocus Sativus.*)

Descrip.—The plant that produces the true Saffron has a round bulbous root, the size of a nutmeg, flatted at bottom, from which spring several white fibres; it is covered outwardly with a yellowish brown skin, but is white in the inside. From this root arise the flowers, inclosed in a thin skin or husk, being naked and without stalks, made up of six long, but roundish-pointed, purple leaves, inclosing in their middle three stamina, of a fiery, yellow, red colour: which being gathered, and carefully dried in a Saffron-kiln, and made into square cakes, is sold in shops.

Place.—It grows in various parts of the world, but it is no better than that which grows in England. At present it grows plentifully in Cambridgeshire.

Time.—The Saffron-flowers bloom in September; but the leaves come not forth till the spring.

Government and Virtues.—It is an herb of the Sun, and under the Lion. Not above ten grains must be given at one time; a cordial if taken in an immoderate quantity, hurts the heart instead of helping it. It quickens the brain; helps consumptions of the lungs, and difficulty of breathing, it is excellent in epidemical diseases, as pestilence, small-pox, and measles. It is a notably expulsive medicine, and a good remedy in the yellow-jaundice. It is a useful aromatic, of a strong penetrating smell, and a warm, pungent, bitterish taste. It is said to be more cordial, and exhilarating than any of the other aromatics, and is particularly serviceable in disorders of the breast in female obstructions, and hysteric depressions. Saffron is endowed with great virtues, for it refreshes the spirits, and is good against fainting-fits and the palpitation of the heart; it strengthens the stomach, helps digestion, cleanses the lungs, and is good in coughs. It is said to open obstructions of the viscera, and is good in hysteric disorders. However, the use of it ought to be moderate and reasonable; for when the dose is too large, it produces a heaviness of the head and sleepiness; some have fallen into an immoderate convulsive laughter, which ended in death. A few grains of this is commonly a dose, though some have prescribed it from half a scruple to a scruple and a half.

SAFFRON (MEADOW.)—(*Colchicum Autumnale.*)

Descrip.—This has a large roundish root, and the leaves are numerous, long, and, when fully expanded, very broad; they naturally appear at a different time from the flower; and if any chance to rise with it they are narrower. The flower rises out of the ground without any stalk, its own tubular base serving for that purpose; it is very large, and of a pale, but elegant purple. The segments are naturally six, but sometimes they are found double that number; and sometimes, instead of an uniform purple, the flower is streaked with white, or is white throughout.

Place.—It is commonly found in meadows.

Time.—It blooms in September.

Government and Virtues.—It is under Saturn. Indiscreetly used, this root is poisonous. A single grain only being swallowed by a person in health, by way of experiment, produced heat in the stomach, and soon after flushing heats in various parts of the body, with frequent shiverings, which were followed by colicky pains, afterwhich an itching in the loins and urinary passages was perceived, and presently there came a continued inclination to make water, with a tremour, pain in the head, great thirst, a very quick pulse, and other disagreeable symptoms. Notwithstanding these symptoms, it is, when properly prepared, a safe, but powerful medicine ; the best way of doing this is to make it into a kind of syrup, by digesting an ounce of the roots, sliced thin, in a pint of white-wine vinegar, over a gentle fire, for the space of forty-eight hours, and then mixing two pounds of honey with the strained liquor, and letting it boil gently afterwards till it comes to a proper consistence. This syrup is agreeably acid, gently bites the tongue, is moderately astringent, and excellent for cleansing the tongue from mucus. In an increased dose, it vomits, and sometimes purges, but its most common operation is by urine, for which it is a remarkably powerful medicine. The dose at first should be but small, half a tea-spoonful twice or three times a day is enough to begin with, and the quantity may afterwards be gradually increased, as the stomach will bear it, or the case may require. It has been given with the most astonishing success in dropsies and tertian agues; and it frequently succeeds as an expectorant, when all other means fail.

SAFFRON (WILD,) OR SAFFLOWER.—*(Carthamus Tinctorius.)*

Descrip.—This is an annual plant, having a small woody root which does not run deep in the earth. The lower leaves are pretty broad, long, and round-pointed; the stalk grows to be two or three feet high, cornered, and without prickles, branching into several divisions towards the top ; beset with lesser leaves an inch broad, and two inches long, pointed, and having a few, not very hard, prickles growing on them. The flowers stand on the heads of the branches, consisting of round scaly heads, having a few spinulæ growing out of them, out of the middle of which spring thrums of a Saffron-coloured fistular flowers, succeeded by white-cornered, longish seed, narrow at one end.

Place.—It is sown in fields and gardens.

Time. It flowers in July. The flower is called Safflower. The seed only is used in the shops.

Government and Virtues.—It is Saturnine, and accounted a pretty strong cathartic, evacuating tough viscid phlegm, both upwards and downwards, and by that means clears the lungs and helps phthisis.

SAGE (COMMON GARDEN.)—*(Salvia Officinalis.)*

Descrip.—This is a shrubby plant found in every garden, and is well known to have long, rough, wrinkled leaves, sometimes of a hoary green, and sometimes of a reddish purple colour, of a pretty strong smell: the flowers grow on long stalks set on verticillatim in spikes; they are large and galeated, having the galea crooked and hollow, and the labella broad, of a blueish purple colour, set in clammy calices; in the bottom of which grow four smooth round seeds.

Place.—It is planted in gardens.

Time.—It flowers in May. Leaves and flowers are used.

Government and Virtues.—Jupiter claims this; and it is good for the liver and to breed blood. A decoction of the leaves and branches made and drank provokes urine, expels the dead child, brings down womens' courses, and causes the hair to become black. It stays the bleeding of wounds, and cleanses foul ulcers or sores. Three spoonfuls of the juice taken fasting, with a little honey, stays the spitting or casting of blood of those in consumptions. These pills are much commended:—Take of spikenard, ginger, of each two drams; of the seed of Sage toasted at the fire, eight drams; all these being brought into powder, put thereto as much of the juice of Sage as may make them into a mass of pills, take a dram of them every morning and night, fasting, and drink a little pure water afterward. It is profitable for all kinds of pains in the head coming of cold and rheumatic humours; as also for all pains of the joints, whether inwardly or outwardly, and helps falling-sickness, the lethargy, lowness of spirits, and the palsy; it is also useful in defluxions of rheum in the head, and for diseases of the chest or breast. The leaves and nettles if bruised and laid upon the imposthumes that rise behind the ears, assuages them much. The juice taken in warm water, helps hoarseness and a cough. The leaves sodden in wine, and laid upon the place affected with the palsy, helps much, if the decoction be drunk also: Sage taken with wormwood is good for the bloody-flux. It also helps the memory, warming and quickening the senses; and the conserve made of the flowers is used for the same purpose, and also for all the former recited diseases. The juice if drank with vinegar, is good for the plague. Gargles are made with Sage, rosemary, honeysuckles, and plantain, boiled in wine or water, with some honey or alum added, to wash sore mouths and throats. Sage is boiled with other hot and comforting herbs, to bathe the body and the legs in the summer-time, especially to warm cold joints or sinews, troubled with the palsy and cramp, and to comfort and strengthen the parts. It is recommended against the stitch, or pains in the side coming of wind, if the place be fomented warm with the decoction thereof in wine, and the herb also after boiling be laid warm thereunto.

SAGE (SMALL,) OR SAGE OF VIRTUE.—(*Salvia Minor Virtutis.*)

Descrip.—This is smaller than the other sages, having less, narrower, and smoother leaves, of a whitish hoary green colour, with two small pieces or ears growing on them next the stalk, which in some plants are wanting, in others but on one side. It is milder in scent than the common, and has smaller flowers, but of the same colour, flowering at the same time, and is also planted in gardens.

Government and Virtues.—It is under Venus, and has the same virtues as the wood sage. An infusion operates powerfully by sweat and urine, and removes female obstructions. The expressed juice drunk for a considerable time is excellent against rheumatic pains; and was formerly celebrated against venereal diseases, but since the introduction of mercury, its use has been set aside.

SAGE (WOOD.)—(*Salvia Agrestis.*)

Descrip.—This rises with square hoary stalks, two feet high, with two leaves set at every joint, like other sage-leaves, but smaller, softer, whiter, and rounder, a little dented about the edges, and smelling somewhat stronger. At the tops of the stalks and branches stand the flowers, on a slender spike, turning themselves all one way when they bloom, and are of a paler and whiter colour, smaller than sage, but hooded and gaping like unto them. The seed is blackish and round; the root is long and stringy, with divers fibres thereat, and abides many years.

Place.—It grows in woods, and by wood-sides; as also in divers fields and bye-lanes in England.

Time.—It flowers in June, July, and August.

Government and Virtues.—The Sages are under Venus. The decoction of Wood-sage provokes urine and womens' courses ; it provokes sweat, digests humours, and discusses swellings and nodes in the flesh, and is therefore good against the venereal disease. The decoction of the green herb, made with wine, is a safe and sure remedy for those who by falls, bruises, or blows, suspect some vein to be inwardly broken, to disperse and void the congealed blood, and to consolidate the veins. The drink used inwardly, and the herb used outwardly, is found to be a sure remedy for the palsy. The juice of the herb, or the powder of it is good for moist ulcers and sores in the legs, and other parts, to dry and heal them more speedily. It is no less effectual in green wounds, to be used upon any occasion.

SALTWORT.—(*Salsola Kali.*)

CALLED also Kali, Glasswort, Sea Grass, and Marsh Samphire.

Descrip.—This plant grows usually with one upright, round, thick, and almost transparent stalk, a foot high, or more; thick set and full of joints, without any leaves; the joints shooting forth one out of another, with short pods at the heads of them, and such like smaller branches on each side which are divided into smaller ones ; the root is small, long and thready. Some other kinds there are differing somewhat in the form of the joints, and one kind wholly reddish, and differing from the other in nothing else. There are four kinds of Saltwort, or Glasswort, viz : 1. *Kali Majus Cochleatum*, Great Glasswort, with snail-like seed. 2. *Kali Minus Album*, Small Glasswort. 3. *Kali Ægyptiacum*, Glasswort of Egypt. And 4. *Kali Geniculatum, sive Salicornia*, Jointed Glasswort.

Place.—The first and third are absolute strangers in this country, but grow in Syria, Egypt, Italy, and Spain : the second, not only grows in those countries but in colder climates, upon many parts of our own coasts, especially in the west. The last grows in all countries, including our own, on the sea-coast where the salt-water flows.

Time.—They all flourish in summer, and those that die give their seed about August ; the last abides all winter.

Government and Virtues.—They are under the dominion of Mars, and are of a cleansing quality, without any great or manifest heat ; the powder of any of them. or the juice which is much better, taken in drink, purges downwards phlegmatically, whitish, melancholy, and adust humours, and is effectual for the dropsy, to provoke urine, and expel the dead child. It opens stoppings of the liver and and spleen, and wastes the hardness thereof; but it must be used with discretion, as a great quantity is hurtful and dangerous. The ashes are sharp and biting, like a caustic, and the lye that is made thereof is so strong that it will fetch off the skin from any part of the body; but it may be mixed with other moderate medicines, to take away scabs, leprosy, and to cleanse the skin.

SAMPHIRE (PRICKLY.)—(*Echinophora Spinosa.*)

Called also Sea Fennel.

Descrip.—It is a much lower plant than the common Fennel, having, broader, shorter, thicker leaves, of a dull green colour; the stalk grows scarcely a foot high, having the like leaves on it; and on the top it bears umbels of small yellowish flowers, and after them roundish seed, like fennel seed, but larger. The root is thick and long, continuing several years. It has an aromatic smell and taste.

Place.—It grows on rocks by the sea-side, in many parts of England, as in Lancashire, Sussex, and Faversham.

Government and Virtues.—This is a martial plant, and is more agreeable as a pickle than useful as a medicine. It is, however, strengthening to the stomach, and procures an appetite, provokes urine, opens obstructions of the bowels, and helps the jaundice.

SAMPHIRE (ROCK OR SMALL.)—(*Crithmum Maritimum.*)

Descrip.—It grows up with a tender green stalk about a half yard or two feet high at the most, branching forth almost from the bottom, and stored with sundry thick and almost round leaves, of a deep green colour, sometimes two together, and sometimes more on a stalk, sappy, and of a pleasant hot and spicy taste. At the tops of the stalks and branches stand umbels of white flowers, and after them come the seed larger than fennel-seed, but somewhat like it. The root is great, white, and long, continuing for many years; and is of a hot and spicy taste likewise.

Place.—It grows on rocks that are washed by sea-water.

Time.—It flowers and seeds in July and August.

Government and Virtues.—It is an herb of Jupiter, and was formerly used more than it is now. It is well-known that indigestion and obstructions are the cause of most of the diseases that the frail nature of man is subject to; both of which might be remedied by a more frequent use of this herb. It is safe, very pleasant both to the taste and stomach, helping digestion, and opening obstructions of the liver and spleen; provokes urine, and helps to take away the gravel and stone engendered in the kidneys or bladder.

SANICLE.—(*Sanicula Europæa.*)

Descrip.—It sends forth many round leaves, standing on long brownish stalks, every one divided into five or six parts, some of them cut like a crow's-foot, and finely dented about the edges, smooth, and of a dark shining colour, and sometimes reddish about the brims; from among which rise up small, round green stalks, without any joint or leaf thereon, except at the top, where it branches forth into flowers, having a leaf divided into three or four parts at that joint with the flowers, which are small round greenish yellow heads, many standing together in a tuft, in which afterwards the seeds are contained, which are small round burs, somewhat like the leaves of Cleavers, and stick in the same manner upon any thing that they touch. The root is composed of many blackish fibres, set together in a long head, which abides green all the winter, and dies not.

Place.—It is found in many shady woods, and other places of England.

Time.—It flowers in June, the seed is ripe shortly after.

Government and Virtues.—Mars owns this herb. It heals green wounds speedily, or any ulcers, imposthumes, or inward bleedings, also tumours on any parts of the body; the decoction or powder in drink taken, and the juice used outwardly, dissipates the humours; and there is not found any herb that can give such present help either to man or beast, when the disease falls upon the lungs or throat, and to heal up putrid malignant ulcers in the mouth, throat, and privities, by gargling with a decoction of the leaves and roots made in water, and a little honey put thereto. It helps to stay womens' courses, and all other fluxes of blood, either by the mouth, urine, or stool, and laxes of the belly; the ulcerations of the kidneys also, the pains in the bowels, and gonorrhœa, or running of the reins, being boiled in wine or water, and drunk.

SARACEN'S CONSOUND, OR GREAT BROAD-LEAVED RAGWORT.—(*Senecio Saracenicus.*)

Descrip.—This is a robust conspicuous plant, which rises sometimes to five feet high; brownish or green stalks, with narrow green leaves snipped about the edges, somewhat like those of the peach tree, or willow leaves, but not of so light a green. The stalk spreads at the top, and is furnished with many yellow star-like flowers, which grow in a cup that is fringed, or surrounded with short leaves at the bottom. The seed is long, small, and of a brown colour, wrapped in down; and, when ripe, is carried away with the wind. The root consists of fibres set together at a head, which survives the winter, although the stalks dry away, and the leaves then disappear. The taste and smell of the whole plant is raw and unpleasant.

Place.—This perennnial commonly grows in the meadows of Yorkshire and Wiltshire, in moist and wet lands, by wood-sides, and sometimes by the water-side.

Time.—It flowers in July: the seed is soon ripe; and is carried away with the wind.

Government and Virtues.—This is an herb of Saturn. It is balsamic and diuretic. If boiled in wine, and drank, it helps the indisposition of the liver, and frees the gall from obstructions; whereby it is good for the yellow-jaundice, and for the dropsy in the beginning of it; for all inward ulcers of the reins, mouth or throat, and inward wounds and bruises; likewise for such sores as happen in the privy parts of men or women: being steeped in wine, and then distilled, the water thereof drank, is singularly good to ease all gnawings of the stomach, or other pains of the body; as also the pains of the mother: and being boiled in water, it helps continual agues; and the said water, or the simple water of the herb distilled, or the juice or decoction, are very effectual to heal any green wound, or old sore or ulcer whatsoever, cleansing them from corruption, and quickly healing them up: briefly, whatsoever has been said of Bugle or Sanicle, may be found herein.

SARSAPARILLA.—(*Smilax Sarsaparilla.*)

Descrip.—This is reckoned among the sorts of prickly Bindweeds, of which there are three sorts: one with red berries, another with black berries, and a third with large leaves, of an oval figure, very entire on the edges, smooth and shining on the surface, of a dark green colour, and supported on shortish leaf-stalks. The flowers are small, and of a yellowish colour.

Place.—The two first grow in Italy, Spain, and other warm countries, throughout Europe and Asia. The third is found only in the West Indies.

Time.—It has ripe berries early in hot countries.

Government and Virtues.—These are all plants of Mars; of a healing quality howsoever used. Both leaves and berries, being drunk before or after taking any deadly poison, are an excellent antidote. If the juice of the berries be given to a new-born child, it shall never be hurt by poison. It is good against all sorts of venomous things. Twelve or sixteen of the berries, beaten to powder, and given in wine, procure urine when it is stopped. The distilled waters, when drank, have the same effect, cleanses the reins and assuages inward inflammations. If the eyes be washed therewith, it heals them thoroughly. The true Sarsaparilla is held generally not to heat, but rather to dry the humours; yet it is easily perceived, that it not only dries them but wastes them away by a secret property, chiefly that of sweating, which it greatly promotes. It is used in many kinds of diseases, particularly in cold fluxes from the head and brain, rheums, and catarrhs, and cold griefs of the stomach, as it expels wind powerfully. It helps all manner of aches in the sinews or joints, all running sores in the legs, all phlegmatic swellings, tetters, or ringworms, and all manner of spots and foulness of the skin. It is reckoned a great sweetener of the blood, and has been found of service in venereal cases. Infants who have received the infection from their nurses, though covered with pustules and ulcers, may be cured by the use of this root without the help of mercurials; and the best way of administering it to them is to mix the powdered root with their food.

SAUCE-ALONE (JACK-BY-THE-HEDGE, OR COMMON GARLIC CRESS.)—*(Alliaria Officinalis.)*

Descrip.—The lower leaves of this are rounder than those that grow towards the top of the stalks, and are set singly on a joint, being somewhat round and broad, pointed at the ends, dented also about the edges, somewhat resembling nettle-leaves in the form, but of a fresher green colour, not rough or prickling; the flowers are white, at the top of the stalks, one above another which being past, follow small round pods, wherein are contained round seed somewhat blackish. The root stringy and thready, perishes every year after it has given seed, and raises itself again of its own sowing. The plant, or any part thereof, if bruised, smells of garlic, but more pleasantly, and tastes somewhat hot and sharp, almost like rocket.

Place.—It grows under walls, and by hedge-sides, and path-ways in fields in many places.

Time.—It flowers in June, July, and August.

Government and Virtues.—It is an herb of Mercury. It warms the stomach, and causes digestion: the juice boiled with honey, is as good as hedge-mustard for the cough, to cut and expectorate the tough phlegm. The seed bruised and boiled in wine, is a good remedy for the wind colic, or the stone, if drank warm: it is given to women troubled with the mother, both to drink, and the seed put into a cloth, and applied while it is warm, is of singular good use. The leaves also, or the seed boiled, is good to be used in clysters to ease the pains of the stone. The green leaves are held to be good to heal the ulcers in the legs.

SAVINE.—(*Sabina Juniperus.*)

Descrip.—This is a small evergreen shrubby tree, having its branches set close together, clothed with short, narrow, somewhat prickly leaves, almost resembling cypress, of a very strong smell; among these, after the tree is old, and has stood long in a place, grow small mossy greenish flowers, which are succeeded by small flattish berries, less than those of Juniper, of the same blackish blue colour.

Place.—Though it does not grow naturally in England, yet it is planted in gardens, where it seldom produces fruit, and has therefore generally been reputed barren.

Government and Virtues.—It is under the dominion of Mars, being hot and dry, in the third degree; and being of exceeding clean parts, it is of a very digesting quality. It is hot and dry, opening and attenuating, and a powerful provoker of the catamenia, causing abortion, and expelling the birth; it is good to destroy worms in children. The juice mixed with milk, and sweetened with sugar, is an excellent medicine for that purpose: beaten into a cataplasm with hog's-lard, it cures children's scabby heads. It is a most powerful detersive, and has so violent an effect upon the uterine passages if used imprudently, that wicked women have employed it to very ill purposes. It is a very fine opener of obstructions of any kind, whence in compositions for the jaundice, dropsy, scurvy, rheumatism,

&c., it makes a very useful ingredient. It is also an enemy to worms, and its chymical oil rubbed upon and about the navel of children. has often had a wonderful effect in expelling them. It deserves the regard of surgeons, as it is a very potent scourer and cleanser of old sordid stinking ulcers, either used in lotions, fomentations, ointments, or even the powder mixed with honey.

SAVORY (SUMMER.)—*(Satureia Hortensis.)*

Descrip.—This has small stringy roots, from which rise a great many woody branches, eight or nine inches high, a little hairy, having two long, narrow leaves at a joint, narrowest next the stalk. The flowers grow next the tops in small whorles, of a whitish colour, with a blush of red, galeated and labiated, set in five-pointed calices, containing four small dark brown seeds.

Place.—It is sown in gardens.

Time.—It flowers in June. The leaves and tops are used.

There is another species of Savory, which is sometimes used, viz.

SAVORY (WINTER.)—*(Satureia Montana.)*

Descrip.—This is more woody and shrubby than the former, with leaves like hyssop, stiffer and harder, and seemingly pierced full of holes, and ending in spinulæ : the flowers are of the colour of the former, and the seed much alike

Place.—This is likewise cultivated in gardens.

Government and Virtues.—They are both under Mercury, being heating, drying, and carminative, expelling wind from the stomach and bowels, and are good in asthma, and other affections of the breast ; they open obstructions of the womb, and promote menstrual evacuations. Winter Savory is a good remedy for the colic and iliac passion; keep it dry, make conserves and syrups of it for your use ; for which purpose the Summer kind is the best. This kind is both hotter and drier than the Winter kind, and is much commended for pregnant women to take inwardly, and to smell often unto. It expels tough phlegm from the chest and lungs ; quickens the dull spirits in the lethargy, if the juice be snuffed up the nose ; dropped into the eyes it clears them of thin cold humours proceeding from the brain. The juice heated with oil of roses, dropped into the ears, eases them of the noises in them, and deafness also ; outwardly applied with wheat flour, as a poultice, it eases sciatica and palsied members. It eases pain from stings of wasps, bees, &c.

SAWWORT (COMMON.)—(*Serratula Tinctoria.*)

Descrip.—This has a white fibrous root. The first leaves are undivided, oblong, broad, of a beautiful green ; sometimes deeply cut in a pinnated form; they vary upon the stalks, being in some plants undivided, and in others very deeply jagged, while the species is the same. In both forms they are regularly notched on the edges. The stalk is round, upright, and slender, about two feet high. The flowers are in small heads, of a fine purple; but the poverty of some soils produce them quite white. The seeds are oblong and large.

Place.—It is common about woods.

Time.—It flowers in August.

Government and Virtues.—This is under Saturn, and is vulnerary and astringent. It has a little sourish, styptic taste. It is very drying and binding, useful for diarrhœa and dysentery, the *fluxus hepaticus*, the excess of catamenia and fluor albus, and against vomiting and spitting of blood.

SAXIFRAGE (GREAT BURNET.)—(*Pimpinella Saxifraga Major.*)

Descrip.—The root is thick at the head, spreading into several branches, growing deep in the earth, of a whitish colour, and a hot taste, from which spring several pinnated leaves, having three or four pinnæ, set opposite, with an odd one at the end ; they are hard in handling. The stalk is about a yard high, stiff, jointed, and full of branches, clothed with narrower leaves, with umbels of white flowers at the ends, followed by very small, dark brown, striated seeds.

Place.—It grows in gravelly places, especially in Kent.

Time.—The seed is ripe in July.

Government and Virtues.—It is under the Moon. The root is hot and dry, expelling wind, good for the colic, and weakness of the stomach ; they are diuretic, useful against the stone, gravel, and scurvy. It has the properties of the parsleys, but eases pains and provokes urine more effectually. The roots or seed used either in powder or decoction, helps the mother, procures the courses, removes phlegm, and cures venom, &c. The distilled water, boiled with castoreum, is good for cramps and convulsions, and the seed used in comfits (like carraway seeds) will answer the same purpose. The juice of the herb dropped into bad wounds in the head, dries up their moisture, and heals them.

SAXIFRAGE (SMALL BURNET.)—*(Pimpinella Saxifraga Minor.)*

Descrip.—This has a round, slender root, divided into several reddish branches, among which are found certain red grains, which are called wild cochineal. The stalks are red, angular, and branched; the leaves are oblong or roundish, dented on the edges, in pairs on the ribs. The flowers grow at the ends of the stalks, in round heads, and consist of a single petal, divided into four parts, of a purple colour; in the middle is a tuft of long stamina; the flowers are of two sorts, one barren, furnished with stamina, the other fruitful, having a pistil. This is succeeded by a quadrangular fruit generally pointed at both ends, of an ash-colour when ripe, containing oblong, slender reddish-brown seeds, with an astringent and somewhat bitter taste.

Place.—It resembles true Saxifrage in its wild state, for which it is often mistaken. It is cultivated in gardens.

Time.—It flowers about the end of June, and the seed is ripe about August.

Government and Virtues.—I is under the dominion of the Moon. The whole plant is binding; the leaves put into wine give it a good flavour and the young shoots make a good salad. It is a cordial and promoter of sweat. The root dried and powdered, stops purgings; and a strong decoction of it, or the juice of the leaves, is good for the same purposes. In the composition of the *Syrupus Altheæ* it is generally used instead of the Great Burnet Saxifrage.

SAXIFRAGE (WHITE.)—*(Saxifraga Alba.)*

Descrip.—This has a few small reddish kernels of roots covered with some skins, lying among small blackish fibres, which send forth round, faint, or yellow green leaves, and greyish underneath, lying above the ground, unevenly dented about the edges, and somewhat hairy, every one on a little footstalk, from whence rise up round, brown, hairy, green stalks, two or three feet high, with such like round leaves as grow below, but smaller, and branched at the top, whereon stand pretty large white flowers of five leaves a-piece, with some yellow threads in the middle, standing in a long crested, brownish, green husk. After the flowers are passed, there rises a round hard head, forked at the top, wherein is contained small black seed, but they often fall away without seed, and it is the kernels of the root that are usually called the White Saxifrage-seed, and so used.

Place.—It grows in many places of this country, as well in the lower, as in the upper dry corners of meadows, and sandy grassy places.

Time.—It flowers in May, and then gathered, as well for that which is called the seed, as to distil, for it quickly perishes down to the ground when any hot weather comes.

Government and Virtues.—This is governed by the Moon. It is very effectual to cleanse the reins and bladder, and to dissolve the stone engendered in them, and to expel it and the gravel by urine; to help the strangury; for which purpose the decoction of the herb or roots in white wine, is most useful, or the powder of the small kernelly root, taken in white wine, or in the same decoction made with white wine, is most usual. The distilled water of the whole herb, root and flowers, is most familiar to be taken. It provokes womens' courses, and frees and cleanses the stomach and lungs from thick and tough phlegm that troubles them. There is no better medicine than this to break the stone.

SAXIFRAGE (WILD, OR MEADOW.)—(*Seselli Pratense Carnifolia.*)

Descrip.—The root is about a finger thick, striking deep in the ground, of a brownish colour on the outside, whitish within, of a hot aromatic taste and smell; and from which spring several winged leaves, not very large, cut into long narrow segments. The stalks are channelled, rising about two feet high, beset with smaller leaves, and having on their tops umbels of pale, yellow, small five-leaved flowers, and after them come short striated reddish brown seeds.

Place.—It grows common in meadows and pasture lands.

Time.—It flowers in August.

Virtues.—The root, herb, and seed are used, being all accounted good to provoke urine, and serviceable in gravel, and distempers of the kidneys ; as also in expelling wind.

There is another more slender Saxifrage, with smaller flowers, white also, but has larger leaves of a deep green. It differs in nothing else from the former.

Place.—It grows in meadows and damp pastures.

Time.—It flowers in May and June.

Virtues.—This little plant is an excellent diuretic ; an infusion of the whole plant operates powerfully and safely by urine, and clears the passages from gravel.

SCABIOUS (DEVIL'S BIT.)—*(Scabiosa Succisa.)*

CALLED also The Blue Devil's Bit.

Descrip.—The lower leaves are rough and hairy, four or five inches long, an inch or more broad, sometimes deeply cut in, and often almost whole, without any incisions, on breaking asunder, drawing out into long threads. The stalks grow to be two or three feet high, round and hairy, having two smaller and more finely cut leaves set at a joint, and on their tops are placed the flowers, which are of a fine cerulean blue.

Place.—It may be found in dry fields, but it is not so plentiful as the Field Scabious.

SCABIOUS (FIELD.)—*(Knautia Arvensis.)*

Descrip.—This rises with many hairy, soft, whitish green leaves, some a little torn on the edges, others much rent on the sides, and have threads, which are seen upon breaking, from which rise up hairy green stalks, three or four feet high, with such like hairy green leaves on them, but more deeply and finely divided, branched forth a little; at the tops, which are naked of leaves for a good space, stand round heads of flowers, of a pale blueish colour, set together in a head, the outermost are larger than the inward, with many threads in the middle, flat at the top, as is the head with the seed; the root is great, white and thick, growing down deep into the ground, and abides many years.

Place.—It grows in meadows, especially about London.

SCABIOUS (LESSER FIELD.)—*(Scabiosa Columbaria.)*

THIS is like the Devil's Bit but smaller. The Corn Scabious is greater in all respects than the Field, its flowers are more inclined to purple. The roots creep under the upper crust of the earth, not so deep as the the first one does.

Place.—It grows in standing corn, or fallow-fields.

Time.—It flowers in June and July, and some abide flowering until it be late in August; and the seed is ripe in the mean time.

Government and Virtues.—Mercury owns the plant. It is effectual for all sorts of coughs, shortness of breath, and all other diseases of the breast and lungs, ripening and digesting cold phlegm, and other tough humour, voiding them forth by coughing and spitting; it ripens all sorts of inward ulcers and imposthumes; pleurisy also, if the decoction of the herb dry or green be made in wine, and drank for some time together. If four ounces of the juice be taken in a morning, fasting, with a dram of mithridate, or Venice treacle, it will free the heart from any infection of pestilence, after taking it the party should get a two hours' sweat in bed ; repeat this medicine as often as necessary. The green herb bruised and applied to any carbuncle or plague sore, will dissolve and break it in three hours. The same decoction drank, helps the pains and stitches in the side. The decoction of the roots taken for forty days together, or a dram of the powder of them taken at a time in whey, helps those that are troubled with running or spreading ulcers, tetters, or ringworms. The juice or decoction drank, helps also scabs and breakings out of the itch, and the like. The juice made into an ointment and used, is effectual for the same purpose. The same also heals all inward wounds by the drying, cleansing, and healing quality therein ; and a syrup made of the juice and sugar, is very effectual to all the purposes aforesaid, and so is the distilled water of the herb and flowers made in due season, especially to be used when the green herb is not in force to be taken. The decoction of the herb and roots outwardly applied, helps all sorts of hard and cold swellings in any part of the body, is good for shrunk sinews or veins, and heals green wounds, old sores and ulcers. The juice made up with the powder of borax and samphire, cleanses the skin of the face and other parts of the body, not only of freckles and pimples, but also of morphew and leprosy ; the head washed with the decoction, cleanses it from dandruff, scurf, sores, itch, and the like, used warm. The herb bruised and applied, in a short time loosens and draws out any splinter, or broken bone lying in the flesh.

SCAMMONY OR GREAT WHITE BINDWEED.—(*Convolvulus Sepium.*)

Descrip.—This is a pernicious weed for the gardener. Its roots creep under the earth to a great distance ; they are larger than those of couch-grass, and would be more easily destroyed if they were not so brittle. The flowers are snowy white, some of a flesh or rose-colour, with a tint of purple.

Place.—It grows most frequently in the Isle of Wight.

Government and Virtues.—This is the plant which produces the Scammony. It does not grow so large here as abroad. The concrete juice of the root is the Scammony of the shops. The best Scammony is black, resinous, and shining, when in the lump, but of a whitish ash-colour, when powdered, of a pretty strong smell, but of no very hot taste, turning milky, when touched by the tongue.

The smallness of our English root prevents the juice being collected as the foreign; but an extract made from the expressed juice of the roots, or any preparation of them, have the same purgative quality, only in less degree.

SCIATICA-WORT, OR SCIATICA-GRASS.—(*Card mantice.)*

Descrip.—The lower leaves are two or three inches long, and about half an inch broad, indented pretty deeply on the edges, growing on long footstalks. The upper leaves are long and narrow, not cut in, and set on without footstalks ; it rises about a foot high, branched, and bearing on the top spikes of small, white, four-leaved flowers, succeeded by round seed-vessels, containing small reddish seed: the root is woody and fibrous, and dies yearly after ripening seed.

Place.—It grows wild in the warmer countries, but with us only in gardens,

Place.—It flowers in June.

Government and Virtues.—It is a very useful Saturnine plant, good for rheumatism. It is little inferior in virtue to the sciatica cress, which it slightly resembles. If the root be bruised in a mortar, mixed with hog's-lard, and rubbed on the parts affected, it will cure the most acute rheumatic.

SCORPION GRASS (MOUSE EAR.)—(*Cerastium Arvense.)*

Descrip.—This is a low creeping plant, sending from a small stringy root, several trailing branches lying on the ground, and shooting out fibres from the joints, by which it takes root. The leaves grow alternately on the stalks, of an oval form, about an inch long, and an inch broad, sharp-pointed, green above, and whitish underneath, covered thick with stiff, long, brown hairs : the flowers stand on footstalks four or five inches long, of the shape of dandelion, but smaller, of a whitish yellow colour above, with several purplish streaks underneath : the stalks, when broken, emit a whitish milk in a small quantity. The flowers pass away in white down, wherein lies small long seed.

Place.—It grows every where upon heaths and commons.

Time.—It flowers most part of the summer.

Government and Virtues.—It is under Mercury. It is of a bitterish styptic taste, and is drying and binding, and a good vulnerary, helpful for all kinds of fluxes: a decoction used as a gargle is commended for ulcers in the mouth.

SCURVY-GRASS (COMMON GARDEN.)—(*Cochlearia Officinalis.*)

Descrip.—This has thick flat leaves more long than broad, and sometimes longer and narrower ; sometimes also smooth on the edges, and sometimes a little waved ; sometimes plain, smooth, and pointed, of a sad green, and sometimes a blueish colour, every one standing itself upon a long footstalk, which is brownish or greenish also, from which arise many slender stalks, bearing few leaves like the other, but longer and lesser for the most part ; at the tops grow many whitish flowers, with yellow threads in the middle, standing about a green head, which becomes the seed-vessel, and is sometimes flat when it is ripe, wherein is contained reddish seed, tasting rather hot. The root is made of many white strings, which stick deeply into the mud, wherein it chiefly delights, yet it will abide in the more upland and drier ground, and tastes brackish there, but not so much as where it feeds upon the salt water.

Place.—It grows upon the sides of the Thames, both on the Essex and Kentish shores, from Woolwich round the sea coasts to Dover, Portsmouth and Bristol plentifully ; the other with round leaves, grows in Lincolnshire, by the sea-coast.

SCURVY-GRASS (DUTCH ROUND-LEAVED.)—(*Cochlearia Rotundifolia.*)

Descrip.—The root is long and full of fibres, from it springs a number of flattish succulent green leaves on long footstalks, which are round and rather hollow, resembling a spoon, whence it has its name *Cochlearia.* The stalks grow eight or nine inches high, brittle, and clothed with the like leaves, which are more angular and pointed ; the flowers grow in tufts on the tops of the stalks, consisting of four small white leaves, which are succeeded by little, round, swelling seed-vessels, parted in the middle by a thin film, and containing small round seeds : both leaves and flowers have a biting hot taste.

Place.—It grows wild in the north of England, by the sea-side ; but is very much cultivated in gardens.

Time.—It flowers in April.

SCURVY-GRASS (GREENLAND.)—(*Cochlearia Grœnlandica.*)

Descrip.—This does not rise so large as the common Dutch Scurvy-grass, yet in some rich lands, the leaves grow very large, not dented on the edges, of a fresh green colour, rising from the root, standing on a long footstalk; from among these rise long slender stalks, with white flowers at the tops of them, which turn into small pods, and smaller brownish seed than the former. The root is white, small, and thready. The taste is not salty, but hot and aromatic.

Place.—It grows in gardens mostly.

Time.—It flowers in April and May.

Government and Virtues.—They are all herbs of Jupiter. This abounds with fine volatile parts; infused or the juice expressed, is better than the decoction, because the volatile parts are lost in boiling: it is a specific remedy against scurvy, purifying the juices of the body from the bad effects of that distemper; it clears the skin from scabs, pimples, and foul eruptions. Officinal preparations are the simple water, the spirit, and a conserve.

SCURVY-GRASS (IVY-LEAVED.)—(*Cochlearia Danica.*)

Descrip.—The only difference in this plant from the others is, the leaves are more divided, so that they appear angular. The colour is light green, and the flowers are smaller, and white like the former.

Place.—It is common on the sea-shore, and in many other places, by the sides of little rills, down the sides of mountains, and in gardens.

Time.—It blooms in April and May.

Virtues.—This plant possesses a considerable degree of acrimony; it is antiscorbutic, and a powerful remedy in moist asthma, or scorbutic rheumatism. A distilled water, and a conserve, are prepared from the leaves, and sold in the shops, its juice together with that of Seville oranges is known by the name of antiscorbutic juices. The leaves bruised, and laid to the face, or any other part, takes away spots, freckles, and sun-burns; but those of delicate complexions cannot bear the application without injuring them

SCURVY-GRASS (HORSE-RADISH.)—(*Cochlearia Armoracia.*)

Descrip.—This has larger leaves than the former species the upper ones are of a lighter green than the lower, of a fleshy substance, and full of juice ; and their colour is an obscure green. The stalks are numerous, thick, juicy, of a pale green, ten or twelve inches high. The flowers, like the former, are small and white, at the tops of the branches.

Place.—It grows upon the muddy parts of the sea-shore.

Time.—It flowers in July,

A species is found in the north with a pale purple flower.

Virtues.—The English Scurvy-Grass is more used for the salt it bears, which opens and cleanses; but the Dutch is of better effect, and oftener used for the scurvy; and purifies the blood, liver, and spleen, by taking the juice every morning fasting, in a cup of drink. The decoction answers the same purpose, and opens obstructions, evacuating cold, clammy and phlegmatic humours both from the liver and the spleen, and bringing the body to a more lively colour. The juice also helps all foul ulcers and sores in the mouth, gargled therewith ; and used outwardly, cleanses the skin from spots, marks, or scars that happen therein.

SCURVY-GRASS (SEA.)—(*Cochlearia Anglica.*)

Descrip.—This grows about as high as the former, but the leaves are thicker, longer, narrower, and more pointed at the ends, frequently finuated about the edges, of a duller green than the garden ; the flowers and seed are alike in both; of a salter taste, but not so hot and pungent as that.

Place.—It grows in salt-marshes, and particularly by the Thames-side, all the way below Woolwich.

Time.—It flowers rather later than the garden kind.

Virtues.—This kind is used along with the others as antiscorbutics, but wanting in fine volatile parts, it is not so prevalent, but abounding more in saline, it may be used to good purpose as a diuretic.

SELF-HEAL.—(*Prunella Vulgaris.*)

Descrip.—This is a small, low, creeping herb, having many small roundish pointed leaves, like leaves of wild mint, of a dark green colour, without dents on the edges; from among which rise square hairy stalks, scarce a foot high, which spread sometimes into branches with small leaves set thereon, up to the tops, where stand brown spiked heads of small brownish leaves like scales and flowers set together, of a blueish purple, in some places sweet, but not so in others. The root consists of many fibres downward, and spreads strings also, whereby it increases. The small stalks, with the leaves creeping on the ground, shoot forth fibres taking hold on the ground, whereby it is a great tuft in a short time.

Place.—It is found in woods and fields every where.

Time.—It flowers in May, and sometimes in April.

Government and Virtues.—This is under Venus, and is a special remedy for inward and outward wounds. Taken in syrups for inward wounds; for outward wounds in unguents and plasters. It is like Bugle in form and qualities, answers the same purposes, and if accompanied with it and sanicle, and other wound-herbs, it is more effectual to wash any wounds or inject into ulcers in the parts outwardly. Where the sharp humours of sores, ulcers, inflammations or swellings need to be repressed, this compound will be effectual; it will also stay the flux of blood from wounds, and solder up their lips, and cleanse the foulness of sores, and speedily heal them. It is a remedy for green wounds. Anoint the temples and forehead with the juice and the oil of roses, to remove the head-ache; the same mixed with honey of roses, cleanses and heals all ulcers in the mouth and throat, and those also in the secret parts.

SENNA (RED-FLOWERED BLADDER.)—(*Colutea Cruenta.*)

Descrip.—It has winged leaves, each entire leaf is composed of six pair of smaller leaves without an odd one at the end, these are of an oblong form, pointed, and of a whitish green colour. The flowers are produced in longish spikes at the tops of the branches, moderately large, of a yellow colour, and striped with red. The root is woody, divided, and spreading.

Place.—It is a native of the East.

Government and Virtues.—It is under Mercury. The leaves (which are the only parts used) are hot, dry, and of a purging quality, but afterwards have a binding effect. It opens obstructions; corrected with carraway-seed, aniseed, or ginger, a dram taken in wine, ale, or broth, fasting, comforts and cleanses the stomach, purges melancholy, choler and phlegm from the head and brain, lungs, heart.

liver, and spleen, cleansing those parts of evil humours; strengthens the senses, procures mirth, and is also good in chronic agues, whether quartan or quotidian. It cleanses and purifies the blood, and causes a fresh and lively habit of the body, and is an especial ingredient in diet-drinks, and to make purging-ale for cleansing the blood. The Common Bladder Senna (*Colutea Arborescens*) works very violently both upwards and downwards, offending the stomach and bowels.

SER MOUNTAIN.—(*Tordylium Officinale.*)

Descrip.—This is sometimes called Hartwort, has a large thick root, that strikes deep into the earth, with many stringy fibres at the bottom. The stalk rises as high as a man, full of branches, having many large winged leaves, as it were encompassing the stalks with a thin sheath, cut into several segments, each of which is usually divided into five, and at the end three oval smaller leaves, smooth, and pointed at the end. It has large umbels of small, five-leaved, white flowers, each of which is succeeded by two large long seeds, striated on the back, having a leafy border on each side, of a brown colour, a pretty strong smell, and a hot bitterish taste.

Place.—It grows upon the Alps, but with us is found only in some gardens.

Time.—It flowers in June.

Government and Virtues.—It is a warm martial plant, both heating and drying; it provokes urine and the menses, expels the birth and after-birth; and is good in disorders of the head and womb. The seeds are put both into Theriaca and Mithridate.

SERVICE TREE (COMMON.)—(*Pyrus Torminalis.*)

Descrip.—This grows to be a pretty large tree, whose branches are clothed with winged leaves, consisting of seven or nine serrated pinnæ, each leaf terminating in an odd one. It has several clusters of five-leaved white flowers, which are followed by fruit of the shape and size of a small pear, growing several together on footstalks an inch long; they are of a greenish colour, with a mixture of red, as they are more or less exposed to the sun; of a rough, austere, choky taste; but when ripe or mellow, sweet and pleasant.

Place.—It is found wild in some parts of England, as in Staffordshire and Cornwall.

Time.—It flowers in May; but the seed is not ripe till November. The fruit is used.

Government and Virtues.—It is under Saturn, and reckoned to be very restringent and useful for all kinds of fluxes; but whe‹ ripe, not altogether so binding. This fruit is seldom to be met with in our markets, and therefore, for a succedaneum, we use the following.

SERVICE TREE (MANURED.)—*(Pyrus Domestica,) (Pyrus Sorbus,) (Sorbus Domestica.)*

Descrip.—This grows tall in good ground, having a whitish bark, and leaves that differ from those of the former, in not being winged, though larger and longer, being cut into seven sharp-pointed and serrated segments, the two next the stalk, being cut in deepest, of a pale green above, and whitish underneath. The flowers grow in clusters like the former, of a yellowish-white colour; and the fruit is set in the same manner on long footstalks, more than twice the size of common haws; they are likewise umbilicated at the top, of a harsh restringent taste when green, but when mellowed, sweet and pleasant, having a stony substance in the middle, including two seeds.

Place.—It grows frequently in woods and thickets, and flowers with the former, the fruit being ripe as late.

Government and Virtues.—It is under the dominion of Saturn. The fruit is used as the former, and is of the same nature, or rather more restringent and binding, being good for all kinds of fluxes, either of blood or humours; when ripe, it is pleasant and grateful to the stomach, promoting digestion, and preventing the too hasty passage of the food out of the bowels; and is commended in fevers attended with diarrhœa. They may be kept all the year, if dried before they are mellow, and may be used in decoctions for the said purpose, either to drink, or bathe the parts requiring it; and are profitably used in that manner to stay the bleeding of wounds, and of the morth o nose, to be applied to the forehead, and nape of the neck.

SHEPHERD'S NEEDLE (COMMON.)—*(Scandix Pecten Veneris.)*

Descrip.—This has a long, slender, white root, hung with a few slight fibres: the leaves are small, and supported on short footstalks; they are finely divided, and their colour is of a very dark green. The stalks are numerous, green, branched, a foot high. The leaves stand irregularly on them, like those from the root; but they are smaller. The flowers are moderately large, and grow in umbels like those of hemlock chervil; they are white, with very little smell.

Place.—It is common in corn-fields.

Time.—It flowers in August.

Government and Virtues.—This is under Venus. When taken as a medicine, it operates by urine, and is good against obstructions of the viscera.

SHEPHERD'S NEEDLE (ROUGH.)—(*Chærophyllum Temulentum.*)

CALLED also Hemlock-Chervil.

Descrip.—This grows from a long, slender, white fibrous root, with finely divided leaves, which are deeply serrated, of a pale green. The stalk is round, upright, green, and a yard high. The flowers grow in little umbels on the tops of the branches, surrounded by slender leaves, forming a kind of cup. The seeds are small, brown, and striated.

Place.—It is common in hedges, on ditch banks, and in gardens.

Time.—It is an annual, and flowers in May.

Government and Virtues.—It is under Venus, and should be gathered when that planet is in exaltation. It is hot and dry, comforting the head and stomach, and helping vertiginous disorders. It is likewise a good deobstruent, opening obstructions of the womb, and procuring the catamenia.

SHEPHERD'S PURSE.—(*Capsella Bursa Pastoris.*)

Descrip.—The root is small, white, and perishes yearly. The leaves are small and long, of a pale green colour, and deeply cut in on both sides, among which spring up a stalk which is small and round, containing small seed upon it even to the top. The flowers are very small and white; after which come the little cases which hold the seeds, which are flat, almost in the form of a heart.

Place.—They frequent the path-ways of this country.

Time.—They flower all the summer; some twice a year.

Government and Virtues.—It is under the dominion of Saturn, and of a cold, dry, binding nature. It helps all fluxes of blood, caused by either inward or outward wounds; as also flux of the belly, and bloody-flux, spitting and voiding of blood, and stops the terms in women; if bound to the wrists, or the soles of the feet, it helps the jaundice. The herb made into poultice, helps inflammation and St. Anthony's fire. The juice dropped into the ears, heals the pains, noise, and matterings thereof. A good ointment may be made of it for all wounds, especially wounds in the head.

SHEPHERD'S ROD.—(*Dipsacus Pilosus.*)

Descrip.—This grows with a fleshy, thick, and somewhat hairy stock. The bottom leaves are large and rough, and grow with thick footstalks, from whence arise two smaller leaves. The upper leaves have a beautiful appearance, of a fine green, and deeply serrated. The flowers are of a gold yellow, and followed by heads of a green and purple colour, stuck round with prickles of a very tenacious substance. In some counties they call it Small Wild Teazle, and sometimes it is found with white flowers.

Place.—It is a biennial, frequently found in hedges.

Time.—It flowers in August.

Government and Virtues.—It is a plant of Mars. The root is bitter, given in a strong infusion strengthens the stomach, and creates an appetite ; it is also good against obstructions of the liver, and the jaundice.

SICKLE-WORT.—(*Diapentia.*)

Descrip.—This plant has a small, stringy, fibrous root, from which rise the leaves on long footstalks ; they are five-cornered, resembling somewhat those of the lesser maple, and are serrated about the edges, of a dark green colour, smooth, and shining : its stalks grow about a foot high, bare of leaves to the top, on which grow little umbels of five-leaved white flowers, small, and full of stamina ; each flower is succeeded by two rough bur-like seeds.

Place.—It grows in woods and thickets.

Time.—It flowers in May. The leaves are used.

Government and Virtues.—This is one of our prime vulnerary plants, and is frequently put in wound-drinks, and traumatic apozems ; and is good for ruptures, inward bruises, spitting of blood, or any hemorrhages, and for wounds both inward and outward. It is under Venus

SILVERWEED.—(*Potentilla Anserina.*)

Descrip.—The root is large, stringy, and full of fibres, sending out pretty large, yellowish, green winged leaves, divided into several deeply serrated segments set opposite to one another, with one cut into three parts at the end, of a pleasant grateful scent. The stalks rise about two feet high, and on the tops are placed the flowers. They are very large and beautiful, composed of five petals of a roundish figure, not dented at the tops; and are of a most beautiful shining yellow; in the middle of each there is a tuft of threads with yellow buttons, but smaller than in cinquefoil, and of a paler yellow.

Place.—It is common by road-sides, and in low pastures.

Time.—It flowers in June.

Government and Virtues.—This plant is under Venus, and deserves to be universally known in medicine. It is of the nature of tansy. The leaves are mildly restringent; dried, and given in powder they cure agues and intermitments; the usual dose is a table-spoonful of the powder every three or four hours. The roots are more astringent than the leaves, and may be given in powder, in doses of a scruple or more in obstinate purgings, attended with bloody stools, and immoderate menses. An infusion of the leaves stops the bleeding of the piles; and, sweetened with a little honey, it is an excellent gargle for sore throats.

SIMSON (BLUE.)—(*Erigeron Acre.*)

CALLED also Sweet Fleabane.

Descrip.—The flowers stand separate, one above another, alternately; they grow in a cylindric cup, with awl-shaped scales, placed erect, and the rays are narrow. The leaves are a dull green, and grow on a ruddy, firm, dry stalk. The flowers are of a purplish blue, and never spread wide open, but the rays always stand open.

Place.—This is a perennial; native of our high dry grounds; a strange plant that appears twice a year, and wears two different aspects.

Time.—In April we see it weak, lying on the ground, and scarce six inches high: in August and September it flowers a second time, and is then robust, upright, about ten inches high, and carries larger flowers.

Government and Virtues.—Mars governs this plant. It is a sharp acrid plant. It is a remedy for disorders of the breast, if they arise from tough phlegm. Yet it is one of those things that should be cautiously tampered with.

SKIRRET.—(*Sium Sisarum.*)

Descrip.—The root is composed of numerous, oblong, tuberous pieces, brownish on the outside, white within, and of a pleasant flower. The stalk is striated, firm, branched, a foot and a half high. The leaves are pinnated, serrated, sharp-pointed, and of a pleasant green. The flowers are white; and, toward the evening, they have a light fragrance. The seeds are small and brown.

Place.—It is a native of Spain, but is cultivated in our gardens for the root, which is pleasant and wholesome.

Time.—It flowers here in June and July.

Government and Virtues.—It is under Venus. The root is opening, diuretic, and cleansing, useful in opening obstructions of the reins and bladder, and frees them from slimy phlegm. It is serviceable against dropsy, by causing great plenty of urine, helps the jaundice, and liver disorders. The young shoots are pleasant and wholesome food, of a cleasing nature, and easy digestion, provoking urine.

SLOE BUSH.—(*Prunis Spinosa.*)

CALLED also Black Thorn.

Descrip.—This is a bush, whose tough branches are hard sharp thorns, sending forth white five-leaved flowers early in the spring, before the leaves appear, which are small and oblong, finely dented on the edges. The flowers are succeeded by small round fruit growing on short stalks, green at first, but when ripe of a fine purplish black colour, of a sour austere taste, and not fit to be eaten until mellowed by the frost.

Place.—It grows every where in the hedges.

Government and Virtues.—This is a Saturnine plant. The fruit is chiefly used, and is restringent and binding, good for all kinds of fluxes and hemorrhages. It is serviceable in washes for sore mouth and gums, to fasten loose teeth, &c. A handful of the flowers infused, is an easy purge; and, if taken in wine and water, is excellent to dispel windy colic. The bark reduced to powder, and taken in doses of two drams, has cured agues. The juice expressed from the unripe fruit is a very good remedy for fluxes of the bowels; it may be reduced by a gentle boiling to a solid consistence, in which state it will keep the year round.

SMALLAGE.—(*Apium Graveolens.*)

Descrip.—The roots are about a finger thick, wrinkled, and sinking deep in the earth, of a white colour, from which spring many winged leaves, of a yellow colour, each single leaf is three square; the stalks rise about three feet high, smooth channelled, rather angular, and very much branched; at the division of the branches, come forth umbels of small yellow flowers, followed by smaller seeds, paler and hotter. The whole plant has a strong ungrateful flavour.

Place.—It grows in marshy, watery places.

Time.—It flowers and ripens seed in the summer months.

Government and Virtues.—It is under Mercury. The roots are diuretic, effectual for the stoppage of urine, and the stone and gravel ; they open obstructions of the liver and spleen; help the dropsy and jaundice, and remove female obstructions. The leaves are of the same nature, and eaten in the spring, sweeten and purify the blood, and help the scurvy : the seed is hot and carminative. The roots, leaves, and seed, are used.

SNEEZEWORT.—(*Achillea Ptarmica.*)

CALLED also Bastard Pellitory.

Descrip.—This has a perennial, long, slender, and fibrous root. The stems are a little angular, upright, woolly and branched, two feet high, having long narrow leaves, finely serrated about the edges, growing on them without any order ; the flowers grow umbel-fashion on the tops of the stalks, and consist of a border of white petala, set about a fistular thrum; they are larger than the flowers of yarrow.

Place.—It grows in moist meadows and watery places.

Time.—It flowers in July.

Virtues.—It has a hot biting taste, and in salads is used to correct the coldness of other herbs. The root held in the mouth helps the tooth-ache, by evacuating the rheum ; the powder of the herb snuffed up the nose, causes sneezing, and cleanses the head of tough slimy humours.

SOAPWORT.—(*Saponaria Officinalis.*)

CALLED also Bruisewort.

Descrip.—It is a species of Lychnis, having many creeping roots arising from a thick woody head ; it sends forth reddish stalks about a foot high, full of knots, which are encompassed by the broad footstalks of the leaves ; these are smooth, of a pale green colour, broad and sharp-pointed, about two inches long, with three pretty high veins on their back. The flowers grow on the tops of the stalks, large, of a pale purple colour, each made of five large round-pointed leaves, set in a smooth long calyx; the seed is small and round, growing in long roundish seed-vessels.

Place.—It grows in watery places, and near rivers.

Time.—It flowers in June.

Government and Virtues.—Venus owns this plant. The whole plant is bitter; bruised and agitated with water, it raises a lather like soap, which easily washes greasy spots out of clothes ; a decoction of it, applied externally, cures the itch. It cures gonorrhœa, by taking the inspissated juice of it to the amount of half an ounce daily.

SOLANUM.—(*Atropa Belladonna,*)

CALLED also Dwale, Solanum Lethale, S. Maniacum.

Descrip.—This is the largest of the Nightshades, having many thick, long, spreading roots, that shoot forth many tall angular stalks, to a man's height or more, beset with dull green leaves, larger than common Nightshade. The flowers are set on among the leaves, singly on long footstalks, and are large, hollow, and bell-fashioned, divided into six segments at the ends, of a dusky brown, greenish colour on the outside, and purplish within ; succeeded by large, round, shining, black berries, the size of cherries, set on a brownish calyx, which contain a purplish juicy pulp of a nauseous sweet taste, full of small flat seeds.

Place.—It grows not unfrequently in many parts of this country, but it is a native of America.

Time.—It flowers in July.

Government and Virtues.—Experience has proved this to be one of the deadly poisons that nature produces. It has a very beautiful appearance, but should be kept out the way of children and others who may be attracted by it.

SOLANUM (BERRY BEARING.)—(*Solanum Bacciferum.*)

Descrip.—The roots of this herb creep along the surface of the earth, are slender, and of a brown colour, shooting up, here and there, round stalks about a foot high, with four, though sometimes five or six leaves, which are broad and roundish, narrowest next the stalk, and ending in a sharp point; from among these a slender stalk arises two or three inches high, bearing a flower, composed of four green leaves, with as many narrow ones under them, of the same colour, with several stamina among them ; in the middle grows a round black berry, the size of a grape, of an insipid taste.

Place.—It is found in good soil in moist shady woods.

Time.—It flowers in May, and the berry ripens in July.

Government and Virtues.—It is under the dominion of Saturn. It is not poisonous, but is an excellent counter-poison, and an alexipharmic, good in malignant and pestilential fevers. The roots boiled in wine help the colic, and the leaves applied outwardly repress inflammations and tumours, especially in the scrotum and testicles, and ripen pestilential tumours.

SOLDIER (COMMON WATER.)—(*Stratoites Aloides.*)

Descrip.—The root is composed of several long, thick, white fibres, with tufted ends ; they are naked from the bottom to the top, but just at the extremity they have several small, short filaments, which spread every way. From this root rise numerous leaves of a singular figure ; they are long and narrow, thickest and broadest at the base, and sharp at the point : they are fleshy, firm, of a deep green purple, and armed with slight prickles along the edges. The stalks rise among these, and are naked, round, thick, and of a pale green. The flowers are large and white, with a pretty tuft of yellow threads in the middle.

Place.—It swims in the water, and is common in the fen countries, as the Isle of Ely, and elsewhere.

Time.—It flowers in July.

Government and Virtues.—It is a cold watery plant, under the Moon in the celestial sign of Pisces. Externally used, it is cooling and repellant. It is a specific against the king's-evil and scrofulous swellings, both taken inwardly, and applied outwardly. It is said likewise to provoke urine, and to be useful in hysteric disorders.

SOLOMON'S SEAL.—(*Polygonatum Multiflorum,*) (*Couvallaria Multiflora.*)

Descrip.—This rises with a stalk half a yard high, bowing down to the ground, set with single leaves one above another, somewhat large, with a blueish eye upon the green, some with ribs, and yellowish underneath. At the foot of every leaf, almost from the bottom to the top of the stalk, come forth small, long, white, and hollow pendulous leaves, with long points, for the most part together, at the end of a long footstalk, and sometimes but one, and sometimes two stalks, with flowers at the foot of a leaf, which are without any scent at all, and stand on one side of the stalk. After they are past, come in their places small round berries, great at first, and blackish green, tending to blueness when they are ripe, wherein are small, white, hard, and stony seeds. The root is a finger or thumb thick, white and knotted in some places, a flat round circle representing a seal, whereof it took its name, lying all along with the upper crust of the earth, and not growing downward, but with many fibres underneath.

Place.—It is frequent in different parts of England.

Time.—It flowers in May ; the root abides and shoots a-new every year.

Government and Virtues.—Saturn owns the plant. The root is available for wounds, hurts, and outward sores, to heal and close up those that are green, and to dry and restrain the flux of humours of old ones. It stays vomitings, bleedings, and fluxes in man or woman. It stays joints that do not remain firm when set, and broken bones in any part of the body, if the roots be bruised and applied. The decoction of the roots bruised in wine or other drink, after a night's infusion, strained and drank, helps both man and beast whose bones have been broken ; it also helps ruptures, if drank or applied outwardly to the place affected. The powdered root in broth acts the same. It dispels congealed blood that comes of blows, bruises, &c., also takes away both the pains and black and blue marks that come from the same cause. The distilled water of the whole plant takes away morphew, freckles &c., from any part of the body

SORREL (COMMON.)—(*Rumex Acetosa.*)

Descrip.—The leaves are smooth, succulent, and tender, long and sharp-pointed, ending next the footstalk in two sharp ears like spinach, of a very sour taste ; the stalk is long and slender, set with two or three smaller leaves, and at the top a long reddish spike of small staminous flowers, succeeded by small shining three-square seed. The root is about a finger thick, branched and full of fibres, of a yellowish brown colour, abiding several years.

Place.—It grows every where in the fields and meadows.

Time.—It flowers in May. The leaves, seed, and root are used.

Government and Virtues.—All the Sorrels are under the dominion of Venus. It is useful to cool inflammation and heat of the blood in agues, pestilential or choleric, or sickness and fainting, arising from the heart; to quench thirst and procure an appetite in fainting or decaying stomachs; for it resists the putrefaction of the blood, kills worms, and is a cordial to the heart, which the seed does more effectually, because it is more drying and binding, and thereby stays the fluxes of womens' courses, or flux of the stomach.

The root in decoction or powder, is effectual for all the said purposes. The decoction of the roots helps the jaundice, and expels the gravel and stone from the reins and kidneys. The decoction of the flowers made with wine, and drunk, helps the black jaundice, and inward ulcers of the body or bowels. A syrup made from the juice and fumitory, is a help to kill those sharp humours that cause the itch. The juice with a little vinegar, serves well to be used outwardly for the same cause, and for tetters, ringworms, &c.

SORREL (MOUNTAIN.)—*(Oxyria Reniformis,) (Rumex Digynus.)*

Descrip.—The leaves are of a glaucous or blueish green colour, broader, shorter, and rounder than the common, and the ears that stand on each side, at their joining to the footstalks, are very large. The stalks are smaller, weaker, and not so erect. They flower and seed much alike.

Place.—It is sown in gardens.

Time.—It flowers in June: the leaves are as sour as the common, and may be used indifferently with it, both in medicines and salads.

SORREL (SHEEP'S.)—*(Rumex Acetosella.)*

Descrip.—This is lower and smaller than the common, with narrow sharp-pointed leaves, each has two large ears growing next the end of the stalk, which makes the leaf appear like a bearded spear; they are sour like the common. The flowers grow in spikes as the former, are small and staminous, and the seed triangular, and less than the seed of that. The root is small and creeping in the ground.

Place.—It grows in dry barren soil.

Time.—It flowers in May.

Virtues.—The leaves of all the Sorrels are very cooling, allaying thirst, and repressing the bile; good in fevers, being cordial, and resisting putrefaction. They are of great use against scurvy if eaten in spring as salad; and the juice is frequently taken among other antiscorbutic juices.

SORREL (WOOD.)—*(Acetosella Oxalis.)*

Descrip.—This grows upon the ground, with a number of leaves coming from the root made of three leaves, like a trefoil, but broad at the ends, and cut in the middle, of a yellowish green colour, every one standing on a long footstalk, which, at their first coming up, are closely folded together to the stalk, but opening themselves afterwards.

Among these leaves rise up slender, weak footstalks, with a flower at the top of every one, consisting of five small pointed leaves, star-fashion, of a white colour, in most places, and in some places dashed over with a small show of blue on the backside only. After the flowers follow small round heads, with yellowish seed in them; the roots are but small strings fastened to the end of a small long piece ; all of them being of a yellowish colour.

Place.—It grows in many parts of England, in woods and wood-sides, where they are moist and shady.

Time.—It flowers in April and May.

Virtues.—This serves all the purposes that the other Sorrels do, but is more effectual in hindering the putrefaction of the blood, to quench thirst, to strengthen a weak stomach, to stay vomiting, and very excellent in any contagious sickness or pestilential fever.

SOUTHERNWOOD.—(*Artemisia Abrotanum.*)

Called also Old Man Tree, Boy's Love, Lad's Love.

Descrip.—This has a perennial root, divided into several parts, which are furnished with fibres. The stems are numerous, of a hard woody substance, covered with a greyish bark, divided into numerous branches, two or three feet high. The leaves are numerous, and divided into many fine bristly segments, of a fine pale green colour, and of a pleasant smell. The flowers are small and yellow.

Place.—It is common in our gardens.

Time.—It flowers for the most part in July and August.

Government and Virtues.—This is a mercurial plant. The seed bruised, heated in warm water, and drank, helps those that are troubled with cramps or convulsions of the sinews, the sciatica, and bringing down womens' courses. The same taken in wine is an antidote against all poisons. The backbone anointed with the oil cures the ague, it removes inflammations in the eyes, if part of a roasted quince, and a few crumbs of bread be boiled, and added. Boiled with barley-meal, it removes pimples, and wheals from the face, or other parts of the body. The seed and dried herb kills worms in children ; the herb bruised and applied, draws out splinters and thorns from the flesh. The ashes mingled with old salad oil, helps those that are bald, causing the hair to grow again on the head or beard. A strong decoction of the leaves is a good worm medicine, but is disagreeable and nauseous. The leaves are a good ingredient in fomentations for easing pain, dispersing swellings, or stopping the progress of gangrenes,

SOUTHERNWOOD (FIELD.)—(*Artemisia Campestris.*)

Descrip.—This has a long, thick, fibrous root. The stalks are shrubby, upright, and much branched, of a whitish colour toward the bottom, and reddish upwards. The leaves are oblong, divided into numerous narrow segments, and their colour greyish green. The flowers stand in thick spikes at the tops of the branches; and they are small and brown.

Place.—It is found in our southern counties by road-sides.

Time.—It flowers in July.

Government and Virtues.—It is a powerful diuretic, and is good in hysteric cases. The best way of using it is in conserve made of the fresh tops, beaten up with twice their weight of sugar. It is a mercurial plant, and worthy of more esteem than it has. The manner of preparing it is thus :—Cut fine four ounces of the leaves, beat them in a mortar, with six ounces of loaf sugar, till the whole is like a paste ; three times a day take a piece of this about the size of a nutmeg : it is pleasant, and very effectual ; and one thing in its favour in particular, it is a composer, and always disposes to sleep.

SOWBREAD.—(*Artanita Cyclamen.*)

Descrip.—The root is round, and somewhat flattish, of a dark brown colour on the outside, with several dark fibres shooting from the bottom ; the leaves grow on thick reddish stalks, of a darkish green above, marked with white spots, and underneath of a reddish or purple colour, round, and hollowed in next the stalk; among these rise the flowers, each on its own footstalk, which is usually slenderest next the ground. They are made up of one single pendulous leaf, divided into five sharp-pointed segments, which turn themselves backward, when they open, and are of a pale purple, when these are fallen, the stalk with the seed-vessel coils itself round towards the earth, like a snake.

Place.—It is a native of the Alps, and the mountains of Austria, but is planted in this country in gardens.

Time.—It flowers in September and October.

Government and Virtues.—This is a martial plant. The root is very forcing, used to bring away the birth and the secundines, and to provoke the menses. The juice is commended against vertiginous disorders of the head, used in form of an errhine; it is good against cutaneous eruptions.

SOWERWEED (KIDNEY-LEAVED.)—(*Oxyria Digyna.*)

Descrip.—This plant grows upright; the root is small and fibrous, tapering towards the top. The leaves are shaped like a kidney, and grow at the end of long foot-stalks, which are so weak that they lie upon the ground: they are greener within than without, and have a soft down on each side: the flowers are small and white, and the seed is so light, that the wind scatters it for many miles.

Place.—It delights in open airy pastures, and open situations. It is plentiful in Westmoreland, Yorkshire, and Wales.

Time.—It flowers in June.

Government and Virtues.—It is a martial plant, and is hot and dry, carminative and expelling wind, and helps the colic and gripes. It is alexipharmic, and good against pestilential distempers. It is of use against the stone and the stoppage of urine, and good in all uterine distempers.

SOW-THISTLE (COMMON.)—(*Sonchus Oleraceus.*)

Descrip.—The leaves of this kind half embrace the stalk, which is slender, hollow, branched, and of a light green, and two feet high. The cups are smooth, the leaves of a fine fresh green, and full of a milky juice. The flowers are numerous, and of a pale lemon colour.

Place.—This is an annual; a robust weed, that rises in all gardens, and waste grounds.

Time.—It blooms from November to June.

Government and Virtues.—This is under Venus. It is divided into many varieties raised from the same seed, viz: the jagged leaved, the entire leaved, the broad and narrow.

SOW-THISTLE (PRICKLY.)—(*Sonchus Asper.*)

Descrip.—This has a yellow, angular, channelled stalk, two feet high, of a fine green, with the lower leaves long, stiff, and much cut in, every indenting ending in a prickle. The flowers are small, numerous, and yellow, and grow several together on the tops of the stalk, shaped like the dandelion, but less, of a paler colour; the under part of the petal is tinctured with purple. The flower turns into down, enclosing long, thin, flattish seeds. The root is thick, long, and whitish; and the whole plant upon breaking, yields a milky, bitter juice.

Place.—This a native of our corn-fields and gardens, and flowers from July to November, until the cold kills it.

Government and Virtues.—This is under the dominion of Venus, and possesses great medicinal virtues; it is cooling and good against obstructions, and the quantity which must at any time be taken, insures its effect, which is mild and aperient. The young tops are good as salad with oil and vinegar, for a scalding of the water. The smooth Sow-Thistle has hollow channelled stalks like the others, and grows as tall ; the leaves are smooth, and free from prickles ; those next the stalk are cut like dandelion, into several segments; that at the end being largest. Those that grow on the stalk seem to encompass it, and have fewer incisions, triangular and pointed at the end. The flowers, seed, and root, are much alike. This grows in the same places as the former, and as frequent.

SOW-THISTLE (TREE.)—(*Sonchus Arvensis.*)

Descrip.—This grows about a yard high. The stalk is tender, hollow, of a yellowish green; and so are the leaves, which, when pressed or broken, run with milk. The flowers are large, and of an orange colour.

Place.—This is frequent in the corn-fields, where the soil is moist and clayey.

Time.—It blooms in August.

Government and Virtues.—Venus governs this plant. Its virtues lie chiefly in its milky juice, which is useful in deafness, either from accidental stoppage, gout, or old age. Four spoonfuls of the juice of the leaves, two of salad-oil, and one teaspoonful of salt; shake the whole together, and put some cotton dipped in this composition into the ears, and you may reasonably expect a good degree of recovery.

SOW-THISTLE TREE (MARSH.)—(*Sonchus Palustris.*)

Descrip.—The stalk is hollow, tender, of a pale green, about a yard and a half high. The leaves are soft and tender, of a light green, and pale underneath, shaped like arrow-heads at their base. The flowers are light yellow, numerous, and they stand in a broad clustering head.

Place.—It is a native of the Thames-side, and frequents other wet places where there is deep mud.

Time.—It blooms in August.

Government and Virtues.—It is under Venus. The whole plant has a very insipid taste. It is cooling and rather binding, it cools a hot stomach, and eases its pains. The herb boiled in wine, and drank, stays the dissolution of the stomach, and the milk that is taken from the stalks, given in drink, is beneficial to those who are short-winded. The decoction of the leaves and stalks causes abundance of milk in nurses, and their children to be well-coloured The juice or distilled water is good for hot inflammations, wheals, eruptions or heat of the skin, and itching of the hemorrhoids. The juice boiled or thoroughly heated in a little oil of bitter almonds in the peel of a pomegranate, and dropped into the ears is a sure remedy for deafness, singings, &c.

SPEEDWELL.—(*Veronica.*)

Descrip.—This grows with weak stalks, frequently taking root, where they trail upon the ground, and thence send up shoots that thicken the tuft. The leaves grow on short footstalks ; they are oval, an inch long, hairy, and crenated about the edges, of a pale green colour. The flowers grow on the upper part of the stalks among the leaves, in short spikes, each of one small blueish purple leaf, cut into four parts ; to each of which succeeds a seed-vessel in the shape of that of the Shepherd's Pouch, full of very small seeds. The root is a bush of fibres.

Place.—It grows in woods and shady places.

Time.—It flowers in June. The whole herb is used.

Government and Virtues.—Venus governs this plant, and it is among the vulnerary plants, used both outwardly and inwardly ; it is also pectoral, and good for coughs and consumptions: and is helpful against the stone and strangury; as also against pestilential fevers.

SPIGNEL.—(*Meum.*)

Called also Mew.

Descrip.—The root spreads deep in the ground, many branches growing from one head, which is hairy at the top, of a blackish brown colour on the outside, and white within, smelling well, and of an aromatic taste, from whence rise long stalks of fine cut leaves like hair, smaller than dill, set thick on both sides of the stalks, of a good scent. Among these leaves rise up round stiff stalks, with a few joints and leaves on them, and at the tops an umbel of pure white flowers; at the edges whereof sometimes will be seen a show of the reddish blue colour, especially before they be full blown, and are succeeded by small roundish seeds, larger than the ordinary fennel, and of a brown colour, divided into two parts, and crusted on the back.

Place.—It grows wild in Lancashire, Yorkshire, and other northern counties, and is also planted in gardens.

Time.—It flowers in June.

Government and Virtues.—This is an herb of Venus. The roots boiled in wine or water, and drank, helps the strangury and stoppings of the urine, the wind, swellings and pains in the stomach, pains of the mother, and all joint-aches. If the powder of the root be mixed with honey, and the same taken it breaks tough phlegm, and dries up the rheum that falls on the lungs.

SPIGNEL (BROAD-LEAVED.)—(*Meum Athamantica.*)

CALLED also Baldmony.

Descrip.—The root is long and thick, fibrous, of an aromatic taste, the bottom leaves are of a dark green colour. The upper leaves are small, very slender, of a dull green colour. The stalk grows about a foot high, not much branched, with a few small leaves growing thereon, bearing on the top umbels of small white five-leaved flowers. The seed is longer and larger than fennel, two growing together, which are striated on the back.

Place.—It is found in our western counties, in rich damp soils, but not common.

Time.—It flowers in June and July.

Government and Virtues.—It is under the dominion of Mercury in Cancer, and is an excellent plant in disorders of the stomach from phlegm, raw crude humours, wind and relaxations, pains, want of appetite and digestion, belchings, ructations, loathings, colic, gripes, retention of the urine, and the menses, and if powdered and given with loaf sugar, and a glass of its infusion in white wine or beer, or water taken evening and morning for some days, mostly brings down the menses and lochia, facilitates the expulsion of birth and after-birth, and eases a windy colic.

SPIKENARD.—(*Nardostachys Jatamansi.*)

Virtues.—This is a native of India, of a heating, drying faculty, good to provoke urine and ease pains of the stone in the reins and kidneys, being drunk in cold water. It helps loathings, swellings or gnawings in the stomach, the jaundice, and such as are liver-grown. It is a good ingredient in Mithridate, and other antidotes against poison; to pregnant women it is forbidden to be taken inwardly. The oil is good to warm cold places, and to digest crude and

.aw humours : it works powerfully on old cold griefs of the head and brain, stomach, liver, spleen, reins, and bladder. It purges the brain of rheum, being snuffed up the nostrils. It comforts the brains, and helps cold pains in the head, and the shaking palsy. Two or three spoonfuls, if taken, help passions of the heart, swoonings, and the colic: and being made into troches with wine, it may be reserved for an eye-medicine, which being aptly applied, represses obnoxious humours thereof.

SPINACH.—*(Spinacia Oleracea.)*

Descrip.—This has a long whitish root, from which rise several broad, sharp-pointed leaves, hollowed in next the stalk, which is flat and succulent, rising about two feet high, with the like but smaller leaves growing on it, with several spikes of green herbaceous flowers, and after them come large prickly seed.

Place.—It is sown yearly in gardens.

Virtues.—It is more used for food than medicine, and is much eaten as boiled salad, and is useful to temper the heat and sharpness of the humours; it cools and moistens, and as a diuretic renders the body soluble.

SPLEEN-WORT.—*(Asplenium Scolopendra.)*

CALLED also Ceterach.

Descrip.—This is a small plant, which consists only of leaves, that rise from a fibrous root, about four inches in length, hardly an inch broad, cut into small roundish segments, which stand opposite to one another, alternately ; they are of a greenish colour on the upper side, and browninish, and full of dusty seed underneath, generally folded inward, resembling the Scolopendra, whence it is named.

Place.—It grows on stone walls and moist shadowy places.

Time.—It abides green all the winter.

Government and Virtues.—Saturn owns it. It is generally used against infirmities of the spleen, helps the strangury, and wastes the stone in the bladder, and is useful against the jaundice and the hiccough.

SPUNK.—*(Agaricus Pedis Equini Facie.)*

CALLED also Touchwood.

Descrip.—This grows to the oak, ash, and other trees. That on old oaks is considered best, the inward part that feels to the touch like buff, must be taken out and beaten a little till it crumbles between the fingers.

Place.—Not only live trees, but decayed ones, and rotten wood, produce this excrescence.

Time.—Warm and damp weather is best for its growth.

Government and Virtues.—This is under the Moon. It is used for stopping blood upon the amputation of a limb, without making any ligature. The softest part should be chosen, and when reduced to powder, as much of it must be applied to the wound as will rather more than cover it; and over this a broader piece must be applied with proper bandages. The moss which grows in old wine-casks is the best thing that can be employed for this purpose.

SPURGE (BROAD-LEAVED.)—*(Euphorbia Portlandica,) (Euphorbia Platyphylla.)*

Descrip.—This does not rise so high, nor are the leaves so broad as some, but they are longer, not dented on the edges; it spreads itself at the top like a tree ; the leaves are very green, and the flowers are white.

SPURGE (CORN.)—*(Euphorbia Segetalis.)*

Descrip.—This has numerous thick blueish green leaves without footstalks ; they are long and narrow, and stand up almost straight. The stalks are round, thick, green, or sometimes reddish, and spead at the top like the others, but the flowers are small and green, and have a pretty appearance at the tops of the stalks.

Place.—It is frequently observed about Cambridge.

Government and Virtues.—Spurges are mercurial plants, and abound with a hot and acrid juice, which, when applied outwardly, eats away warts and other excresences.

SPURGE (DWARF.)—*(Euphorbia Exigua.*

Descrip.—This has a less root than the Petty Spurge, and sends forth many stalks not much branched, about a foot high, thick-set with long narrow leaves like toad-flax, but rounder pointed : the tops of the stalks are divided into several partitions like umbels, with hollow cup-like leaves pierced through the stalks of the flowers, which are small and yellow ; the seed-vessel is three-square.

Place.—A native of France, but it grows in our gardens.

Virtues.—The virtues are same as the former, a strong and violent cathartic and emetic, but now out of use.

SPURGE (GARDEN.)—(*Euphorbia Hortense.*)

Descrip.—This grows with a thick reddish stalk, beset with long and narrow blueish green leaves, and so continues, without running into branches, till the next year, when it rises three or four feet high, with many branches toward the top; on which, at every division, grow broader and somewhat triangular leaves, set on without footstalks; the flowers are small and yellow, standing in round hollow leaves, which encompass the stalk like a cup, and these are followed by three square seed-vessels, containing three oblong seeds. The whole plant is so full of milk, that if you cut off a branch, it will run out by drops in some quantity, which milk is of a hot fiery burning taste, inflaming the mouth and throat for a great while.

Place.—It grows in gardens, where it springs of its own sowing, dying after it has brought its seed to perfection.

Virtues.—This is much of the nature of the foregoing plant, but is rather stronger and more violent in its operation. The milk is good to take away warts.

SPURGE (GREATER.)—(*Euphorbia Major.*)

Descrip.—This plant grows as tall as a little tree, with a smooth jointed hollow stalk, about a finger thick, covered with a glacuous mealiness. The leaves are large, roundish, but cut into five, seven, or sometimes nine sharp-pointed, and serrated divisions; the footstalks are long, in the centre of the back part of the leaves. The flowers are small and staminous, growing on the top of the stalks; but lower down, and upon the body of the plant, grow bunches of rough triangular husks, each including three white seeds less than horse-beans, which, in their brittle shells, contain spotted kernels of a sweetish oily taste.

Place.—It grows in Essex, and other counties.

Time.—It flowers in August.

Virtues.—The kernels, which are the only parts used, purge watery humours both upwards and downwards with great violence. The expressed oil from the seeds, is good to kill lice in children's heads.

SPURGE (KNOTTY-ROOTED.)—(*Euphorbia Hyberna.*)

Descrip.—The stalks are numerous, weak, round, of a pale green, and a foot high; the leaves are many, thick, of a pale green: they are not at all indented, and terminate in a round blunt end. The flowers are small and yellow and form a kind of umbel at the tops of the branches.

Place.—This is frequent in the corn-fields of Ireland.

SPURGE (OLIVE.)—(*Daphne Mezereum.*)

Descrip.—This is a low shrubby tree, with many flexible branches, seldom growing above four or five feet high, shooting out clusters of flowers, all round the upper parts of the branches, early in the spring, before the leaves appear: they are of a pale purple, or peach colour, of a single tuberous leaf, cut into four segments at the end, of a pleasant, sweet smell; and are succeeded by small, longish round berries, of a red colour. The leaves grow thick together on the tops of the twigs, two inches long, and scarce half so broad at the end, where they are broadest. The root is full of branches, and runs deep in the earth

Place.—It is planted here in gardens.

Time.—It flowers in February and March. The root, bark, leaves, and berries, are used.

Virtues.—All the Spurges agree in their qualities. They purge serous and choleric humours very violently, and help the dropsy and inveterate asthma.

SPURGE (PETTY.)—(*Euphorbia Peplis.*)

Descrip.—This has a very large thick root, many times the size of a man's arm, spread out into many branches, and sending up many tough stalks, two or three feet high, reddish and much divided, having smooth, long, narrowish, green leaves, broadest at the end. The flowers which grow on the tops of the stalks are small and yellow, which are followed by triangular seed-vessels containing three roundish seeds. The whole plant is full of a caustic milk, burning and inflaming the mouth for a great while.

Place.—It grows in several parts.

Time.—It flowers in June. The root is used, and of that the bark only.

Virtues.—It is a strong cathartic, working violently by vomit and stool, but is very offensive to the stomach and bowels by reason of its sharp corrosive quality, and therefore ought to be used with caution.

SPURGE (PORTLAND.)—(*Euphorbia Portlandica.*)

Descrip.—This has fair green leaves, and the flowers are of a blueish green : in every other respect it resembles the other kinds already described.

Place.—They are found upon the Island of Portland

SPURGE (RED.)—(*Euphorbia Characias.*)

Descrip.—This has long, narrow, sharp-pointed ends ; they have short footstalks, and are smooth, of a dead green at first, but afterwards red : they are of a hard, firm substance, and differ as much in that as colour from those of the preceding species. Towards the top the stalk divides in a number of branches, on which stand the flowers in umbels ; they are small, numerous, and of so deep a purple, that they appear nearly black. The seed is very large, and the whole plant becomes red, after standing some time.

Place.—It is found wild in Staffordshire : and also on the mountains in the north of Ireland.

Time.—It flowers in May.

SPURGE (ROUGH FRUITED.)—(*Euphorbia Verrucosa.*)

Descrip.—The leaves stand irregularly ; and are broad, short, sharp-pointed, smooth, of a pale green, and somewhat serrated at the edges. The flowers stand in small tufts at the top of the plant, they are a little round, of a yellowish green. The seed-vessel is roundish, large and rough, it is more conspicuous than in the other kinds, and has been compared to a wart, the seeds are as large.

SPURGE (SEA.)—(*Euphorbia Paralias.*)

Descrip.—This has a singular appearance ; the leaves encompass the stalk : and has. small greenish flowers at the top of the stalk ; the whole plant is perfectly smooth, and a blueish green colour.

SPURGE (SUN.)—(*Euphorbia Helioscopia.*)

Descrip.—The leaves are numerous, oblong, of an invert-oval figure, and serrated at the edges : they have no footstalks, and are smallest at the base, when they are broader all the way to the end : their colour is blueish green. The flowers stand at the top of the stalk, in a broad spreading umbel ; they are of a yellowish green.

Place.—This sort is often cultivated on garden borders, and on other cultivated grounds.

Time.—It flowers in July and August.

SPURGE (WOOD.)—(*Euphorbia Amygdaloides.*)

Descrip.—The stalks are numerous and firm, they are thick, upright, and round, and have a reddish bark, and under that a green one; they grow a yard high, and not branched, except where they spread at the top for flowering. The leaves are large and numerous; they are long, narrow, and soft to the touch; their colour is a deep greyish green, and they are hairy on the upper side, but more so underneath, and their middle rib is red toward the base. The flowers are greenish, small, and very numerous, they stand at the top of the stalks on small divided branch es which spread into a kind of umbel, and which have at their insertions and divisions, shorter leaves than those on the stalks. The figure and disposition of the petals of the flower, form numerous crescents. insomuch, that the whole top in flower has a beautiful appearance. The whole plant is full of a caustic milky juice.

Place.—This is frequent in woods and on heaths.

Time.—It flowers in June.

SQUILL.—(*Scilla Maritima,*) (*S. Ornithogalum.*)

Called also Sea Onion.

Descrip.—This has a perennial root, consisting of a very large coated bulb, full of a thick slimy juice, and a large cluster of long, thick, white fibres, proceeding from its base. The leaves are three or four inches broad, of a thick juicy substance, smooth on the surface, entire at the edges, and of a fine bright green colour. The stem sometimes grows to be three feet high, is round, slender, and of a tender succulent substance. The flowers grow in longish spikes, and they are small and white.

P ace.—It is a native of the sea-coasts of Italy and Spain, but here it is found only in the gardens of the curious.

Time.—It flowers here in the middle of summer.

Government and Virtues.—This is a hot biting martial plant. The root is bitter to the taste, and so acrid as to blister the skin if it is much handled; taken internally in doses of a few grains, it promotes the expectoration and urine; in larger doses it vomits, and sometimes purges. It is one of the most certain diuretics in dropsical cases, and expectorants in asthmatical ones, where the lungs or stomach are oppressed by tough viscid phlegm, or injured by the imprudent use of opiates. Being disagreeable in taste, it is given in the form of pill, made of the powdered root beaten into a mass, with the addition of syrup, or mucilage of gum arabic.

STAR-WORT (GARDEN.)—(*Aster Hortense.*)

Descrip.—This grows to about a foot and a half high, with hairy leaves set on the branches, without order: toward the top it is divided into three or four branches, at the end of which grows a yellow flower like a marigold, but with a broader thrum and narrower petala; close under each flower grow six or seven stiff roundish leaves, in form of a star, whence it takes its name; the seed is oblong, thin, and flat, of a blackish colour: the root is small and fibrous, perishing every year.

Place.—It is a native of the southern part of Europe, and grows in this country only in gardens.

Place.—It flowers in July.

Government and Virtues.—This is under the dominion of Mercury. The leaves are only used, which are commended against buboes and swellings in the groin.

STAR-WORT (SEA.)—(*Aster Tripolium,*) (*Tripolium Vulgare.*)

Descrip.—This grows spontaneously in the fields. It is a perennial; native of our damp grounds near the sea, and great rivers; a handsome plant, of a yard high, with a ruddy branched stalk. The leaves are smooth, narrow, of a fine green. The flowers are numerous, large, and blue.

Time.—They bloom in August.

Government and Virtues.—This is under the dominion of Mercury. The leaves are cooling, and good for burns, scalds, and inflammations, in any part. The seed is narcotic and soporiferous, and rarely used. A slight tincture or infusion of the plant promotes perspiration, and is good in feverish complaints. The juice boiled into a syrup with honey, is excellent in asthmatical complaints, and other disorders of the lungs; and outwardly applied, is a cure for the itch, and other cutaneous disorders.

STAR-WORT (SPRING-WATER.)—(*Callitriche Verna.*)

Descrip.—This is like Fleabane, but smaller. The root is small and fibrous; the stalk is round, reddish, upright, and a foot high; the leaves are long, narrow, and of a lively green ; the flowers stand at the tops of the branches, which they terminate, and are small and white.

Place.—It is found in many parts of England, but seems owing to seeds scattered and blown out of gardens.

Time.—This sort flowers in May.

STAR-WORT (AUTUMNAL WATER.)—(*Callitriche Autumnalis.*)

Descrip.—This differs from the former only in the time of flowering and the colour of the flower, which is sometimes of a pale blue, sometimes purplish, just according to the accidents of the soil. Another of the species is found frequently in our salt-marshes with yellow flowers, but their shape and virtues are the same.

Government and Virtues.—These are under Mercury, but are seldom used ; however, it would be worth trying ; they are unpleasant, but are excellent pectorals.

STAVES-ACRE.—(*Delphinium Staphisagria.*)

CALLED also Lousewort.

Descrip.—This plant grows from a foot and a half to two feet high; the lower leaves are large and round, divided into seven sharp-pointed segments deeply cut in. The leaves grow on the stalk, which is round and somewhat downy, are less, but alike in shape. The flowers grow on the tops of the stalk, of a blue colour, each flower is succeeded by three or four crooked pods which contain two or three large brown wrinkled angular seeds.

Place.—A native of warm countries, but grows in gardens.

Time.—It flowers in July. The seed only is used.

Virtues.—It is seldom taken inwardly, being of a hot burning taste. It is sometimes used in masticatories and gargarisms for the tooth-ache. The powder is used to kill lice. The seed is given in small doses against rheumatic and venereal disorders ; they roughly vomit and purge, and it is better to omit their use internally. Chewed in the mouth, they largely expel watery humours from adjacent parts, and are of service in disorders of the head.

STONE CROP.—(*Sedum Acre.*)

CALLED also Prick Madam, Small Houseleek, and Wall Pepper.

Descrip.—It grows with trailing branches on the ground, set with many thick, flat, roundish, whitish green leaves, pointed at the ends. The flowers stand together loosely. The roots are small, and run creeping under ground.

Place.—It is found on stone and mud walls, upon the tiles of houses, among rubbish, and in gravelly parts.

Time.—It flowers in June and July, and the leaves are green all the winter.

Government and Virtues.—It is under the dominion of the Moon, cold in quality, and somewhat binding, very good to stay defluxions, especially such as fall on the eyes. It stops bleeding, both inwardly and outwardly, helps cankers, and fretting sores and ulcer; it prevents diseases that arise from choleric humours, expels poison, resists pestilential fevers, and is good for tertian agues; the decoction answers the same purposes. It is a harmless herb, bruised and applied to the place, it helps king's-evil, and other knots or kernels in the flesh: as also the piles, but it should be used with caution. The juice taken inwardly excites vomiting. In scorbutic cases, and quartan agues, it is a most excellent medicine, under proper management.

STORAX TREE.—(*Liquidambar Styraciflua.*)

Descrip.—This tree grows like the Quince tree both in size and form ; the leaves are long and round, white underneath and stiff. The flowers stand both at the joints with leaves, and at the ends of the branches, and consist of five or six white ones, with some threads in the middle, after which come berries set in the cups that were flowers before, pointed at the ends, and hoary all over, each on a long footstalk, containing within them certain kernels in small shells, and yields a clear fragrant gum of the colour of brown honey. Another kind has three or five broad leaves, which come forth out of knots from a round root, covered with a crested, or jointed bark, standing on small blackish long stalks, divided into three or five parts, full of veins, dented about the edges, and pointed at the ends. A third sort is called the Red Storax.

Place.—The first grows in France, and Italy, Candy, Greece, and Turkey, where it yields no gum ; but in Syria, Cilicia, Pamphylia, Cyprus, and those hotter countries, it thrives considerably.

Time.—It flowers in spring, yields fruit in September.

Government and Virtues.—This is a Solar plant, and only the gum is used. It is hot in the second degree, and dry in the first. It heals, mollifies, and digests, and is good for coughs, catarrhs, distillations of rheum and hoarseness. Pills made with a little turpentine, gently loosens the belly. It resists cold poisons. Dropped into the ears, it helps the singing and noise in them.

STRAWBERRIES.—*(Fragaria Vesca.)*

THIS plant is so well known that it needs no description.

Place.—It grows in woods, and is planted in gardens.

Time.—It flowers in May, the fruit ripens soon after.

Government and Virtues.—Venus owns the herb. The fruit when green, is cool and dry; but when ripe cool and moist; the berries cool the liver, the blood, and the spleen, or a hot choleric stomach; refresh and comfort fainting spirits and quench thirst; they are good for inflammations, yet it is best to refrain from them in a fever, lest by their putrefying in the stomach, they increase the fits. The roots and leaves boiled in wine and water, and drank, cool the liver and blood, and assuage all inflammations in the reins and bladder, provoke urine, and allay their heat and sharpness. The same if drank, stays the bloody flux and womens' courses, and helps the swelling of the spleen. The water of the berries carefully distilled, is a remedy and cordial in the panting and beating of the heart, and good for the jaundice. The juice dropped into foul ulcers, or washed therewith, or the decoction of the herb and root, cleanses and helps to cure them. Lotions and gargles for sore mouths, or ulcers therein, or in the privy parts or elsewhere, are made with the leaves and roots thereof; it is also good to fasten loose teeth, and to heal spongy gums. It helps to stay catarrhs, or defluxions of rheum in the mouth, throat, teeth, or eyes. The juice or water is singularly good for hot or inflamed eyes, if dropped into them, or they bathed therewith.

STRAWBERRY CINQUEFOIL.—*(Potentilla Fragariastrum,) (Fragaria Sterilis.)*

Descrip.—The root is large, reddish, and woody, divided at the the top into several heads, and has a few fibres. The footstalks of the leaves are four inches long, tender, and hairy. The leaves are broad, oblong, hairy, serrated, and not unlike those of strawberry, but less, of the winged kind, not fingered as in the ordinary Cinquefoils. The stalk is round, firm, erect, about two and a half feet high The flowers are numerous large, and white. They stand at the tops of the branches, succeeded each by a cluster of seeds, resembling a strawberry, whence the name.

Place.—It grows wild in Cumberland and Wales.

Time.—It flowers in May and June.

Government and Virtues.—It is under Jupiter. The root possesses a considerable astringency, and is excellent in the overflowing of the menses, and in bloody stools. The best way of giving it is in powder, its dose is a scruple. The young leaves in an infusion are diuretic. It is good in intermittant fevers.

SUCCORY (GARDEN.)—(*Cichorium Sativum.*)

Descrip.—This has longer and narrower leaves than the Endive, and more cut on the edges, the root abides many years. It bears blue flowers, and the seed is hardly distinguishable from the seed of ordinary Endive.

SUCCORY (WILD.)—(*Cichorium Intybus.*)

Descrip.—The difference between this and the garden kind is, its growing wild, and not rising on the ground, much cut in on both the edges, even to the middle rib, ending in a point; sometimes it has a rib down to the middle of the leaves, from among which rises up a round, hard, woody stalk, spreading into many branches, set with smaller and lesser divided leaves on them up to the tops, where stand the flowers, which are like the garden kind, and the seed is also; the root is white, but more woody and hard than the garden kind. The whole plant is exceedingly bitter.

Place.—It grows in many parts of England, in waste, untilled and barren fields. The other only in gardens.

Government and Virtues.—It is under Jupiter. The garden kind, as it is more dry and less cold than Endive, so it opens more. A handful of the leaves or roots, boiled in wine or water, and drank fasting, drives forth choleric and phlegmatic humours, opens obstructions of the liver, gall, and spleen, helps the jaundice, the heat of the reins, and of urine. A decoction made of the wine, and drank, is effectual against lingering agues; and a dram of the seed in powder, drank in wine, before the fit of ague, helps to drive it away. The distilled water of the herb and flowers has the like properties, and is good for hot stomachs, and in agues, either pestilential or of long continuance; for swooning and passions of the heart, for heat and head-ache in children, and for the blood and liver. The water, or the juice, or the bruised leaves applied outwardly, allays swellings, inflammations, St. Anthony's fire, pushes, wheals and pimples, especially used with a little vinegar; as also to wash pestiferous sores. The water is effectual also for sore eyes that are inflamed, for nurses' breasts that are pained by the abundance of milk.

SUCCORY (YELLOW.)—(*Cichorium Hieracioides.*)

Descrip.—This has a thick taper root, brown on the outside, and white within, full of bitter milk. It grows deep in the ground; the lower leaves resemble those of the dandelion in shape, and tooth-like sections; but they are larger and hairy; the stalk rises about a yard high, striated, hairy, and angular, with leaves set on without footstalks, almost encompassing the stalk, being sharp-pointed at the end. Among these grow the flowers, set on close to the stalk several together, of a fine gold yellow, composed of several rows of flat petala indented at the ends: the seed is brown and longish, and grows not in down like the seed of the Dandelion.

Place.—It is planted in gardens.

Time.—It flowers in June.

Government and Virtues.—It is under Jupiter, and is aperative and diuretic, opening obstructions of the liver, and is good for the jaundice: the seed partakes of the same virtues, in a lower degree; it is also good to destroy worms. The root, leaves, flowers, and seed, are used.

SUMACH.—(*Rhus Cotinus.*)

Descrip.—The root is large, long, divided, and woody. The stem is shrubby, thick, and covered with a brown rough bark; it is divided into several branches, the bark of which is of a lighter colour, set with thorns. The leaves are winged; they grow in pairs, are notched round the edges, attached to the middle rib, and terminated by an odd one; their colour is dark green. The flowers are produced in spikes at the extremities; these spikes are long, thick, and woolly, and the flowers are small and purple.

Place.—It is a native of the warmer climates, but we have it in our gardens.

Time.—It flowers in the summer months.

Government and Virtues.—It is under the dominion of Jupiter. The seeds dried, reduced to powder and taken in small doses, stop purgings and hemorrhages, the young shoots have great efficacy in strengthening the stomach and bowels, if taken in a strong infusion The bark of the roots has the same virtues, but in an inferior degree.

SUN DEW.—(*Drosera Anglica.*)

Descrip.—It has small, round, hollow leaves, somewhat greenish, but full of red hairs, which make them look very red, every one standing upon its own footstalk, reddish, and hairy likewise. The leaves are continually moist in the hottest day, yea, the hotter the sun shines, the moister they are, the small hairs always holding this moisture. Among these leaves rise up slender stalks, reddish also, three or four fingers high, bearing small whitish knobs one above another, these are flowers, which afterwards contain small seed. The root is a few small hairs.

Place.—It grows usually in bogs and wet places, and sometimes in moist woods.

Time.—It flowers in June, and then the leaves are fittest to be gathered.

Government and Virtues.—The Sun rules it, and it is under the sign Cancer. The leaves, bruised and applied to the skin, erode it, and bring out such inflammations as are not easily removed. The juice destroys warts and corns, if a little be frequently put upon them.

SWALLOW-WORT.—(*Asclepias Syriaca.*)

Descrip.—The roots are slender and stringy, spreading much in the ground, sending up many tough stalks, about two feet high, very slender, set opposite to one another, on very short footstalks, round at the base, an inch and a half broad at the widest part, and about three inches long, growing narrower, and sharp-pointed; on the tops of the stalks come forth small bunches of five-leaved star-fashion white flowers ; each of them in warm countries where it is natural, is succeeded by two long slender pods, which contain small flat seed, lying among a silky down.

Place.—It grows with us only in gardens.

Time.—It flowers in June.

Government and Virtues.—Jupiter owns this plant. The root, which is the only part used, is a counter-poison, both against the bad effects of poisonous herbs, and the bites and stings of venomous creatures ; it is helpful against malignant pestilential fevers, which it carries off by sweat; it is likewise good against the dropsy and jaundice.

SYCAMORE TREE.—(*Acer Pseudo-platanus.*)

Descrip.—There are two sorts of this tree, the one bearing fruit out of the body and greater arms of the tree only, the other upon stalks without leaves. The first grows larger than the mulberry-tree, with round long leaves, pointed at the ends, and dented about the edges; it bears fruit, but no flower, differing in that from all other trees. The whole tree abounds with milk. The root is solid and black, and abides fresh long after it is felled. The other, which is called the Sycamore of Cyprus, grows as tall as a plum tree, with broad and somewhat round leaves.

Place.—The first grows chiefly in Egypt, Syria, and Arabia, and the other in Cyprus, Caria, Rhodes, &c.

Government and Virtues.—They are under the particular influence of Venus. The fruit makes the belly soluble, but by its over-much moisture troubles the stomach and gives little nourishment. The milk taken from the tree, by gently piercing the bark, afterwards dried and made into troches, softens and dissolves tumours, and solders and closes together the lips of green wounds. The fruit, being applied as a plaster, has the same effect.

TAMARISK-TREE.—(*Tamarix Gallica.*)

Descrip.—This never grows to any great size in England, though in its native country it does, with a brown rough dark bark. The younger branches are a chestnut colour, clothed with fine tender green leaves, thinner and finer than those of cypress; the flowers grow in rough spikes at the ends of the younger shoots, about an inch long, several spikes growing together, each consisting of a great many small, five-leaved, pale red flowers, which are succeeded by very small seed, included in a downy substance.

Place.—It is planted only in gardens in England, its native place is Spain, and the southern parts of France The wood, bark, and leaves are used.

Time.—It flowers about the end of May, or in June; and the seed is ripe in the beginning of September.

Government and Virtues.—This a Saturnine herb. The root, leaves, young branches, or bark boiled in wine, and drank, stays the bleeding of the hemorrhoidal veins, the spitting of blood, the too abounding of womens' courses, the jaundice, the colic, and the bites of venomous serpents; outwardly applied, it is powerful against the hardness of the spleen, the tooth-ache, pains in the ears, red and watering eyes. The decoction, with some honey added, is good to stay gangrenes and fretting ulcers, and to wash those that are subject to nits and lice. Its ashes heal burns and scalds. It helps the dropsy, arising from the hardness of the spleen, and therefore to drink out of cups made of the wood is good for splenetic persons. It is helpful for melancholy, and the black jaundice that arises therefrom.

TANSY (COMMON.)—*(Tannacetum Vulgare.)*

Descrip.—The leaves are of a bright and pleasant green, and a very fragrant smell, not coarse as that of the garden Tansy, but a pleasant aromatic. The stalk grows upright, branchy, of a light green, and a yard high; the flowers are large, of a bright yellow. The leaves are winged, the small ones deeply cut in; and the root is of a dark brown colour.

Place.—This sort is most frequently found wild on high grounds, and dry pastures. It is a perennial.

Time.—It blooms in July and August.

Government and Virtues.—This is under Venus. It is an agreeable bitter, a carminative, and a destroyer of worms, for which a powder of the flowers should be taken from six to twelve grains at night and morning. Care is required in collecting them, to obtain their virtue. Clip off a quantity of Tansy-flowers, before they are over-blown, close to the stalk. This must be done in the middle of a dry day; spread them on the bottom of a hair-sieve turned upside down; shake them often about, and let the wind pass through them, but keep them from the sun, and thus you may have them always. The leaves only are used, and are astringent and vulnerary, good to stop all kinds of fluxes and preternatural evacuations, to dissolve congealed blood, to help those who are bruised by falls: outwardly it is used as a cosmetic, to take off freckles, sun-burn, and morphew; as also in restringent gargarisms. The powder of the herb taken in some of the distilled water, helps the whites in women, but more especially if a little coral and ivory in powder be put to it. It helps children that have a rupture, if boiled in water and salt. If boiled in water and drank, it eases the griping pains of the bowels, and is good for the sciatica and joint aches. The same boiled in vinegar, with honey and alum, and gargled in the mouth, eases the tooth-ache, fastens loose teeth, helps the gums that are sore, settles the palate of the mouth to its place, when it has fallen down. The distilled water cleanses the skin of all discolourings, as morphew, sun-burns, pimples, freckles, &c. ; dropped into the eyes, or cloths wet therein and applied, takes away their heat and inflammations.

TANSY (GARDEN.)—*(Tannacetum Hortis.)*

Descrip.—This is a low plant, which never rises up to stalk, but creeps upon the ground, emitting fibres from the joints, by which it roots in the earth, and spreads out much ; the leaves are made up of several pinnæ set opposite, each about an inch long, and not half so broad, serrated about the edges, covered with a shining silver-coloured down : the flowers grow at the joints, on long foot-stalks, of five leaves, like Cinquefoil. The root is slender, with many fibres of a dark brown colour.

Place.—It grows in gardens, and botanical plantations.

Government and Virtues.—Venus owns this herb, which when bruised and applied to the navel, stays miscarriages. It consumes phlegmatic humours which the cold and moist constitution of winter usually affects the body with, and that was the first reason for eating Tansies in the spring. The decoction, or the juice drank in wine, is a remedy for all disorders that come by the stopping of urine, helps the strangury, and weak reins and kidneys. It is profitable to to expel wind from the stomach, belly, and bowels, to procure womens' courses, and expel windiness in the matrix, if bruised and applied to the lower part of the belly. The herb fried with eggs, helps to digest and carry downwards those bad humours that trouble the stomach. The seed or juice given in drink to children is effectual to cure worms. If boiled in oil, it is good for shrunken sinews, or when pained with cold, if applied thereto.

TARE (VETCH COMMON BLACK.)—*(Ervum Hirsutum,) (Vicia Hirsuta.)*

Descrip.—The stalks are angular, weak, and leaning, beset alternately at the joints with long leaves, with a tendril at their end, made of ten or a dozen small roundish pinnæ, a little hollowed in, with a spinula at the end: they are sometimes a little hairy. The flowers usually grow two together, upright, of a purple colour, followed by small flattish pods, containing three or four small black seeds.

Place.—It is sown in the fields.

Time.—It flowers in May, the seed is ripe in August and September.

Government and Virtues.—It is under the Moon in an airy figure. It is rarely used in medicine, but it is given in a decoction made of milk, to drive out the small-pox and measles.

TARRAGON.—(*Artemisia Dracunculus.*)

Descrip.—This has many round stalks full of branches, clothed with long narrow leaves, sharp-pointed, smooth, and shining; on the top of the stalks grow the flowers small and greenish, few in number, and thin set, on long footstalks. The leaves have a strong smell and taste.

Place.—It is planted in gardens.

Time.—It flowers in July and August.

Government and Virtues.—The leaves, which are chiefly used, are heating and drying, and good for those that have the flux, or any preternatural discharge. It is a mild martial plant. An infusion of the young tops increases the urinary discharge, and gently promotes the menses.

TEA.—(*Thea Bohea,*) (*Camellia Bohea.*)

Descrip.—It has a woody spreading root, several slender branches, with numerous oblong leaves, flowers like those of the dog-rose, and a fruit composed of one, two, or three berries. Only one species is known, and the difference there is when it comes to us proceeds from the soil, age, climate, method of collection, and curing. The preparation of the leaves consists in drying and roasting them over the fire in an iron pan, and rolling them, while hot, with the hand on a mat, till they become curled, it is then sent to this country in air-tight chests of tin and lead.

Place.—It is a native of China and Japan, and is cultivated in all the Eastern parts.

Virtues.—Green Tea (*Thea Viridis,*) (*Camellia Viridis,*) is diuretic, and carries an agreeable roughness with it into the stomach, which gently astringes the fibres of that organ, and gives such a tone as is necessary for a good digestion: the Bohea is softening and nutritious, and proper in all inward decays. Strong tea is prejudicial to weak nerves, but is salutary for violent head-ache and sickness occasioned by inebriation.

TEASEL (MANURED.)—(*Dipsacus Fullonum.*)

Called also Fuller's Thistle.

Descrip.—This grows tall, with a stiff, hard-furrowed, very prickly stalk. The lower leaves are long, large, and sharp-pointed, indented about the edges, smooth above, but with the middle rib of the upper part full of prickles. The leaves, which grow on the stalks, like a trough, catch the dew or rain which falls, and are likewise prickly underneath. The stalks are divided into several branches, bearing on their tops large heads full of crooked prickly hooks, among which grow several purplish hollow flowers, each in a particular cell; and after them come longish, square, striated seed. The root is pretty large and whitish.

Place.—It is cultivated in the field.

Time.—It flowers in July.

TEASEL (WILD.)—(*Dipsacus Silvestris.*)

Descrip.—This grows larger and higher than the former with the like stiff-crested and prickly stalk, especially in the upper part; the stalk is single, divided into branches; the lower leaves are long, narrow, and prickly underneath. The leaves, which grow on the stalk, are joined together, encompassing the stalk, and catching the rain; but it more particularly differs in the heads, which have their prickles growing erect, not hooked like the former; and each head having at the bottom several stiff prickly radii growing in a circle; the flowers grow like the former, succeeded by the like seed. The root is thick, and full of fibres.

Place.—It grows upon banks in the borders of fields.

Time.—It flowers in June and July.

Government and Virtues.—The virtues of both Teasels are the same; the roots, which are the only parts used, are said to have a cleansing faculty. The water found in the hollow of the leaves is commended as a collyrium to cool inflammation of the eyes, and as a cosmetic to render the face fair. They are under the dominion of Venus.

THISTLE (BLESSED.)—(*Carduus Benedictus.*)

Descrip.—From a small woody root, which perishes, after the seed is ripe, there rises several reddish hairy stalks, about two feet high, on which rise long hairy green leaves, cut in on both sides into several laciniæ or jags, each terminating in a small harmless spinula. On the top of the stalks grow the flowers in round heads, encompassed with leaves smaller and shorter than those below, less jagged, somewhat more prickly: they are yellow and fistular, standing in scaly calices, each scale of which ends in a slender long spine, denticulated on both sides. The seed is longish, round, and striated, of a brown colour, encompassed at the top with a crown of stiff bristles, standing out like the feathers of a shuttlecock. The whole plant is very bitter.

Place.—It is sown every year in gardens.

Time.—It flowers in June.

Government and Virtues.—Mars rules this Thistle. It is cordial and sudorific, good for all sorts of malignant and pestilential fevers, and for agues of all kinds. It destroys worms in the stomach, and is good against all sorts of poison.

THISTLE UPON THISTLE.—(*Polycantha Crispa.*)

Descrip.—This has long thick roots with many fibres; the leaves are long and narrow, of a deep green, divided at the edges, and very prickly; the stalks are numerous, tough, upright, branched, and edged with sharp prickles; the flowers stand on the tops of the branches in numerous heads, and they are of a pale red.

Place.—It is common under edges.

Time.—It flowers in July.

THISTLE (DWARF MAY.)—(*Polycantha Acaulos.*)

Descrip.—In some placed it is called the Dwarf Carline Thistle. It has a long and thick root, with many fibres; the leaves lie spread upon the ground, long and large, set with sharp prickles; the flowers grow low and large in the middle, scarcely rising from the ground, of a fine purple.

Place.—It is common in dry pastures in many of our southern counties, and likewise upon Blackheath.

Time.—It flowers in July.

THISTLE (LADY'S.)—(*Carduus Marianus,*) (*Silybum Marianum.*

Descrip.—This is a stately and beautiful plant. The root is long, and furnished with many fibres. The stalk is upright, firm, regularly branched, five feet high. The leaves very large, long, broad, irregularly notched at the edges, of a deep green, veined and variegated with blueish white. The flowers are large and purple, with prickly heads.

Place.—It is common in open pastures and waste places.

Time.—It flowers in July.

THISTLE (LANCED GENTLE.)—(*Cnicus Lanceolatus,*) (*Cirsium Lanceolatum.*)

Descrip.—It grows upright, from which it is denominated a lance. The root is long and slender, but the stalk, though soft, is tough, three feet high, not divided into branches. The leaves are greyish green, regularly notched and sinuated at the edges. The stalk as well as the leaves is beset with many sharp prickles. The flower grows in a stately manner single upon the top of the branches, and is of a beautiful blueish purple.

Place.—It grows in damp ground.

Time.—It flowers in July.

THISTLE (MARSH.)—(*Cnicus Palustris,*) (*Cirsium Palustre.*)

Descrip.—The root has tough brown fibres, with an upright root, not much branched, seven feet high, usually of a brownish colour, tinged with purple, and very prickly. The leaves are broadish and long, of a deep green, set with thorns. The flowers stand at the tops of the stalks, six or eight together ; and they are of a deep purple.

Place.—It is frequent in meadows in the Isle of Ely.

Time.—It flowers in June.

THISTLE (MUSK.)—(*Carduus Nutans.*)

Descrip.—The root is thick, long, and furnished with fibres. The stalk is five feet high, upright, of a brownish colour. The leaves are many, large, and divided at the edges, of a dusky colour, and beset with prickles. The flowers are large and purple, and frequently there is one at the extremity of the stalk, which hangs drooping.

Place.—It is frequent in damp pastures.

Time.—It flowers in June.

THISTLE (SAINT BARNABY'S.)—(*Carduus Solstitiaria Flava.*)

Descrip.—The root is long, slender, black, and has few fibres. The first leaves spread circularly on the ground ; they are long, deeply divided, of a faint green. The stalk is tough, firm, upright, and two feet high : the leaves on it resemble those from the root ; and they are of a faint green also. The flowers stand in small prickly heads at the tops of the branches ; and they are of a beautiful yellow.

Place.—We have it in dry pastures in some parts of England ; but it is not common.

Time.—It flowers in June.

THISTLE (SPEAR.)—(*Ascalea, Carduus Lanceolata.*)

Descrip.—The root is long and has many fibres. The stalk is upright, six feet high, very prickly, and divided into many branches. The leaves are long and large : their colour is a pale green, and they are deeply divided at the edges into pointed segments; and at the end are formed in the same manner, like the point of a spear. The flowers grow at the tops of the branches, and are large and purple.

Place.—It is common in waste grounds.

Time.—It flowers in July.

THISTLE (STAR.)—(*Centaurea Calcitrapa.*)

Descrip.—This has narrow leaves lying next the ground, cut deeply on the edges, soft, a little woolly, green all over, among which rise up weak stalks parted into branches, all lying to the ground, so it seems a pretty bush, set with the same kind of leaves up to the tops, where severally stand small whitish green heads, set with sharp white pricks, which are somewhat yellowish; out of the middle whereof rises the flowers, composed of many small reddish purple threads; and in the heads, after the flowers are past, come small whitish round seed lying down as the others do. The root is small, long, and woody, perishing every year, and rising again of its own sowing.

Place.—It grows wild in the fields about London.

Time.—It flowers early, and seeds in July, and sometimes in August.

Virtues.—The seed made into powder, and drank in wine, provokes urine, and helps to break the stone, and expel it. The root powdered, and taken in wine, is good against the plague and pestilence; drank in the morning fasting, it is very profitable for a fistula in any part of the body.

THISTLE (WAY.)—(*Cnicus Arvensis,*) (*Cirsium Arvense,*) (*Serratula Arvensis.*)

Descrip.—The root is white and creeping; the stalks are numerous, tough, of a pale green, smooth, not much branched, and a yard high. The leaves are numerous, long, moderately broad, and of a strong green; they are deeply and irregularly notched and sinuated on the edges, beset by long prickles. The flowers terminate the branches in numerous small heads, and are of a pale purple.

Place.—It is common in fields and under hedges.

Time.—It flowers in July.

THISTLE (WELTED MAY.)—(*Carduus Acanthoides.*)

Descrip.—The root is long, thick, and furnished with many fibres. The stalk is three feet high, with prickly membranes from the base of the leaves, of a dusky green.

The leaves are oblong, very broad, dented and sinuated at the edges, and very prickly. The flowers grow in small heads at the tops of the stalks, and among the upper leaves, and they are of a pale red.

Place.—It is usually found on ditch-banks in loamy soils.

Time.—It flowers in August.

Government and Virtues.—The Thistles in general are under Jupiter. Their medicinal properties are very few. They are celebrated by German physicians as stomachic and sudorific, but are not esteemed by our physicians.

THISTLE (WILD CARLINE.)—(*Carlina Vulgaris.*)

Descrip.—The root has numerous fibres connected to a large head. The stalk is upright, firm, branched towards the top, seven or eight feet high. The leaves are large, long, and very broad, of a fine deep green, and divided in the spear-pointed manner at the sides and ends. The flowers terminate the branches: they are very large, of a fine purple, and when quite open, have a grand appearance.

Place.—It is common in our northern counties, and is also found in the neighbourhood of Bristol.

Time.—It flowers in July and August.

THISTLE (WOOLLY-HEADED.)—(*Cnicus Eriophorus.*)

Descrip.—The root is fibrous. The stalk upright, thick, branched, and five feet high. The leaves are long, and rather broad, beautifully divided, like Spear Thistles, but with more numerous and more regular segments. Their colour is deep green. The flowers grow at the tops of the branches in large woolly heads; of a fine deep purple.

Place.—It is found in our western counties, but is scarce.

Time.—It flowers in August.

THORN-APPLE.—(*Datura Stramonium.*)

Descrip.—It has a large divided and fibrcus root; the stem is thick, firm, upright, branched, and two or three feet high: the leaves are large, broad, sharp-pointed, supported on short, firm leaf-stalks, a little indented at the edges, of a firmish texture, and a dark green colour. The flowers come out at the divisions of the stem and branches; large and white; the seeds are many and kidney-shaped.

Place.—It is a native of the southern parts of America, but flourishes very well in our gardens.

Time.—It flowers in April.

Government and Virtues.—Jupiter governs this plant. The juice pressed out of the fresh plant, and inspissated to an extract, has been taken in doses from half a grain to a dram, in twenty-four hours, in epileptic disorders, convulsions, and madness. An ointment made of the leaves is cooling and repelling.

THORNBERRY (BLACK.)—(*Acacia Germanica.*)

Descrip.—This shrub rises about four feet high. The branches are thorny, and have a deep brown bark; the leaves are oblong, broad, and of a fine green; the flowers are white; and the berries when ripe of a dark purple, and covered with a greyish dust.

Place.—It grows in the hedges and borders of fields.

Time.—It flowers in March and April, but the fruit ripens after all other plums whatsoever, and it is unfit to eat until the autumn frost mellows it.

Government and Virtues.—All the parts of this bush are binding, cooling, and dry, and all effectual to stay bleeding at the nose and mouth, or any other place, the lax of the belly or stomach, or the bloody-flux, or the too much abounding of womens' courses, and helps to ease the pains of the sides, and bowels, that come by over-much scouring, to drink the decoction of the bark of the roots, or the decoction of the berries, either fresh or dried. The leaves are good to make lotions to gargle and wash the mouth and throat wherein are swellings, sores, or kernels, and to stay the defluxions of rheum to the eyes, or other parts; to cool the heat and inflammations of them, and to ease hot pains of the head, by bathing the temples and forehead therewith.

THOROUGH-LEAF.—(*Beupleurum Campestris.*)

Descrip.—This sends forth a straight round stalk, two feet high, whose lower leaves are of a blueish colour, and smaller and narrower than those higher up, and stand close thereto. The flowers are small and yellow, standing in tufts at the heads of the branches, where afterwards grow the seed, which is blackish. The root is small, long, and woody, perishes annually, after seed-time, and rises again plentifully of its own sowing.

Place.—It is found in corn-fields.

Time.—It blooms in July.

Government and Virtues.—Saturn has the dominion of

this plant. It is useful for all sorts of bruises and wounds either inward or outward; and old ulcers and sores likewise, if the decoction of the herb with water and wine be drunk, and the place washed therewith, or the juice of the green herb bruised, or boiled, either by itself, or with other herbs, in oil or hog's-grease, to be made into an ointment to serve all the year.

THOROUGH-WAX (COMMON.)—(*Bupleurum Rotundifolium.*)

Descrip.—The root is long, slender, white, and furnished with a few fibres. The leaves are large, broad, oblong, undivided, of a blueish green. The flowers stand at the tops of the branches, and are moderately large and yellow. The seeds are large and round.

Place.—It is sometimes found in corn-fields.

Time.—It flowers in August.

Government and Virtues.—This is under Jupiter, and is excellent to stay all kinds of fluxes of blood, or humours in man or woman, whether at nose, mouth, or belly. The juice of the herb or root, or the decoction, taken with some Venice treacle, and the person laid to sweat, expels any venom or poison, or the plague, fever, or other contagious diseases.

THOROUGH WAX (WHITE.)—(*Bupleurum Rotundifolium Album.*)

Descrip.—This has a small fibrous, sticky root, from which rise smooth, and frequently reddish stalks. The leaves are of a blueish green colour, of an oval shape, smooth, not indented on the edges, full of nerves, which run obliquely from the centre to the circumference of the leaf; they are perforated by the stalk, which runs through them, and is divided towards the top into several branches, at the ends of which grow small umbels of yellow flowers, usually five together, upon one stalk, with as many small leaves under each umbel, the three outermost being largest; each flower is succeeded by two oblong seeds.

Place.—It grows only among the corn.

Time.—It flowers in June and July. The whole plant is used.

Government and Virtues.—This is a plant of Jupiter in Virgo. It is among the vulnerary plants, serviceable in green wounds, bruises, ruptures, contusions, old ulcers and sores, either given in powder or the decoction.

THRIFT (COMMON.)—(*Armeria Maritima,*) (*Armeria Vulgaris,*) (*Statice Armeria.*)

Descrip.—This has long, narrow, grassy green leaves; they are smooth, undivided at the edges, and sharp-pointed. The stalk rises in the centre of a tuft of these leaves, and is round, upright, simple, naked, and of a pale, greyish green colour. The flowers stand at the top, a number together, in a round cluster, pretty large, of a pale fleshy purple. The seed is small, round, and of a pale brown.

Place.—It is most common about the sea coast.

Government and Virtues.—It is a plant of Saturn; very astringent, but not often used.

THYME (COMMON GARDEN.)—(*Thymus Vulgaris.*)

Descrip.—The root is fibrous, the stalks numerous, hard, woody, brown, much branched, and ten inches high. The leaves are short, broad, pointed, and of a dusky green. The flowers are small, very numerous, and of a pale red; the seeds are roundish, small, brown, and glossy.

Place.—A native of India, but is found in every garden.

Time.—It flowers in June.

Government and Virtues.—It is a strengthener of the lungs; a good remedy for the chin-cough in children. It purges the body of phlegm, and is an excellent remedy for the shortness of breath. It kills worms in the belly, and being a notable herb of Venus, provokes the terms, gives safe and speedy delivery to women in travail, and brings away the after-birth. An ointment made of it takes away hot swellings and warts, helps the sciatica and dullness of sight, and takes away pains and hardness of the spleen: it is excellent for those that are troubled with the gout; as also, to anoint the testicles that are swelled. It eases pains in the loins and hips. The herb taken inwardly, comforts the stomach much, and expels wind.

THYME, (WILD, OR MOTHER OF.)—(*Thymus Serpyllum.*)

Descrip.—This plant has a small, stringy, creeping root, from which rise a great number of very slender, leaning, woody stalks, having two small, roundish, green leaves, set at a joint, on short footstalks. The flowers grow on the tops of the stalks among the leaves, in small loose spikes of a reddish purple colour. The leaves and flowers have a strong pleasant smell

Place.—It is frequent on hilly heaths, in dry pastures, and by road sides.

Time.—The flowers appear in July.

Government and Virtues.—The whole plant is fragrant, and yields an essential oil that is very heating. An infusion of the leaves removes head-ache, occasioned by inebriation. It is under Venus, and is excellent for nervous disorders. A strong infusion, drank as tea, is pleasant, and a very effectual remedy for head-ache, giddiness, and other disorders of that kind; and a certain remedy for that troublesome complaint, the night-mare.

TOBACCO.—(*Nicotiana Tabacam.*)

Descrip.—It rises from a long fibrous root; the stem is robust, round and hairy, branched, and two or three feet high; the leaves are large, numerous, of an oblong form, pointed at the end, entire in the sides, of a dusky green colour, and clammy to the touch. The flowers are numerous, large, of a reddish colour; they terminate the stem and branches, and make a pretty appearance at a distance. The seeds are numerous, round, and small.

Place.—A native of the West Indies, but grows in gardens.

Time.—When sown in a hot-bed in spring, it arrives at a tolerable degree of perfection in summer.

Government and Virtues.—It is a hot martial plant. A slight infusion of the fresh gathered leaves vomits roughly; is a good medicine for rheumatic pains; an ointment made of them, with hog's-lard, is good for painful and inflamed piles. The distilled oil dropped on cotton cures the tooth-ache, if applied. The powdered leaves, or a decoction of them, kill lice, and other vermin. The smoke of Tobacco injected in the manner of a clyster, is of efficacy in stoppages of the bowels, for destroying small worms, and for the recovery of persons apparently drowned.

TOOTHCRESS (BULBIFEROUS.)—(*Dentaria Bulbifera.*)

Descrip.—The root is thick, and of an irregular figure, and runs obliquely under the surface. The first leaves are oblong, narrow, undivided, and of a pale green; they have short footstalks, and rise in little tufts. The stalk is round, slender, a pale green, and is a foot and a half high. The leaves are placed alternately on it from the bottom to the top, and they resemble those from the root: they have short footstalks, long, narrow, sharp-pointed, a little undulated at the edges, and of a pale green. The flowers stand in a short spike at the top of the stalk, which droops; they hang all on one side, large, white, with a blush of purple.

Place.—It is scarce, sometimes found among bushes in open situations, in some parts of England.

Time.—It flowers in July and August.

Government and Virtues.—It is under Mars, and is a good vulnerary. It is recommended to stop all kinds of fluxes and hemorrhages; helps to consolidate wounds, fractures and ruptures, especially the root. A cataplasm of the root takes away black marks occasioned by contusions.

TORMENTIL.—(*Tormentilla Officinalis.*)

Descrip.—The root is thick and large, reddish in the inside, with small fibres; the stalks are long and slender, and unable to support themselves. It has seven long narrow leaves rising at a joint, serrated only at the ends. The flowers are small and yellow, of four leaves with a few stamina in the middle; the seed is small, growing naked on the calyx.

Place.—It grows in woods, and on commons.

Time.—It flowers in June and July. The roots are used.

Government and Virtues.—This is a herb of the Sun. It is excellent to stay all kinds of fluxes of blood or humours in man or woman, whether at nose, mouth, or belly. The juice of the herb or root, or the decoction thereof, taken with some Venice treacle, and the person laid to sweat, expels any venom or poison, or the plague, fever, or other contagious diseases; it is an ingredient in all antidotes or counter-poisons. The root taken inwardly is most efficacious to help any flux in the belly, stomach, spleen, or blood; and the juice opens obstructions of the liver and lungs, and thereby helps the jaundice. It is very powerful in ruptures, and bruises or falls, used outwardly or inwardly. The root made up with Pellitory of Spain and alum, and put into a hollow tooth, not only assuages the pain, but stays the flux of humours which causes it. It is a no less effectual remedy against outward wounds, sores and hurts, than for inward, and is therefore a special ingredient in wound drinks, lotions, and injections, for foul corrupt rotten sores and ulcers of the mouth, secrets, or other parts of the body

TORMENTIL (CREEPING.)—*(Tormentilla Reptans.)*

Descrip.—The root has a small head, with many fibres, which are brown, tough, and of an austere taste. The leaves are divided, and stand on short, reddish footstalks, a little hairy: they are of a fine green colour, and deeply serrated. The stalks rise in the centre of these, four or five feet from each head of the root; they are long, slender, reddish, and run upon the ground, sending roots downwards at every joint, and tufts of leaves, and often stalks upwards. The flowers are large, of a beautiful yellow, with a little tuft of paler threads in the centre, and when these fall, the seeds ripen, in a small oval cluster.

Place.—It is found on the edge of Charlton forest, Sussex.

Virtues.—Its virtues are same as former, but less in degree. The flowers are binding and drying, good for dysenteries and diarrhœas, especially attendant upon malignant fevers; they are also alexipharmic. They are serviceable in hemorrhages of the nose, mouth, or womb; they fasten loose teeth, and help the falling of the uvula.

TREFOIL.—*(Trifolium.)*

CALLED also Honey-Suckle.

Descrip.—The root grows long and slender, with many fibres. The first leaves are supported on long slender footstalks, of a pale green; three leaves grow on each footstalk; and they are of a deep green, broad, short, and marked with a crescent-like white spot, in the middle. The stalks are numerous, short, and procumbent: they are divided into branches as they run upon the ground, and send out a great many leaves of the same form and structure with the first, and the stalks of the flowers among them; these are slender, like those of the leaves, and of the same pale green. The flowers are small and white, numerous, in a round thick head, each cell containing four small seeds.

Place.—It grows in almost every place in this country.

Time.—It flowers in June.

Government and Virtues.—Mercury has dominion over the common sorts. The leaves and flowers are good to ease the pains of the gout, if the herb be boiled and used as a clyster. If the herb be made into a poultice, and applied to inflammations, it will ease them. The herb boiled in lard, and made into an ointment, is good to apply to the bites of venomous creatures. The decoction of the herb and flowers, with the seed and root, taken for some time, helps those troubled with the whites. The seed and flowers boiled in water, and made into a poultice with some oil, and applied, helps hard swellings and imposthumes.

TREFOIL (HEART.)—*(Trifolium Cordatis.)*

Descrip.—Besides the ordinary kind, here is one which may be called Heart Trefoil, not because it is triangular, like a heart, but because each leaf contains the perfect icon of a heart, and that in its proper colour, viz., a flesh colour.

Place.—It grows by the way-side in various parts.

Government and Virtues.—It is under the dominion of the Sun, and is a great strengthener of the heart, and cherisher of the spirits, relieving those who faint and swoon; it is a remedy against poison and pestilence, and defends the heart against the noisome vapours of the spleen.

TREFOIL (PEARL.)—*(Trifolium Lotus.)*

Descrip.—It differs from the common sort, only in one particular, it has a white spot like a pearl, on the leaf. It is under the Moon, and its icon shows its virtues to be against the pin and web in the eyes.

TURNIP.—*(Brassica Rapa.)*

This root is so well known that it needs no description.

Place.—It is sown in fields and gardens.

Time.—It flowers in April.

Government and Virtues.—It is under the Moon in Pisces. It is a nourishing food, more useful in the kitchen, than as a medicine. The juice of the sliced root extracted with brown sugar-candy, *strata super stratum*, baked in an oven, is a good pectoral, and helps coughs and consumptions.

TURNSOLE.—*(Heliotropium Europæum.)*

Called also Heliotrope.

Descrip.—This rises with one upright stalk, about a foot high, dividing itself into small branches, of a hoary colour; at each joint of the stalk and branches grow small broad leaves, rather white and hoary. At the tops of the stalks and branches stand small white flowers, consisting of four small leaves, set in order one above another, upon a small crooked spike, which turns inwards with a bowed finger, opening by degrees as the flowers blow open; after which, in their place, come forth cornered seed, four for the most part standing together; the root is small and thready, perishing every year, and the seed shedding every year, raises it again the next spring.

Place.—It grows in gardens.

Government and Virtues.—It is an herb of the Sun. If boiled in water and drank, it purges both choler and phlegm, and boiled with cummin, helps the stone in the reins, kidneys, or bladder, provokes urine and womens' courses, and causes an easy and speedy delivery in child-birth. The leaves bruised and applied to places pained with the gout, or that have been out of joint, and newly set, and full of pain, give much ease; if the juice of the leaves, with a little salt be rubbed upon warts or wens, and other kernels in the face, eye-lids, or any other part, it will take them away.

TUTSAN.—(*Hypericum Androsæmum.*)

CALLED also Park Leaves.

Descrip.—The stalks grow three feet high, smooth, reddish, not much branched, with two large oval brown green leaves set opposite at every joint, on short footstalks, those next the ground being smallest. The flowers grow several together, on long footstalks, of five small yellow roundish leaves each, with stamina in the middle of the same colour, yielding a reddish juice, and are succeeded by berry-like seed-vessels, green at first, and afterwards of a deep purple, almost black, containing small seed in purplish juice; the root is thick, of a reddish colour, with many fibres.

Place.—It grows in woods, groves, parks, forests, and by hedge-sides, in many parts of this country.

Time.—It flowers later than St. Peter's wort.

Government and Virtues.—It is an herb of Saturn, and an anti-venerean. It purges choleric humours, helps the sciatica and gout, and heals burns; it stays the bleeding of wounds, if the green herb bruised, or the powdered herb be dried and applied. It is a sovereign remedy for either wound or sore, either outwardly or inwardly, if used in drinks, lotions, balms, or ointments; and also in any other sort of green wounds, old ulcers, &c.

VALERIAN (GARDEN.)—(*Valeriana Hortense.*)

Descrip.—This has a thick, short, greyish root, lying above ground, shooting forth small pieces of roots, which have all of them many long green strings and fibres under them in the ground, whereby it draws nourishment. From the head of these leaves spring up many green leaves, rather broad and long, without any divisions on the edges; but those that rise up after them are dented on the edges, some being winged to the middle rib; the stalk rises a yard or more, sometimes branched at the top, with many small white flowers, of a purplish colour, there follows small brownish white seed, that is easily carried away with the wind; the root smells more strong than either leaf or flower, and is of more use in medicines.

Place.—It is generally kept with us in gardens.

Time.—It flowers in June and July, and continues until the frost pulls it down.

Government and Virtues.—This is under Mercury. The decoction of this herb takes away pains of the sides, provokes womens' courses, and is used in antidotes; the root boiled with liquorice, raisins, and aniseed, is good for difficulty of breathing, coughs, and to expectorate phlegm, and clear the passages. If boiled in wine and drank, it is good for venomous bites and stings: it helps to drive wind from the belly, and is of excellent property to heal inward sores or wounds, and for outward cuts or wounds, and drawing away splinters or thorns from the flesh.

VALERIAN (GREEK.)—*(Polemonium Ceruleum.)*

Descrip.—The root is about a finger thick, of a brown colour, growing not in the earth, but spreading itself across with many white strings on each side; it shoots out several hollow channelled stalks two or three feet high, having the hollow leaves long and round-pointed, some whole, and others cut in, resembling those of scabious, but that they are smooth; the leaves which grow on the stalks are also much more cut in; the stalks are divided towards the top into several branches, having at each divarication a long narrow leaf, and at the ends grow the flowers in a kind of umbels, each flower being a small, long, narrow tube, divided at the top into five segments, with as many apices, of a white colour.

Place.—It is planted in gardens, and is found wild in some parts of Yorkshire.

Government and Virtues.—It is under Mercury, and is alexipharmic, sudorific, and cephalic, and useful in malignant fevers, and pestilential distempers; it helps in nervous complaints, head-aches, trembling, palpitations of the heart, vapours, &c. It is good in hysteric cases, and epilepsies have been cured by the use of this herb.

VALERIAN (WATER.)—(*Valeriana Aquatica.*)

Descrip.—The roots are long, slender, and creeping, sending out a few small white fibres. The leaves which spring from them are almost round, but somewhat pointed. The leaves which grow on the stalks, are like those of the garden kind, but less. We have two species of this Valerian, one rises higher than the other, having three pairs of leaves set opposite; the umbels grow closer, and the flowers are a great deal smaller than the other, which rise not so high, and has but two pairs of leaves on the stalks. The flowers are much larger, and like the garden Valerian, but of a pale purple colour, as are also the former.

Place.—They grow promiscuously in marshy grounds and moist meadows.

Time.—They flower in May.

VALERIAN (TRUE WILD.)—(*Valeriana Sylvestris.*)

Descrip.—This has a root divided into several white thick strings, of no scent when taken out of the ground, but smelling very strong when dry. The stalks rise about a yard high, hollow, and channelled, having several long winged leaves, whose pinnæ are long, sharp-pointed, and serrated about the edges, high-veined, and rather hairy; the leaves which grow on the stalks are narrow. The flowers are of a purple colour; both flowers and seeds are shaped like the garden Valerian. It grows in woods and dry places; and flowers in May.

Place.—It is found on dry heaths and in high pastures.

Virtues.—The root has a strong and disagreeable smell, warm to the taste, bitter, and a little acrid. In habitual costiveness, it is an excellent medicine, and will loosen the belly when other purgatives prove ineffectual. It is excellent against nervous affections, such as head-aches, trembling, palpitations, vapours, and hysteric complaints.

VERVAIN (COMMON.)—(*Verbena Officinalis.*)

Descrip.—This has broad leaves next the ground, deeply gashed about the edges, of a blackish green colour on the upper side, somewhat greyish underneath. The stalk is square, branched into several parts, rising about two feet high, with a long spike of flowers of a blue colour and white intermixed, after which come small round seeds in small rather long heads; the root is small, but of no use.

Place.—It grows in waste grounds almost every where.

Time.—It flowers in July, and the seed ripens soon after.

Government and Virtues.—This is an herb of Venus, and excellent for the womb to strengthen and remedy all the cold distempers of it, as plantain does the hot. It is hot and dry, opening obstructions, cleansing and healing: it helps the yellow jaundice, the dropsy and the gout, kills and expels worms in the belly, and causes a good colour in the face and body, strengthens as well as corrects the diseases of the stomach, liver and spleen; helps the cough, wheezings, shortness of breath. and the defects of the reins and bladder, expelling the gravel and stone. It is excellent against venomous bites, and tertian and quartan agues. It consolidates and heals all wounds, both inward and outward, stays bleeding, and used with honey, heals old ulcers and fistulas in the legs and other parts of the body, and ulcers that come in the mouth; or used with lard, it helps the swellings and pains in the secret parts.

VINE TREE.—(*Vitis Vinifera.*)

Descrip.—The root is woody, divided, and spreading. The stem is covered with a rough brown bark, divided into many long straggling branches, which are too weak to support themselves. The leaves are large, numerous, and very beautiful, of a roundish figure, but deeply divided into five or more lobes, sharp-pointed, notched at the edges; they are supported on longish leaf-stalks, and from the base of these there frequently rises long, and very robust tendrils. The flowers are produced in clusters on long leaf-stalks, which rise together with the leaf-stalks and tendrils; they are small, and of a green or whitish colour.

Government and Virtues.—This is a fine plant of the Sun. The dried fruit, as it comes from abroad under the names of raisins, and currants, is good in coughs, consumptions, and other disorders of the breast. The leaves of the English Vine boiled, make a good lotion for sore mouths; if boiled with barley-meal into a poultice, it cools inflammations of wounds; the droppings of the Vine, when it is cut in the spring, boiled with sugar into a syrup, and taken inwardly, is excellent to stay womens' longings when pregnant. The decoction of the leaves in white wine, does the same; or the tears of the Vine, drank two or three spoonfuls at a time, breaks the stone in the bladder. The ashes of the burnt branches make discoloured teeth white by rubbing in the morning. It is a most gallant tree of the Sun, very sympathetical with the body; that is the reason why spirit of wine is the greatest cordial among vegetables.

VIOLET.—(*Viola Odorata.*)

Descrip.—The root is perennial ; it is long, slender, crooked, and fibrous ; they are supported on long slender leaf-stalks, of a roundish figure, heart-shaped at the base, slightly notched at the edges, and of a dark green colour, several slender creeping stems rise from among them, which take root at the joints, and so propagate the plant. The flowers are supported singly on long, slender, fruit-stalks, which rise direct from the root; they are large, of a beautiful deep blue or purple, and extremely fragrant. The seeds are egg-shaped, numerous, and furnished with appendages.

Place.—It is common on warm banks, and produces its blossoms in March and April.

Time.—It flowers until the end of July, but it is best in March, and the beginning of April.

Government and Virtues.—It is a fine, pleasing plant of Venus, of a mild nature, and no way hurtful. It is cold and moist while fresh and green, and is used to cool any heat or distemperature of the body, either inwardly or outwardly, as inflammations in the eyes, in the matrix or fundament, in imposthumes also, and hot swellings, to drink the decoction of the leaves and flowers made with water or wine, or to apply them as poultices to the affected parts ; it eases pains in the head, caused through want of sleep; or any pains arising from heat, if applied in the same manner, or with oil of roses. A dram weight of the dried leaves or flowers purges the body of choleric humours, if taken in a draught of wine or other drink ; the powder of the purple leaves of the flowers, only picked and dried, and drank in water, helps the quinsy, the falling-sickness in children, especially at the beginning of the disease. The flowers of the white Violets ripen and dissolve swellings. The herb or flowers, while they are fresh, or the flowers that are dry, are effectual in the pleurisy, and all diseases of the lungs, to lenify the sharpness of hot rheums, and hoarseness of the throat, heat and sharpness of urine, and all pains of the back, or reins, and bladder.

VIOLET (WATER.)—(*Hottonia Palustris.*)

Descrip.—The root is a tuft of long, black, and slender fibres, which penetrate deep into the mud. The leaves are long, large, and beautifully pinnated; they consist each of ten, twelve, or more pairs of long and narrow segments, regularly disposed, and an odd one at the end. From the base of this cluster of leaves, there are propagated some long, slender stalks, which take root again as they run on the surface of the mud, and in those places send up fresh clusters of leaves. In the centre of these leaves rises the stalk which is to support the flowers; this is tall, upright, round, slender, and naked. The flowers stand in little clusters at and near the top; they are moderately large, very pretty, and of a whitish colour tinged with red. The seed is single and small.

Place.—It is frequent on the muddy bottoms of waters.

Time.—It flowers in June.

Government and Virtues.—Saturn governs this plant. The leaves are cooling, externally applied; but they are more used by country-people than by physicians. The flowers are accounted a specific against the fluor albus, and are frequently made use of in a conserve or decoction for that purpose, which is to be continued for some time. Some commend the herb as of great use against the king's evil, and all scrofulous swellings.

VIPER'S BUGLOSS.—(*Echium Vulgare.*)

Descrip.—This has many long rough leaves lying on the ground, from which rise up hard round stalks, whereon are set rough, hairy, or prickly sad green leaves, rather narrow; the middle rib for the most part being white. The flowers stand at the top of the stalk, branched forth in many long spiked leaves of flowers, all opening for the most part on one side, which are long and hollow, turning up the brims a little, of a purplish violet colour in them that are fully blown, but more reddish while they are in the bud, but in some places of a paler purple colour, with a long pointel in the middle, feathered or parted at the top. After the flowers are fallen, the seeds become ripe, blackish, cornered, and pointed like the head of a viper. The root is somewhat great and blackish.

Place.—It grows wild almost every where.

Time.—It flowers in summer, the seed ripens soon after.

Government and Virtues.—It is an herb of the Sun. It is an especial remedy against both poisonous bites, and poisonous herbs. The seed drank in wine, produces abundance of milk in nurses' breasts. The same if taken, eases the pains in the back, loins, and kidneys. The distilled water when the herb is in flower, or its chief strength, applied inwardly or outwardly, is good for the same purposes.

WAKE ROBIN (GOLDEN.)—(*Arum Maculatum.*)

Descrip.—This neglected plant has a roundish tuberous root, brown on the outside, white within, placed at no considerable depth, and furnished with a few fibres. The leaves, which are marked with beautiful gold-coloured veins, rise alternately across the stock; they are oblong, smooth at the edges, pointed at the ends, and of a fine fresh green, and often some spots of white are visible on them. The stem is round, thick, and ten inches or a foot high. On its top stands a single flower, of a fine yellow, which is afterwards succeeded by fine bright red berries.

Place.—It is found under hedges, and in moist meadows.

Time.—It flowers in May.

Government and Virtues.—It is under the dominion of the Sun. The root is a powerful antiscorbutic, and by the activity of its subtle parts, it cuts all viscidities, and is of service in humourous asthmas, in which case it should be bruised and gently boiled in a closed vessel, in half white-wine, and half water, and sweetened with honey of roses. The root bruised and mixed with cows' dung, and applied warm in a fit of gout and rheumatic pains will ease them. The root beat up with vinegar and laid upon a bruised part will dissipate stagnant blood. and prevent blackness of the skin.

WALL-FLOWER (COMMON.)—(*Cheiranthus Cheiri.*)

Descrip.—The root is divided into a number of straggling parts, each furnished with numerous fibres. The stalk is round, firm, upright, hard, and very much branched. The leaves are long, narrow, and of a fresh green; They have no footstalk, they adhere by the base, and are undivided at the edges. The flowers grow in spikes at the top of the stalks and branches, and are large, yellow, and sweet scented. The pods are long, slender and whitish; the seeds are flatted and small.

Place.—It is common on old walls, and in some places on rocks; and has thence, for its beauty and fragrance, been introduced into gardens, where the flower, and indeed the whole plant, grow much larger than in the wild state.

Time.—It flowers in May and June.

WALL-FLOWER (SEA.)—(*Cheiranthus Tricuspidatus.*)

Descrip.—This is less than the foregoing, with a long, slender root, furnished with a few fibres. The stalks are numerous, weak, branched ; they stand irregularly, of a pale colour, and a little hairy. The leaves are long, narrow, and deeply indented at the edges ; they grow without footstalks, and are somewhat hairy, and their colour is a pale whitish green. The flowers stand at the tops of the stalks and branches ; and they are large and white.

WALL-FLOWERS (WILD.)—(*Leucoium Sylvestris.*)

Descrip.—The common single Wall-flowers, which grow wild abroad, have sundry small, long, narrow, dark green leaves, set without order upon small, round, whitish woody stalks, which bear at the tops single yellow flowers one above another, every one bearing three leaves each, and of a very sweet scent ; after which come long pods, containing a reddish seed. The roots are white, hard, and thready.

Place.—It grows upon old walls; the other sort in gardens only.

Time.—All the single kinds flower many times in the end of autumn ; but double kinds do not.

Government and Virtues.—The Moon rules them. It cleanses the blood, and frees the liver and reins from obstructions, provokes womens' courses, expels the secundine, and the dead child ; helps the hardness and pains of the mother, and of the spleen also ; stays inflammations and swellings, comforts and strengthens any weak part, or out of joint; helps to cleanse the eyes from films, and to cleanse filthy ulcers in the mouth, or any other part, and is a singular remedy for the gout, and all aches and pains in the joints and sinews. A conserve made of the flowers, is used as a remedy both for the apoplexy and palsy.

WALNUTS.—(*Juglans Regia.*)

Descrip.—This tree rises to a great height, and spreads irregularly into branches. The leaves are pinnated ; the pinnæ vast, oblong, and of a fine green. The catkins are brownish, with a tinge of green, and the fruit is covered with a green rind.

Place.—It grows wild in many places in Scotland ; and is planted every where for the fruit.

Time.—It blossoms early before the leaves come forth, and the fruit is ripe in September.

Government and Virtues.—This is a plant of the Sun. Let the fruit of it be gathered accordingly, which has the most virtue whilst green, before it shells. The bark binds and dries very much, and the leaves are much of the same temperature, but when they are older, are heating and drying in the second degree, and are harder of digestion than when fresh; if taken with sweet wine, they move the belly downwards, but if old they grieve the stomach; and in hot bodies, cause the choler to abound, producing headache, and are an enemy to those that have the cough; but are less hurtful to those that have a colder stomach, and kill the broad worms in the stomach or belly. If taken with onions, salt, and honey, they help the bites of mad dogs, or poisonous bites of any kind. The juice of the green husks boiled with honey, is an excellent gargle for sore mouths, or the heat and inflammations in the throat and stomach. The kernels, when they grow old, are more oily, and unfit to be eaten, but are then used to heal the wounds of the sinews, gangrenes, and carbuncles. If burned, these kernels are very astringent, and will stay laxes and womens' courses, when taken in red wine, and stays the falling of the hair, and makes it fair, being anointed with oil and wine. The green husks will act the same, if used in the same manner. The kernels beaten with rue and wine, and applied, helps the quinsy: bruised with honey, and applied to the ears, eases pains and inflammations therein. The distilled water of the green leaves in the end of May, cures foul running ulcers and sores, to be bathed with wet cloths or sponges applied to them every morning.

WATER-WORT (CHICKWEED.)—(*Elatine Alsinastrum.*)

Descrip.—This has often been mistaken for Fluellin. It has a small white fibrous root. The first leaves are small, narrow, and pointed; they increase in size as they rise to the middle, and then gradually diminish to the top; they have no footstalks, and are of a grassy green colour: the stem is so weak, it scarce holds itself upright, but trains some part of its length on the ground. The flowers grow in the bosom of the leaves; they are small, and supported on slender and short footstalks; they are of a yellowish and dark purple. The seed is very minute and brown.

Place.—It grows upon the borders of corn-fields, and by running shallow waters.

Time.—It is in flower in May.

Government and Virtues.—It is a moist, cooling plant, under the Moon. The juice cleanses and heals old ulcers; and it has at former times been in esteem as an inward medicine for internal bruises. The flowers and leaves beaten into a conserve, is the best way of taking it for any inward purpose.

WELD, OR WOLD.—(*Reseda Luteola.*)

CALLED also Dyers' Weed and Willow-leaved Yellow Herb.

Descrip.—It grows about a yard high, having hollow channelled stalks, covered with long narrow green leaves, set on without footstalks; of a dark blueish green colour, a little crumpled, as it were round-pointed, which so abides the first year; and the next spring, from among them, rise up divers round stalks, two or three feet high, beset with many such-like leaves thereon, but smaller, and shooting forth small branches, which, with the stalks, carry many small yellow flowers, in a long spiked head at the top of them, where afterwards come the seed, which is small and black, inclosed in heads that are divided at the tops into four parts. The root is long, white, and thick. The whole herb becomes yellow, after it has been in flower a while.

Place.—It grows every where by way-sides, in moist grounds.

Time.—It flowers about June.

Government and Virtues.—The root cures tough phlegm, digests raw phlegm, thins gross humours, dissolves hard tumours, and opens obstructions. It is commended against venomous bites, to be taken inwardly and applied outwardly to the hurt place, as also for the plague or pestilence.

WHEAT.—(*Triticum.*)

THIS useful plant is so well known that it needs no description.

Place.—It is sown in fields every where.

Time.—It is reaped in July and August.

Government and Virtues.—It is under Venus. The oil pressed from Wheat by means of plates of iron or copper, heals tetters and ringworms, if used warm. The green corns chewed, and applied to the bites of mad dogs, heals them; wheat-bread poultices made with red wine, and applied to hot, inflamed, or blood-shot eyes, helps them. Hot bread poultices applied three days together, heals kernels in the throat. Wheat-flour mixed with juice of henbane, stays the flux of humours to the joints, if laid thereto; or mixed with the yolk of an egg, honey, or turpentine, draws, cleanses, and heals boils, plague sores, or foul ulcers. It is more useful for food than medicine; though a poultice made of it with milk, eases pains, ripens tumours and imposthumations; and a piece of toasted bread dipped in wine, and applied to the stomach, is good to stay vomiting.

WHITLOW-GRASS.—(*Draba Verna.*)

Descrip.—It has an annual fibrous root; the stem is round, branchy, hairy, of a red colour, and four or five inches high; the leaves are pretty numerous, small, broadest at the extremity, and divided into three segments; their colour is reddish. The flowers terminate the stem and branches in considerable numbers; white, small, but conspicuous. The seeds are numerous and very minute.

Place.—It grows on the roofs of houses, old walls, and among rubbish.

Time.—It flowers in April.

Government and Virtues.—It is under Jupiter. A strong infusion of the whole plant, fresh gathered, is an excellent sweetener of the blood and juices, and good against scorbutic complaints in general. Those who wish to use it all the year, should make a syrup of its juice in the spring, or beat the leaves into a conserve with sugar, for the dried plant loses all its virtues, and is only to be had fresh for a short time in the spring.

WHORTLE.—(*Vaccinium Myrtillus.*

Descrip.—It is a small shrub, with slender purplish branches. The leaves are round, obtuse at the ends, and not serrated on the edges. The flowers are greenish, with a tinge of red; the berries are round, red, and well tasted.

Place.—This species of the Bilberry-bush is common in our northern counties on boggy ground.

Time.—It flowers in May.

Virtues.—The bark of the root is warm and dry, it opens obstructions of the liver and spleen. The unripe fruit is drying and binding, good for fluxes of all kinds, and inflammations in the mouth and throat. The ripe fruit is cooling, good to allay the heat of burning fevers; it is grateful to the stomach, and creates an appetite.

WILLOW-HERB.—(*Lysimachia Nemorum.*)

Descrip.—This is a shrubby plant. It has large, hollow channelled stalks, divided into many branches full of leaves, three growing together on long footstalks, indented a little about the edges. The flowers grow in short round spikes, set on long stalks, of a pale blue, small and papilionaceous, set each in a particular calyx, succeeded by short pods, containing small yellow seeds. The root is woody and fibrous.

Place.—It grows in damp woods and marshy places, and has been observed near the banks of the Severn.

Time.—It flowers in July.

WILLOW-HERB(CREEPING.)—(*Epilobium Alpinum.*)

Descrip.—The root is small and fibrous ; the stalks are round, weak, and slender : they trail on the ground and take root as they lie, only part approaching to an erect posture. The leaves stand in pairs : they are short, broad, and of an oval figure, pointed at the ends, smooth, round, of a deep green ; and those towards the tops of the stalks are smaller and narrower. The flowers are small, pale red.

Place.—It grows in our woods and meadows.

Time.—It flowers early in summer.

WILLOW-HERB (GREAT FLOWERED.)—(*Epilobium Ramosum.*)

Descrip.—This is a fine tall plant. The stem is thick, firm, upright, and five feet high. The leaves are broad, regularly notched, terminating in a point, of a beautiful green, and lightly hairy ; they have no footstalks, and the flowers are large, of a pale red, and grow in a deep cup. The tops of this plant have a light fragrance.

Place.—It is found by waters, and in shady copses.

Time.—It flowers in June.

Government and Virtues.—All the species of Willow-Herbs have the same virtues : they are under Saturn, and are cooling and astringent. The root dried and powdered, is good against hemorrhages: the fresh juice acts the same.

WILLOW-HERB (HAIRY.)—(*Epilobium Hirsutum.*)

Descrip.—This is smaller, but is like the preceding. The leaves are notched at the edges, of a deep green. The stalks are round, firm, upright, two and a half feet high. They are large, of a bright red, at the tops of the branches.

Place.—It is an inhabitant of our damp meadows.

Time.—It flowers in July.

WILLOW-HERB (MARSH.)—(*Epilobium Palustre.*)

Descrip.—The root has a small head, with many large fibres. The first leaves are oblong, of a dead green, and pointed at the ends. The stalk is round, erect, robust, much branched, about two feet high. The leaves on this are large and moderately broad, of a dead green, hairy, not indented, fixed to the base of the stalk. The flowers are numerous at the tops of the stalks, small, of a lively pale red.

Place.—It is very common in many parts of England.

Time.—It flowers in June.

Virtues.—The flowers, stalks, roots and all, may be used. They are cooling and drying, good to stay fluxes and loosenesses, gonorrhœa and nocturnal pollutions. The leaves are good to be applied to hot tumours and inflammations.

WILLOW-HERB (MONEY.)—(*Lysimachia Nummularia.*)

Descrip.—The root is knotty at the head, sending forth long strings and fibres ; the stalks are tough and limber, growing low, with leaves set alternately upon them, that are hard, firm, full of nerves, of an oval shape, but sharp-pointed at the end, about two inches long ; on the middle of the back of each grows a small mossy green flower, that is succeeded by the seed, which is small and brown.

Place.—It is found in damp woods.

Time.—It flowers in July

WILLOW-HERB (PURPLE MONEY.)—(*Lysimachia Tenella Purpurea.*)

Descrip.—This is a tender succulent plant, very slender, with many oval divided leaves, of a whitish green colour. The stalks are hollow and cornered, much branched, not rising very high, having on their tops long spikes of flowers, purple above and whitish underneath, having a spur in the hinder part, the footstalk being inserted in the middle of the flower; they are succeeded by single round seed.

WILLOW-HERB (ROSE-BAY.)—(*Epilobium Angustifolium.*)

Descrip.—This is the most beautiful of all the Willow-Herbs. The root is large and spreading. The first leaves rise in a thick tuft, and are long, narrow, deep green on the upper side, and silvery grey underneath; they have no footstalks, are even at the edges, and terminate in a point. The stalk rises in the centre of the leaves : it is thick, firm, upright, and five feet high. The leaves stand irregularly upon it; they are long, narrow, even at the edges, of a deep green on the upper side, and a silvery white below. The flowers are large and beautiful, in a long spike, deep red. The seed-vessels are long, and the seeds winged with down.

Place.—It is found in damp meadows in Yorkshire.

Time.—It flowers in June and July.

WILLOW-HERB (MOUNTAIN.)—(*Epilobium Montanum.*)

Descrip.—This is thicker set with leaves, and more robust than the former. It grows upright; the stalk is round, reddish, and four feet high. It is thick set with leaves, of a pale greyish green, soft to the touch, oblong, broad, indented, they stand irregularly on the base of the stalk. The flowers are large, of a pale red, on the tops of the stalks. The seed grows in a pod with a silvery down amongst it.

Place.—It is common in pasture grounds, and shady hedges, in our northern and western counties.

Time.—It flowers in June.

WILLOW-HERB (SPURGE.)—(*Epilobium Tetra gonum.*)

Descrip.—This has a singular appearance. The stem is slender, and upright : the leaves narrow, smooth at the edges, long, and pointed; they are numerous, soft, and of a deep green. The flowers are moderately large, and grow at the tops of the branches ; of a beautiful bright red.

Place.—It is frequent in damp meadows under hedges, and by the sides of brooks.

Time.—It flowers in July.

WILLOW-HERB (TUFTY.)—(*Lysimachia Thrysiflora.*)

Descrip.—This rises from a long, thick, and fibrous root. The stalk is round, firm, upright, and two feet high. The leaves are narrow, oblong, and pointed. They grow at the joints without footstalks below, but alternately above, and yet sometimes three are found at a joint; their colour is a grassy green. The flowers are small, of a pale red; they grow on long footstalks, which rise with the leaves. The seed-vessels are round, and the seeds small and brown.

Place.—It is found in damp places in the west of England.

Time.—It flowers in July.

WILLOW-HERB (YELLOW.)—(*Epilobium Lysimachia.*)

Descrip.—This grows very large, and resembles in its form common yellow Loosestrife, for which it is often mistaken. The stem is thick, firm, upright, hard, four feet high, and towards the top it sends out a few branches which rise from the joints. The leaves grow two or more at a place, without footstalks; they are large, broadest in the middle, and pointed at the end, of a beautiful green. The flowers are numerous, large, and of a beautiful gold yellow; they have five petals, and buttons in the threads.

Place.—It is not unfrequently found wild by water-sides.

Time.—Its time of flowering is from May to July.

Virtues.—This the most powerful of the whole species. It opens obstructions of the liver and spleen, provokes urine, is good for the dropsy, if infused in common drink. The ashes infused in ale or wine, are used against the same distemper, causing great discharges of water by urine.

WILLOW-TREE.—(*Salix Alba.*)

Descrip.—The White Willow grows to be a large tree. The bark is rough, of a pale brown colour on the trunk, but on the branches it is whitish grey. The leaves are long, narrow, sharp-pointed, and light green. The catkins are brown.

Place.—It is common by water-sides all over the land.

Time.—The flowers appear early in spring.

Government and Virtues.—The Moon owns it. The leaves, bark, and seed are used to stanch the bleeding of wounds, and at mouth and nose, spitting of blood, and other fluxes of blood in man or woman, to stay vomiting, and the provocation thereto, if the decoction of them in wine be drunk. It helps to stay thin, hot, sharp, salt distillations from the head upon the lungs, causing consumption. The leaves bruised with pepper, and drank in wine, help in the wind-colic. Water that is gathered from the

Willow, when it flowers, the bark being slit, is very good for dimness of sight, or films that grow over the eyes, staying the rheums that fall into them; it provokes urine, if drank, and clears the face and skin from spots and discolourings. The decoction of the leaves or bark in wine, takes away scurf and dandrif by washing the place with it.

WINTER GREEN.—(*Pyrola Minor.*)

Descrip.—The leaves resemble those of the Pear-tree, but not so large; they grow on footstalks two or three inches long, smooth, and of firm texture. The stalks grow a foot high, bearing on their tops several small five leaved white flowers, having a few stamina in the middle, rising one above another in a loose spike, succeeded by cornered seed-vessels, full of small seed; the root is small, slender, and fibrous.

Place.—It grows in woods, both in the north and west.

Time.—It flowers in July.

Government and Virtues.—This is another Lunar plant. The leaves are the only part used, are cooling and drying, and a good vulnerary both for inward and outward wounds and hemorrhages, ulcers in the kidneys or bladder: as also against making bloody water, and excess of the catamenia.

WOAD (COMMON.)—(*Isatis Tinctoria.*)

Descrip.—It has large leaves, long and broad, of a greenish colour, somewhat blue. From among these leaves rises up a lusty stalk, three or four feet high, with leaves set thereon; the higher the stalk rises, the smaller are the leaves; at the top it spreads divers branches, at the end of which appear very pretty little yellow flowers, and after they pass away, come husks, long, and rather flat; in form they resemble a tongue; in colour they are black, and hang downwards. The root is white and long.

Place.—It is sown in fields, and reaped three times a year.

Time.—It flowers in June, but it is long after before the seed is ripe.

Government and Virtues.—It is a cold and dry plant of Saturn. An ointment made of the leaves stanches bleeding. A plaster made thereof, and applied to the region of the spleen which lies on the left side, takes away the hardness and pains thereof. The ointment is good in such ulcers as abound with moisture, and takes away the corroding and fretting humours; it cools inflammations, quenches St. Anthony's fire, and stays defluxion of the blood to any part of the body.

WOODRUFFE (SQUINANCY.)—(*Asperula Cynanchica.*)

CALLED also Woodrow and Woodrowel.

Descrip.—The stalks grow about a foot high, square and slender, and but little branched, having seven or eight long green leaves, growing in a circle at every joint, with little or no roughness : the flowers grow on the tops of the stalks in small umbels, of little single-leaved white flowers, spread like a bell, of a sweet smell ; each is succeeded by two roughish seed. The root is small, slender, and creeping under the upper surface of the earth.

Place.—It grows in woods and copses.

Time.—It flowers in May.

Government and Virtues.—Mars rules it. The green herb should be used. It is good in the jaundice, and all diseases of the stomach and liver, opening obstructions, and causing appetite. Bruised, it heals fresh wounds and cuts.

WOODRUFFE (SWEET.)—(*Asperula Odorata.*)

Descrip.—This has a spreading fibrous root, with a square stock, upright, not much branched, and eight inches high : of a pale green, and slender substance. The leaves, like the former, are placed at the joints in a stellated manner, but more considerable, broader and larger ; they are sharp-pointed, smooth, of a dark green. The flowers are small and white, but a variety is found with pale blue flowers. The seeds are small and round.

Virtues.—It is nourishing and restorative, good for weak consumptive people : it opens obstructions of the liver and spleen, and is said to be a provocative to venery.

WORMSEED (TREACLE.)--(*Erysimum Cheiranthoides.*)

Descrip.—The roots are long, slender, and furnished with many strings ; the leaves are long and narrow, of a pale green; the stalk a yard high. It is not much branched, at the top grow the flowers in a spiky order; they are small and yellow, and the seed-vessels resemble pea-pods, only they are angular. The seed is small and brown, and the whole plant very much resembles hedge mustard.

Place.—It grows upon rotten moist grounds.

Time.—It flowers in May and June.

Government and Virtues.—It is under the dominion of Mars. The whole plant has a hot taste, and so have the seeds, which are good in rheumatic complaints, and in obstructions of the viscera, and in scorbutic disorders. A poultice of the roots disperses hard tumours in any part of the body. Small doses of the juice given in white wine, promote the menses, and hasten delivery; and in larger doses it is an excellent medicine in the jaundice, dropsy, and complaints of the like nature. Made into syrup with honey, and a small quantity of vinegar, it is beneficial in asthmatic complaints It kills worms in the stomach and intestines; and it is good in small quantities in hysteric cases, if the use be continued for some time.

WORMWOOD.—(*Artemisia Absynthium.*)

Descrip.—This useful plant grows about a yard high; the stalk is pale green, tough, upright, and divided wildly into many branches: the leaves are of a pale green on both sides, divided into many parts, soft to the touch, but make the fingers bitter. The flowers are numerous, small, chaffy, hang down, and of a pale olive colour at first; but, after standing a while, they grow brownish.

Place.—This is a perennial plant, growing every where.

Time.—It blooms in June and July.

Government and Virtues.—This is a martial herb, and is governed by Mars. This is the strongest, the Sea Wormwood is the second in bitterness, and the Roman joins a great deal of aromatic flavour, with but little bitterness; to acquire and enjoy the full powers they possess, they must be well known, for each kind has its particular virtues. The two first grow wild in this country; the third is frequent in our botanic gardens, but is not confined to these places. The common kind is excellent in weakness of the stomach, gout and gravel. The leaves and flowers are used.

WORMWOOD (COMMON BROAD-LEAVED.)—(*Absynthium Latifolium Vulgare.*)

Descrip.—The root is thick and woody, divided into several branches, enduring many years, holding its lower leaves all winter, which are large and winged, and divided into small parts, very much cut in; greenish above, and white underneath. In summer it sends out woody, striated, hoary stalks, two or three feet high, full of white pith, having lesser leaves growing upon them; those towards the top are long, narrow, and a little indented. The flowers rise among these in a kind of loose spikes at the tops of the stalks, and look naked; they are brownish yellow, growing many together, hanging down their heads, inclosing small seed. The whole plant has a very bitter taste.

Place.—A wild plant, and frequent by way-sides, ditch-banks, and in church-yards.

Time.—It flowers in July and August.

Government and Virtues.—It is a martial herb, as before observed. The tops of the plant are to be used fresh gathered; a very slight infusion is excellent for all disorders of the stomach, prevents sickness after meals, and creates an appetite; but if made too strong, it disgusts the taste. The tops with the flowers on them, dried and powdered, are good against agues, and have the same virtues with wormseed in killing worms; in fact, they are much better than the wormseed sold in the shops, which is generally too much decayed. The juice of the large leaves of Wormwood, which grow from the root, before the stalk appears, is the best against the dropsy and jaundice, for it opens obstructions, and works powerfully by urine. It is good in all agues, in decoction or infusion, in water, ale, wine, or in the juice only; but its infusion in wine or ale is an easy, and as good a preparation as any. The infusion, drank morning and evening for some time, helps hysterics, obstructions of the spleen, and weakness of the stomach. Its oil, taken on sugar, and drank after, kills worms, resists poison, and is good for the liver and jaundice. The root has a slow bitterness, which affects not the head and eyes, like the leaves, hence the root should be accounted among the best stomachics. The oil of the seed, given from half a scruple to half a dram, in some liquor, or a spoonful of the juice in some wine, taken before the fit comes on, and the patient put to bed, cures quotidians and quartans. In a looseness from eating too much fruit, after the use of rhubarb, Wormwood wine is excellent. A fomentation of the herb boiled with water, and strained, has been successfully applied to a spreading gangrene. Poultices of Wormwood boiled in grease, barm, or wine, may be applied with good success to white swellings. Boiled in lard, and laid to swellings of the tonsils and quinsey, is serviceable. Its internal use is good in such diseases as come from gross blood, or obstructions of the capillaries, or in viscidities or phlegm, which line the insides of the stomach, bowels' or vessels, or in too great sharpness of the blood, by its opening obstructions, cleansing, bracing, and promoting perspiration and urine. It is admirable against surfeits. It not only cures the pain of the stomach, weakness, indigestion, want of appetite, vomiting, and loathing, but hard swellings of the belly. This, with rosemary, saffron, and turmeric root infused in rhenish wine, is a cure for the jaundice, and brings down the menses; or a decoction of it, broom-tops, greater celandine, white horehound, lesser centaury, flowers of hypericon, barberry-bark, turmeric, and madder-roots, strained, and hoglice-wine added, is very good to cure the jaundice. Wormwood and vinegar are an antidote to the mischief of mushrooms and henbane, and the biting of the sea-fish, called *Draco marinus*, or quaviver; mixed with honey, it takes away blackness after falls, bruises, &c. All other Wormwoods, the nearer they approach in taste to pleasant or palatable, they are so much the worse, for they are weaker, their use requires so much longer time, larger doses, and yet less success follows. The herb and Pellitory of the Wall boiled in water till they are soft, then strained, and a fomentation of the liquor used, and the herbs laid on after in a poultice, eases all outward pains ; or the herb boiled in oil till the oil is almost wasted, strained, and anointed, cures the pains of the back. Placed among woollen cloths, it prevents and destroys the moths.

WORMWOOD (ROMAN.)—(*Artemisia Pontica.*)

Descrip.—This is less than the former, about two and a half feet high, the leaves are smaller and finer, the divisions narrower and slenderer, hoary, and white both above and underneath. The leaves that grow on the upper part of the branches, are long, narrow, and undivided, resembling more the leaves of common Southernwood in figure, than either of the other Wormwoods. The flowers are numerous, growing on the tops of the branches as the former, of a darker colour, but vastly smaller. The root is creeping and spreading, and composed of fibres ; it is in all respects a more neat and elegant plant.

Place.—This species is a native of the warmer parts of Europe, and grows with us only in gardens.

Time.—Like all the Wormwoods, it flowers in July.

Government and Virtues.—It is also a martial plant. The fresh tops are used, and the whole plant dried. It is excellent to strengthen the stomach ; the juice of the fresh tops is good against obstructions of the liver and spleen, and has been known singly to cure the jaundice. For this purpose the conserve of the leaves is recommended; and indeed this is the sort of Wormwood that conserve ought only to be made of. The flowery tops are the right part. These made into a light infusion, strengthen digestion, correct acidities, and supply the place of gall, where, as in many constitutions, that is deficient. One ounce of the flowers and buds should be put into a vessel, and a pint and a half of boiling water poured on them, and thus to stand all night. In the morning, the clear liquor, with two spoonfuls of wine, should be taken at three draughts, an hour and a half distant from one another. This regularly observed for a week, will cure all complaints arising from indigestion and wind; and a fourth part of the dose repeated afterwards will make the cure more lasting. An ounce of these flowers put into a pint of brandy, and steeped for the space of six weeks, will produce a tincture, of which a tablespoonful taken in a glass of water twice a day, will, in a great measure, prevent the increase of the gravel, and give great relief in the gout. Medicines prepared in the shops from Wormwood are—A simple water. A greater and a lesser compound water. A simple and a compound syrup. An oil by decoction or infusion. An oil by distillation. An extract, and a fixed salt.

The Roman Wormwood differs from the Sea in the following. The leaves are finer cut, and less woolly. This is the most delicate kind, but of least strength. The Wormwood wine, so famous with the Germans, is made with this Roman Wormwood, put into the juice, and worked with it: it is a strong and excellent wine, not unpleasant, yet of such efficacy to give an appetite, that the Germans drink of it so often, that they are able to eat for hours together, without sickness or indigestion.

WORMWOOD (SEA.)—(*Artemisia Maritima,*) (*Absynthium Serippium.*)

Descrip.—The stalk is white, woolly, hard, two feet high, and has a few, short irregular branches. The leaves are long, narrow, tough, firm, white, and hoary; very much like Southernwood. The root lies deep, and is woody; the flowers are of a yellowish brown, and the shoots from which they depend hang drooping.

Place.—This is a perennial, that covers many acres of sea-coast in different parts of the kingdom.

Time.—This species flowers in July.

Government and Virtues.—This is an herb of Mars. It is a very noble bitter, and succeeds in procuring an appetite, better than common Wormwood, which is best to assist digestion. The flowery tops, and the young leaves and shoots, possess the virtues; the older leaves, and the stalk, should be thrown away as useless. Boiling water poured upon it produces an excellent stomachic infusion: but the best way is, taking it in a tincture made with brandy. For lighter complaints, the conserve, such as directed to be made of field Southernwood, agreeably answers the purpose. Hysteric complaints have been completely cured by the constant use of this tincture. In the scurvy, and in the hypochondriacal disorders of studious sedentary men, few things have greater effect; for these it is best in strong infusions; and great good has arisen from common Wormwood, given in jaundices and dropsies. The whole blood, and all the juices of the body, are affected by taking this herb. It turns the milk bitter in the breasts of nurses, if taken while suckling. It is sold in the shops instead of the Roman Wormwood, and is often used in medicine instead of the former, though it falls far short of it in virtue.

YARROW (COMMON.)—(*Achillæa Millefolium.*)

CALLED also Nose-bleed, Milfoil, and Thousand-leaf.

Descrip.—It has many leaves cut into a multitude of fine small parts, of a deep green colour and tough substance; the stalk is upright, of a dull greyish green, and the flowers are usually white, but not all of a whiteness and grow in knots. Some of these, among others, will grow of a delicate crimson, which are those that produce seed, and from this seed will rise red flowered plants.

Place.—This is an upright, and not unhandsome plant, common in our pasture grounds, and, like many others, of much more use than is generally known. It is perennial, and grows to two feet high.

Time.—It blooms from July to the latter end of August.

Government and Virtues.—It is under the influence of Venus. As a medicine it is drying and binding. A decoction of it boiled with white wine, is good to stop the running of the reins in men, and whites in women; restrains violent bleedings, and is excellent for the piles. A strong tea in this case should be made of the leaves, and drunk plentifully; and equal parts of it, and of toad flax, should be made into a poultice with pomatum, and applied outwardly. This induces sleep, eases the pain, and lessens the bleeding. An ointment of the leaves cures wounds, and is good for inflammations, ulcers, fistulas, and all such runnings as abound with moisture.

YARROW (SNEEZEWORT.)—(*Achillæa Ptarmica.*)

Descrip.—The root is long, slender, and hung with many fibres. The stalk is round, upright, and two feet high, of a pale green, and branched. The leaves are long, narrow, of a deep green, rough on the surface, sharp-pointed, and serrated at the edges. The flowers are very numerous small and white, and they terminate the branches. The seed is oval.

Place.—It is common on ditch banks.

Time.—It flowers in August.

Government and Virtues.—Venus governs this useful plant. The leaves dried and powdered, and snuffed up the nose, occasions sneezing, and are excellent against inveterate head-aches. The young tops are of a sharp, but pleasant taste, and may be eaten in salads. It is a good vulnerary, both inwardly taken in infusion, decoction, &c., and outwardly applied in fomentations; for it is a drier and astringent, and therefore proper to be used in all immoderate fluxes, whether of the bowels, or other parts, especially of the menses, and in female weaknesses.

YEW.—(*Taxus Baccata.*)

Descrip.—It grows to be an irregular tree, spreading widely into branches. The leaves are long, narrow, and placed with a beautiful regularity. The flowers are yellowish, and and the berries are surrounded with a sweet juicy matter.

Place.—It grows in woods, and in gardens.

Government and Virtues.—This is a tree of Saturn. The leaves are said to be poisonous; but the wood, if it grew with more regularity, would be very valuable. This tree, though it has no place among medicinal plants, yet it does not deserve (at least in our climate), so bad a character as the ancients gave it, viz, a most poisonous vegetable, the berries of which threaten present death to man or beast that eat them; many have eaten them in this country and survived. However that may be, it has very powerful poisonous qualities, that rise by distillation. In this form, it is the most active vegetable poison known in the whole world, for in a small dose it instantly induces death without any previous disorder; and its deleterious power seems to act upon the nervous system, without exciting the least inflammation in the part to which it more immediately enters. It totally differs from opium and all other sleepy poisons, for it does not bring on the lethargic symptoms, but more effectually penetrates and destroys the vital functions, without immediately affecting the animal. These observations are made as a caution against any rash application of it, for, though it is sometimes given usefully in obstructions of the liver and bilious complaints, those experiments seem too few to recommend it to be used without the greatest caution. The deleterious qualities of laurel-water are more than equalled by this.

YUCCA, OR JUCCA.—(*Yucca Gloriosa.*)

CALLED also Adam's Needle.

Descrip.—This Indian plant has a thick tuberous root, spreading in time into many tuberous heads, whence shoot forth many long, hard, and hollow leaves, very sharp-pointed, compassing one another at the bottom, of a greyish green colour, abiding continually, or seldom falling away, with sundry hard threads running in them, and when withered, become pliant to bind things with. From the midst of these spring forth a strong round stalk, divided into several branches, whereon stand divers somewhat large white flowers, hanging downwards, consisting of six leaves, with divers veins, of a weak reddish, or blueish colour, spread on the back of the outer leaves from the middle to the bottom, not reaching to the edge of any leaf, which abide not long, but quickly fall away.

Place.—It grows in divers places of the West-Indies, as in Virginia and New England.

Time.—It flowers about the latter end of July.

Virtues.—It has no properties, as yet known of, for medicinal use. The natives in Virginia use the roots for bread. The raw juice is dangerous, if not deadly, and it is supposed the Indians poisoned the heads of their darts therewith.

DIRECTIONS FOR MAKING SYRUPS, &c.

HAVING in divers places of this Treatise promised you the way of making Syrups, Conserves, Oils, Ointments, &c. of herbs, roots, flowers, &c. whereby you may have them ready for your use at such times when they cannot be had otherwise; I come now to perform what I promised, and you shall find me rather better than worse than my word.

That this may be done methodically, I shall divide my directions into two grand sections, and each section into several chapters, and then you shall see it look with such a countenance as this is.

SECTION I.

OF GATHERING, DRYING, AND KEEPING SIMPLES, AND THEIR JUICES.

CHAP. I. Of leaves of herbs &c.
—II. Of Flowers.
—III. Of Seeds.
CHAP. IV. Of Roots.
—V. Of Barks.
—VI. Of Juices.

SECTION II.

OF MAKING AND KEEPING COMPOUNDS.

CHAP. I. Of distilled Waters.
—II. Of Syrups.
—III. Of Juleps.
—IV. Of Decoctions.
—V. Of Oils.
—VI. Of Electuaries.
—VII. Of Conserves.
—VIII. Of Preserves.
CHAP. IX. Of Lohocks.
—X. Of Ointments.
—XI. Of Plaisters.
—XII. Of Poultices.
—XIII. Of Troches.
—XIV. Of Pills.
—XV. The way of fitting Medicines to compound diseases.

Of all these in order.

CHAPTER I.

Of Leaves of Herbs, or Trees.

1. Of leaves choose only such as are green and full of juice; pick them carefully, and cast away such as are declining, for they will putrify all the rest. So shall one handful be worth ten of those you buy in Cheapside.

2. Note what places they most delight to grow in, and gather them there; for betony that grows in the shade is far better than that growing in the sun, because it delights in the shade; so also such herbs as delight to grow near the water, shall be gathered near it, though haply you may find some of them upon dry ground. The treatise will inform you where every herb delights to grow.

3. The leaves of such herbs as run up to seed are not so good when they are in flower as before, (some few excepted, the leaves of which are seldom or never used) in such cases, if through ignorance they were not known, or through negligence forgotten, you had better take the top and the flowers than the leaf.

4. Dry them well in the sun, and not in the shade, as the saying of the physician is; for if the sun draw away the virtues of the herb, it must needs do the like by hay, by the same rule, which the experience of every country farmer will explode for a notable piece of nonsense.

5. Such as are astrologers (and indeed none else are fit to make physicians) such I advise; let the planet that governs the herb be angular, and the stronger the better; if they can, in herbs of Saturn, let Saturn be in the ascendant; in the herb of Mars, let Mars be in the Mid-heaven, for in those houses they delight; let the Moon apply to them by good aspect, and let her not be in the houses of her enemies; if you cannot well stay till she apply to them, let her apply to a planet of the same triplicity; if you cannot wait that time neither, let her be with a fixed star of their nature.

6. Having well dried them, put them up in brown paper, sewing the paper up like a sack, and press them not too hard together, and keep them in a dry place near the fire.

7. As for the duration of dried herbs, a just time cannot be given, let authors prate at their pleasure; for,

1st. Such as grow upon dry grounds will keep better than such as grow on moist.

2dly. Such herbs as are full of juice will not keep so long as such as are dryer.

3dly. Such herbs as are well dried, will keep longer than such as are slack dried. Yet you may know when they are corrupted by their loss of colour, or smell, or both: and, if they be corrupted, reason will tell you that they must needs corrupt the bodies of those people that take them.

4. Gather all leaves in the hour of that planet that governs them.

CHAPTER II.

Of Flowers.

1. The flower, which is the beauty of the plant, and of none of the least use in physic, groweth yearly, and is to be gathered when it is in its prime.

2. As for the time of gathering them, let the planetary hour, and the plant they come off be observed, as we shewed you in the foregoing chapter: as for the time of the day, let it be when the sun shines upon them, that so they may be dry; for if you gather either flowers or herbs when they are wet or dewy, they will not keep.

3. Dry them well in the sun, and keep them in papers near the fire, as I shewed you in the foregoing chapter.

4. So long as they retain the smell and colour, they are good; either of them being gone, so is their virtue also.

CHAPTER III.

Of Seeds.

1. The seed is that part of the plant which is endowed with a vital faculty to bring forth its like, and it contains potentially the whole plant in it.

2. As for the place, let them be gathered from the place where they most delight to grow.

3. Let them be full ripe when they are gathered, and forget not the celestial harmony before mentioned; for I have found by experience that their virtues are twice as great at such times as others: "There is an appointed time for every thing under the sun."

4. When you have gathered them, dry them a little, and but a very little, in the sun before you lay them up.

5. You need not be so careful of keeping them so near the fire as the other before mentioned, because they are fuller of spirit, and therefore not so subject to corrupt.

6. As for the time of their duration, it is palpable they will keep a good many years; yet they are best the first year, and this I make appear by a good argument. They will grow soonest the first year they be set, therefore then they are in their prime; and it is an easy matter to renew them yearly.

CHAPTER IV.

Of Roots.

1. Of roots choose neither such as are rotten or worm-eaten, but proper in their taste, colour and smell, such as exceed neither in softness nor hardness.

Give me leave to be a little critical against the vulgar received opinion, which is, that the sap falls down into the root in the autumn, and rises in the spring, as men go to bed at night and rise in the morning; and this idle talk of untruth is so grounded in the heads, not only of the vulgar but also of the learned, that a man cannot drive it out by reason. I pray, let such sap-mongers answer me this argument: If the sap falls into the roots in the fall of the leaf, and lies there all the winter, then must the root grow only in the winter. But the root grows not at all in winter, as experience teacheth, but only in summer; therefore if you set an apple kernel in the spring, you shall find the root grow to a pretty bigness in the summer, and be not a whit bigger next spring. What doth the sap do in the root all that while? Prick straws? 'Tis as rotten as a post.

2. The truth is, when the sun declines from the tropic of Cancer, the sap begins to congeal both in root and branch: when he touches the tropic of Capricorn, he ascends to usward, it begins to wax thin again, and by degrees, as it congealed. But to proceed.

3. The drier time you gather the roots in, the better they are, for they have the less excrementitous moisture in them.

4. Such roots as are soft, your best way is to dry in the sun, or else hang them in the chimney corner upon a string; as for such as are hard, you may dry them anywhere.

5. Such roots as are great, will keep longer than such as are small; yet most of them will keep all the year.

6. Such roots as are soft, it is your best way to keep them always near the fire, and take this general rule for it. If in winter time you find any of your herbs, roots, or flowers begin to be moist, as many times you shall (for it is your best way to look to them once a month) dry them by a very gentle fire, or, if you can, with convenience, keep them near the fire, you may save yourself the trouble.

7. It is in vain to dry roots that may commonly be had, as parsley, fennel, plantain, &c. but gather them only for present need.

CHAPTER V.

Of Barks.

1. Barks, which physicians use in medicine, are of these sorts: of fruits, of roots, of boughs.

2. The barks of fruits are to be taken when the fruit is full ripe, as oranges, lemons, &c. but because I have nothing to do with exotics here, I pass them without any more words.

3. The barks of trees are best gathered in the spring, if of oak or such great trees; because then they come easier off, and so you may dry them if you please; but indeed the best way is to gather all barks only for present use.

4. As for the bark of roots, 'tis thus to be gotten: Take the roots of such herbs as have a pith in them, as parsley, fennel, &c. slit them in the middle, and when you have taken out the pith, which you may easily do, that which remains is called, though improperly, the bark. and indeed is only to be used.

CHAPTER VI.

Of Juices.

1. Juices are to be pressed out of herbs when they are young and tender, out of some stalks, and tender tops of herbs and plants, and also out of some flowers.

2. Having gathered the herb, if you will preserve the juice of it when it is very dry (for otherwise the juice will not be worth a button) bruise it well in a stone mortar with a wooden pestle, then having put it into a canvass bag, the herb I mean, not the mortar, for that will give but little juice, press it hard in a press, then take the juice and clarify it.

3. The manner of clarifying it is this: Put it into a pipkin or skillet, or some such thing, and set it over the fire; and when the scum ariseth take it off; let it stand over the fire till no more scum arise; when you have your juice clarified, cast away the scum as a thing of no use.

4. When you have thus clarified it, you have two ways to preserve it all the year.

1st. When it is cold put it into a glass, and put so much oil on it as will cover it to the thickness of two fingers; the oil will swim at the top, and so keep the air from coming to putrify it. When you intend to use it, pour it into a porringer, and if any oil come out with it, you may easily skim it off with a spoon, and put the juice you use not into the glass again, it will quickly sink under the oil.

2nd. The second way is a little more difficult, and the juice of fruits is usually preserved this way. When you have clarified it, boil it over the fire, till being cold it be of the thickness of honey. This is most commonly used for diseases of the mouth, and is called roba and saba.

And thus much for the first section, the second follows.

SECTION II.

THE WAY OF MAKING AND KEEPING ALL NECESSARY COMPOUNDS.

CHAPTER I.

Of Distilled Waters.

HITHERTO we have spoken of medicines which consist in their own nature, which authors vulgarly call Simples, though something improperly; for in truth, nothing is simple but pure elements; all things else are compounded of them. We come now to treat of the artificial medicines, in the form of which, because we must begin somewhere, we shall place distilled waters; in which consider,

1. Waters are distilled of herbs, of flowers, of fruits, and of roots.

2. We speak not of strong waters, but of cold, as being to act Galen's part, and not Paracelsus's.

3. The herbs ought to be distilled when they are in the greatest vigour, and so ought the flowers also.

4. The vulgar way of distillations which people use because they know no better, is in a pewter still; and although distilled waters are the weakest of artificial medicines, and good for little but mixtures of other medicines, yet they are weaker by many degrees than they would be were they distilled in sand. If I thought it not impossible to teach you the way of distilling in sand, I would attempt it.

5. When you have distilled your water, put it into a glass covered over with a paper pricked full of holes, so that the excrementitious and fiery vapours may exhale, which cause that settling in distilled waters called the mother, which corrupt them, then cover it close and keep it for your use.

6. Stopping distilled waters with a cork makes them musty, and so does paper if it but touch the water; it is best to stop them with a bladder, being first put in water, and bound over the top of the glass.

Such cold waters as are distilled in a pewter still (if well kept) will endure a year; such as are distilled in sand, as they are twice as strong, so they endure twice as long.

CHAPTER II.

Of Syrups.

1. A Syrup is a medicine of a liquid form, composed of infusion, decoction, and juice. And

1st. For the more graceful taste.

2dly. For the better keeping of it; with a certain quantity of honey or sugar hereafter mentioned, boiled to the thickness of new honey.

2. You see at the first view that this aphorism divides itself into three branches, which deserves severally to be treated of, viz.

1. Syrups made by infusion.
2. Syrups made by decoction.
3. Syrups made by juice.

Of each of these, for your instruction's sake, kind countrymen and women, I speak a word or two apart.

1st. Syrups made by infusion are usually made of flowers and of such flowers as soon loose their colour and strength by boiling, as roses, violets, peach-flowers, &c. My translation of the London Dispensatory will instruct you in the rest. They are thus made: Having picked your flowers clean, to every pound of them, add three pounds, or three pints, which you will, for it is all one, of spring water, made boiling hot; but first put your flowers into a pewter pot with a cover, and pour the water on them; then shutting the pot let it stand by the fire to keep hot twelve hours, and strain it out; (in such syrups as purge, as damask roses, peach-flowers, &c. the usual, and indeed the best way is to repeat this infusion, adding fresh flowers to the same liquor divers times, so that it may be stronger) having strained it, out, put the infusion into a pewter bason, or an earthren one well glazed, and to every pint of it add two pounds of sugar, which being only melted over the fire without being boiled, and then skimmed, will produce you the syrup you desire.

2ndly. Syrups made by decoction are usually made of compounds, yet may any simple herb be thus converted into syrup. Take the herb, roots, or flowers you would make into a syrup, and bruise a little; then boil it in a convenient quantity of spring water; the more water you boil it in the weaker it will be; a handful of the herb or root is a convenient quantity for a pint of water; boil it till half the water be consumed, then let it stand till it be almost cold, and strain it through a woollen cloth, letting it run out at leisure, without pressing. To every pint of this decoction add one pound of sugar, and boil it over the fire till it comes to a syrup, which you may know if you now and then cool a little of it with a spoon; skim it all the while it boils, and when it is sufficiently boiled, whilst it is hot strain it again, through a piece of woollen cloth, but press it not. Thus you have the syrup perfected.

3rdly. Syrups made of juice are usually made of such herbs as are full of juice, and indeed they are better made into a syrup this way than any other; the operation is thus: having beaten the herb in a stone mortar with a wooden pestle, press out the juice and clarify it, as you are taught in the juices; then let the juice boil away till about a quarter of it be consumed; to a pint of this add a pound of sugar, and boil it to a syrup, always skimming it, and when it is boiled enough, strain it through a woollen cloth, as we taught you before, and keep it for your use.

4. If you make a syrup of roots, that are anything hard, as parsley, fennel, and grass roots, &c. when you have bruised them, lay them to steep in that water that you intend to boil them in, hot, so will the virtues the better come out.

5. Keep your syrups either in glasses or stone pots, and stop them not with cork or bladder, unless you would have the glass break and the syrup lost, only bind paper about the mouth.

All syrups, if well made, will continue a year with some advantage; yet such as are made by infusion keep shortest.

CHAPTER III.

Of Juleps.

1. Juleps were first invented, as I suppose, in Arabia, and my reason is, because the word julep is an Arabic word.

2. It signifies only a pleasant potion, as is vulgarly used by such as are sick and want help, or such as are in health, and want no money to quench their thirst.

3. Now-a-day it is commonly used,

1. To prepare the body for purgation.
2. To open obstructions and the pores.
3. To digest tough humours.
4. To qualify hot distempers, &c.

4. Simples, juleps, (for I have nothing to say to compounds here) are thus made: Take a pint of such distilled water as conduces to the cure of your distemper, which this treatise will plentifully furnish you with, to which add two ounces of syrup conducing to the same effect; (I shall give you rules for it in the next chapter) mix them together and drink a draught of it at your pleasure. If you love tart things, add ten drops of oil of vitrol to your pint, and shake it together, and it will have a fine grateful taste.

5. All juleps are made for present use, and therefore it is in vain to speak of their duration.

CHAPTER IV.

Of Decoctions.

1. All the difference between decoctions, and syrups made by decoction, is this: syrups are made to keep, decoctions only for present use; for you can hardly keep a decoction a week at any time; if the weather be hot, you cannot keep it half so long.

2. Decoctions are made of leaves, roots, flowers, seeds, fruits, or barks, conducing to the cure of the disease you make them for, and are made in the same manner as we have shewed you in syrups.

3. Decoctions made with wine last longer than such are made with water; and if you take your decoction to cleanse the passage of the urine or open obstructions, your best way is to make it with white wine instead of water, because this is penetrating.

4. Decoctions are of most use in such diseases as lie in the passage of the body, as the stomach, bowels, kidneys, passages of urine and bladder, because decoctions pass quicker to those places than any other form of medicine.

5. If you will sweeten your decoction with sugar, or any syrup fit for the occasion you take it for, which is better, you may, and no harm.

6. If in a decoction you boil both roots, herbs, flowers, and seed together, let the roots boil a good while first, because they retain their virtues longest; then the next in order by the same rule, viz. 1. the barks, 2. the herbs. 3. the seeds. 4. the flowers. 5. the spices, if you put any in, because then the virtues come soonest out.

7. Such things as by boiling cause sliminess to a decoction, as figs, quince-seed, linseed, &c. your best way is, after you have bruised them, to tie them up in a linen rag, as you tie up calf's brains, and so boil them.

8. Keep all decoctions in a glass close stopped, and the cooler place you keep them in the longer they will last ere they be sour.

Lastly. The usual dose to be given at one time is two, three, four, or five ounces, according to the age and strength of the patient, the season of the year, the strength of the medicine, and the quality of the disease.

CHAPTER V.

Of Oils.

1. Oil Olive, which is commonly known by the name of salads oil, I suppose, because it is usually eaten with salads by them that love it; if it be pressed out of ripe olives, according to Galen, is temperate, and exceeds in no one quality.

2. Of oils, some are simple, and some are compound.

3. Simple oils are such as are made of fruits or seeds by expression, as oil of sweet or bitter almonds, linseed and rape seed oil, &c. of which see in my dispensatory.

4. Compound oils are made of oil of olives, and other simples, imagine herbs, flowers, roots, &c.

5. The way of making them is this; having bruised the herbs or flowers you make your oil of, put them into an earthen pot, and to two or three handfuls of them pour a pint of oil, cover the pot with a paper, set it in the sun about a fortnight or so, according as the sun is in hotness: then having warmed it very well by the fire, press out the herb, &c. very hard in a press, and add as many more herbs to the same oil; bruise the herbs (I mean not the oil) in like manner, set them in the sun as before; the oftener you repeat this, the stronger your oil will be; at last, when you conceive it strong enough, boil both oil and herbs together, till the juice be consumed, which you may know by its leaving its bubbling, and the herbs will be crisp; then strain it while it is hot, and keep it in a stone or glass vessel for your use.

6. As for chemical oils, I have nothing to say here.

7. The general use of these oils is for pains in the limbs, roughness in the skin, the itch, &c. as also for ointments and plaisters.

8. If you have occasion to use it for wounds or ulcers, in two ounces of of oil, dissolve half an ounce of turpentine, the heat of the fire will quickly do it; for oil itself is offensive to wounds, and turpentine qualifies it.

CHAPTER VI.

Of Electuaries.

Physicians make more a quoil than needs by half about electuaries. I shall describe but one general way of making them up; as for ingredients you may vary them as you please, and as you find occasion, by the last chapter.

1. That you may make electuaries when you need them, it is requisite that you keep always herbs, roots, flowers, seeds, &c. ready dried in your house, that so you may be in readiness to beat them into a powder when you do need them.

2. It is better to keep them whole than beaten; for being beaten, they are more subject to lose their strength, because the air soon penetrates them.

3. If they be not dry enough to beat into powder when you need them, dry them by a gentle fire till they are so.

4. Having beaten them, sift them through a fine tiffany searce, that no great pieces may be found in your electuary.

5. To one ounce of your powder add three ounces of clari-

fied honey; this quantity I hold to be sufficient. If you would make more or less electuary, vary your proportion accordingly.

6. Mix them well together in a mortar, and take this for a truth, you cannot mix them too much.

7. The way to clarify honey, is to set it over the fire in a convenient vessel till the scum arise, and when the scum is taken off it is clarified.

8. The usual dose of cordial electuaries is from half a dram to two drams; of purging electuaries, from half an ounce to an ounce.

9. The manner of keeping them is in a pot.

10. The time of taking them is either in a morning fasting, and fasting an hour after them; or at night going to bed, three or four hours after supper.

CHAPTER VII.

Of Conserves.

1. The way of making conserves is two-fold; one of herbs and flowers, and the other of fruits.

2. Conserves of herbs and flowers are thus made: if you thus make your conserve of herbs, as of scurvy grass, wormwood, rue, and the like, take only the leaves, and the tender tops (for you may beat your heart out before you can beat the stalks small) and having beaten them, weigh them, and to every pound of them add three pounds of sugar; you cannot beat them too much.

3. Conserves of fruits, as barberries, sloes, and the like, are thus made; first scald the fruit, then rub the pulp through a thick hair sieve made for that purpose, called a pulping sieve; you may do it for a need with the back of a spoon, then take this pulp thus drawn and add to it its weight of sugar, and no more; put it into a pewter vessel and over a charcoal fire: stir it up and down till the sugar be melted, and your conserve is made.

4. Thus you have the way of making conserves; the way of keeping them is in earthern pots.

5. The dose is usually the quantity of a nutmeg at a time, morning and evening, or (unless they are purging) when you please.

9. Of conserves, some keep many years, as conserve of roses; others but a year, as conserve of borage, bugloss, cowslips, and the like.

7. Have a care of the working of some conserves presently after they are made; look to them once a day, and stir them about. Conserves of borage, bugloss, and wormwood, have an excellent faculty at that sport.

8. You may know when your conserves are almost spoiled

by this; you shall find a hard crust at the top with little holes in it as though worms had been eating there.

CHAPTER VIII.

Of Preserves.

Of preserves are sundry sorts, and the operation of al being somewhat different, we shall handle them all apart. These are preserved with sugar.

1. Flowers.
2. Fruits.
3. Roots.
4. Barks.

1. Flowers are very seldom preserved; I never saw any that I remember save only cowslip flowers, and that was a great fashion in Sussex when I was a boy. It is thus done. Take a flat glass, we call them jar-glasses, strew on a laying of fine sugar, on that a laying of flowers, and on that another laying of sugar, on that another laying of flowers, so do till your glass be full; then tie it over with a paper, and in a little time you shall have very excellent and pleasant preserves.

There is another way of preserving flowers, namely with vinegar and salt, as they pickle capers and broom buds; but as I have little skill in it myself, I cannot teach you.

2. Fruits, as quinces and the like, are preserved two different ways.

1st. Boil them well in water, and then pulp them through a sieve, as we shewed you before; then with the like quantity of sugar boil the water they were boiled in into a syrup, viz, a pound of sugar to a pint of liquor; to every pound of this syrup add four ounces of the pulp, then boil it with a very gentle fire to their right consistence, which you may easily know if you drop a drop of syrup on a trencher; if it be enough, it will not stick to your fingers when it is cold.

2nd. Another way to preserve fruits is this: First pare off the rind, then cut them in halves and take out the core, and boil them in water till they are soft; if you know when beef is enough you may easily know when they are, then boil the water, with its like weight of sugar into a syrup; put the syrup into a pot, and put the boiled fruit as whole as you left it when you cut into it, and let it remain till you have occasion to use it.

3. Roots are thus preserved: First scrape them very clean, and cleanse them from the pith, if they have any, for some roots have not, as eringo and the like: boil them in water till they be soft, as we shewed you before in the fruits: then boil the water you boiled the root in into a syrup as we shewed you before, then keep the root whole in the syrup till you use them.

4. As for barks, we have but few come to our hands to be done, and of those the few that I can remember, are oranges, lemons, citrons, and the outer barks of walnuts which grow, without-side the shell, for the shells themselves would make but scurvy preserves; these be they I can remember, if there be any more put them into the number.

The way of preserving these is not all one in authors for some are bitter, some are hot: such as are bitter, say authors, must be soaked in warm water, oftentimes changing till the bitter taste be fled; but I like not this way, and my reason is this, because I doubt when their bitterness is gone so is their virtue also; I shall then prescribe one common way, the same with the former, viz. first boil them whole till they be soft, then make a syrup with sugar and the liquor you boil them in, and keep the barks in the syrup.

5. They are kept in glasses or in glazed pots.

6. The preserved flowers will keep a year, if you can forbear eating of them; the roots and barks much longer.

7. This art was plainly and first invented for delicacy, yet came afterwards to be of excellent use in physic; for

1st. Hereby medicines are made pleasant for sick and squeamish stomachs, which would else loath them.

2dly. Hereby they are preserved from decaying a long time.

CHAPTER IX.

Of Lohocks.

1. That which the Arabians call lohocks, and the Greeks eclegmia, the Latins call linctus, and in plain English signifies nothing else but a thing to be licked up.

2. Their first invention was to prevent and remedy afflictions of the breast and lungs, to cleanse the lungs of phlegm, and make it fit to be cast out.

3. They are in body thicker than a syrup, and not so thick as an electuary.

4. The manner of taking them is often to take a little with liquorice stick, and let it go down at leisure.

5. They are easily thus made: Make a decoction of pectoral herbs, and the treatise will furnish you with enough, and when you have strained it with twice its weight of honey or sugar, boil it to a lohock; if you are molested with much phlegm, honey is much better than sugar, and if you add a little vinegar to it you will do well; if not, I hold sugar to be better than honey.

6. It is kept in pots, and may be kept a year and longer.

7. It is excellent for roughness of the wind-pipe, inflammations and ulcers of the lungs, difficulty of breathing, asthmas, coughs, and distillations of humours.

CHAPTER X.

Of Ointments.

1. Various are the ways of making ointments, which authors have left to posterity, and which I shall omit, and quote one which is easiest to be made, and therefore most beneficial to people that are ignorant in physic, for whose sake I write this. It is thus done:

Bruise those herbs, flowers, or roots, you will make an ointment of, and to two handfuls of your bruised herbs add a pound of hog's grease dried, or cleansed from the skins, beat them very well together in a stone mortar with a wooden pestle, then put it into a stone pot, (the herb and grease I mean, not the mortar) cover it with a paper, and set it either in thé sun or some other warm place, three, four, or five days, that it may melt; then take it out and boil it a little, and whilst it is hot strain it out, pressing it out very hard in a press; to this grease add as many more herbs as before, let them stand in like manner as long, then boil them as you did the former. If you think your ointment not strong enough, you may do it the third and fourth time; yet this I will tell you, the fuller of juice the herbs are, the sooner will your ointment be strong: the last time you boil it, boil it so long till your herbs be crisp, and the juice consumed, then strain it, pressing it hard in a press, and to every pound of ointment add two ounces of turpentine and as much wax. because grease is offensive to wounds as well as oil.

2. Ointments are vulgarly known to be kept in pots, and will last above a year, sometimes above two years.

CHAPTER XI.

Of Plaisters.

1. The Greeks made their plaisters of divers simples, and put metals into most of them, if not all; for having reduced their metals into powder, they mixed them with the fatty substances whereof the rest of the plaister consisted whilst it was yet hot, continually stirring it up and down lest it should sink to the bottom; so they continually stirred it till it was stiff; then they made it into rolls, which when they needed for use, they could melt it by the fire again.

2. The Arabians made up theirs with oil and fat, which needeth not so long boiling.

3. The Greeks' emplaisters consisted of these ingredients, metals, stones, divers sorts of earth, fœces, juices, liquors, seeds, roots, excrements of creatures, wax, rosin, and gums.

CHAPTER XII.

Of Poultices.

Poultices are those kind of things which the Latins call

cataplasmata, and our learned fellows, that if they can read English, that's all, call them cataplasms, because 'tis a crabbed word few understand; it is indeed a very fine kind of medicine to ripen sores.

2. They are made of herbs and roots fitted for the disease aforesaid, being chopped small and boiled in water to a jelly; then adding a little barley meal, or meal of lupins, and a little oil or rough sweet suet, which I hold to be better, spread upon a cloth and applied to the grieved part.

3. Their use is to ease pains, to break sores, to cool inflammations, to dissolve hardness, to ease the spleen, to concoct humours, and dissipate swellings.

4. I beseech you to take this caution along with you: Use no poultices, if you can help it, that are of an healing nature, before you have first cleansed the body, because they are subject to draw the humours to them from every part of the body.

CHAPTER XIII.

Of Troches.

1. The Latins call them *placentula*, or little cakes, and the Greeks *prochikois*, *kukliscoi*, and *artiscoi*; they are usually little round flat cakes, or you may make them square if you will.

2. Their first invention was, that powders being so kept, might resist the intermission of air, and so endure pure longer.

3. Besides, they are easier carried in the pockets of such as travel; as any man, for example, is forced to travel whose stomach is too cool, or at least not so hot as it should be, which is more proper, for the stomach is never cold till a man be dead; in such a case it is better to carry troches of wormwood or galangal, in a paper in his pocket, than to take a gallipot along with him.

4. They are made thus: At night when you go to bed, take two drams of fine gum tragacanth; put it into a gallipot, and put half a quarter of a pint of any distilled water fitting for the purpose you would make your troches for to cover it, and the next morning you shall find it such a jelly as the physicians call mucilage: with this you may, (with a little pains taken) make a powder into a paste, and that paste into cakes called troches.

5. Having made them, dry them in the shade, and keep them in the pot for your use.

CHAPTER XIV.

Of Pills.

1. They are called *pilulæ*, because they resemble little balls; the Greeks call them *catapolia*.

2. It is the opinion of modern physicians, that this way of making medicines was invented only to deceive the palate,

that so by swallowing them whole, the bitterness of the medicine might not be perceived, or at least might not be insufferable; and indeed most of their pills, though not all, are very bitter.

3. I am of clean contrary opinion to this. I rather think they were done up in this hard form that so they might be the longer digesting. The first invention of pills was to purge the head; now, as I told you before, such infirmities as lie near the passages were best removed by decoctions, because they pass to the grieved parts soonest; so here, if the infirmity lies in the head or any other remote part, the best way is to use pills, because they are longer in digesting, and therefore better able to call the offending humours to them.

4. If I should tell you here a long tale of medicines working by sympathy and antipathy, you would not understand a word of it; they that are set to make physicians may find it in the treatise. All modern physicians know not what belongs to a sympathetical cure, no more than a cuckoo what belongs to flats and sharps in music, but follow the vulgar road, and call it a hidden quality, because it is hidden from the eyes of dunces, and indeed none but astrologers can give a reason for it; and physic without reason is like pudding without fat.

5. The way to make pills is very easy, for with the help of a pestle and mortar, and a little diligence, you may make any powder into pills, either with syrup or the jelly I told you before.

CHAPTER XV.

The way of mixing Medicines according to the cause of the Disease, and part of the body afflicted.

This being indeed the key of the work, I shall be somewhat the more diligent in it. I shall deliver myself thus:

1. To the vulgar.

2. To such as study astrology; or such as study physic astrologically.

1st. To the vulgar. Kind souls, I am sorry it hath been your sad mishap to have been so long trained in such Egyptian darkness, even darkness which to your sorrow may be felt. The vulgar road of physic is not in my practice, and I am therefore the more unfit to give you advice. I have now published a little book, (Every Man his own Doctor) which will fully instruct you, not only in the knowledge of your own bodies, but also in fit medicines to remedy each part of it when afflicted; in the mean season take these few rules to stay your stomachs.

1. With the disease regard the cause, and the part of the body afflicted; for example, suppose a woman be subject to miscarry through wind, thus do:

(1.) Look out abortion in the table of diseases, and you shall be directed by that how many herbs prevent miscarriage.

(2.) Look out wind in the same table and you shall see how many of these herbs expel wind.

1. These are the herbs medicinal for your grief.
2. In all diseases strengthen the parts of the body afflicted.
3. In mixed diseases there lies some difficulty, for sometimes two parts of the body are afflicted with contrary humours, as sometimes the liver is afflicted with choler and water, as when a man hath had the dropsy and yellow jaundice; and this is usually mortal.

In the former, suppose the brain to be too cold and moist, and the liver to be hot and dry; thus do:

1. Keep your head outwardly warm.
2. Accustom yourself to the smell of hot herbs.
3. Take a pill that heats the head at night going to bed.
4. In the morning take a decoction that cools the liver, or that quickly passeth the stomach, and is at the liver immediately.

You must not think, courteous people, that I can spend time to give you examples of all diseases. These are enough to let you see so much light as you without art are able to receive. If I should set you to look at the sun, I should dazzle your eyes and make you blind.

2ndly. To such as study astrology, (who are the only men I know that are fit to study physic, physic, without astrology, being like a lamp without oil) you are the men I exceedingly respect, and such documents as my brain can give you at present, being absent from my study, I shall give you.

1. Fortify the body with herbs of the nature of the Lord of the Ascendant, 'tis no matter whether he be a Fortune or Infortune in this case.
2. Let your medicine be something anti-pathetical to the Lord of the Sixth.
3. Let your medicine be something of the nature of his sign ascending.
4. If the Lord of the Tenth be strong, make use of his medicines.
5. If this cannot well be, make use of the medicines of the Light of Time.
6. Be sure always to fortify the grieved part of the body by sympathetical remedies.
7. Regard the heart, keep that upon the wheels, because the sun is the foundation of life, and therefore those universal remedies *Aurum Potabile*, and the Philosopher's stone cure all diseases by fortifying the heart.

AN ALPHABETICAL LIST
OF
ALL HUMAN DISEASES,
WITH THE
NAMES OF THE HERBS THAT WILL CURE THEM,
AND THE
Number of Page upon which each Herb can be found.

The whole being a Complete Guide to Culpeper's Herbal.

S

———:o:———

DIRECTIONS FOR MAKING SYRUPS, ETC.

———

SECTION I.

SECTION II.

THE END